露地

the japanese tea garden

marc peter keane

Stone Bridge Press • Berkeley, California

Published by
Stone Bridge Press
P. O. Box 8208
Berkeley, CA 94707
TEL 510-524-8732 • sbp@stonebridge.com • www.stonebridge.com

All translations by the author, under the tutelage of Kyōko Selden, unless noted otherwise.

Photographs taken and illustrations and line art drawn by the author, unless noted otherwise.

Book design and layout by Linda Ronan.

2015 2014 2013 2011 2010 2009   10 9 8 7 6 5 4 3 2 1

Manufactured in China.

LIBRARY OF CONGRESS CATALOGING-IN-PUBLICATION DATA
Keane, Marc P. (Marc Peter)
  The Japanese tea garden / Marc Peter Keane.
    p. cm.
  Includes bibliographical references and index.
  ISBN 978-1-933330-67-9
  1. Japanese tea gardens. 2. Japanese tea gardens—Pictorial works. I. Title.
  SB458.K433 2009
  712.0952—dc22
              2008043112

contents

acknowledgments

My understanding of tea and tea gardens comes from many sources. The books are listed in full in the bibliography; the people deserve more immediate notice. To begin, I would like to say thank you to all my Kyōto "tea-friends" who shared *ippuku* with me: John McGee and Alexandre Avdoulov, Gary Caldwaller and Joseph Justice, and Michiko Yuwasa of Hiden'in temple. Several scholars also kindly shared of their time, in particular Tsutsui Hiroichi of the Ura Senke Foundation in Kyōto, Nakamura Toshinori of the Kyōto University of Art and Design, Tani Akira of the Nomura Art Museum, Dennis Hirota of Ryūkoku University, as well as all the researchers associated with the Research Center for Japanese Garden Art at the Kyōto University of Art and Design. I am especially grateful to many people at Cornell University, where a great deal of this book was written, including Fred Kotas, bibliographer of the Japanese collection; Anyi Pan, Chinese art historian; and John Whitman and Laurie Damiani of the East Asian Program, of which I am a visiting scholar. Kendall Brown, Kathy Gleason, Clifton Olds, Barbara Ruch, and John Whitman supported me in my application for the Graham Foundation grant for which I am so grateful. I did receive that grant and so must thank everyone at the Graham Foundation for their support, which helped me acquire the many images within. Ken Rodgers combed through the raw text to clean out the burrs, and Beth Cary polished the final text with a rare bilingual skill only few editors have. Finally, I would particularly like to express my many, many heartfelt thanks to Kyōko Selden, who worked carefully with me on all the translations, offering me a window into the world that forms the very basis of this book. Without her, this book would not have been possible.

CRAWL THROUGH DOOR. Mushanokōji Senke, Kyōto. The small square door, *nijiri-guchi*, slides open to the left, requiring guests to bow down and crawl through it in order to enter the tea room. In this way, the door acts as a divider or threshold between the outside world and inner world of the tea room. Photograph by Ōhashi Haruzō.

an invitation to tea

You have been invited to tea. The city is Kyōto. The season, early spring. Together with three other guests, you wait around the corner from the entrance to the garden in order to make certain you arrive at the gate just on time. Not early, not late. Just on time.

You and the other guests wear patternless *kimono*, though more and more these days people wear Western clothes to tea: suits and ties, simple dresses. The important thing is that a guest be neat and clean as an expression of respect for the host and of purity of mind. No one wears jewelry or uses perfume or cologne, those being too worldly and distracting. The four of you wait there at the side of the street in your *kimono*, an anomaly in modern Kyōto.

It is a warm day made warmer still by the treeless asphalt streets and tall concrete buildings that surround you. The center of Kyōto is, by and large, a dis- mal place, not rundown, just not pretty—aside from the occasional old townhouse. In general the recently built parts of the city are not well designed, consisting of a haphazard collection of cheap apartment buildings and convenience stores. It was not always this way. Historical photos of Kyōto, as well as the paintings and woodblock prints that predate photographs by hundreds of years, show a sea of scalloped tile roofs cresting over row after row of elegant, low-rise wooden buildings like silver waves. After visiting even a single *machiya*, the traditional wooden townhouses, one understands how elegant they can be, and if you project that mental image backward through time, you can imagine a city of preeminent beauty. And yet, oddly, this is not, for the most part, how the city was perceived by its residents.

The aristocrats of the Heian period (794–1185),

for instance, seem to have loved their capital, their *miyako*, better than life itself. Even something as seemingly minor as being assigned a bureaucratic position in Uji just a few miles to the south (let alone to a lonely rock in another province) was tantamount to exile and stirred thoughts of desperation. Yes, the aristocrats loved their *miyako*, but it was not the city as a whole they loved; rather their affection was limited to the grand estates within the city that they called home. Their idealized vision of the city was framed by the strong rammed-earth walls that encircled their properties and limited to the gardens and residences within those walls. It was the society of the city they loved, not the city itself. The streets beyond the walls of their estates in the northeast quarter, as well as whole districts of the city elsewhere where only commoners lived, were regarded disparagingly, if at all.

The city that you see around you was laid to waste in medieval times and rebuilt, burned again and built again, yet still, although the quality of the architecture steadily improved throughout history—the materials used and the skill with which they were created—the expressions of affection for the city were still assigned to the grand estates of military lords, *daimyō*, the temples and shrines, and the gay quarters full of cloth-bannered theaters and tea houses. Not the streets. Not the city itself, as a city. In fact, as we shall examine later, the "city" became a symbol of all things worldly and defiled, especially the marketplace within the city where the stamping and milling of people buying and selling raised a storm of dust. The physical dirt, as well as the spiritual impurity of monetary transactions, gave rise to the expression "the dust of the marketplace," *shijin*, the epitome of defilement.

The practice of *chanoyu*, commonly called the tea ceremony in English, was developed in urban centers in Japan during the 15th and 16th centuries. Although some parts of those cities, such as where provincial lords had their residences, were described as being beautiful in contemporary records, other districts, such as the "downtown" areas where the merchants lived, were not. It is very telling, therefore, that *chanoyu* began precisely in those places that were thought of so poorly. Not in the palaces of the military lords and aristocrats, or in the temples of the Zen Buddhist priests, but in the lowly merchant quarters, where you stand now, waiting for the tea gathering to begin. It is not coincidental. The reason is (or at least one of the reasons is) that *chanoyu* was created as an escape from what was perceived as a defiled world—a means to escape from the city, within the city—and the tea garden was created to be very much the antithesis of ugly streets and dusty marketplaces. At first, just very, very simple and clean and then, later, mossy, green, and forest-like.

The tea garden, which was called a *roji* at first and *chaniwa* in later years, was intended to be a path away from that urban world, or as was recorded in a 17th-century text about the beginnings of tea, "The *roji* is simply a path beyond this transient world; how then does it scatter all the dust from the spirit?"[1] When seen in this light, dismal present-day Kyōto might not be all that far from its historical roots. That is to say, allegorically, the ideal of escaping the physical and social ills of the city within the rusticity and communion of a tea gathering is as possible, and as necessary, today as it was in the era when *chanoyu* was first being developed.

The appointed time for tea has come. Along with the other guests, you walk to the host's house. Turning the corner you see, lodged between two nondescript apartment buildings, a roofed wall made of broad clear-grained wooden boards and, above them, stippled brown-clay plaster, in all about twice the height of a person. Above the wall you can see the tops of tall, neatly tended broadleaf evergreen trees. Off to the right side, the subtly contorted branches of a large red pine hang over the roof of the entry gate. From where you stand it looks as if there is a forest inside, somehow forgotten and still thriving within the city. It couldn't be more perfect.

You walk in single file to the gate, the oldest and most proficient at tea among you going first. You are second in line but that does not make you second in rank at the gathering. That place is reserved for the person who is last in line because, even as there are responsibilities with going first, so too are there duties assigned to the person who goes last in line.

The leader of the guests is called the *shōkyaku*, the guest of honor, and he is expected to do everything first. He will go first through the garden and into the tea house, receive tea first, and take on the role of guiding the other guests through the gathering, for instance, by initiating conversation with the host. The last among the guests, called the *makkyaku* or *otsume*, plays the opposite part, taking on the role of finishing things or closing things up. You will find this out as soon as you enter the tea garden.

The doors of the gate have been unlocked and left slightly ajar as a signal from your host, the *teishu*, that preparations have been completed, as an invitation to enter. You let yourselves in. A narrow walkway of tiny flat-topped stones, laid out with great precision so they form a smooth walking surface, extends back through the trees toward a two-story wooden townhouse. The walkway is overarched by graceful Japanese maples, which let a dappled light fall on the path. Bordered on the right by the wall of the neighboring building and on the left by a low garden fence, the walkway is tunnel-like, edged with moss and the sparsest planting of ferns and the diminutive *senryō*.

You walk most of the way down the path but, before you reach the entry to the house, you find, off to the left, a small roofed gate, this one not grand and imposing like the one on the street, not solid and defensive, but lightly built, open and airy. If your invitation today had been to a formal, full-session tea gathering, a *chaji*, you would have proceeded to the main house and gone inside to wait in a room set aside for that purpose, the *machiai*, where the host or her assistant would have served you cups of hot water made with the same water that she would use to make tea later on. This would have allowed you to taste the water and have given you time to prepare yourselves to arrange your clothes and such.

Today, however, the tea gathering is more informal, a *chakai*. There will be no meal served, and many of the aspects of the longer *chaji*, such as entering the *machiai*, are being dispensed with.

As with the large gate by the street, this light garden gate has been left unlocked, and you let yourselves in. This is the *roji-mon*, the garden gate. When you have all entered, the *otsume*, the last among you, begins his role by turning to close the gate and lock it with a wooden bar laid horizontally across the twin swinging doors. Although the separation is in fact ephemeral, by locking the gate, the outside world has been symbolically left behind. Your host has been waiting inside the tea house all this time. Her preparations are complete and she has been sitting quietly. Listening. The sound of the gate closing and the dull clack of wood on wood as the *otsume* locks the gate comes to her and alerts her to your arrival.

Entering the tea garden, you find yourself in what appears to be a small forest, mossy-floored and exceedingly tidy. The ground is swept and watered, the trees trimmed to maintain an unaffected airiness. A light cover of tree branches extends over you like layered lace umbrellas. If you had just been standing on a modern city street, you cannot sense it now, the broader schema of things now forgotten: the location of the garden, the year, the urgencies of your day-to-day life. What remains is the atmosphere of a forest trail: the glint of pale light off water droplets on the ferns, the meandering line of the narrow path leading back through the trees to the tea house, the hue of a bark-shingle roof that can be just barely glimpsed through the trees.

There are no flowers in the garden. No prized boulders. The design is restrained for the same reason that guests do not wear patterned clothes or perfume or jewelry, namely, so that it will offer nothing to distract from the intention of the gathering. The tea garden is clearly not a "showy garden," and yet much can be discerned. You know it is spring by the pale green of the new leaves. You sense the hospitality of the owner in every well-tended detail. Nothing is astounding about this garden and yet, in its subtlety (and *because* of its subtlety), you find that it encourages you to open your senses and pay attention: to listen closely, scent the air, examine the most minute recesses for their secrets.

This is the tea garden, what has come to be known as the "dewy path." A garden that is not a garden. Yet

how did it come to be? And why? In the early Muromachi period (1333–1568) there were no such gardens in Japan, though people did drink tea. By the early Edo period (1600–1868), tea gardens were common, found in the residences of urban merchants, military lords, and aristocrats, and also in Buddhist temples. What happened? The story of how that came to be is the story of this book.

Since it is the development of the *roji* in medieval times that marks the beginning of tea gardens—and since tea gardens have had such a broad impact on garden design in Japan thereafter—understanding how the *roji* came into being is of great importance to understanding Japanese gardens as a whole. Accordingly, the storyline of this book falls into three main sections, pivoting on the period when the *roji* was first created. Chapters 1 and 2 present background material—the history of tea, gardens, and architecture that predated and became the foundation for the development of *chanoyu* and the *roji*. Chapters 3 and 4 give an in-depth look at Japanese society during the 15th and 16th centuries, showing the confluences of cultural, social, economic, and other forces that allowed for the development of *chanoyu* and the *roji* at that time. The final chapters of the book follow up by looking at how the *roji*, which was so simple in its original configuration, continued to be developed over the centuries into the more complex form of tea garden that exists today.

The gate is open. Join me.

1

a brief history of tea

茶史

The tea garden, in its most incipient form, began to make its appearance in historical texts during the 16th century. But what came before then? What precedents were there in Japan, and in China (where tea culture originated), that may have informed the development of *chanoyu* and its special garden? The tea garden didn't simply emerge out of thin air—its appearance was the end result of a long evolution of traditions regarding tea and gardens. To understand this, first we must look at the development of tea culture in general.

The term "tea culture" includes a wide spectrum of cultural attributes including the manner of drinking tea, the utensils used in its preparation and service, the artwork displayed during a tea gathering, the philosophical or literary themes that informed the culture, the form of architecture associated with tea gatherings, and, of course, the garden or other physical setting within which tea was served or through which one passed in order to reach the place of the tea gathering.

The history of tea drinking from a Japanese perspective, from its beginnings in Tang-dynasty China (618–907) to the full development of *chanoyu*, would fill volumes; indeed it has filled volumes.[2] What follows here is a cursory historical introduction for those readers who may not be familiar with the big picture, and then, following that, an in-depth look at that same history with a particular eye on how it led to the development of tea gardens in Japan.

To begin with, in Japan (and in China and many other places as well) tea is called *cha*. All tea, everywhere—whether red, brown, or green; leaf-tea or powdered; roasted, scented, or plain—is derived from a single species, Camellia sinensis, the "Chinese camellia." The variety of the species, the manner in which the leaf is picked—from what part of the stem, at what time of the growing season, and so on—and the way the leaves are processed after picking, all define whether the tea will become Earl Grey, *oolong*, or *matcha*.

In terms of its effect on the evolution of Japanese tea gardens, the cultural practice of tea drinking in Japan up to the 15th century can be seen as developing in three stages. The first stage took place dur-ing the Nara period (710–84) when the tea culture of Tang-dynasty China was introduced and tea drinking became an important part of Japanese culture for the first time. The second stage occurred during the Kamakura period (1185–1333) when the tea culture of the Song dynasty (960–1279), and to some degree the Yuan dynasty (1271–1368), was introduced, along with many other aspects of Chinese culture including Zen Buddhism. The third stage came during the Muromachi and Momoyama periods (1333–1600) in Japan while China was under the rule of the Ming dynasty (1368–1644).

Tea was a common beverage in China by the Tang dynasty. The newly picked tea leaves were pressed into "cakes" of which small pieces would be later broken off and crushed in order to make a pot of tea. Japanese priests studying Esoteric Buddhism in China in the 9th century learned about the healthful and potentially medicinal properties of tea and brought the custom of tea-drinking back to Japan, where it spread throughout the priestly and aristocratic classes of society.

Through the 10th, 11th, and 12th centuries, Japan had little or no official contact with China. At the end of the 12th century, however, the military families in Japan wrested control of society from the civil aristocratic class.[3] Under the new leadership, envoys were once again sent to China, then under control of the Song dynasty. Upon their return to Japan, the envoys, who included Buddhist priests and merchants as well as other private citizens, introduced many aspects of Song culture including Zen Buddhism, the artistic sensibilities and practices of the Chinese literati such as ink landscape paintings (*sansuiga*) and tray plantings (*bonsai*), and the culture of drinking whisked, powdered tea, called *matcha* in Japanese.

In Japan, *matcha* became part of life in Zen Buddhist temples, where it was used in formal ceremonies as an offering, and during meditation as a mild stimulant. The military class then began incorporating the drinking of *matcha* into their daily lives, too, collecting Chinese tea utensils with great fervor and holding lavish tea-tasting parties. Finally, the merchant classes in cities such as Sakai, Nara, and Kyōto began to take part in *matcha* tea culture, collecting and dealing in tea utensils and practicing as tea masters. The confluence of these three social classes—Zen priests, military lords, and urban merchants—and the increasing social status and influence of artists and artisans set the scene for a new form of tea culture.

Beginning in the early 15th century, and continuing over a period of two hundred years, a series of tea masters and their disciples began creating a new manner of tea gathering that would eventually be called *chanoyu*. *Chanoyu* tea masters moved away from the technological control of Chinese-style tea, finding new beauty instead in rusticity, using roughly made or naturalistic utensils such as local Japanese ceramics and simple bamboo wares. They rejected the lavishness of earlier tea parties and began holding tea gatherings for a limited number of guests in small, rustic tea houses called *sōan*, or grass-roofed arbors. Being adept at this form of tea gathering came to be of great social importance and, at times, of political significance. Ideally, tea gatherings were also intended to be contemplative in nature, an inward-focused activity with overtones of Zen Buddhist and Daoist spirituality.

The *sōan* were often situated in the privacy of the back part of urban properties. Small gardens were developed as entry paths to the *sōan*, modeled after deep evergreen forests—unadorned, naturalistic, and subdued. It is these "entry path gardens," known as *roji*, that mark the beginning of tea gardens.

Tang-Dynasty China (618–907)

The capital of the Tang dynasty in China was the city of Chang'an, present-day Xian, far inland directly on the land routes that led west to the Middle East and south to India, supporting the cosmopolitan atmosphere of the age. The arts and literature flourished (the latter encouraged by the development of block printing), and Confucian ideals of an ordered society were put into effect through a system of scholar-officials. These officials, career bureaucrats chosen through civil service examinations, acted as intermediaries between the imperial government and provincial communities. They were often proponents of tea culture, and their taste in art and philosophy would influence the development of rustic tea and tea gardens in Japan many centuries later.

By the Tang dynasty, the drinking of tea in China had developed into a refined art. Newly picked tea leaves were steamed, pounded, and then pressed into molds until they formed a solid block: ball-shaped, brick-shaped, and petal-shaped among others. Because of this shaping, the tea was known as caked tea or brick tea—*tuancha* in Chinese and *dancha* in Japanese. The caked tea would then be baked and packaged for distribution and sale. To drink the tea, a piece of the block would be broken off, roasted, ground in a wheel pestle, and the resulting powder sifted and boiled in water.[4] It was common for salt or spices to be added to the tea, even though tea purists disagreed with this habit.

The art of tea was recorded in a three-volume book called the *Chajing*, the *Classic of Tea* (*Chakyō* in Japanese), which was written in the late 8th century by Lu Yu, whose background is not well documented. Opening with the famous line "Tea is a noble tree from the south," which Japanese tea masters many centuries later would make reference to, the book details the origins of tea, as well as the methods of gathering, preparing, and drinking tea. Utensils for preparing and serving tea had been developed to a high level by Lu Yu's time, and he mentions fifteen tools for the manufacture of tea (including the boiler, pestle, and storage containers) and twenty-five tools associated with the service of tea (including the brazier, the measure, the water filter, and, of course, tea bowls). Lu Yu also compares tea and water from different areas, but he does not describe a particular form of architecture associated with the service of tea nor a garden setting within which tea gatherings were held.[5]

Nara-Period Japan (710–84)

During the Nara period in Japan, the capital was called Heijō-kyō, located where the city of Nara is today. The era is marked by the formalization of social, political, religious, and artistic culture that had initially been imported from Korea and China during the previous Kofun (300–552) and Asuka (552–710) periods. The imperial lineage became firmly established, as did many other aristocratic family lines; certain esoteric Buddhist sects became institutionalized through the support of the imperial government; and, in the arts, it is the sculptures and paintings of Buddhist themes that are best known from that era.

At the end of the 8th and beginning of the 9th centuries, Japanese Buddhist priests began making trips to Tang China to study at established temples. Among them were Eichū, Saichō, and Kūkai[6] all of whom are credited with bringing back the first tea from China—either the seeds or the tea leaves. Eichū had been in China the longest, for over thirty years beginning in the 770s or 780s. Saichō and Kūkai only stayed a year or two, both going once in 804 and Kūkai again in 806. But it is unlikely that any of these three were actually the first to introduce tea seeds to Japan. An entry for 729 in Ōgishō records a ceremonial tea offering, chagi, held at the imperial court, implying that tea use was already well established by that time. Moreover, tea seeds were found at the Tōro archeological dig in Shizuoka Prefecture dating from the Yayoi period (300 B.C.–A.D. 300), perhaps the 2nd century A.D., lending credence to the theory that a native Japanese tea plant existed before Chinese tea was introduced.[7]

Nevertheless, in the Nara period and certainly by the Heian period (794–1185), tea had become an accepted part of the lives of Japanese aristocrats. Tea was used, in part, as a means to affect an air of Chinese sophistication, but also for the healthful and invigorating properties of the drink. Recently, tea has been praised for its anti-oxidant and anti-bacterial properties, which could explain tea's healthfulness, and for a long time now it has been known to contain caffeine, which certainly would explain its invigorating properties. Green tea, however, contains less caffeine than black teas (perhaps a third the amount), and much less than coffee (perhaps a fifth the amount).

The tea used by the Japanese court and Buddhist priests was dancha, which was imported from China. They also imported tea utensils, and it is thought that the manner in which tea was prepared and served in Japan was very much like that of China at that time. Also, in Japan, as in China, there was no specific architecture designated for tea, nor was there any exterior space that could be called a tea garden.

In terms of how contact with the Tang dynasty, and the introduction of tea drinking into Japan in the Nara period, affected the development of the tea garden, we should understand that period as one of cultural foundation building. To begin with, the introduction of tea drinking to Japan was significant in the sense that it established tea as a drink of great importance, associated with the priestly and aristocratic classes of society, and known for its healthful properties. This meant that several hundred years later, when powdered-tea drinking was introduced to Japan from Song-dynasty China, it was received as something very new and very old at the same time, filling the antipodal roles of the *traditional* and the *avant-garde* simultaneously, and found ready acceptance because of that dual character.

Also of great importance to the development of rustic tea and tea gardens, as we shall look at in detail later on, was the ideal of the "hermit-scholar" that formed one of the philosophic foundations of rustic tea culture. Although tea gardens would not develop in Japan until the 16th century, the Chinese tradition of hermit-scholars dates back to the Tang dynasty, and men such as Wang Wei (701?–761), the Tang-dynasty landscape poet, were well-known to medieval Japanese tea masters. So, although Tang-dynasty tea culture—the exact manner of drinking tea, the architecture and gardens associated with tea (or lack thereof)—did not directly influence the development of Japanese tea gardens in the 16th century, it did lay a cultural foundation that supported the development of tea gardens many hundreds of years later.

Song-Dynasty China (960–1279)

The Song dynasty is divided into two periods: Northern Song (960–1127), when the capital was based in the city of Kaifeng, in today's Henan province, and Southern Song (1127–1279), when those members of the imperial court who survived an attack from the north set up a new capital at Lin'an (Hangzhou). Again, scholar-officials were instrumental in establishing the new dynastic order as were members of the mercantile class, a newly ascendant group of commoners who fostered private trade and a market economy. The Song dynasty is known for its many cultural developments including calligraphy, painting, and ceramics. It is these three that most strongly influenced the development of tea culture in Japan, and when Japanese travelers came to China during the later Yuan and Ming dynasties it was primarily Song-style artifacts they were seeking.

Regarding tea, by the end of the Tang dynasty a new manner of preparing and serving tea had been developed in China called powdered tea, *mocha* in Chinese or *matcha* in Japanese. This method was refined during the Song dynasty and has become associated with that era. To make *mocha*, freshly picked tea leaves were first steamed to fix them, then partially dried, ground in stone grist mills, and sieved to create a very fine powder, about the consistency of talcum powder, but brilliant green in color. This powder was then stored in containers until it was used. To drink the tea, a small amount would be taken from the container with a scoop, placed in a ceramic bowl, hot water added to it, and the mixture whisked until a light froth developed on the surface. In formal situations, the bowl would then be placed in a ceramic or lacquer stand to elevate it, symbolizing the respect in which the tea was held.

Paintings from the Song period give a good sense of the settings in which tea was served. Loosely defined, there are three categories of settings: garden pavilions, outdoor courtyards, and wild nature.

A good example of the first category—pavilions as a setting for tea—can be seen in the painting *Literary Gathering*, executed by an unknown painter (fig. 1). The painting shows tea being served in an open-walled

I. SONG-DYNASTY TEA PAVILION. In Song-dynasty China, the pavilions in which tea was served were not used exclusively for tea gatherings but rather for all manner of cultural pastimes. One can see tea being prepared in the side room but, as the servant carrying a tray and walking toward the gate implies, preparations were also made at other locations. *Literary Gathering*, anonymous, Song dynasty (960–1279). National Palace Museum, Taiwan.

pavilion that looks out onto a walled courtyard garden. Other paintings from the same era, such as *Reading in an Open Hall* by Chao Po-su (1124–82), depict pavilions that look out over broader natural landscapes. In either case, however, the pavilions are not devoted entirely to the service of tea but were apparently used for any of the pastimes of literary gentlemen, such as the Four Accomplishments that were often pictured in paintings of the Song dynasties: playing the lute, playing *qi* (a strategic board game with black and white beads), calligraphy, and painting.[8] In *Literary Gathering* we see tea being prepared in a room on the left-hand side of the pavilion. Two or three blackish tea stands sit on a table at which a man is brewing tea in white porcelain cups. In the central part of the room, two guests sit talking with their host, awaiting their tea. Just outside the gate to the left, however, another servant is carrying a tray with two bowls, implying that some preparations were made elsewhere. Similarly, in *Reading in an Open Hall*, tea is being carried on a tray to a pavilion by a retainer, which indicates that tea was not always made within the hall but rather at some location apart from it.

As depicted in *Literary Gathering*, the pavilions were tile-roofed, built on raised stone platforms, and made with squared posts and beams. The courtyards surrounding the pavilions seem, in places, to have been no more than leveled ground, and in other parts to have been developed as gardens with plantings of pine, willow, and bamboo and the placement of carefully balanced rockery. In fact, one cannot tell whether the rockery is intended to represent a created, garden-like landscape or simply to imply the pavilion was built next to an existing outcropping. Neither of the pavilions appears to be in an urban location.

The second type of setting for tea service was

out-of-doors in an open courtyard as seen in paintings such as *The Eighteen Scholars*, anonymous (fig. 2); *Eighteen Scholars of Tang*, attributed to Emperor Hui-tsung (1082–1135); and *Preparing Tea*, attributed to Liu Sung-nien (ca. 1174–1224). The last two paintings are intended to be images of Tang literati tea parties, but the utensils shown are from the Song period, making the images primarily representative of the Song period. In each of the paintings we can see good examples of the kind of tea service utensils that will eventually be brought to Japan during the Kamakura (1185–1333) and Muromachi periods (1333–1568). There are the *tianmu* tea bowls (Japanese, *tenmoku*) with their saucer-like pedestal stands, tall bronze water kettles (some shown placed directly in a brazier), and a stone grist mill for grinding tea into powder. These aspects of the tea service were imported to Japan and used in precisely the same manner as they were in China—at least until the development of rustic tea in the 15th and 16th centuries. The courtyard garden that forms the setting for tea service, however, is very different from what would be found in Japan.

In *The Eighteen Scholars*, only the presence of a white stone balustrade in the background lets us know that the scene is in a garden or courtyard and not in wild nature. This image is one of four scrolls that depict the Four Accomplishments. Here we see some gentlemen, seated on a low, bench-like table, absorbed in a game of *qi*. Their backs are protected from the wind by a large screen on which has been painted a landscape scene. In the foreground are a stone table and a carved stone planter in which has been set an ornamental stone. Along the left-hand side of the painting, in the foreground, we see elaborately shaped rockery and a short palm tree poking out from behind the rock. In the background, behind the gathering, is a kind of banana tree,

2. **SONG-DYNASTY TEA CUSTOMS.** While some gentlemen interest themselves in a game of *qi*, two of their servants pour hot water into a porcelain cup that sits on a black ceramic or lacquer pedestal. Powdered tea would already have been put in the bowl. These utensils are the same as those that Japanese Zen priests brought to Japan and used in their temples. *The Eighteen Scholars*, anonymous, Ming-dynasty copy of an original attributed to the Song dynasty (960–1279). National Palace Museum, Taiwan.

a tall, ornately hollowed rock (probably decomposed limestone such as the *taihu* stones) that had been set in the courtyard as an ornament, and a large willow tree.

Eighteen Scholars of Tang and *Preparing Tea* depict very sparsely decorated, flat courtyards. It is more than likely that the painterly conventions of China—which called for a rarefaction of the painted image and the use of open, unpainted space—may have contributed to the apparent simplicity of the garden design. Nevertheless, it appears from these paintings that the courtyards were composed mostly of flat, open spaces surfaced with compacted soil or sand, were enclosed in some way by walls or balustrades, and were punctuated with only occasional plantings, groupings of rockery, and a few pieces of furniture for the comfort of the guests: tables, chairs, benches, and an assortment of tea paraphernalia.

The third setting for tea revealed in Song-dynasty paintings is out in nature, as seen in *Mountain Retreat* by Li Kung-lin (1049–1106; fig. 3). Here we see images of Li and his friends out enjoying the scenery at Lung-mien Mountain Retreat in Shuzhou.[9] All the tea utensils were carried there, a portable brazier was used to heat water, and tea was served using the same *tianmu* tea bowls as seen in the paintings mentioned above.

These paintings give an impression of what a Japanese visitor to China in the Song dynasty would have experienced if he had gathered in the company of the literati, joining them for tea at a country estate, or while visiting a famous scenic spot. Most likely, however, Japanese visitors would not have had the opportunity to join in such a group of famous literati. They were, after all, just foreign visitors of minor rank from a little-known country off the coast of China. Instead, it is the paintings themselves that the Japanese would have known best, seen in the halls of the Buddhist temples where they were studying or in the studios of the painters they were apprenticing to.

What these paintings reveal to us is that, during the Song period in China, although there were garden pavilions that often were the setting for gatherings that included the service of tea, there was no architecture specifically devoted to tea gatherings. Similarly, although there were courtyard-like, semi-enclosed spaces in which selected trees and rockery were arranged as the setting for gatherings at which tea was served, there was no garden developed specifically to be a setting for tea gatherings or an entry to a tea house.

3. TEA IN THE MOUNTAINS. The scene is the Lung-mien Mountain Retreat at which the painter, Li Kung-lin, and his friends are enjoying themselves. The utensils used for tea were simple and portable; the setting was wild nature—a riverbank by a crashing waterfall. *Mountain Retreat* (detail), Li Kung-Lin (1049–1106), Song dynasty (960–1279). National Palace Museum, Taiwan.

Kamakura-Period Japan (1185–1333)

The Kamakura period marks a point in time of dramatic shifts in the structure of Japanese society, four aspects of which were crucial to the development of the tea garden: the usurpation of societal control from civil aristocratic families by military aristocratic families (*bushi*), the introduction of Zen Buddhism from Song-dynasty China and the activity of Zen priests (*zensō*), the development of a merchant class (*shōnin*), and the development of professional and semi-professional artists and artisans (*geinōsha, shokunin*).[10] In Chapter 3 of this book, we will examine all four groups in detail, looking at how their confluence was essential to the development of *chanoyu* during the late Muromachi period. But for now, in terms of the Kamakura period, we will look at the use of tea within the context of just the first two, the Zen priests and the military families.

For at least two hundred years before the military government (*bakufu*) was formally established in the provincial city of Kamakura, military families such as the Taira and Minamoto, who served civil aristocratic families, had been developing their own independent power bases. At the end of the 12th century, these evolving social changes reached a tipping point and those families took the reins of power, setting up a new, military-based government. One of the most important decisions the new government made, not only in terms of the development of tea gardens but for Japanese culture in general, was to restore official contact with China after a hiatus of several hundred years. The last official embassy had been sent to the Tang court from the imperial Heian court in A.D. 894. In 1185, when the Kamakura *bakufu* was established, China was under control of the Song dynasty, and the renewed contact between the two countries allowed new ideas and products to be introduced to Japan. With regard to the development of tea gardens, two of the most important cultural imports were Zen Buddhism and the new way of drinking powdered tea, *matcha*, both brought back to Japan by traveling priests and, soon afterward, adopted by families of the new military aristocracy for use in their households.

EARLY TEA USE AMONG ZEN PRIESTS

Zen Buddhism (*Zen* is pronounced *Chan* in China) had, in fact, been introduced to Japan during the Heian period (794–1185), but the civil aristocratic class of that time was more interested in the flourish of the esoteric sects of Buddhism than the personal rigors required by the Zen sect. The military lords, however, actively supported the newly imported Zen sect, partly because its core philosophy of self-training appealed to them but also because, politically, the new sect had no established power base in Japan and could be molded to their needs.

Several sects of Zen Buddhism were introduced to Japan during the Kamakura period, and of them two in particular established themselves most effectively: the Rinzai sect (Chinese, *Linji*) and the Sōtō sect (Chinese, *Caodong*). Of these two, it is the Rinzai sect that is primarily associated with the medieval Japanese arts such as ink landscape painting (*sansuiga*), dry landscape gardens (*karesansui*), and, of course, the artistic practice of tea, *chanoyu*. The fact that the Rinzai sect developed this unique relationship to the arts does not have to do with anything inherent in the dogma or practice of the sect, nor with its history in China. Rather, it is due to the manner in which it settled in Japan and to the associations it developed there.

Whereas the Sōtō sect established its temples in the countryside, the Rinzai sect found fertile ground in the urban areas of Japan—Kyōto and Kamakura—and established its most powerful temples in those cities. Cities, and city dwellers, being what they are, the Rinzai sect naturally became associated with urbane things including the various fine arts.

The Rinzai sect was introduced to Japan by a priest named Eisai (1141–1215), who traveled to China in 1168 and then again in 1187. Along with the teachings of Rinzai Buddhism, he is also credited with bringing back seeds of the tea plant, some of which he gave to the priest Myōe (1173–1232) of Kōzanji temple in Toganoʻo, a mountainous village district just north of Kyōto.[11] Myōe successfully raised the seeds, and this is traditionally considered to be the beginning of the cultivation of tea plants in Japan. In the following years, tea plantations were established to the south of Kyōto in Uji and elsewhere around Japan.

The Rinzai Zen temples were organized into a hierarchical system known as the Five Mountains, Gozan, based on a Chinese model (wushan). The temples that were placed within the system, and which position they occupied in the hierarchy of the system, shifted with the vagaries of the times. In fact, eventually, there were five designated temples in Kamakura and five more in Kyōto, so the total was actually "ten mountains." Temples within the Five Mountains system received the most direct financial support from the government and wielded the most political power. It is interesting to note, therefore, that the one temple which, more than any other, was associated with the development of the arts, such as painting and tea, was Daitokuji, a Zen temple that was *not* in the Gozan system. This was not coincidental. Rather, it was because the temple was free from the direct control of the military government's bureaucracy that creative expression was able to flourish within its precincts.

The use of tea in Rinzai temples during the Kamakura period was primarily as a healthful beverage, a means to stay alert during meditation, and as an offering in formal ceremonies called *sarei* (tea rituals). In 1211, Eisai wrote a treatise on the healthful qualities of tea called *Kissa Yōjōki* (*The Book of Tea for Health*) that he would eventually present to the *shōgun*, chief military lord, Minamoto no Sanetomo. Revealed in his text are two aspects of how tea was regarded during his time. The first is, as the title implies, that tea was a healthful drink with medicinal properties. The second can be deduced from how he couches his expressions in a mixture of Buddhist and Daoist terminology, revealing the commingling of those philosophies in Zen Buddhism, in general, and with regard to tea, in particular.

One of the formal ceremonies, *sarei*, that is still practiced today is called *yotsugashira*, the Ceremony of the Four Heads, which loosely translated means the ceremony for the Four Honored Ones (fig. 4). It is held at Kenninji temple in Kyōto each year in April. The ceremony is an important clue to understanding the development of tea culture in Japan because it is an excellent example of the formality that pervades *chanoyu*—the precise, ritualistic manner of serving and receiving tea. In the *yotsugashira* ceremony an incense burner is placed on a stand in the middle of the prayer hall of the temple. The floor is wooden, but around the perimeter of the room a single row of *tatami* mats is laid out to allow priests (or other guests) to sit comfortably. In the center, facing the incense burner, are four chairs in which the four guests of honor will be seated. Tea is brought out and offered first to the portrait of Eisai hung at one end of the room, then to the four main guests, and finally to all others in attendance.

To serve the tea, attendants carry in *tenmoku* tea bowls, each on its own pedestal. They hold the bowls with great care, grasping the pedestal with two hands and holding it just in front of their chest. The attendants walk with a slow, steady rhythm bringing a bowl in turn to each guest, a scoop of *matcha* already placed inside each bowl. A second attendant follows with a tall bronze kettle (just like the ones seen in *Eighteen Scholars of Tang*), from which he pours hot water into the bowl and whisks it with a bamboo whisk until a pale froth forms on top. The honorific quality of the event, the precise, ritualized movements, the silence within which all is carried out, the attention to detail—all these things were incorporated into *chanoyu* at a later date. There were not, however, any spaces in Zen temples during the Kamakura period that were specific to the service of tea, either architectural or garden-like.

EARLY TEA USE AMONG MILITARY FAMILIES

The military families developed their own distinctive culture over the course of the late Heian and Kamakura periods. The drinking of *matcha* as it was practiced in Zen temples was incorporated as part of their household culture, including the use of a portable tea shelf called *daisu* in Japanese (fig. 5). The form of the *daisu* was, for all intents and purposes, identical to that used in Song-dynasty China and had been brought to Japan by Zen priests. It was a small piece of furniture, usually finished in highly polished black lacquer, with a low shelf for heavy objects such as the charcoal brazier, *furo*, and water container, *mizusashi*, and a higher shelf for lighter utensils such as the *tenmoku* tea bowls and their stands. Because the service of tea in the residences of the military class at that time was associated with the *daisu*, that style of service has come to be called *daisu-cha*.[12]

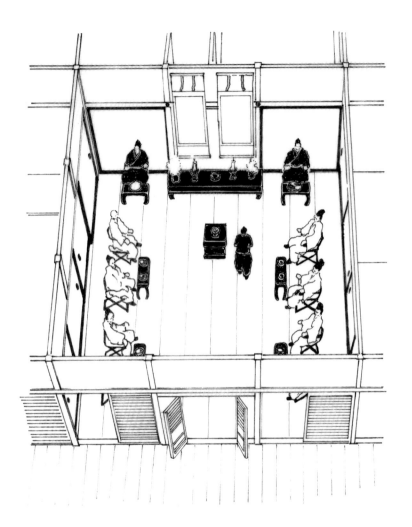

4. YOTSUGASHIRA TEA CEREMONY. One of the formal ceremonies, *sarei*, held in Zen Buddhist temples and the residences of military lords was called *yotsugashira*, the Ceremony of the Four Honored Ones. The formal, ceremonial procedure of these occasions influenced the development of tea gatherings in the 1500s. This is an imaginary view of a gathering like a *yotsugashira* taking place at Lord Ashikaga Yoshinori's Muromachi-dono Palace in 1437. Redrawn from Nakamura, *Chanoyu Quarterly*, vol. 70, p. 37.

By the end of the Kamakura period, gatherings specifically designed for the drinking of *matcha* had become frequent. These were known as *chayoriai*, literally, "tea gatherings," and were typically held in rooms called *kaisho*, literally, "meeting rooms" (but "reception rooms" or "parlors" fits the use better). The *kaisho* was, at first, just a name for any room in the residence that was being used as a parlor, but, by the end of the Kamakura period, the name referred to a specific room and, at times, a separate hall. One important aspect about a room being used as a *kaisho* is that it was required to have some shelving to display the host's valuables, which in that era generally meant things imported from China. These were known as *kara-mono*, "Chinese things," and included ceramic bowls, bronze vases, and calligraphic or painted scrolls.[13] The tea gatherings became progressively more lavish and the intent of showing off one's wealth more obvious.

The drinking of tea also developed into a game or contest of sorts. The host would present several types of tea in separate bowls and the guests would compete to see if they could determine which type of tea was being served. Specifically, the point of the game was to determine which tea was *honcha* ("true tea"; the tea from Togano'o) and which was *hicha* ("false tea"; any tea not from Togano'o). The competition was known as *tōcha*, "contest tea." In some ways, *tōcha* follows from the Heian-period pastime of *mono-awase*, "comparing things," in which court ladies would attempt to match any manner of similar objects, be they flowers, shells, or tree roots. The "matching" of a tea to a location in *tōcha* followed in this tradition, but the setting, with its lavish display of wealth, as well as the copious quantities of food, alcoholic drink, and expensive prizes, meant that medieval *tōcha* was different in its atmosphere from Heian-period *mono-awase*.

In summary, we find that in Kamakura-period Japan the drinking of tea had become widespread among both Buddhist priests and the military aristocracy. In particular, the drinking of whisked powdered tea, *matcha*, had become the vogue, and it was common for Zen temples and the houses of the military aristocracy to have the utensils required for the preparation and service of tea. There were also rooms, such as the *kaisho*, that were used for tea gatherings, although they were not used exclusively for that purpose. There was not, however, in Zen temples, or the residences of the military aristocracy, or anywhere else, an exterior garden-like space that had been developed exclusively as a place for serving tea or as an entry garden to a tea house.

Yuan-Dynasty China (1271–1368)

The Yuan dynasty can be said to have begun either in 1271, when Kublai Khan founded the Yuan lineage, or in 1279, when Khan finally subdued the last of the Song dynasty at their southern court. It ended in 1368 with the Mongol expulsion. The Yuan capital was at Khanbaliq (present-day Beijing), and, although the government was modeled on Chinese systems, it was staffed by people from all over Central Asia, a custom that was typical of the racially and culturally mixed Mongolian armies. Even a person from distant Italy, Marco Polo, was able to be granted the governorship of Hangzhou, the capital of the destroyed Southern Song dynasty.

The connections between the Yuan court and Japan were unusual to say the least. Kublai Kahn had tried to invade Japan twice, in 1274 and again in 1281. Both fleets met with disaster, falling prey to typhoons (the *kamikaze*, "winds of the gods"). In 1275, the Mongol emissaries who were sent to call on the Kamakura government were all beheaded. Despite this, by the early 1300s, just at the end of the Kamakura period and into the following Muromachi period (1333–1568), trade vessels were again being sent to China. The first groups were arranged by temples, or in the name of temples, and at times by Shintō shrines as well. The profits of the voyages, which may have reached as much as a hundred times the investment, were intended to support those temples' activities. The ships included those supporting Shōmyōji (temple of the Shingon Risshū sect in Kanagawa, 1306), Tōfukuji (Zen temple in Kyōto, 1323), Kenchōji (Zen temple in Kamakura, 1323), Kamakura Daibutsu (the Great Buddha sculpture of Kamakura, 1330), Sumiyoshi Taisha (a Shintō shrine in Ōsaka), and Tenryūji (Zen temple in Kyōto, 1342). In terms of the development of tea culture in Japan, these voyages were important not only for the goods they imported but because they reawakened Japanese society to an "international mind-set" that expanded further during the following Ming dynasty, even if only for a brief time.

The Mongols traditionally drank their tea with milk, a practice that the Han Chinese under their rule abhorred and that the Japanese travelers did not seem to appreciate or import. The Song style of drinking continued among the Han Chinese during the Yuan-dynasty Mongol rule, and it is this style that the Japanese continued to import during this time. A process of roasting tea leaves to improve their flavor, called *chaoqing*, or "green roasting," that developed during the Yuan dynasty would allow for a revolutionary change in tea drinking during the following Ming dynasty. Just

5. CHINESE-STYLE TEA SHELF. The formal practice of making and serving whisked powdered tea was imported from Song-dynasty China. It included the use of a Chinese-style tea shelf, known as a *karamono daisu* in Japanese. On the top shelf, to the left, is the cloth bag that holds the tea caddy, *shifuku*, and a black tea bowl, *tenmoku*, on its red pedestal, *tenmoku-dai*. On the bottom shelf, from the left, is the cast iron kettle, *kama*, set into the bronze brazier, *furo*; a bamboo water ladle, *hishaku*, and a pair of fire tongs, *hibashi*, set into a tall bronze urn, *shakudate*; a bowl to collect waste water, *kensui*; and a lidded pot for clean water, *mizu-sashi*. In the front, on a square lacquer tray, are the tea caddy, *chaire*, and the tea spoon, *chashaku*. Redrawn from *Chadō Shūkin*, vol. 2, p. 89.

as the Mongol-style tea service typical of the Yuan dynasty was not imported to Japan, neither was there any specific tea architecture or tea garden introduced to Japan from China at this time.

Ming-Dynasty China (1368–1644)

The people revolted against their Yuan rulers, and in 1368 Chu Yüan-chang, a former Buddhist monk who had become the leader of the rebellion, proclaimed himself emperor and founder of the Ming dynasty. The capital was initially in the southern city of Nanjing and then moved to Beijing under Emperor Yung Lo in 1421. The administration began a "tally" system under which trade ships wishing to enter Chinese ports were required to have official passports, or "tallies," from the government. These tallies were called *kangō* in Japanese, and the ships that made the voyages at that time were known as *kangōsen,* or "tally ships."

The aforementioned development of the *chaoqing* process made loose leaf tea more than just palatable; it became good enough for the emperor to drink. In 1391, an imperial edict disallowed the making of caked tea in China, and from then on tea in China was primarily made from loose leaf that was steeped in hot water to extract the flavor, much as it is today.

Paintings of tea gatherings in the Ming period show a similar arrangement to those from the Song period. As in Song paintings, some depict tea being served in formal pavilions in which the host and his guests sit inside the hall and are served by attendants who prepare tea in an adjacent room or just outside. One such example is *The Villa of Master Donglin,* in which we can see attendants busily preparing tea in a grove of trees off to the right of a pavilion where the host and his guest sit (fig. 6).

Another motif, as in Song paintings, is tea being served outdoors. In *The Gathering in the Apricot Garden,* for instance, we see two gentlemen sitting under flowering trees (fig. 7). They are, in fact, Ts'ui Tzu-chung, the painter himself, and his host, the patron who commissioned the painting. While the setting looks like wild nature, with craggy rocks here and there, the title makes one think this may have been an agricultural setting. The setting was most likely Beijing where the patron lived, and it was not uncommon for well-to-do urbanites to have argricultural lands as part of their estates in the city.

A third motif we find is tea being served in a rustic arbor in a place that seems to be far away from any city or town, deep in the mountains. One painting that shows this third type is *Brewing Tea* by Wen Cheng-ming, who made tea the focus of his paintings and poems (fig. 8). In *Brewing Tea* we see two small thatch-roofed huts, set in the wilds of a mountain landscape beneath an ancient pine tree. Placing tea houses by large pine trees or in groves of pines would eventually become a classic form in Japan. Cheng-ming's hut is simple, remote, and away from human settlements. The owner is receiving a guest in the main hut while, off to the side in a smaller hut, an attendant is brewing tea.

6. MING-DYNASTY TEA PAVILION. Here we see tea being prepared by attendants in a grove of trees. Although tea is an important part of Ming-dynasty culture, neither the pavilion, nor the garden associated with it, is reserved exclusively for tea gatherings. *The Villa of Master Donglin,* attributed to Qiu Ying (1494–1552). Museum fuer Asiatische Kunst, Staatliche Museen zu Berlin.

There is a book on the table, and one can tell from that, and from the dress and hair fashion of the people in the scene, that this is not a poor farmer's hut but rather that of a literate man who has chosen to be in reclu-

7. TEA IN THE ORCHARD. The setting of this outdoor tea is most likely the apricot grove of the gentleman sitting in the large chair, the patron of the painting. The stone mortar seen in the foreground, which is used for grinding tea leaves into powder, is very much like those that were brought to Japan and are still used to this day. *The Gathering in the Apricot Garden*, 1638, Ts'ui Tzu-chung (d. 1644). Chazen Museum of Art, University of Wisconsin–Madison.

sion. The image presented here—of tea service being associated with detachment from the affairs of urban life—would become an essential part of the development of *chanoyu* in the 15th and 16th centuries in Japan and would be a fundamental impetus for the design of the tea gardens that were developed at that time.

So far, we have looked at the Tang, Song, Yuan, and Ming dynasties in China and at the Nara, Heian, and Kamakura periods in Japan to see if there were any specific precedents for the tea garden and, more generally, to see if there were any cultural precedents that could have informed its development. What we have found can be summarized in the following four steps.

- **Initial Introduction of Tea Culture**: It goes without saying that tea gardens would not have developed in Japan unless, first, tea service had become an important part of Japanese society. Seen in that light, the roots of the tea garden can be found in the initial introduction of tea and tea service to Japan during the Tang/Nara periods. This culture of tea formed the fundamental platform upon which Japanese *chanoyu* culture would be built in a much later era and from which the tea garden would evolve. There were not, however, specific exterior spaces in China or Japan at that time that could be called "tea gardens" and that served as direct role models for the development of the tea garden.

- **Introduction of Zen Buddhism**: The importation from China of Zen Buddhism beginning in the 12th century introduced a number of cultural aspects to Japan that would later influence the development of tea gardens. One is the particular world view associated with Zen Buddhism,

8. THE IDEAL HUT FOR TEA. The ideal of a cultured man who shares quiet time over tea with a guest in his simple thatch-roofed hut was a major thematic undercurrent in the development of *chanoyu* in Japan. One difference: this gentleman does not prepare tea for his guest himself but instead has an attendant do so in the side room. *Brewing Tea*, 1531, Wen Cheng-ming (1470–1559), Ming Dynasty. National Palace Museum, Taiwan.

which will be examined in more detail in Chapter 3. Specific to the development of *chanoyu* was the introduction through Zen temples of the use of powdered tea, *matcha*. Powdered tea was regarded as a healthful drink, was used to maintain alertness during meditation, and was also offered in formal temple ceremonies, called *sarei*. As we shall see in more detail later, the early forms of *chanoyu* in Japan used all of the utensils that were found in Zen temples. Also, the formality of *chanoyu*—its precise movements and placement of objects and its requirement for extreme cleanliness in all aspects of a tea gathering—can be said to have derived, in great part, from the precedent of the *sarei*. There were not, however, within Japanese Zen temples of the Kamakura period, specific exterior spaces that were used as tea gardens.

◆ **Introduction of Chinese Literati Culture:** The ideal of the literate scholar/official, who involves himself in a life of culture through activities such as the Four Accomplishments, was an important precedent in the development of Japan's cultural life styles. In particular, the literate scholar who leaves behind the trappings of society for a life as a recluse in the wilds of nature proved to be a fundamental ideal in the development of *chanoyu* and the tea garden.

◆ **Adoption of Powdered Tea Culture by the Military Aristocracy:** The fourth important development during this time was the transfer of tea culture from its initial footing in Zen temples to the residences of the military aristocracy where it was developed into a new manner of serving tea. In those residences it did not serve a ceremonial function but was part of the social life of the military lords. It was this new residential tea culture that eventually led to the development of *chanoyu*, and of the tea garden. And, as with the Zen temples during the Kamakura period, so too in the residences of the military aristocracy: there were not yet any exterior, garden-like spaces that could be called tea gardens.

2

文化

cultural background

Having just seen how tea culture developed in Japan in the centuries preceding the appearance of the tea garden, we will now take a look at four other aspects of Japanese culture that also informed its development. To begin with, by the time the tea garden developed, there was already a long tradition of garden design in Japan. So, one wonders, did those older gardening traditions influence the design of the *roji*? Were they used as models for its design or, conversely, were their traditions specifically rejected in favor of something new? Second, as we will see in detail later on, the first true tea gardens—and the culture of *chanoyu* that gave birth to them—developed in the townhouses of the urban merchants. These townhouses, called *machiya*, formed the physical context within which the *roji* were first developed. Understanding the history of that particular form of architecture helps in comprehending the reasons why the tea garden developed as it did. Third, the development of *chanoyu* and the tea garden was deeply influenced by the archetype of a literate and artistic recluse or hermit, so a look at this effect is in order. And, last, we will examine the particular aesthetics—such as *wabi* and *sabi*—that informed the development of *chanoyu* and the *roji*.

Garden History

For those readers who may not be familiar with Japanese gardens, what follows is a brief introduction to the history of gardens up to the 16th century when the *roji* developed, to show in what ways the *roji* was influenced by preexisting traditions, and in what ways it was a departure from those traditions.

Gardens were first built in Japan during the Asuka period (552–710) by artisans who had traveled from the Korean kingdoms as part of a more extensive cultural importation that included architecture, writing, religion, cloth making, and so on. Through the following Nara period (710–84), gardens were developed into a distinctly Japanese form so that by the Heian period (794–1185), Japanese gardens had evolved into a highly complex art form.[14] The gardens of the Heian period, the age when civil aristocrats reigned, were built in essentially two environments: the residences of civil aristocrats and the temples of esoteric Buddhist sects.

The aristocratic gardens, known today as *shinden* gardens after the style of residential architecture they were associated with, featured a flat court of sand to the south of the main residence hall (*shinden*) that acted as an entry and gathering place, and a pond or stream garden beyond that court to the south. The gardens incorporated images of wild nature drawn from nature directly, as well as from poetry, and allegorical images taken from Buddhist teachings. They were also shaped by the requirements of Chinese geomancy and a complex set of taboos that circulated among the aristocratic class.

The *Sakuteiki*, a gardening treatise from the mid-Heian period, describes in detail the technique and theory of garden design for that period. Whereas most Heian period garden design can *not* be said to have been directly influential on the development of *roji*, one of the gardening styles mentioned in the *Sakuteiki* that seems to presage the *roji*, in its intent if not its actual design, is the *yamazato no yō*, or the "mountain village style." The *Sakuteiki* states:

> To create a garden scene that evokes the feeling of a mountain village (*yamazato*), first build a high hill by the building, and then set stones from the top to bottom in such a way as they appear as bedrock breaking the surface of the ground.[15]

This image of a rocky hillock is very unlike the design of tea gardens as they actually came to be, but the idea of basing a garden's design on the image of a mountain village—a bucolic yet melancholy scene often described by recluse poets—was very much a theme in the design of early tea gardens.

The temple gardens of note from the Heian period are referred to as Pure Land gardens because they evoke, through their design and spatial layout, images of Buddhist Pure Lands, *jōdo*. Again, there is not a direct link between the design of Pure Land gardens and that of the medieval *roji*. However, Buddhist imagery was eventually interwoven in the *roji*, and it is important to note that incorporating Buddhist imagery in gardens was an ancient theme in Japanese gardens. In fact, the very first reference to a gardener in *Nihon Shoki* (also *Nihongi*), *Chronicles of Japan*, relates that he built an image of Mount Sumeru (Jp: Shumisen), the central mountain of the Buddhist cosmological scheme, in the garden of the Empress Suiko.[16]

The military aristocracy of the Kamakura period did little to change the taste in gardening of their predecessors among the Heian-period civil aristocrats. Low-level military men did not build gardens at their residences because the garden was a cultural attribute for which they had no affinity, not to mention the financial wherewithal. Those more powerful military families that developed a hereditary culture like that of the civil aristocrats mimicked many aspects of the aristocratic court culture, including many aspects of the design of their residential architecture and gardens.

Unlike the military families, Zen Buddhist priests began to develop gardens at their temples in a new direction during the Kamakura period. Although

the outward design was not, at first, radically different from the previous Heian-period *shinden* gardens, these garden building priests (*ishitatesō*) began to set stones in groupings that had new allegorical Buddhist meaning, as well as a painterly compositional style. These gardens were called *karesansui*, or "dry landscape," gardens (fig. 9).

In the Muromachi period, gardens in Zen temples and in the residences of military families combined styles derivative of the earlier civil aristocrats' gardens with the developing *karesansui* style. They featured ponds with boulder-encrusted shorelines, artfully pruned trees, and arrangements of large, sometimes unusually colored stones. Stones had always been a central feature of Japanese gardens—the opening line of the *Sakuteiki* makes this clear. It reads, *ishi wo taten koto*, which literally means the "art of setting stones" but was commonly understood at that time to mean the "art of garden making." The setting of stones was so important to the art of garden making that instead of saying, "making a garden," one simply said, "setting stones." True to this tradition, the gardens of Zen temples and of the military families' residential gardens prominently featured stone arrangements.

Conversely, an early collection of writings on *chanoyu* called *Usoshū* states, "no stones are to be set [in the garden; that way] the attention of the guests will not be distracted and, as they put their spirit into the tea gathering, they will be able to focus on the excellent tea wares presented within."[17] Considering how important stones were in the tradition of garden making in Japan, the fact that stones were expressly deemed to be unacceptable for use in the *roji* reveals a great deal about the counter-culture mentality that existed among the creators of *chanoyu*.

Machiya: Merchant Townhouses

The very first *roji* were created in the confines of urban properties amid the bustle of the merchant districts in cities like Kyōto and Sakai. Early records of tea gatherings mention the Shimogyō (Lower Capital) district of Kyōto in particular, which was then, as now, a mercantile district. After the time of the Ōnin War, which ravaged central Kyōto, the northern and southern parts of the city were split at around Nijō Street. Shimogyō effectively comprised the area bordered by Nijō Street to the north, Rokujō Street to the south, Takakura Street to the east, and Horikawa Street to the west.[18] The homes of the merchants—which acted as both residence and shop—were called *machiya*, and it was within this physical environment that the *roji* developed.

When the capital of Heian-kyō was built in 794 it was designed according to the planning systems of ancient Chinese cities to support the hierarchical bureaucracy of the imperial household and the civil aristocracy. The streets were laid out in a north-south, east-west grid dividing the city into a mesh of rectangular lots. Initially those lots were not privately owned but rather were assigned to the population depending on a person's status within the system. The higher echelon of aristocrats, those of the third rank or higher, received a property 1 *chō* in size. A *chō* was 400 *shaku* square or about 121.2 meters square, yielding a plot about 11,698 square meters in size. Fourth and fifth ranks received one half *chō*, the six, seventh, and eighth ranks received one quarter *chō*, and commoners received a small lot called a *henushi* (literally the "door owner"). To create *henushi*, a *chō*-sized block was divided into thirty-two individual lots of approximately the same size laid out in four north-south columns and eight east-west rows. The *henushi*, therefore, was one thirty-second of a *chō* or about 460 square meters, a small lot for the time but still much larger than the average size of a private lot in Kyōto today. The inner lots faced onto an alleyway called an *ainomachi*, and, because they relinquished some of their size to allow for the alleyway, they were slightly smaller than the outer lots—9.25 by 5 *jō* for the inner as opposed to 10 by 5 *jō* for the outer lots.[19] Being smaller and facing a narrow alleyway, the inner lots were consequently more difficult to access than those lots that were facing one of the surrounding streets. Over time, the inner lots fell into disuse, a situation that was augmented by the development of a mercantile society in which access to the street meant a greater chance of success in business. By the 16th century, the inner core of the *chō*-sized blocks had evolved into open space, at times used communally and at times privately. With more people competing to share the street-front, the typical lot of an urban merchant was narrow, although it had depth into the block.

A map from 1587 of a neighborhood in Kyōto called Manjūya-chō, which was considered to be the center of the city, shows the average frontage to be only 3 *ken*, or about 5.5 meters.[20] There were, however, larger lots with broader frontage, such as the one owned by Dōtetsu that had a 5-*ken* frontage as well as a separate alleyway just a little over 1 meter in width that connected to the street on the opposite side of a neighboring

9. DRY LANDSCAPE GARDENS. Daisen'in, Kyōto. *Chanoyu* developed during the late Muromachi period (1333–1568). At that time, many Zen temples, as well as the residences of military lords, had sculptural gardens called *karesansui*, which created abstract images of the natural landscape through a sparse arrangement of boulders, raked sand, and a few plantings. Photograph by Ōhashi Haruzō.

property and led back to the rear of Dōtetsu's plot (fig. 10). The alleyway was called the *sukiya tōrimichi*, or "tea house path," revealing the function of the entryway. In addition to *tōrimichi*, another name for these long narrow alleyways that led back to the rear of urban properties was *roji*, and it was just such long, narrow entries that were the precursors to the first tea gardens, also known as *roji*. The linguistic connection between these names will be looked at further in Chapter 5.

The shape of the properties of urban merchants in medieval times—specifically, narrow properties leading deeply back from the street—created the physical context within which the tea house developed. Another influence was the architecture of the merchants' residences, called *machiya*, literally, "town-house." At present the remaining *machiya* in Kyōto are built in a manner indicative of the late 18th to early 19th century. They have tiled roofs (*kawara yane*), white lime-plaster exterior walls (*shiro-kabe*), and bare clay-plaster interior walls (*tsuchi-kabe*). The walls are plastered in such a way as to allow the wooden structure of posts and beams to be revealed (*shin-kabe*). The floors are covered with *tatami* mats, and the openings to the outside are covered with sliding doors covered in translucent paper (*shōji*) and wooden night-panels (*amado*). The typical pattern of buildings built on a long narrow plot is to have one unit along the street for a shop (*omoteya, mise*), a second unit slightly further back as a residence (*omoya*), and one or more thick-walled storage structures (*kura*) at the very back of the property.

This layout is more elaborate than the *machiya* of the 15th and 16th centuries when *chanoyu* was first being developed (fig. 11). Paintings from the 16th and even the 17th centuries show that the roofs were not tiled but rather made of wooden planks or shingles, sometimes held down with a grid of bamboo poles in turn weighted down with round stones. An occasional roof seen in the paintings is still thatched with reeds—the most ancient method of roofing. The outer walls (and what can be seen of the inner walls, too) are typically not covered with white lime plaster but are

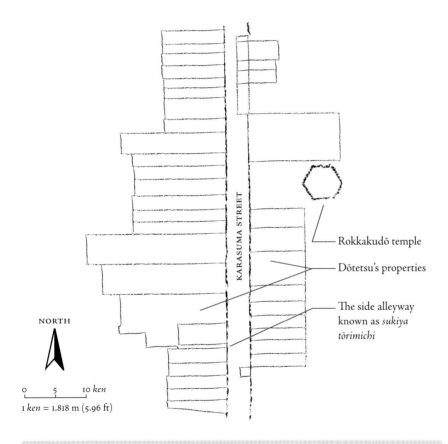

KARASUMA STREET

Rokkakudō temple

Dōtetsu's properties

The side alleyway known as *sukiya tōrimichi*

NORTH

0   5   10 *ken*

1 *ken* = 1.818 m (5.96 ft)

10. TEA GARDEN PRECURSOR. Dōtetsu owned two lots on Karasuma Street that were much larger and had broader frontage than his neighbors—a sign of wealth. Leading to the rear area of one of his properties was a narrow alleyway called a *sukiya tōrimichi*, or "tea house path." Redrawn from a 1587 map of Manjūya-chō found in *Teien Gaku Kōza 2*, p. 17.

bare clay plaster. The use of *tatami* seems to be widespread, but the openings to the outside are either wide open, closed with heavy wooden grill-work (*kōshi*), or hung with cloth doorway curtains (*noren*)—they do not have *shōji*. The arrangement of the three structures—*omoteya*, *omoya*, and *kura*—had not yet begun, that being a result of the social stability and greater general wealth of the Edo period (1600–1868).

The *machiya* of the merchants also differed from the *shoin* residences of the aristocrats, priests, and upper-class military lords in the kind of wood used in their construction. The *shoin* architecture employed clear wood (knotless wood) that was cut and planed into square posts and beams in a process called *kiwari*.[21] Nowadays, and probably from the late Edo period onward, *machiya* are also built with fine, knotless wood wherever the wood is exposed, though of smaller dimensions. In the Muromachi period, however, merchants' houses, like farmhouses, used available wood of a lesser grade. Whereas aristocrats, priests, and upper-class military lords paid for their residences through land taxes and used conscripted labor, merchants paid for their residences with their own money. The difference in building materials is reflective of the disparity in the social and financial power of their respective classes. It also meant that the kind of irregular, "natural" materials that would be used in the construction of the rustic tea houses, *sōan*, were perhaps not so unfamiliar or distasteful to the merchants as they were to members of the upper echelons.

There was another aspect of *machiya* design that led to the development of the *sōan*. In this case it was related to the life-style of the merchants, as well as the architecture. According to the economic and social structure of the middle ages, the custom among merchants was for the owner of a business (typically, the father of a household) to pass on the reins of the business to his eldest son and "go into retirement" before he became old and infirm. This was expressed as becoming an *inkyo*, or a "recluse." To what degree the father actually retired from active involvement in the business probably depended on each family's situation. In some cases the retirement may have simply been for show, in others for real, but whether it was real or not, the *inkyo* would move out of the main house, the *omoya* or *nushiya*, and into a small structure at the back of the property called an *an* (rhymes with "Khan"), a polite term for a simple arbor or hermitage.

Normally when the character for *an* is used by itself, it is pronounced *iori*, and when it is used in combination with other Chinese characters it is pronounced *an*, as in *sōan*. In *Hōjōki*, for instance, which will be presented below in the section on hermits, the same character is pronounced *iori*. Historical records of the residences of urban merchants, however, show the word as *an* not *iori*. Both pronunciations, *an* and *iori*, will be used throughout this book but they refer to the same type of simple, rustic structure.

A survey from the late 1480s of the community near Tōdaiji in Nara shows numerous examples of a main house occupied by two to nine people with an associated *an* occupied by one or two people, undoubtedly the retired householder and his wife.[22] João Rodrigues, a Jesuit missionary from Portugal who lived in Japan from 1577 to 1610, described the process of becoming an *inkyo* in his *História da Ingreja do Japão* (*The History of the Church in Japan*):

> The Japanese are in general of a melancholy
> disposition and nature. Moved by this natural
> inclination, they take much delight and pleasure
> in lonely and nostalgic places, such as woods with

II. WOODEN TOWNHOUSES IN MEDIEVAL KYŌTO. The residence/shops of urban merchants are called *machiya*, literally, "townhouses." In the late Muromachi period (1333–1568), they were still simple affairs, made with a post and beam structure infilled with mud/straw wattle on bamboo lath. The front was more or less open, shielded during the day with cloth curtains and closed at night with wooden panels. The roof was made of wooden boards held down against the wind with a crisscross of tied bamboo poles weighted at the intersections with heavy stones. The front of the *machiya* adjoined the city street and the back opened onto an enclosed communal courtyard formed by a block of *machiya* called a *chō*. In these courtyards can be seen some sparse plantings—pine and bamboo being most common—and in the top center, a person drawing water from the communal well. *Rakuchū Rakugaizu* (Rekihaku Kōhon, formerly Machida-bon), 16th century (depicts Kyōto between 1525 and 1536), middle of the fourth panel of the right-hand set of screens. National Museum of Japanese History, Tōkyō.

shady groves, cliffs, and rocky places, solitary birds, torrents of fresh water flowing down from rocks, and in every kind of solitary thing imbued with a natural artlessness and quality. All this fills their souls with this inclination and melancholy, producing a certain nostalgia.

Hence they are much inclined towards a solitary life, far removed from all worldly affairs and tumult. Thus in olden days many solitary hermits devoted themselves to contempt of the world and its vanities. They gave themselves over to a solitary and contemplative life, believing that in this way they purified their souls and obtained salvation in their false sects. Thence arose the custom of *inkyo*; that is, during their lifetime they hand over their house, estates, and public affairs to their heirs, and take a house for themselves where they lead a quiet and peaceful life, withdrawn from all worldly business and disturbance. They shave their heads and beard, and exchange their secular robes for religious and sober dress. They are called *nyūdō* or *zenmon*, which is a certain kind of religious state of bonzes and is the first rank of those who begin to devote themselves to the things of salvation and religious cult. The beginning and origin of this *cha* meeting [*chanoyu*] and the various ceremonies performed therein are founded on this natural disposition.[23]

Whether the reason was spiritual in nature, as Rodrigues describes, or simply a matter of business and society, it is clear that this procedure of becoming an *inkyo* was a widespread phenomenon by the time that *chanoyu* began to develop. The *an* that the *inkyo* would live in was a smaller building than the main house (most likely, much smaller) and did not have the architectural components required of a shop that the structure along the street would have had. Neither was the *an* a "tea house" *per se*, although it may have had some of the attributes of that kind of architecture, for instance, an in-floor brazier (for warmth) and a display alcove or shelves for the display of objects that the *inkyo* enjoyed. The *an* of urban merchants can be considered one of the antecedents of the rustic tea house, and the path that led from the street back to the *an*—the *roji*—was the space that would develop into the tea garden.

Another name given to these rooms in the back of merchant residences was *zashiki*, or sitting parlor. As *tatami* mats grew more affordable, people began to cover whole rooms with the mats, fitted into a precise wall-to-wall pattern. *Inryōken Nichiroku*, a diary kept in succession by the head priests of Inryōken, a sub-temple of the powerful Zen temple Shōkokuji, records a visit to "backyard *zashiki*."

> "Went to stay at the home of Tokuzō, the *saké* dealer. There was a garden in the back and a sitting parlor, more beautiful than any other in Kyōto. It had a hearth and a privy. So restful and convenient."[24]

The Hermit in the City

The art of tea, *chanoyu*, the elegantly rustic tea house, *sōan*, and the early tea garden, *roji*, all developed as part of the culture of the literate and artistic recluse that has pervaded Chinese and Japanese culture for millennia. In Japanese, the recluse is called an *intonsha*, *inja*, or simply *in* (rhymes with "seen"). Some of the figures from Chinese history who were well-known in Japan include Laozi, Tao Yuanming, and Hanshan. These three figures neatly represent three possible intentions for a recluse life: Daoist, Confucianist, and Buddhist.

Laozi is the legendary ancestral figure of Daoism who purportedly lived in the Spring and Autumn period, between the years 770 B.C. and 476 B.C. He is envisioned as the father of Daoist thought, the author of the geomantic treatise *Daodejing*, and, as such, his reclusion is seen in light of Daoism—of finding truth within the geomantic systems of nature, such as Yin and Yang and the Five Phases.[25]

Tao Yuanming, known as a poet, was born into a lower-level gentry family and served as a government official, but retired to the life of a farmer saying, "Whenever I have been involved in official life, I was mortgaging myself to my mouth and belly."[26] His motive for reclusion—the intentional refusal to allow himself to be bound by the requirements of society—can be seen in light of Confucianist thought, even though it was a rebellious act within a system that idealizes loyalty in a hierarchical social structure. Tao Yuanming was well-known to Muromachi-period society for his poetry and through paintings that depict him with other well-known historical figures such as *The Four Admirers*, *The Three Laughers of the Tiger Glen*, and *The Three Sages Tasting Vinegar*. These were themes originally seen in imported paintings by Chinese artists and then, later, in paintings produced by Japanese artists as well. *The Four Admirers*, which depicts four figures known for their appreciation of four different flowers, idealizes the hermit's love for nature. *The Three Laughers of the Tiger Glen* and *The Three Sages Tasting Vinegar* depict three figures, each of whom represents a different religion/philosophy (Daoism, Confucianism, Buddhism), symbolizing an idealized harmony among them.[27]

Hanshan was an eccentric Tang-dynasty Chan priest who wrote poetry and eventually became sanctified as an incarnation of the Buddhist deity Monjū. Hanshan and his compatriot, Shide, were immortalized in countless paintings that were also well known during the Muromachi period.[28] Hanshan was a wildly eccentric, anti-establishment figure much like the Muromachi-period Zen priest Ikkyū, who is reputed to have been the religious mentor to several early tea masters. Hanshan represents the Buddhist ideal of the recluse who casts away attachment to worldly things as a method of attaining enlightenment.

These Chinese figures are introduced here because they represent three reasons for reclusion, but there were, of course, many other figures who were known to Muromachi-period society, primarily through the media of literature and painting. Moreover, the ideal of a recluse was not limited to examples from China; there were others that were closer to home, of which the four best known were Saigyō, Yoshishige no Yasutane, Kamo no Chōmei, and Yoshida Kenkō.

Saigyō (1118–90) was born Satō Norikiyo. As a young man, he was a palace guard, *hokumen no bushi*, for Emperor Toba. When only 23 years of age, he left the palace society and began traveling around the country writing poems along the way. Ninety-four of the more than two thousand poems he wrote were included within the medieval anthology *Shinkokin Wakashū*. There are various reasons given for Saigyō becoming a recluse: the death of a close friend, a love affair with a lady of the court, an unquenchable desire for freedom, and a love of being among pastoral scenes. When not traveling, he lived in simple huts in Sagano and Ōhara, both farming villages on the outskirts of the capital. His poetry often captured images of bucolic mountain villages, *yamazato*, and the simple thatch-roofed huts, *kusa no iori*, where he lived or would spend the evening while traveling (fig. 12). Both the *yamazato* and *kusa no iori* (the latter written with the same characters as *sōan*) would become central to the culture of the tea garden. He wrote,

> I have given up
>> even on visitors
> If not for the loneliness
>> of this mountain village
>>> how hard it would be to live here

> Moonlight leaks
>> into this thatch-roofed hut
>>> so rough and broken
> I gaze on it reflecting
>> off my tear-wet sleeves[29]

Saigyō's poems also contain another expression that has become inextricably linked with *chanoyu*—*matsu kaze*, or "the wind in the pines." This poetic image is not Saigyō's invention; it shows up in Japanese writing as far back as the 7th-century *Manyōshū* and in countless works after that, such as the *Tale of Genji* (*Genji Monogatari*, 11th century) and the *nō* plays of Kan'ami (1333–84) and Zeami (1363?–1443?). When *chanoyu* culture fully developed in the 16th century, *matsu kaze* became so commonly associated with *chanoyu* it could be called cliché. Pine groves or large, single pine trees were often mentioned as the setting for tea arbors—both permanent arbors as well as temporary ones that were set up while traveling or on military campaigns—and many prized tea utensils were given the name *Wind in the Pines*. One reason for the connection between *matsu kaze* and *chanoyu* is that the quiet, hissing sound wind makes when blowing through the

needles of a pine tree is similar to the sound produced by the gently simmering kettle of water used to boil water for tea in a tea house. In *chanoyu* terminology,

12. AN IDEAL HUT FOR A HERMIT. This woodblock is of the hut of a mid-Edo-period (1600–1868) priest named Jiun who styled his life after Saigyō's—never living in one place too long. The poem in the colophon reads, "My abode always shifts—In autumn the red leaves of Saga / In spring, the cherries of Yoshino." Looking at this, one can imagine Saigyō watching the moonlight leaking into his desolate thatch-roofed hut, *kusa no iori*. *Saikoku Sanjūsansho Meisho Zue*, Akatsuki Kanenari (1793–1860). Rinsen Shoten, Kyōto.

the sound of boiling water has come to be referred to as "the wind in the pines." That is a specific connection, but, more generally, the connection between *matsu kaze* and *chanoyu* stems from the fact that, in poetry, the image of pines was related to lonely places—windswept beaches or mountain retreats—and it was this sublime loneliness that matched so well with the aesthetic of *chanoyu* as aptly reflected in this poem by Saigyō:

> Gazing up upon
> > the early morning moon
> > > filtering through the trees
> My loneliness carried deeper
> > by the pine wind along the ridges[30]

Yoshishige no Yasutane (?–1002), also known as Kamo no Yasutane, was a mid-Heian-period poet who built himself a place to live in the undeveloped lands in the west of the capital on Rokujō Street. He describes his home in detail in one of his books, *Chiteiki (The Pond Garden Records)*, that is said to have influenced the writing of *Hōjōki* by Kamo no Chōmei. He built a small hill and dug out a pond, adding a pine-covered isle, a little bridge and boat, scarlet carp, and white herons (though the last probably added themselves). He also built a small hall on the west side of the lake to enshrine the Amida Buddha and would visit there to pray, entering his library after dinner to read and find himself "in the company of worthy men of another era." His house, with its Amida Hall, library, pond garden, and so on, however humbly he expresses it, was not a simple hut like Saigyō's. His way of living, however, did emulate the ideals of the recluse. In the following quote from *Chiteiki*, Yasutane expressed eloquently his desire for a separation from worldly society and an earnest communion with companions of like

mind—the same sentiments that would later inform the development of *chanoyu*.

> As for the people and the affairs of the contemporary world, they hold no attraction for me. If, in becoming a teacher, one thinks only of wealth and honor, and is not concerned about the importance of literature, it would be better if we had no teachers. If, in being a friend, one thinks only of power and profit, and cares nothing about the frank exchange of opinions, it would be better if we had no friends. So I close my gate, shut the door, and hum poems and sing songs to myself.[31]

Kamo no Chōmei (1155?–1216), an early-Kamakura-period poet, was born into a family of shrine priests from Shimogamo Shrine in Kyōto. He studied *waka* poetry with Shune and, in 1204, took the tonsure. He built a small house for himself in the hills outside the capital and wrote poetry and essays. Among his best-known works is *Hōjōki (Tales of the Ten Foot Square Hut)*, written in 1212, which captures the spirit of *mujōkan*, a Buddhist perception of the evanescence of life. *Hōjō* means "a square the sides of which are one *jō* in length." One *jō* being about 10 feet, the expression translates as "10 feet square."[32] Chōmei's *hōjō* is an allegorical reference to the residence of Vimalakirti (Jp: Yuima), a wealthy Indian contemporary of the historical Buddha, Shakamuni, whose understanding of Buddhism is described in the Vimalakirti sutra. Although a wealthy man, Vimalakirti chose to live in a ten-foot-square hut, an expression of piety and abstinence. This parable was symbolically incorporated into Zen temple life by naming the main hall of the temple the *hōjō*. Originally, in Chinese Chan temples, there were two *hōjō*. Along an axial line extending from the outer gate of the temple and heading south to north (or west to east) were the following halls: Buddha Hall, *butsuden*; Dharma Hall, *hattō*; Front Main Hall, *zenhōjō*; and the Main Hall, *hōjō*. In most Japanese temples however, especially after the advent of private cloisters called *tatchū*, there is only one *hōjō*.

The *hōjō* is, traditionally, where the head priest lives (in the northern half of the hall) and where the Buddhist images are enshrined (in the southern half of the hall). Whereas temple monks receive their lectures on Buddhism in the Dharma Hall, temple patrons and other important lay people are greeted or receive lectures in rooms on the south side of the *hōjō*. Of course, in reality the *hōjō* of Zen temples are much bigger than 10 feet square, but the name remains as a symbol of the austere ideals of Zen life.

The size of a tea room is often four and a half *tatami* mats, known as *yojōhan* (literally, "four and a half"). There are, in fact, many different sizes and shapes of tea rooms, from two to ten mats or more, but the classic tea room, the standard from which all others diverged, is a square-shaped room that is four and a half mats in size. *Tatami* have been made in various sizes depending on the era and location, but the proportion has always remained "one by two." The *tatami* in the region around Kyōto are about 1.91 meters long (6 feet 3 inches), so when a room is laid out with four and a half of these *tatami* mats, it forms a square that is about 2.87 meters (9 feet 5 inches) on a side or about 10 feet square—literally a *hōjō*.

In *Hōjōki*, Chōmei refers to his hut as a *hōjō* only once. However, there are many references to *iori*, arbor or hermitage. There is the "brushwood arbor," *shiba no iori*; the "temporary arbor," *kari no iori*; the "one-room arbor," *hitoma no iori*; and the "grass (roofed) arbor," *kusa no iori*. These images are very similar to, and are very likely to have been role models for, the *sōan*, grass-roofed arbor, that was developed as a part of *chanoyu* centuries later.

Sixty years about to disappear like morning dew,
I decided to build a new lodging for my last days,
something like the hut a hunter builds for just
one night or the cocoon of an old silkworm. Compared to the home I had in my middle years, this
is but a hundredth of the size. As the time passes,
the older I get, the smaller becomes my home.

This is no ordinary residence! It is but ten-feet-square (*hōjō*) with [a ceiling] less than seven feet. As I have in mind no fixed place to live, it was built without being fastened down to the ground. I packed earth for the foundation, thatched the roof, and held it together with simple metal clasps at every joint. By doing so, if I ever have a change of heart, I could move the thing somewhere else just like that. When it comes time to reassemble it, what trouble would it be to me? To carry it away would take but just two carts, requiring nothing more than the labor of hauling it.

Now, having hid myself away in the mountains of Hino [I made my home like this]. On the southern side, I added a temporary trellis off the eaves as a sun-screen and beneath that a narrow veranda made of bamboo. To the west, I made a shelf as a Buddhist altar (*akadana*) and along the western side I enshrined a painting of Amida Buddha so that the setting sun illuminates its forehead. On the doors [of the altar], I hung an image of Fugen and Fudō. Above the sliding paper doors (*shōji*) on the northern side, I made a little shelf to hold three or four black leather baskets storing books on poetry (*waka*), music (*kagen*), and copies of the *Essentials of Salvation* (*Ōjōyōshū*) and such.[33] Next to that are a harp (*koto*) and a lute (*biwa*)—a so-called foldable harp and a jointed lute. In the east I set up a quilt of woven bracken as my evening's bed. In the eastern wall there is a window opening and a desk for writing. Near where I would set my pillow is a charcoal brazier that I use to burn my brushwood kindling. There is a small plot to the north enclosed by a small open-wattle fence that I use as a garden, planted with every kind of medicinal herb. Such is the nature of my makeshift arbor (*kari no iori*).

About the place itself, to the south [of the hut] water flows from a bamboo pipe and is held in a pool by stones that I set there. The woods grow so close to the eaves that I will never want for firewood. Called by the name Toyama, it is covered thickly in *masaki* vines,[34] the valleys overgrown yet open to the west—not half bad for philosophic meditations.[35]

It is uncanny how many aspects of this description match that of the tea houses used for *chanoyu* three hundred years later, so much so that one cannot help but be led to believe that Chōmei's *Hōjōki* (which certainly would have been known by tea masters in the 16th century), above all other records of literate recluses, formed the archetypal model for their design. Looking through the passage we find the following points that are similar in rustic tea houses.

- A structure built as if to be temporary, like a mountain hut, easily dismantled and moved. He called it his makeshift arbor, which can also translate as temporary arbor. Tea houses are also built lightly and, although they are in fact very carefully crafted, are intended to symbolize impermanence.

- A small structure—only 10 feet square. This size is, to repeat, precisely the same as the classic four-and-a-half-mat (*yojōhan*) that is the classical or standard form of tea house architecture.

- A narrow veranda called a *sunoko*. The entry to the earliest tea houses was not through a small crawl-through door, as became typical in the late 1500s; rather they were accessed by stepping up and across a narrow veranda, *sunoko*.

- A pervasive atmosphere of Buddhism, in particular Pure Land Buddhism, which focuses on the Amida Buddha. A painting of Amida is enshrined within the arbor; *Essentials of Salvation* is a text that focuses on three Pure Land sutras, and, in most variants of *Hōjōki* (though not this one), Chōmei also mentions keeping a copy of the Lotus Sutra. During the Edo period (1600–1868), the tea garden would be assigned specific Buddhist meanings that were drawn from that sutra.

- A life of refined culture. For Chōmei, this was expressed through the references to poetry and music. In fact poetry plays merely a small role in *chanoyu* and music none at all. However, *chanoyu* tea masters saw themselves, and still see themselves, as attaining a particularly refined cultural life through the practice of tea.

- A life of austerity. Chōmei's bracken bed is

indicative of the simplicity and austerity that was the ideal of *chanoyu* tea masters.

♦ A small enclosed garden. Although Chōmei's garden was planted with medicinal herbs, which play no role in tea gardens, the overall atmosphere of a small space enclosed by a rustic fence is very much in keeping with the design of a tea garden.

♦ Water available just outside. In a tea garden, water for ritual cleaning is placed in the garden in a water basin. This is the single most essential element of a tea garden. Chōmei's water was running through a bamboo pipe, *kakehi*, undoubtedly drawn from a nearby well-spring. In tea gardens that are actively used for *chanoyu*, a *kakehi* is not used. Instead, the water basin is filled by the host using a wooden bucket so the guests can either see or hear it being done. Water running constantly from a *kakehi* into a water basin to produce a burbling sound is an effect employed in some parks and gardens, but not normally in actively used tea gardens.

♦ Firewood and water. The woods nearby the arbor provide firewood; the bamboo pipe water. References to "chopping firewood and carrying water" found in tea literature symbolize an austere life that has been pared down to the essentials.

♦ Mountains surrounding the arbor that are thick with trees. A tea garden is, in fact, carefully maintained, yet the archetype that tea masters sought to reflect in the design of their gardens was the kind of evergreen forest that Chōmei mentions.

♦ And, last but certainly not least, the ability of the arbor to provide a place of undisturbed meditation. This, of course, is the fundamental purpose behind the practice of *chanoyu* and the design of a tea house and tea garden.

Kenkō (ca. 1282–after 1352), a late-Kamakura, early-Muromachi-period poet, was born Urabe no Kaneyoshi. His family acted as the priests of the Yoshida Shrine in Kyōto, thus his name in later years of Yoshida Kenkō (Kenkō and Kaneyoshi are written with the same *kanji*). Kenkō served on the staff of the Hosokawa family and then went to serve Emperor Gonijō (1285–1308, reign: 1301–8) as *sahyō no suke*, vice minister of the office of the military guards of the eastern ward. After the death of Emperor Gonijō, Kenkō took the tonsure and began his life as a recluse poet. He was not much older than Saigyō when he did so. Among his works, *Tsurezuregusa* (*Essays in Idleness*) is the best known. Like Saigyō, Kenkō mentions mountain villages, *yamazato*, and rustic huts, *iori* or *kusa no iori* from time to time in his writings.

About the tenth month I had the occasion to visit a village (*yamazato*) beyond the place called Kurusuno. I made my way far down a moss-covered path (*koke no hoso michi*) until I reached a lonely-looking hut (*iori*). Not a sound could be heard, except for the dripping of a water pipe buried in the fallen leaves. Sprays of chrysanthemum and red maple leaves had been carelessly arranged on the holy-water shelf. Evidently someone was living here. Moved, I was thinking, "One can live even in such a place," when I noticed a tangerine tree, its branches bent with fruit, that had been enclosed by a forbidding fence.

Rather disillusioned, I thought now, "If only the tree had not been there!"

The soldier who goes to war, knowing how close he is to death, forgets his family and even forgets himself; the man who has turned his back on the world and lives in a thatched hut (*kusa no iori*), quietly taking pleasure in the stream and rocks of his garden, may suppose that death in battle has nothing to do with him, but this is a shallow misconception. Does he imagine that, if he hides in the still recesses of the mountains, the enemy called change will fail to attack? When you confront death, no matter where it may be, it is the same as charging into battle.[36]

The image in the first passage, of a narrow, moss-covered path leading back to a lonely-looking hut, is precisely the *form* that 16th-century tea masters tried to emulate in their gardens (fig. 13). Similarly, the image in the second passage, of a hut as a place of detachment from the world, is precisely the *theme* that those tea masters chose as the basis of *chanoyu*.

By the middle of the Muromachi period, there was no shortage of role models for the ideal of a literate and artistic recluse, both Chinese and Japanese. The image of the mountain village (*yamazato*) and the rustic huts of the recluses (*iori, kusa no iori, kari no iori,* etc.) were concepts that were well known among the contemporary elites of society: the military and civil aristocrats and priests of the Zen sect, as well as men of the merchant class. Many of the previously mentioned recluses began life in bureaucratic service (Tao Yuanming, Saigyō, Yasutane) or some other aspect of upper-echelon society (like Chōmei and Kenkō, who were from priestly families). The reason they gave for choosing a life of reclusion was the overbearing quality of life within urban society. The merchants, however, were not directly part of the military or civil aristocracy, or the ruling bureaucracy, so the reasons they had for wanting to escape would have been different. At least four can be postulated.

The first possibility is that there was a personal reason. For instance, it may well have been that the physical conditions of the urban center, with its dusty streets, crowded markets, hectic pace, and lack of open green space, inspired a longing for a simple life among pastoral fields and streams. This is similar to the Daoist ideal of the recluse enjoying nature for nature's sake though it lacks the Daoist interest in nature for geomantic reasons.

A second possibility is that there was a social basis for the interest in reclusion. The merchants may have felt that they were trapped in an insurmountable situation, being labeled as lowly individuals in a world run by military men. The escape they sought may not have been from the physical city but rather from the social system that they lived in and that regarded them as second class. This is not unlike the Confucianist recluse who leaves society for political reasons.

A third possibility is that the impetus toward a life of reclusion had a religious or philosophical basis. The Zen Buddhist ideal that the path to enlightenment required a severing of attachment to worldly things may have been genuinely appealing to the merchants, in part because their daily lives were so inherently connected to physical goods. Certainly many of the merchants whose names are associated with the early development of *chanoyu* are also known to have consorted with Zen priests and even studied Zen Buddhism as lay practitioners, so the possibility of influence is understandable. It is entirely possible that some of the early tea masters practiced tea as a form

13. THE GARDEN AS PATH. Omote Senke, Kyōto. The tea garden is fundamentally a simple, understated path as can be understood by the original name, *roji*, which means alleyway or pathway. In its simplest interpretation the *roji* is just a mossy path that leads to the tea room—in its wider understanding it is the beginning of an inward journey. Photograph by Ōhashi Haruzō.

of Zen training. Early records of tea gatherings kept by merchants, however, do not reveal this. They focus primarily on the material aspects of the gatherings, consisting mostly of extensive and exacting lists of the various tea utensils used and the food served at each gathering, bringing into question the degree to which rustic tea was actually perceived by them as a means of separating oneself from worldly things.

The fourth possibility for the merchant's interest in the recluse life was simply a choice by default. The aesthetics and cultural attributes of the powerful classes, such as *shoin* architecture, were disallowed to the merchants by their social status. They were prevented, for instance, from acquiring large estates with extensive gardens and spacious halls. The simple *sōan* hut of a recluse and the other rustic accoutrements of *chanoyu*, however, were not off limits to them. In fact, *chanoyu* was something a merchant could make his own, enjoy developing, and be better at than the elite classes. It was a cultural territory *in which he could be superior.*

The reasons why merchants found the ideal of the recluse appealing are several and complexly interwoven—it is likely that all are true in composite rather than any single one above the others—but what is certain is that what lay behind the shift from the lavish tea gatherings of the military lords to the rustic style of *chanoyu* gatherings held by the merchants was an attempt to emulate the life of the aesthetically sensitive, culturally aware, and philosophically disposed recluse. Unlike the aforementioned recluses, however, the merchants did not actually go into reclusion in the deep mountains or in a mountain village on the outskirts of the cities they lived in. Instead, they built their places of reclusion right on their properties in the middle of the city.

One term for these urban properties that were designed to be recluse hermitages was *yamazato*, moun-

tain village. As we have seen, this expression has a long history. It shows up in the Heian-period gardening treatise *Sakuteiki* as a style of gardening, and recluse poets such as Saigyō and Kenkō used it to describe the bucolic places they lived in or passed through. In the Muromachi period, one such urban *yamazato* was the estate of Toyohara Muneaki (1450–1525), a court musician, who also associated with *renga* poets and *chanoyu* practitioners. He built an arbor for himself under a big, old pine tree and called the place Yamazatoan, the Mountain Village Arbor. The traveling poet Sōchō described it this way:

> When even the mountains
>   may leave me only gloomily
>   the best hideaway
> Is right in the middle of the City
>   my Arbor Beneath the Pines[37]

The most famous example of a *yamazato* comes at the peak of the development of *chanoyu* as Sen Rikyū (1522–91) is coalescing the art in his position as tea master for the military ruler Toyotomi Hideyoshi. In 1583, Hideyoshi had part of the grounds of his Ōsaka Castle sectioned off and made into a garden with tea arbors. It was called Yamazato-maru (*maru* being a suffix given to denote a section of a castle's grounds) and, following that, other *yamazato* were also built at Hideyoshi's Nagoya Castle at Hizen in northern Kyūshū and at the Fushimi Castle south of Kyōto. These belong not to the age when *chanoyu* and the *roji* were initially being devised, but to a slightly later age and will be described in more detail below. It is also interesting to note where the urban *yamazato* just mentioned were built—not at the residences of merchants but on the properties of people in service to the court (a court musician) and at the residence of the *shōgun* himself.

The merchants expressed their ideal of reclusion in different language. *Nisuiki*, also known as *Isshiki*, is one of the records that captures this other language. The diary of aristocrat Washino'o Takayasu (1484–1533), *Nisuiki* was written between the years 1504 and 1533. Although it primarily records scenes of court proceedings, it also describes various events related to the arts, including *chanoyu*. An entry from 1526 records a visit Takayasu made to a tea gathering held on an island in the pond of Awataguchi-Shōren'in temple in Kyōto. He notes that tea was "served by tea master Sōshu, a lower-class lay monk of Shimogyō, greatly skilled at the refinements of *chanoyu*."[38] He was referring to Murata Sōshu, an apprentice in tea to Murata Shūko.

Some six years later, on the 6th day of the 9th month in 1532, Takayasu mentions visiting Sōshu at his tea house, Goshoan, the Arbor of the Noon-day Pine. The word he uses for "tea house" is *chaya* (literally, "tea house"), an early use of this expression.[39] He writes, "On our way home, we stopped by to see [Murata] Sōshu's tea house. It had the appearance of a mountain cottage. It should truly be called an hermitage in the city—a moving thing to see. Sōshu is the leader of contemporary *chanoyu*."[40] The expression "appearance of a mountain cottage" was written *sankyo-no-tei*, and the "hermitage within the city" was written *shichūin*. *Sankyo-no-tei* was not commonly used, but *shichūin* was used often in Zen Buddhist circles in Japan and, before that, in China. The fact that *shichūin* and *sankyo-no-tei* were used to describe the residences of merchants hints at the influence of Zen Buddhist and eremitic cultures on their lifestyles.

Shichūin is written with three *kanji*: *shi, chū, in*. The character for *shi* means marketplace: the busiest,

most "urban," part of a city.[41] One can imagine a mass of people milling about, engaged in worldly activities, buying and selling things, and raising a storm of dust (fig. 14). The marketplace became a symbol of all things bad about city life and, in particular, the dust of the marketplace became a symbol for spiritual contamination. The expression "the dust of the marketplace," *shijin*, is found in writings both religious and secular as an epithet for worldly impurity. The character *in* of *shichūin* means to hide or conceal. It can be applied to a person or a place and can thus mean either a hermit or hermitage. The character *chū* simply means "in the middle of," and in fact the expression is found at times without that middle character, written simply as *shi'in*. *Shichūin* can mean the "hermit in the city," "hermitage in the city," "hermit in the marketplace," and "hermitage in the marketplace." It refers to both the person who removes himself from the trappings of urban society (wealth, position, power) without physically removing himself from the urban context itself, as well as to the location—the hermitage—where that urban reclusion takes place.[42]

Another similar expression for a place of urban reclusion is *shichū no sankyo*, the "mountain cottage in the city." João Rodrigues recorded this in his *História da Ingreja do Japão*. As mentioned before, Rodrigues lived in Japan from 1577 to 1610, and this record of the "xichu no sankio" in Sakai probably reflects what he would have seen in the latter part of his stay, around the turn of the century. He writes:

> So they [the merchants of Sakai City] entertained each other with *cha* in these small huts within the city itself and in this way made up for the lack of refreshing and lonely places around the city. Indeed, to a certain extent this way was better than real solitude because they obtained

and enjoyed it in the middle of the city itself. They called this in their language *shichū no sankyo*, meaning a lonely hermitage found in the middle of the public square.[43]

The *Vocabulario da Lingoa de Iapam*, a Japanese-Portuguese dictionary published in Nagasaki in 1603–4 by Portuguese missionaries, defines *shichū no sankyo* thus: "to be a hermit in the middle of the square or market or among people, and remaining religious and recollected."[44] The use of these related terms—*shichū no sankyo, shichūin, sankyo-no-tei*—all of which refer to being a recluse in the city, makes clear that one ideal of *chanoyu* was to provide a place of temporary escape from the realities of day to day life and from the limitations of everyday perceptions.

14. THE MEDIEVAL MARKETPLACE. This painting depicts an ecstatic *nenbutsu* dance led by the itinerant priest, Ippen, taking place in an unused marketplace. The marketplace, pronounced *ichi* or *shi*, was quintessentially urban—exciting, loud, bustling, dusty, and materialistic. The expression *shijin*, "the dust of the marketplace," became an epithet for worldly impurity. *Shichūin*, the "hermit in the marketplace," was used to express the ideal of escaping worldly concerns, like a hermit, but doing it while still "in the marketplace," in other words while living one's life in the city. *Ippen Shōnin Eden*, 1299, Hōgan En'i (dates unknown). Tōkyō National Museum.

Tea Aesthetics

This brief look at the history of gardens, the townhouses of the merchants, and the ideal of the "hermit in the city" should have helped to define the context in which *chanoyu* and the tea garden developed. Before going on to the development of the tea garden itself, there is one last aspect of Muromachi-period culture that needs to be introduced—the language of tea aesthetics—an understanding of which sheds light on the art and practice of *chanoyu*. Some of the terms that follow, like *hie*, are rarely used these days, while others, like *wabi* and *sabi*, are well known in Japan and, to some degree, around the world.[45]

The aesthetics of tea are fundamental to its practice. This is not only in the sense of aesthetics as "an appreciation of beauty or good taste"—which certainly was fundamental to the practice of *chanoyu*—but also in the sense that aesthetics represent an underlying principle, or set of principles, that is manifested in the outward appearance of an object or in a mode of behavior. So it is with *chanoyu*, in particular the early phases of its development. The first aesthetic that comes to mind in a discussion of *chanoyu* would probably be *wabi*, and yet *wabi* was not, surprisingly, where the story began but rather where it came to rest.

Before *chanoyu* developed, there already existed among medieval artists and connoisseurs an aesthetic associated with things that were plain, subdued, self-revealing, mysterious, and natural—all of the things that the aesthetic called *wabi* would eventually encompass. These can be found most clearly in two other arts: *nō* theatre and *renga* poetry. The aesthetic usually associated with *nō*, *yūgen*, which translates as subtle profundity, has roots in Chinese Daoist teachings and was illuminated by such figures as Yoshida Kenkō

(mentioned in the preceding section) and Shōtetsu (mentioned in the section in Chapter 3 on artisans), as well as by the *renga* poet Shinkei.

The aesthetics of *renga* influenced the development of *chanoyu* even more directly than those of *nō*. *Renga*, linked-verse poetry, is a communal art in which several poets gather to write a single "linked" poem by taking turns composing sections according to a prescribed formula. Those tea masters who were most directly involved with the early development of tea, such as Murata Shukō (1423–1502), were also known to keep company with *renga* poets and in some cases were *renga* poets themselves, as was the case with Takeno Jōō (1502–55). There were several, interrelated aesthetics sought by *renga* poets with names such as *hie* (chill), *kare* (withered), and *yase* (gaunt). These terms were often used in combination; thus we find *hie-yase* (chill and gaunt), or *hie-kare* (chill and withered).[46]

While the aesthetics of paucity, age, and evanescence were expressed with words like *hie*, *kare*, and *yase* at the time of Shukō, by the time of Jōō, *wabi* and *sabi* were being used, even as they are today. *Wabi*, which can be described as the beauty of frugality, is a common word that existed long before the advent of *chanoyu*. As an adjective, *wabishii*, it means loneliness; the verb, *wabu*, means to languish. In Heian-period poetry it was used to express the forlorn feelings associated with unrequited love, as in this poem from *Manyoshū*, an 8th-century anthology of poetry:

> You do not come
>   no reason clear to me
>   and I   like rising waves
> Am washed over and over by loneliness
>   yet still you will not come[47]

At times, *wabi* was related to the sadness of autumn, as in this poem from the 10th-century anthology *Kokin Wakashū*:

Never again
    will I plant   nor even hope to see
        that Silver Grass
When it sets its plumes
    autumn is just too sad to bear[48]

For Jōō, a poem by Fujiwara no Teika (1162–1241) from the *Shinkokinshū* anthology best expressed his ideal of *wabi*:

As I look around
    there are no cherry blossoms
        no autumn colors
Just a fisherman's cottage by the bay
    bleak in the autumn dusk[49]

For Rikyū, however, *wabi* was defined best by a different poem, this one by Fujiwara Ietaka (1158–1237) from the *Minishū* anthology:

For those who only
    might be waiting on the cherry blossoms
        how I wish I could show them Spring
In the new grasses that part the snow
    around this mountain village[50]

The *Yamanoue Sōjiki* introduces another use of the word *wabi*, in the form *wabi-suki*.

According to the people of old, once you have become a master of tea, if you can have only one set of tea utensils, it is best to concentrate on the *wabi* taste (*wabi-suki*). Shinkei commented on linked-verse poetry (*renga*), "As far as *renga* goes, it's good to be withered and cold." According to Tsuji Gensai, Jōō always said that, at its best, tea should be like that, too.[51]

Wabi, therefore, can be seen as a form of beauty, a melancholy beauty such as found in autumn, golden-warm yet tinged with the cold of oncoming winter. It can be seen as a sense of loneliness, a positive loneliness as felt by a hermit who voluntarily removes himself from society, but also a bitter loneliness, the awareness of the inherent human condition—of being utterly alone within oneself. It can be seen as frugality, the cutting away of the superfluous trappings of human existence. And, it can be seen as the beauty of rebirth, the deeply felt shock of seeing fresh grasses (rather than gaudy tree blossoms). Expressed in ideal terms, when a tea master realizes the proper mode of living—being frugal, humble, and attuned to subtleties—the aesthetic expressed in his life and in his manner of practicing *chanoyu* can be termed *wabi* (fig. 15).

A companion word to *wabi* is *sabi*. As an adjective, *sabishii*, it means to be lonely (as a personal feeling) or desolate (as with a physical place). The *Manyōshū* contains the following poem by Takechi Kurohito on the ruins of the Capital at Ōmi in which "withered with grief" is the translation of *sabi*:

The hearts of the gods
of the land of Sasanami
    by the rippling waves
have withered with grief,
and the capital lies in ruins.
Gazing, I am filled with grief. [52]

Whereas the word *sabi* was used to mean desolation in a critique of poetry by Fujiwara Shunzei (1114–1204), in the *nō* theater of Zeami and the *renga* poetry of Shinkei, *sabi* took on meanings similar to *hie* and *kare*. *Sabi* can also refer to the patina gained by an object made of a material that weathers well with age. Objects with this patina are greatly prized by tea masters. The word for "rust" is also pronounced *sabi* (although the *kanji* are different), but iron rust is something that tea masters generally dislike. The reason for this difference is that iron rust is usually a sign of poor care and, thus, decrepitude, whereas the preferred patinas—such as that taken on by bronze, bamboo, or ceramic objects that have been well maintained—are a sign of good care and graceful aging.

Another aesthetic expression that became inextricably linked with the practice of *chanoyu* is *suki*. In modern Japanese, *suki* is typically used to mean "liking something or someone." In Heian-period poetry it had a similar meaning, connected with love affairs.

In the early medieval period, the meaning of *suki* shifted to encompass a devotion to the arts, as seen in Kamo no Chōmei's *Hosshinshū*, in which the pursuit of art is expressed within the context of the life of a recluse, *suki no tonsei*, literally, "the recluse with taste." A recluse's separation from society and closeness to nature was seen as bringing him to a higher level of aesthetic appreciation and onto the path toward Buddhist enlightenment. *Suki* became linked with the life of the recluse and the Buddhist path and, as *chanoyu* practice spread through many social classes during the Muromachi period, *suki* became associated with that art as well. Shōtetsu used the term *cha no suki*, tea enthusiast, in the mid-15th century, which is thought to be the first time the word *suki* was used in terms of tea practice.

Suki, used in relation to tea practice, came to mean "taste" or "style." We find the words *karamono-suki* and *wamono-suki*, for instance, which translate as "a taste for Chinese-style tea wares" (literally, "Chinese-style things" not "tea wares") and "a taste for Japanese-style tea wares." Tea practitioners became known as *sukisha* (*sha* means person), which can be translated as "a man of taste" or "a man of style." But the word *suki* was so strongly associated with the practice of *chanoyu* that it

15. FLOWERS FOR TEA. The essential component of *chabana*, flower arrangements for tea gatherings, is simplicity. Often a single flower is used, and the vase is usually very simple—an old basket, a rough ceramic vase, or just a section of bamboo. This flower is named *robiraki* ("opening of the hearth") and is a cross between the tea plant, Camellia sinensis, and the native Japanese camellia, Camellia japonica. Flower arranged by Watanabe Sōjitsu. Photograph by Tabata Minao.

came to be a synonym for *chanoyu*. *Sukiya*, for instance (*ya* means house), does not mean a "tasteful house" or a "stylish house" but simply a "tea house," a house where *chanoyu* is practiced. Rodrigues has this to say about the advent of *suki*:

> There were many people in the kingdom, but especially in Miyako [Kyōto] and Sakai, who devoted themselves to this pastime and took great pains therein so that they won the acclaim of the world in this art. As such they were regarded and esteemed by all. They continued to improve this way of *chanoyu* more and more, and partly changed Higashiyama Dono's [Shōgun Ashikaga Yoshimasa] ancient method by reducing some less essential things and then adding others that they believed were opportune and in keeping with the purpose of the exercise. In this way they established another way called *suki* and this is now in current use. Its teachers are known as *sukisha*, and the items used therein as *sukidōgu*.[53]

People began to use the word *suki* in relation to tea practice earlier than *wabi*. To differentiate between the two, it can be said that the word *suki* becomes connected with *chanoyu* as people start to develop a new artistic sense about tea—an experimental, playful, and refined aesthetic toward tea practice—while *wabi* follows the development of the rustic tea among the urban merchants, such as those living in Shimogyō, which happens somewhat later. Naturally, the practice of *suki*-style tea (stylish tea) and of *wabi*-style tea (rustic tea) predates the use of the words themselves and, more so, the recording of those words in historical texts. Although *suki* was first mentioned in relation to tea by Shōtetsu around 1450, and *wabi* shows up regu-

larly for the first time in *Yamanoue Sōjiki* at the end of the 1580s, the oral uses of those words are certain to be older, and the actual practice of *suki*-style tea and *wabi*-style tea even older still.[54]

Judging from most early historical descriptions of *suki*-style tea and *wabi*-style tea, the initial impression one is left with is that *suki* referred to fashion, design, and style—a cultural practice requiring refined taste in ceramics, architecture, tea, and more. *Wabi*, on the other hand, appears to have had the potential to be inherently spiritual—its essential frugality seems to have been born of the Zen Buddhist predilection for stripping away unneeded and superficial elements. In all truth, however, the terms cannot be categorized so easily. Rodrigues, for instance, claimed that *suki*-style tea had a deep spiritual meaning, recording that its practitioners involved themselves in tea in the manner of Zen Buddhist ardents. Conversely, he felt that *wabi*-style tea, what he called *wabizuki*, was a lower, base version of true tea practice, which he called *honzuki*. By the later 1500s, what constituted *suki*-style tea and what constituted *wabi*-style tea, and how the two were separate, became blurred, even as the term *wabizuki* implies.

For the purposes of this book, however, we will use the term *chanoyu* to refer to the practice of rustic tea, namely, a gathering between a host and a small number of guests in a rustic setting (such as the simple *sōan* of urban residences) at which frugality rules in all aspects of the tea service—the utensils, meal, and display of flower and scroll. During the last decades of the 16th century, *chanoyu* grabbed the attention and passion of Japanese upper-class society, and for thirty to forty years the urban merchants who were the creators and developers of that practice of tea held sway in society as the arbiters of taste. And, it was at that time that those very same tea masters created the very first tea gardens.

3
muromachi society

The Muromachi period began in 1338 when Ashikaga Takauji moved the seat of government from Kamakura to the Muromachi district of Kyōto. There were aspects of the society at that time that were crucial to the development of *chanoyu* and, thus, to the development of the tea garden: namely, the culture of the military aristocratic families (*bushi*), the institutionalization of Zen Buddhist temples and the cultural activity of Zen priests (*zensō*), the development of the merchant class (*shōnin*), and the flourishing of professional and semi-professional artists and artisans (*geinōsha, shokunin*). Each of these groups had ideals that they strove to reach and each of them had worldly means by which they lived. *Chanoyu* was the result of the confluence of all of these.

In short, very short, the story of the development of *chanoyu* is this: The service of *matcha* transferred from Zen temples to the residences of the *bushi*, where it became a lavish event, complete with the presentation of food and wine and the display of artwork and other symbols of wealth. In the 15th and 16th centuries, certain tea masters began to experiment with another mode of serving *matcha*, one that drew on the popular ideal of the scholar-hermit who detaches himself from worldly cares by retreating into wild nature. The eventual result of this experimentation was a subdued tea service incorporating rough, locally made utensils, held in simple structures at the back of the urban properties that were accessed by passing through understated gardens emulating forest paths. The forms those gardens took were shaped by the ideals held by each of the four groups mentioned above, as well as by the less than idyllic ways in which they may have lived their lives.

Bushi: *Military Aristocracy*

The society of the military aristocracy, *bushi*, was ordered in a neo-Confucian manner, in other words in a hierarchical system in which each person held a position within society, not as an individual but based upon relationships of allegiance. Among the military classes, the hierarchy consisted of the allegiance of a warrior (*samurai*) to his lord (*daimyō*), a lord to the chief military lord (*shōgun*), and the *shōgun* to the emperor. The emperor was, by this point in time, a figurehead leader who gave legitimacy to the social order but did not wield actual political power. Although loyalty and allegiance were held as ideals in the society, they were not always carried out in practice. Indeed, the era when *chanoyu* and the *roji* were developed—a time bracketed by the Ōnin War of 1467–77 (which left Kyōto in utter ruins) and the eventual consolidation of Japan under the Tokugawa shogunate in 1603—was particularly fraught with civil disturbance and constant power-grabbing between various lords. One term that represents the period best is *gekokujō*, "the inferior rising above their superiors." These antipodal characteristics of *bushi* society—a Confucian-based ideal of hierarchical order and the reality of violent social struggle—formed the broad historical context within which *chanoyu* was born.

The residences of the military aristocracy through the Kamakura period more or less emulated those of the civil aristocracy they had replaced, a style known as *shinden*, named after the central hall of the complex (fig. 16).[55] As mentioned earlier, rooms used for social gatherings were called *kaisho*, meeting halls or parlors, and by the end of the Kamakura period the *kaisho* had become not just a name for any room used as a parlor but a room dedicated to social gatherings. In addition to the development of the *kaisho*, there were other changes in the residential architecture of the military aristocracy that, taken in combination, gave rise to a new form of architecture called the *shoin* style.[56] Primary among these changes was the introduction of the

16. MEDIEVAL MILITARY LORD'S RESIDENCE. Called the Willow Palace, Yanagi no Gosho, this residence was the seat of the head military lord, *shōgun* Ashikaga Yoshiharu (1511–50). Built in 1525, it contained aspects of both *shoin* and *shinden* styles. The property was surrounded by a strong rammed-earth wall, *tsuijibei*, and the halls were roofed with cypress bark shingles, *hiwadabuki*. The meeting hall, *kaisho*, in which tea competitions would have been held, faces southward over a pond garden. In the garden we can see elaborate rockery and plantings, including a plum tree in bloom. *Rakuchū Rakugaizu* (Rekihaku Kōhon, formerly Machida-bon), 16th century (depicts Kyōto between 1525 and 1536), middle of the first panel of the right-hand set of screens. National Museum of Japanese History, Tōkyō.

bushi

shoin itself, a well-lit writing alcove built into an outer wall that was the sign of a literate householder. The changes also included the use of squared and planed posts and beams; single-layer, translucent paper doors, *shōji*, to separate rooms from the outside; an alcove for the display of scrolls and flowers, *tokonoma*; another alcove with shelves for the display of ceramics and other possessions, *chigai-dana*; and the covering of the entire floor with *tatami* mats, rather than simply using small movable mats as seats. The walls were made of clay plaster on a bamboo wattle and were usually finished with white plaster, *shikkui*, on the exterior and white paper (perhaps *torinoko* paper) on the interior. This gave the architecture a bright, clean, and formal atmosphere.[57]

In part, these changes were a natural outcome of newly developing technologies. Improved techniques in paper making, for instance, and the ensuing drop in cost of translucent paper, were key to the use of *shōji*. Other changes came about because of the social needs of the military class, such as the increase in literacy (thus the reading alcove) and the competitive desire to conspicuously exhibit their wealth (thus the display shelves).

The *kaisho* and other rooms for gathering with visitors were typically found on the south side of the residences, referred to as the *hare* direction. Pronounced "ha-reh" and written with the character for "clear" (as in clear weather), the *hare* side was the formal side and, in social terms, the outward-facing side. Contrary to this, the private rooms of a residence were typically on the north side of the building referred to as the *ke* side. *Ke* means "private" but is written with a character that means "unclean," a typically self-deprecating gesture toward one's own family or private space. Tea gatherings began as *hare* events, but the development of *chanoyu*,

as we will look at in more detail later on, brought them into the realm of the *ke* side of the house.

Tea gatherings, *chayoriai*, and the tea-tasting competitions, *tōcha*, that took place therein, are examples of tea events carried out in the *kaisho* and were "bright, open, and outward-facing" in character. Because of its physical location within the residence, as well as the social characteristic of the gathering, the *chayoriai* of that period are now also referred to as *hare-no-cha*. By the early Muromachi period, these gay events had gone so overboard in terms of lavish display, they gained the appellation *basara*, which means an unabashed, gaudy show. *Chanoyu*, which was developed at the end of the Muromachi period, was the aesthetic and philosophic antithesis of the *basara*. Rather than a sumptuous meal, *chanoyu* focused on the service of tea itself with only a simple meal to accompany it. Instead of exhibiting great quantities of artwork or other symbols of wealth, *chanoyu* focused on the presentation of only one thematic piece of artwork (calligraphy or painting) and a simple flower arrangement (fig. 17). It cannot be said that a display of wealth was not also a part of *chanoyu* from early on, but that was not its overt purpose.

The ideals of the *bushi*, as well as the more pragmatic realities of their way of life, played a role in the development of *chanoyu*. As mentioned, a Confucian, hierarchical social arrangement was the ideal for the *bushi*. *Chanoyu*, however, was based on a gathering that was, ideally, non-hierarchical. Of course the existence of the *shōkyaku* and *makkyaku*, guests who have leading roles within the gathering, means that there is a hierarchy of sorts among the guests. Also, in some tea rooms there is a slightly raised platform (*jōdan*) for the use of guests of extremely high social standing (the *shōgun* or emperor) or a high door (*kinin-guchi*) to allow high-ranking guests (from aristocratic families) to enter without humbling themselves by bowing through the crawl-through door (*nijiri-guchi*). But these examples are rare, and the ideal of social equality in *chanoyu* is revealed in the guest lists of many tea gatherings recorded in historical texts. Not only did warriors of different ranks gather in the intimate quarters of a *sōan* tea house in a way they would not have elsewhere, but members of different social groups—including military aristocrats, Buddhist priests, merchants, aristocrats, artists, and others—would be invited to the same tea gathering on an equal basis. *Chanoyu* developed among the merchant class as a rejection of the values of military society—the raucousness of their *basara* and the restrictions of their hierarchies.

The realities of life among the military class during the period of the development of *chanoyu*—the betrayals and rivalries that led to conflict between lords and rampant warfare—also informed the evolution of *chanoyu*. The tea room was one of the few places where a military man was required to remove his swords. At first, swords were set outside the entry door, sometimes being hung from nails to protect them from becoming soiled.[58] Later, a double-tiered rack was hung on the wall at the entry of the tea house for the express purpose of holding swords when they were removed. *Samurai* carried two swords, a long and a short one. The longer top tier was for the long sword and the shorter bottom tier for the short one. As "undefended"

17. A SUMPTUOUS TEA GATHERING. A military-class couple entertain a priest with a sumptuous meal as the men debate the benefits of drinking *sake* (rice wine). The floor is covered fully with *tatami* and important objects are displayed on a red lacquer tray in the alcove, *oshiita*, a precursor to the larger display alcove called a *tokonoma*. The purpose of the gathering is clearly conspicuous consumption. In a separate room off to the left called a *chatate-dokoro*, a man is busily making tea, blowing on the brazier through a bamboo tube to heat the coals. The areas for private, household activity off to the left were referred to as *ke* while the elegant room for entertaining was called *hare*, thus the expression *hare no cha* for fancy tea gatherings that took place in that space. *Shuhanron Ekotoba*, 16th century. Chadō Shiryōkan, Kyōto.

space, the tea room could be used as a place of parlay and peace-making. Tea records, however, do not record this sort of conversation as having taken place but, conversely, admonish against "commonplace" conversation. No matter what the conversation tended toward, the intimacy of the space brought the participants into close physical proximity unlike any other room where they normally gathered. Although the military class participated in the development of *chanoyu*, it was inherently a rejection of, or a loosening of, certain strictures of their social culture.

In military family residences, tea was usually served in large, bright, open rooms, the *kaisho*. One oft-cited example, however, of a "small room for tea" in a military residence is Dōjinsai, a four-and-a-half-mat room at the Higashiyama palace of Ashikaga Yoshimasa (1435–90), the eighth *shōgun* of the Ashikaga line. Dōjinsai (which is still extant although it has been shifted from its original location) is located within the Tōgudō hall, which was built in 1486. The room is in the *shoin* style and has many of the components mentioned above: reading alcove, white-plastered walls, square-planed post and beam structure, staggered shelves, *tatami* mats, and one wall of *shōji* screens that open onto the large garden outside.

Originally, the room was thought to be simply a study, but during recent renovations it was revealed that the floor structure had been set up to have an in-floor brazier. Resulting theories have suggested that Dōjinsai was not simply a study room but was in fact a tea room. There are other examples of in-floor braziers in private, *shoin*-style rooms such as those of Kisen Shūshō, the priest of Shōkokuji who kept the diary *Inryōken Nichiroku*. He had a brazier in his private study, but it was apparently used for heating the room or for informally warming water for tea, not for

any formal practice of tea.[59] Likewise with Dōjinsai. The room was most likely used as Yoshimasa's private study, and the brazier was not installed as part of a dedicated tea room but rather to provide heat and for warming water as needed for refreshment. In any case, the garden at Yoshimasa's estate (then called Higashi-yama-dono and now called Jishōji or Ginkakuji, the Silver Pavilion) was designed as a painterly landscape scene with boulder-encrusted shorelines, islands in the pond, and carefully pruned pine trees on those islands. There was no dedicated tea room and certainly no tea garden at Yoshimasa's estate.[60]

One historical record that reveals the use of tea within the residences of the military class in the early Muromachi period is called *Kissa Ōrai (Correspondence on Drinking Tea)*. The opening passages describe the setting of a tea gathering.

It is terribly regrettable that you weren't able to attend the tea gathering the other day. Everyone there was terribly disappointed [at your absence]. May I ask the reason? Now let's see, [what shall I tell you about] the Parlor (*kaisho*)? In the Guest Room (*kyakudono*) there were hanging screens of finely cut bamboo (*misu*) and the garden out front was spread with beautiful sand. A length of cloth had been hung from the eaves and silk cloth hung by the windows. The guests began to gather bit by bit and when they were finally arranged, we began with three ceremonial offerings of rice wine. Next we shared one serving of slim noodles (*sōmen*) and tea, and then a meal with some delicacies from the mountains and the sea. When we were finished, we savored the sweetness of some beautiful fruits from the orchard, after which we rose and left the room. Some of the group went to the hillock in the garden that could be seen through the northern window and escaped the heat of the day in the shade of the pines and oaks. The rest of the group went to look at the waterfall by the southern eaves, spread open their lapels and let the cool breeze wafting off the splashing water refresh them. There was a splendid building there with a sitting room on the second floor, towering high [above the garden], open all four sides to the view. This is the tea pavilion (*kissa no tei*) and is also used to view the moon. On the left side was a colorful painting by Shikyō majestically presenting the image of Shaka giving a sermon at Mount Ryōsen. To the right was a black ink painting by Mu Xi, a charming scene of the Kannon Bosatsu at her home on Mount Fudaraku.[61]

The first thing made obvious in this passage is how sumptuous the tea gathering was at the time, including gourmet food, rice wine, and relaxing in the garden. Tea was served in two rooms: the parlor, *kaisho*, which was not used exclusively for tea service, and the tea pavilion, *kissa no tei*, which was named for tea but seems to have primarily been an elegant viewing platform from which to see the garden. The garden had two parts with distinct characteristics: an area spread with sand up close to the *kaisho* and a heavily treed section further back. This was typical of the design of the residential gardens of civil aristocrats in the Heian period. At that time, the sand-covered area close to the residence, called the *niwa* (or *nantei*, Southern Court), was used for all manner of gatherings from dances to archery contests. The planted section further back, with tall shade trees and flowing water, could be viewed from the rooms and verandas of the resi-

dences or strolled through, in much the same way that is described in *Kissa Ōrai*. The descriptions in *Kissa Ōrai* indicate that the residential gardens of military aristocrats followed those of the civil aristocrats in the Heian period. What we can deduce from *Kissa Ōrai* is that, although there seems to have been architectural settings for tea in the residences of the military class in the early Muromachi period—the *kaisho* and the *kissa no tei*—they were not solely dedicated to that function. Moreover, there were not gardens within those residences that were designed to function exclusively as part of a tea gathering.

Zensō: *Buddhist Priests*

Zen Buddhism was introduced to Japan from China during the Kamakura period and, under the patronage of the military class, Zen temples grew in number and influence. Other new sects of Buddhism that developed within Japan at the same time, such as Jōdoshinshū (True Pure Land sect, which focuses on simple prayers to the Amida Buddha), were more popular among the majority of the populace, but Zen (in particular, the Rinzai sect of Zen) became strongly associated with the military class. After initial difficulties experienced trying to introduce a new religion, the institutionalization of Rinzai Zen Buddhism followed a Chinese precedent when, in the late Kamakura period, the Rinzai monks modeled the organization of their temples after the Chinese Wushan system, or Five Mountain system, pronounced Gozan in Japanese. The Gozan system began with five hierarchically ranked temples in the city of Kamakura and then added five more ranked temples in Kyōto during the Muromachi period. Which temples held which ranking changed with the times and, in fact, at times more than five temples were in each list, showing that the specifics of the Chinese system were not being followed even if the general parameters were. The Five Mountain temples were those officially recognized by the shogunate and, as such, wielded particular power. Their official position also gave them the wherewithal, financially and politically, to be patrons of the arts but, naturally, only those arts that were in favor with the establishment.

As one might expect, this was not the kind of environment that would sponsor experimental work, and *chanoyu* was, at the time of its initial creation, a radical declination from the norm. Interestingly enough, the temple most closely associated with the development of *chanoyu* was Daitokuji in Kyōto, which was not part of the Gozan system and as such was correspondingly free from the political control of the shogunate. Although that freedom alone may not fully explain the relationship between Daitokuji and *chanoyu*, it is more than mere coincidence, and there are many ways in which the Zen Buddhist community influenced the development of tea practice and, eventually, the development of the tea garden.

Zen priests were not the originators of *chanoyu* or the *roji*. They were, however, influential in their development. Many of the early tea masters are known to have had strong ties with Zen temples, some to have studied with Zen priests, and in a few cases to have become lay-priests themselves. In those cases Zen priests were mentors to aspiring tea masters. Murata Shukō was reputed to have been a student of the famously eccentric Zen priest Ikkyū, although their actually having met is not documented in any

text. Sōkyū and Rikyū were both known to have associations with Nanshūji, in Sakai, and Daitokuji, both men having given large financial contributions to the latter (fig. 18).

As mentioned earlier, the manner of serving tea in Zen temples, especially the formal customs associated with tea service called *sarei*, formed the basis of the tea service in the houses of the military class. This is an example of a very literal and direct influence Zen priests had on the development of tea culture. In a broader context, though, their influence can be seen in the inherent frugality of the practice of *chanoyu*. Nothing is extravagantly used, nothing is wasted—an attribute that can be seen in the design of tea architecture, in the movements of the host and guests as they move about the room and prepare and receive tea, in the small quantities of food and tea that are served, and even in the sparse design of the tea garden.

Much is made of the links between Zen and tea. The more recent the document, the more likely it is to state this connection clearly; earlier documents tend to be mostly silent on this issue. One early document, however, that reveals a connection between Zen and tea is a colophon written in 1549 by the Zen priest Dairin Sōtō on a portrait of the tea master Takeno Jōō. Sōtō was a priest of Nanshūji in Sakai and Jōō was his lay-apprentice in Buddhism. The portrait was done on the occasion of Jōō receiving from Sōtō the Buddhist name Ikkan. The colophon reads:

> Formerly, he had bonds with the unhindered
> cause of enlightenment, Amida's vow,
> Then changed schools and actively endeavored
> [in Zen].
> Realizing that the taste of tea and the taste of
> Zen are the same,

He scoops up the all the wind in the pines, his
mind undefiled.[62]

This phrase, "the taste of Zen and tea are one and the same," was often repeated after that and shows up in a number of texts from the Edo period onward.

Another record that links Zen and tea—dating from about fifty years later than the colophon but still contemporary with the development of *chanoyu*—is found in *História da Ingreja do Japão* (*The History of the Church in Japan*) by João Rodrigues. He did not write the manuscript while he was in Japan; he compiled it from memory in Macao in the 1620s. Yet the book still stands as a fairly accurate record of life in Japan during the late 16th century at the time that the practice of *chanoyu* was being coalesced by Sen Rikyū and others. We see in Rodrigues's comments that, at least by the late 16th century, the practice of *chanoyu* was clearly correlated with the practices of the Zen sect. Rodrigues has a habit of describing his subjects in honorific terms, speaking highly of the places he writes about and praising the various qualities of the Japanese people in general. His description of *chanoyu*, therefore, might be considered to be an idealized version—something that his hosts made pains he understand and that he, in turn, wished to pass on to his countrymen in the best light. Still, despite any embellishment he may have made, he did live in Japan for over thirty years, was fluent in the language, and could hardly have been convinced of something that was patently not true. The following is from Rodrigues's account of Japan.

Those who practice *chanoyu* try to imitate these
solitary philosophers [of the Zen sect] and hence
all pagan followers of this art [as opposed to
those followers whom were Christian converts
of which there were a few] belong to the Zenshū
sect, or else join it even though their forefathers
had hitherto belonged to another sect. Although
they imitate the Zenshū sect in this art, they
do not practice any superstition, cult, or special
ceremony related to religion; for they have taken
none of this from the sect, but imitate it merely
as regards its eremitical seclusion and withdrawal

18. ZEN TEMPLE GROUNDS. Daitokuji, Kyōto. Historically, Daitokuji has been known for its sponsorship of the arts and those of artistic mind. Sōchō, the poet, used to stay there when in Kyōto, and many early tea masters are known to have undergone lay-training at Daitokuji, including Rikyū. Sōchō began the construction of this main gate, *sanmon*, but ran out of funds. Rikyū stepped in to support the construction of the second floor, Konmōkaku, for which service a carved figure of him was enshrined there. This meant that anyone entering had to walk "beneath Rikyū's feet." The arrogance of this act is reputed to be one reason Rikyū was forced to commit suicide by the ruling military lord, Toyotomi Hideyoshi.

from all dealings in social manners, its resolution and alertness of mind in everything, and its lack of tepidity, sluggishness, softness and effeminacy. They imitate them as well in the contemplation of things of nature, not as regards its end (that is, the knowledge of the being and perfection of the First Cause through external things) but only in the natural part which they see on the surface, for this moves and inclines the spirit to solitude, nostalgia and withdrawal from worldly, ostentatious activity and business.

Apart from some general principles, they do not teach anything by word but rather by deed, and they leave everything else to the contemplation of each individual, until he understands the purpose and essentials of the art through his own efforts; he adapts anything merely incidental as he thinks fit and suitable, provided it does not go against the general rules of *suki*. The purpose of this art, *cha*, then is courtesy, good breeding, modesty and moderation in exterior actions, peace and quiet in body and soul, exterior humility, without any pride, arrogance, fleeing from all of the exterior ostentation, pomp, display and splendor of social life; instead, sincerity without any deceit as befits a hermit in the wilderness, honest and decent attire, with certain order, neatness and plainness in everything in use and in the house, in keeping with such a calling.[63]

Other records that make explicit the connections between *chanoyu* and Zen, such as *Nanbōroku* (*Records of the Priest Nanbō*, c. 1690), *Chawa Shigetsu Shū* (*Pointing at the Moon Anthology*, 1701), and *Zencharoku* (*Zen Tea Record*, 1828), date from later eras. It may be that they were recording in written form a pre-existing oral

tradition that *chanoyu* was a reflection of Zen, but it could also be that the authors were pointedly trying to encourage their readers to perceive a connection between tea and Zen.[64]

Nanbōroku is purported to be the records of a Zen monk named Nanbō who was a close disciple of Sen Rikyū. The title was originally *Kissa Nanpōroku (Tea Records of the Southern Way)*, in which "southern way" refers to the opening line of Lu Yu's classic on tea, *Chajing*, which states, "Tea is a noble tree from the south." At a later date, the title was changed to *Nanbōroku*, to refer to the purported author. The *Records* were, again allegedly, found by Tachibana Jitsuzan (1655–1708), who compiled them into the form we have now at the end of the 17th century. For over a century, just a few copies of the book were kept in private hands; it became widely circulated only in the early 19th century. There is, however, no historical record of a Zen monk named Nanbō (or any of the other names he used) ever being at one of Rikyū's tea gatherings or having been his apprentice in tea. This seems suspect, since the author is purported to have been a very close confidant of Rikyū's, recording in detail his deepest thoughts on tea. It seems most likely that, even if *Nanbōroku* was based on some original historical notes or hearsay, it was certainly embellished by the person who edited it into the version we know today.

It is interesting to note, however, that references to Buddhism in tea texts sometimes include ideas from both Zen and Pure Land sects indiscriminately. In the Metsugo section of *Nanbōroku*, which is purportedly a recollection of Rikyū's words after his death, we find the following:

(1) eagerly made inquires of the masters of Daitokuji and Nanshūji. Day and night, with the

monastic rules of Zen temples as my basis, I simplified the measurements regulating the highly refined manner of the *shoin* room; I unfolded the world of the Pure Land in the locus of the *roji*, brought the spirit of *wabi* to its culmination in a thatched hut of two mats, endeavored in practice through gathering firewood and drawing water, and at last realized, though faintly, that there is the taste of the real in a bowl of tea.[65]

Another historical text that reveals a connection between Zen and *chanoyu* is *Chawa Shigetsu Shū*, a collection of anecdotes about the life of Rikyū, observed by his grandson Sōtan (1578–1658). What Sōtan saw and heard he then related to one of his own most important apprentices, Fujimura Yōken (1613–99), and this was written down by one of Yōken's apprentices (and son-in-law), Kusumi Soan (1636–1728).[66] The collection is, of course, narrative rather than verbatim when it quotes Rikyū as saying, "Since it [tea] was originally formulated on the basis of Zen, there is no 'way' that need be further specified. If you simply take the tea stories of our predecessors that I often recount as a pointer to the moon, you will naturally come to understand."[67] Still, whether verbatim, narrative, or assigned to Rikyū by Soan, it represents the common belief of people involved with *chanoyu* that, at the time of Rikyū, the foundation of *chanoyu* was Zen Buddhist thought.

Zencharoku, or *Zen Tea Record*, as the name clearly states, is pointedly and entirely about the relationship between *chanoyu* and Zen Buddhism. The date of writing and authorship of *Zencharoku* are in doubt. Although there are conflicting ways to assess its history, it was first published in 1828 and was most likely the product of the early 19th century, not before that.

The text is filled with phrases such as "At the heart of *chanoyu* lies the way of Zen," "The preparation of tea is a wholly Zen activity; it is an effort to realize self nature," and "The spirit of tea is the spirit of Zen; there is no 'spirit of tea' independent of the spirit of Zen. If you do not know the taste of Zen, you do not know the taste of tea." The clarity with which this text makes the connection between *chanoyu* and Zen undoubtedly stems from the desire of the author/publisher to present tea in its most spiritual mode, to reawaken practitioners in their day and age to what they felt was the spiritual core of *chanoyu*. However, while it is clear that Zen thought informed the development of *chanoyu* in many ways, this exclusionary tone—Zen is Tea, Tea is Zen—was not the language used in the era when *chanoyu* was first being created.

Zen is a sect of Buddhism which proposes that the path to enlightenment is to be found through meditative practices rather than prayer to higher beings, as is true of the other sects of Buddhism. Zen practice is thus termed *jiriki*, "self-empowerment," and the other sects, *tariki*, "external empowerment." The tenets and practices of Zen very much set the cultural tone in the Kamakura and Muromachi periods, at least among the upper-echelon military class, and they also shaped the development of *chanoyu*. There are three ways in which the practice of Zen—how Zen priests lived their lives and carried out their teachings—influenced *chanoyu*: the premise of "teaching through action," the practice of "moving meditation," and a "detachment from material things."

Kyōge betsuden, "transmission of doctrine without the use of sutras," and *ishin denshin*, "transmission from mind to mind," are two ways that Zen priests state the concept of not teaching through words, written or spoken, but through direct action. The teacher guides the pupil by the way he leads his own life; the student comes to realization through direct experience. Rodrigues noted the same thing about tea.

> Those who practiced *chanoyu* were also greatly versed in the subject [*suki*], and when they changed something or added something new, they did not explain in words the reason for such a change and addition. For it is a rule of this art that its experts do not explain the reason and cause of the things they do in this matter by words but by deeds only, for they leave everything to the consideration and reasoning of their pupils. In this way, the pupils may come to understand the reason through their own efforts by watching what the teacher does. This is how the masters of Zen sects teach their doctrine, and this art imitates them.[68]

Another text that reveals the characteristic of "teaching through practice" is found in *Rikyū Ichimai Kishōmon (One-Page Testament of Rikyū)*, the oldest extant copy of which is from 1602, within a decade of Rikyū's death. Proclaiming what *chanoyu* is, and how it differs from tea practice of the past, Rikyū is "quoted" as saying that tea is not something to be taught, but simply understood by doing.

> *Chanoyu* as we now practice it is not the *chanoyu* that has been discussed and proclaimed in the past by accomplished teamen of China and Japan. Neither is it to partake of tea having grasped its essence through scholarly study. It is simply to drink tea, knowing that if you just heat the water, your thirst is certain to be quenched. Nothing else is involved.[69]

The practice of meditation most widely associated with Zen is *zazen*, seated meditation, in which the practitioner sits on the floor, usually on *tatami* mats, usually in a darkened room. At Zen temples this room is called a *zendō*, meditation hall. The practitioner's legs are crossed over themselves in a full- or half-Lotus position, hands folded in front of the navel, and eyes half-closed or shut. This, however, is not the only form of meditation. The various chores that are done around the temple, which are collectively called *samu*, are also considered to be a form of "moving meditation." These chores can be anything from cleaning rooms to working in vegetable patches to cooking meals—the proverbial chopping wood and carrying water. Meditation through physical work is a basic premise of all of the so-called "Zen arts," be they martial arts or fine arts, in which the art form itself is seen as a means of focusing the mind and opening awareness to new levels. The institutionalization of these arts into the grand master system, *iemoto seido*, and the custom of terming them *dō* or "Way" is an Edo-period development. Some common examples are *sadō* (the Way of Tea), *kyūdō* (the Way of the Bow), and *kadō* (the Way of the Flower, commonly called *ikebana*). The opening lines of *Oboegaki*, which is the first book of *Nanbōroku* and can be considered an Edo-period text, make clear that *chanoyu* was also considered in this manner by this time.

> [Rikyū said] *chanoyu* of the small room is above all a matter of performing practice and attaining realization in accord with the Buddhist path. To delight in the refined splendor of a dwelling or the taste of delicacies belongs to worldly life. There is shelter enough when the roof does not leak, food enough when it staves off hunger. This

is the Buddhist teaching and the fundamental meaning of *chanoyu*. We draw water, gather firewood, boil the water, and make tea. We then offer it to the Buddha, serve it to others, and drink ourselves. We arrange flowers and burn incense. In all of this, we model ourselves after the acts of the Buddha and the past masters. Beyond this, you must come to your own understanding.[70]

In the Muromachi period these various practices—*sadō*, *kyūdō*, *kadō*, etc.—had not coalesced into the formalized lineages of the grand master system and were not yet termed "Zen arts." But, looking at the social and cultural environment of the Muromachi period, as well as the background and experience of the people who fundamentally shaped the practice of these arts, it is reasonable to assume that the various arts could have been considered, by some of the practitioners, to be direct-action methods for the expression and realization of Zen Buddhist enlightenment.

Detachment from material things is a fundamental part of Zen practice. As one example, acolytes in Zen temples, *unsui*, are given the space of one *tatami* mat within the *zendō* as their "room." They have their robes, a bowl, and a set of chopsticks, and that's about it. No more than is absolutely necessary. This attribute of paring down things to the absolute minimum is also the sentiment of *chanoyu*. Again, from the opening of *Oboegaki*: "To delight in the refined splendor of a dwelling or the taste of delicacies belongs to worldly life. There is shelter enough when the roof does not leak, food enough when it staves off hunger."[71] *Roji Seicha Kihaku* (Zen Rules for the Roji, in which case "*Roji*" means the tea garden and tea house together) states, "The host will emerge to invite the guests in. He is poor; the utensils for tea and rice, irregular; the food

lacking any refinement in flavor. The trees and rocks in the garden are simply as in nature. Any who find this incomprehensible should leave forthwith."[72]

In reality, the practitioners of *chanoyu*, throughout history, have rarely been poor. The creation of tea house and garden often require a higher than average construction budget, and many of the tea utensils have a great monetary value. This was understood by the initial designers of *chanoyu*. They were not giving up all their worldly goods, nor were they just playing at being poor. Rather, they were creating places—physically, temporally, and socially—within which they and their guests could step out of the ordinary understanding of things in terms of monetary value and social standing and come in touch with a new means of perceiving the world (fig. 19).

In addition to the practice of Zen—teaching through action, moving meditation, and material detachment—certain scriptural and doctrinal aspects of Zen are evident as having influenced the development of *chanoyu* and the *roji*. Most obvious of the scriptural examples is the word *roji* itself. This will be described fully in Chapter 4, but suffice it to say here that the word originally meant simply "an alleyway" and later was assigned new *kanji* (also pronounced *roji*) that were taken from the Lotus Sutra, *Myōhō Rengekyō*, giving the word a Buddhist meaning.

In terms of how the doctrine of Zen may have shaped the development of *chanoyu*, the first thing that comes to mind is the core concept of *kū*, or "emptiness." The translation of *kū* as "emptiness" is literally correct, but it is also misleading.

The English word "emptiness" makes it sound like a nihilistic concept—a denial of the actual existence of anything. But in fact *kū* is rather different. When Buddhism was first developing in India, one of the aspects that set it apart from the older Hindu practice was the Buddhist disbelief in the existence of a fixed soul. Hindu practice centered on a belief in individual souls, *atman*, and a greater, pure soul, *brahman*. The ideal of the religion was the alignment of lesser to greater, the synchrony of *atman* with *brahman*. Buddhists took a different point of view. They looked at the world and saw all things at all times in an on-going process of change and concluded that if the world is in a constant state of flux, nothing can be fixed, not even souls. Furthermore, they perceived that all things arise out of, and because of, this state of flux. It is the very interaction between things that gives rise to all other things. Given this, Buddhist thinking posits that since everything is dependent on causation for its existence, no phenomenon is permanent and immutable. Expressed another

19. TEA SERVICE IN A BUDDHIST TEMPLE. The method of drinking whisked, powdered tea was imported from China by Buddhist priests along with many other aspects of Song-dynasty culture. Here we see a gathering at Kiyomizu Temple in Kyōto, a temple of the Hossō sect; the situation would have been similar in a Zen temple. While a number of priests are copying sutras, in a separate room, another priest and two young attendants prepare tea for the refreshment of the scribes. The black *tenmoku* tea bowls on red *tenmokudai* pedestals, the brazier, and the kettle are all exactly like those depicted in earlier paintings from China. *Kiyomizudera Engi*, Dosa Mitsunobu (dates unknown), 1517. Tōkyō National Museum.

way, phenomena are "empty" of static existence. The Indians called this emptiness, *sūnyatâ*—the Japanese say *kū*. Although the English word "empty" is linguistically correct, the words "impermanence" and "interconnectivity" seem to capture the essence better.

Impermanence and interconnectivity are basic attributes of *chanoyu* as well, and illuminate two of the most important changes in the shift away from the sumptuous entertainment of *hare-no-cha* to the quiet communion of *chanoyu*. The structure of the tea house is lightly made; the aesthetics of the gathering are those of the patina gained from weathering and age. Impermanence is understood as a basic reality of life and reveled in. The gathering itself, as well, is no more than a brief meeting of a small group of people, a coming-together that happens once, and then is gone. This is expressed in the phrase *ichigo ichie*, which translates literally as "one time, one meeting" but, more loosely, can be described as meaning that a communion of people at any particular time happens only once and never again the same way. The origins of the statement are to be found in *Yamanoue Sōjiki* (*Yamanoue Sōji's Records*), tea records written around 1590 by tea master Yamanoue Sōji (1544–90), a primary disciple of Sen Rikyū. Here we find the expression "*ichigo ni ichido no kai*," "a once in a lifetime meeting."[73] In this statement we also find expressed the aspect of interconnectivity. The *chanoyu* gathering, in its ideal form, allows those gathered to share the moment, to feel the close communion of people, even if only for a brief moment, and also, through such utterly simple things as the taste of water in the water basin in the garden and a single flower placed in the display alcove of the tea house, to be reminded of the interconnections that link them with all other elements of nature.

This is one of the ideals of Zen Buddhist thought that certainly informed the development of *chanoyu*. Whether it is always practiced by those doing *chanoyu* today is beside the point. In fact, it is not. It may even be rare. Going back two hundred years to *Zencharoku*, we find a person writing a text about the connections between Zen and tea specifically because he saw so many people around him practicing *chanoyu* as fanciful entertainment and thought he needed to remind them that they were missing the point of the core principles. Going back three hundred years to *Nanbōroku*, we find the same admonishments; and if *Nanbōroku* is believed to be the words of Rikyū, then we find the person who coalesced the practice of *chanoyu* himself expressing those sentiments at the very time that he is creating the practice. The fact that *chanoyu* is not practiced by most people as a form of moving meditation does not lessen the obvious impact that the ideals of Zen had on changing the drinking of tea from the festive activity of *hare-no-cha* to the introspective practice of *chanoyu*.

Shōnin: *Merchants*

The man credited with coalescing the art of *chanoyu* into the form we know today was Sen Rikyū (1522–91). He was not a military lord, nor was he a Buddhist priest. He was a merchant. Or, more properly put, he came from a family of merchants, because by the later years of his life, when he was fully defining his ideas of *chanoyu* and serving as tea master to the rulers Nobunaga and Hideyoshi, his main daily occupation was not the running of the family mercantile business. The fact that Rikyū was from the merchant class is not coincidental; in many ways the story of *chanoyu* and the *roji* is the story of the merchant class.

In the Heian period (794–1185), the financial support of the civil aristocracy was based on privately controlled manors called *shōen*. The products required by the aristocratic class were provided by craftsmen and artisans who were also somehow bonded to the *shōen*. Since most *shōen* and farming villages strove to be more or less self-sufficient in their needs for daily life, markets in villages or towns were sporadic events. As the control of the *shōen* by civil aristocratic families declined toward the end of the Heian period due to lack of direct managerial policies, and as the needs of provincial military families grew more culturally complex, the craftsmen and artisans whose skills were previously provided only to one *shōen* became sought after over a wider range. Markets where their products could be found (as well as other, more basic products such as rice and salt) became more common events in towns, eventually developing into regular marketplaces, *teiki-ichi*. With the advent of regular marketplaces and available quantities of goods from free-trading craftsmen, there arose a need for systems of distribution, storage and sales of products, handling of money (or its equivalent in rice), and even "marketing," if you will. The people who began to provide those services developed into what we now call the merchant class, *shōnin*.

The attitude of society toward the merchants was not always favorable. The civil aristocrats had justified their own position of control over society through claims of divine ancestry, in the case of the imperial lineage, and connections to that ancestry in the cases of the other aristocratic families and retainers. The military families, as they began to take over control of society, justified their right to control through military prowess and the ability to provide protection and sta-

bility. The farmers and artisans found their place in society guaranteed by the food they raised and products they made. The merchants, however—being neither civil nor military elites, nor producers of goods—were viewed as preying on the labors of society, and not altogether trustworthy. A contemporary adage was *Byōbu to akyūdo to wa sugu nareba, mi ga tatanu*, "Folding screens and merchants are a lot alike, they both need to be crooked to stand."[74] In the Edo period, this pejorative view would be codified in the class system that ranked members of society with the military families at the top and merchants at the bottom known as *shi-nō-kō-shō*, which stands for military families (*shi*), farmers (*nō*), artisans (*kō*), and merchants (*shō*). In the early Muromachi period and, before that, in the Kamakura period, although it was not codified in the legal structure, this sentiment already existed, especially among those in the civil and military aristocracies.

The services provided by the merchants, however, were essential to the growth of villages into towns and towns into cities, and vital to the power bases of the

20. LIFE IN THE MERCHANT DISTRICT. This scene, from around the Muromachi-Sanjō area of Kyōto, depicts life in the merchant district in the mid-16th century. Various shops display their wares on shelves along the street, or invite customers inside the main, earthen-floored room, *doma*, to do business. The streets are unpaved; the architecture is still relatively simple. One house is having its roof reworked with wood shingles and a bamboo lattice, which will be weighted with stones at the intersections to hold the roof against strong winds. *Rakuchū Rakugaizu* (Uesugi-bon), Kanō Eitoku (1543–90), 16th century (depicts Kyōto between 1532 and 1555), lower half of the fourth panel of the left-hand set of screens. Uesugi Museum, Yonezawa City.

very classes that despised them (fig. 20). Consequently, they flourished. Commercial and craft guilds, called *za*, became social forces to be contended with, as did the wholesalers of goods, *ton'ya*, and warehousers of goods, *dosō*. *Dosō* means "earth-walled storehouse" and referred to the large, fireproof structures where the merchants kept their stock, but was also an appellation for those merchants involved in that business. The *dosō*, by virtue of having standing stocks and an ability to protect their goods, also became bankers and money lenders. They were able to provide the financial base that the civil and military aristocracies required but did not always have themselves. The warehouses on the coast in the port city of Sakai (south of Ōsaka), which by virtue of its position on the Inland Sea became a center for intercoastal and international trade, were called *naya*, and the families that controlled them, *nayashū*. The tea masters Takeno Jōō and Sen Rikyū were both from *nayashū* families: Takeno's traded in leather, Rikyū's in fish.

The merchants' wealth, and their expertise in business, gave them an important role supporting international trade. When ships were sent overseas on tributary or trade missions to China, Korea, and the Ryūkyū islands (present-day Okinawa), the merchants were able to bid for the right to supply the vessels. Those supplies included goods that were needed for the trip itself, such as food and water, and special trade goods required as tribute (especially true during the tally trade with the Ming dynasty). Beyond that, there was also room on board for merchants to take goods privately on speculation. The tally trade was a system of control imposed by the Chinese government to regulate and limit the number of incoming ships. An official passport, or tally, was required in order to obtain entry to a Chinese port. The tallies were sup-

plied by the Chinese government to the Japanese administration, who, in turn, dispensed them to their supporters. At first, from their inception in 1403 until about 1410, the tally ships were arranged directly by the military government, *bakufu*, but then, later, until the end of the system in 1547, they were administered by a conglomerate of the *bakufu*, military lords (*daimyō*), and merchant sponsors, with the merchants playing an increasingly important role. The possible profits were staggeringly high compared to the investment.

The role of merchants in these international trade expeditions brought them into the circles of Zen priests and military families. The priests traveling to China, in part, to study at Chan temples were the most literate members of the retinue. Also, because their motives were, ostensibly, nonpolitical in character, they were often given the role of emissary. The military, in particular the *shōgun* and some *daimyō* families, such as the Hosokawa and Ōuchi families, were connected with the Ming tally trade as sponsors and as holders of the tallies required to enter Chinese ports.

Participation in international trade brought merchants closer to the upper echelons of society and gave them access to artwork and tea wares from overseas. It is not by chance that so many of the tea masters whose names remain in records from the 16th century were from the port cities of Sakai and Hakata, the two major international trading ports in Japan. Although merchants were, by the nature of their trade, considered second class *as a class*, it was an interesting aspect of Muromachi-period urban culture that individuals from base origins were able to rise within society, sometimes to extremely high positions, simply by virtue of their skills. The epitome of this is the story of a peasant boy born near present-day Nagoya with no family name, just the moniker Hiyoshimaru, who ended up rising through the ranks of soldiering to become the leader of Japan, Toyotomi Hideyoshi.[75] There were social restrictions by class, but not so clearly for individuals.

Rikyū was a merchant, yet managed to become cultural advisor to both Oda Nobunaga and Toyotomi Hideyoshi, successive leaders of Japan, because of his skills: as a chief tea master (sadō), as an adept advisor, and as a diplomat. The connection of merchants to chanoyu is related to this possibility of social mobility through skill. The military families were the power brokers of Muromachi society, the Zen priests were learned, the aristocrats held a lineage to antiquity. Merchants could supply them all with goods, lend them money, underwrite their adventures, but they couldn't socialize with them *as merchants*, something they could do as tea masters. For merchants, being a tea master, known at the time as *chanoyusha* or *sukisha*, was a means of accessing social circles that were otherwise closed to them.

Several merchants kept detailed records of the tea gatherings they attended, which give us an inkling of what the merchants found important. In some cases, these records were kept going for many generations; *Matsuya Kaiki* (*Matsuya Family Tea Records*), for example, continued for three generations. Though no single entry can be considered typical of all others, the following entry from 1596 is fairly representative of the genre.

> 4th year of Bunroku, 1595, 1st month
> Morning of the 7th day.
> Went to the residence of the Honorable Chūbō
>   Gengo. Food was served in the formal room
>   (*shoin*), tea in the four-and-a-half-mat room
>   (*yojōhan*).
> In the display alcove (*toko*) was a large bamboo

flower vase with chrysanthemums (*kiku*) and narcissus (*suisen*). On the display shelf was a tea caddy (*katatsuki*) in a white-and-gold-thread cloth bag. The ladle (*hishaku*) was hung on the wall, the water container (*mizusashi*) was made of Seto pottery with tortoise shell lid, ceramic tea bowl (*yaki cha-wan*), linen tea cloth (*chakin*), bamboo tea scoop (*chashaku*).
First Sitting: Okaya Dōga, Kinuya Jukkan, Kusuriya Munakata, [Matsuya] Hisamasa, Kureya Sōho, Genji Bussha; Six Guests.
Second Sitting: Hantōya Jūkan, Nabeya Sōritsu, Koya Sōyū, Imonoya Kyūtai, Kitanohashi Gyosa, Sanjō Nunoya; Six Guests.
Third Sitting: Ōhigashi Jōkyū, Taramiya Zen'emon, Haruta Matazaemon, [Matsuya] Hisayoshi, Ushiroiya Gorozaemon, Kokiya Zenshirō; Six Guests.

- Grilled salmon, soup with chicken and wheat-gluten bread, followed by pickles and grilled chicken
- Thin sliced Sea Bream (*tai*) and Sea Perch (*suzuki*) in vinegar,[76] rice, clear broth with octopus (*tako*), cherry flowers (*sakura-iri*), and new shoots (*kukutachi*)
- Three tastes of salmon, taro and *konnyaku* jelly.[77]

As is usually the case with the tea records of merchant tea masters, there are only brief notes on several aspects of the gathering: Where and when the gathering was held, what the tea room was like, what artwork/flowers and tea utensils were displayed, who attended the gathering, and what was served for the meal. The three meals mentioned were most likely three separate servings; one for each of the sittings. It is interesting to note that many of the guests (this was a large gathering with three sittings) were merchants, as can be told just by their names: for instance, Kinuya (silk merchant), Kusuriya (pharmacist), Nabeya (kitchen utensil dealer), and Imonoya (cast-iron goods). As is typical, the entry does not mention the tea garden, nor does it wax philosophic with references to Buddhist thought.

The lack of philosophy and spirituality in merchant tea records leads one to think their view of *chanoyu* was materialistic and worldly. *Chanoyu*, however, has a deeper connection with the merchant class than just as a means of social climbing. It was not originally created as a method for accessing higher social circles, although it certainly was used that way by some as it began to be accepted by the upper echelon as part of their culture. As we have seen, the custom of drinking *matcha* came over from Song China with Zen priests and existed in Zen temples in both prosaic and ritual forms. Members of the military class took on this culture as their own and created, or their servants created, the *shoin* style of tea. But it was within the community of the merchants that the drinking of *matcha* was transformed into *chanoyu*.

The first inklings of a change from the formal *shoin-cha* to the rustic *chanoyu* come in texts such as *Shōtetsu Monogatari*, a poetic commentary written around 1450. There is a reference at the end comparing tea people and poetry people that includes the expression *cha no suki*.[78] This is the first use of the word *suki*—which means variously affection, refinement, and taste—in connection with tea, revealing the beginnings of an aesthetic sensitivity toward tea that eventually resulted in the development of *chanoyu*. The reference in *Shōtetsu Monogatari* is not specific to the

merchant class, but soon after, a merchant/tea connoisseur named Murata Shukō (1423–1502) revealed his thoughts on *chanoyu* in a letter written to his disciple Furuichi Chōin (1459–1509). The letter has come to be known as known as *Kokoro no Fumi, The Letter of the Heart*, and in it Shukō states the need for tea masters to move away from the tradition of Chinese-styled *shoin-cha* toward a practice that incorporates native tea wares, is based on the aesthetics of "chill and withered" (precedents to *wabi*), and takes place in a small tea hut.

Many other pivotal tea masters at this time were merchants. Shukō's successor was Murata Sōshu (also written as Sōju, dates unknown), the tea master mentioned in Chapter 2's section on hermit culture who had a tea house named Goshoan, the Arbor of the Noon-day Pine. He lived in Shimogyō (Lower Capital), a bustling merchant district of Kyōto, on Shijō Street, one of the main cross-streets. It can be assumed that men who appear in tea records as having lived in Shimogyō were men of the merchant class. It is not clear if he was the biological son of Shukō, his adopted son, or simply a follower of Shukō who took his name, but he is widely regarded as Shukō's principal apprentice. Another tea master who lived in Shimogyō was Jūshiya Sōgo (dates unkown), who was a pupil of Kogaku Sōkō, a Zen priest at Daitokuji. The dates of Sōgo's birth and death are unknown, but his name appears in *Matsuya Kaiki* as the host of a tea gathering in 1537, and he is thought to have died by the late Tenbun era, which ended in 1555. He is recorded in *Nanbōroku* as having been mentor in *chanoyu* to Takeno Jōō and in *Yamanoue Sōjiki* (and *Matsuya Kaiki*) in relation to his tea utensils. Also reputed to have been a Shimogyō tea master, pupil of Shukō, and mentor to Jōō was Fujita Sōri (dates unknown).[79]

Originally, this ideal of a scholar hermit was not a merchant ideal. The notion of a "hermit in the city" would not be naturally associated with the mind-set of an urban merchant—Chinese literati and Zen priests, certainly, but not merchants. In the confluence of social groups and cultures that made up Muromachi-period Kyōto, however, that ideal was transplanted to, and found fertile ground to root in, the merchant quarters. Shimogyō was a dense, urban area. Merchants did not have a lot of room to spread out. They could obtain wealth in the form of coin, rice, or other valuable possessions such as art work, but they were not able to build lavish residences for themselves. Large-scale use of land for personal reasons was restricted to the *shōgun*, some *daimyō* and aristocrats, and temples. The development of a form of *chanoyu* that is inherently inward-focused, spatially compressed, and escapist or transcendental (depending on your point of view), grows directly out of the social and physical conditions of the urban merchants' lives.

Shokunin/Geinōsha: *Artisans/Artists*

The fourth social class in the Muromachi period that influenced the development of *chanoyu*, and thus the creation of the *roji*, were the artisans, *shokunin*, and artists, *geinōsha* or *geinōmin*. Perhaps social group is a better expression than class because they were not identified in the Muromachi period as a single group. In the following Edo period, the *shokunin* would be identified as the *kō* of *shi-nō-kō-shō*, but the *geinōsha* were of various backgrounds and have never been specifically identified as a single group. A good indicator of the rise of importance of the *shokunin* within medieval society is the appearance, from the Kamakura period onward, of various books with titles that include the term *Shokunin Uta-awase* (*Poetry Contests Between "Skilled People"*). These depict imaginary poetry competitions between people of various occupations. The term *shokunin* had the broad meaning of any urban resident with a particular occupation—from carpenter to priest—but the books do give a good insight into the wide variety of artisans who plied their trade at the time.

One such edition is *Shichijūichi-ban Shokunin Uta-awase* (*Seventy-one Poetry Competitions Between "Skilled People"*) that lists 142 various people and their work in 71 pairs, depicting each with a short poem and a drawing. The list includes many we would today call *shokunin*, such as the carpenter who is listed at the very beginning. Assuming there was an intentional choice to the order the artisans were presented in, the fact that the carpenter is listed first tells a bit about his position in the society, or at least his omnipresence. Also revealing is that he is pictured wearing a military family hat, *samurai eboshi*, and a sword in his belt, both signs of an elevated status. Among the tradesmen are the roof-tile maker, *kawara-yaki*; the shingle maker, *hiwadabuki*; the weaver, *hata-ori*; the wheelwright, *kuruma-zukuri*; and the charcoal maker, *sumi-yaki*. There are also people whom we would today call artists or performers, such as the lute player, *biwa-hōshi*; the festival performer, *dengaku*; the musician, *gakunin*; and the dancer, *maibito*. We also find linked-verse poets, *rengashi*, who were mentioned earlier, and street sellers of whisked tea, known as *ippuku issen*, a name that translates literally as "penny for a drink." It is interesting to note, however, there is no profession of gardener listed among these 142 skilled people.

During the Muromachi period, the artisans who were involved with the development of *chanoyu* included those related to tea architecture, such as carpenters, *tatami* makers, and paper makers; those related to tea utensils, such as the potters who made ceramic tea bowls, vases, and water containers; and those related to the gardens, such as the people who collected special materials for gardens (trees, stones, lanterns) and had the skills to install them. The skills of these artisans, and the degree to which they perfected the tools they used, were critical to the development of

21. CONNOISSEURS IN THE LORD'S COURT. The Ashikaga *shōgun* (green and red jacket, left center) is seen making a pilgrimage to Wakamiya Hachimangū Shrine with his retainers. Among them are three men, in the lower center, who have shaved heads (as Buddhist priests have) but also carry swords (as *samurai* do). These are the *dōbōshū*, connoisseurs employed at the courts of military lords to advise them on cultural and artistic matters including tea practice. *Ashikaga Shōgun Wakamiya Hachimangū Sankei Emaki*, 16th century. Wakamiya Hachimangūsha, Kyōto.

chanoyu. Carpenters had, for instance, over the years since the Heian period, refined their metal tools (saws and chisels) and improved their use of those tools to such a degree that they were able to execute the highly detailed and demanding work required in the creation of the *sukiya* tea house. They also had a sense of where to collect the various natural materials required in the execution of the design. They were not the designers, however, at least not initially. By the late Edo period, when *chanoyu* culture had existed for two hundred years and the grand master system had fully developed, craftsmen had been producing works for tea for many generations. They were fully aware of *chanoyu* culture and were so well practiced at their various crafts that a novice tea practitioner could turn to them and request any needed object, from tea caddy to tea house, and be confident that they could advise him in the proper form. In the beginning this was not so, and the tea masters who first tentatively began experimenting with *chanoyu* needed to instruct the artisans in their desires. Nevertheless, those artisans were able, because of the skills and tools they had developed for other applications, to create what was requested of them.

Artisans, therefore, were essential to the early development of *chanoyu* in a secondary, or supporting, role. The artists, *geinōsha*, however, played a much more direct role in its development. The medieval period in Japan saw the flourishing of many forms of artists, from street performers to poets. Part of the cultural development of society within merchant towns allowed those arts that had been theretofore part of aristocratic culture to become part of townsfolk culture and, conversely, allowed activities that had long been part of commoner or rural peasant culture to become more highly developed. The way in which tea drinking (once the reserve of aristocrats and priests) became part of military and merchant culture is an example of the former, and the way in which *dengaku*, rural theater originally performed during rice plantings, transformed into *nō* theater performed for the military aristocracy exemplifies the latter. Traveling performers and storytellers such as *biwa-hōshi* and *etoki-hōshi* became instruments by which these newly developing cultures were spread from place to place.

Of the many types of *geinōsha* who were active during the Muromachi period, there are two groups that influenced the development of *chanoyu*, and thus the tea garden. The first are linked-verse poets, *rengashi*. The *renga* poets did not develop *chanoyu* themselves, but they did incorporate an aesthetic in their poetry that influenced tea masters and presaged the aesthetic called *wabi* as was described in the section on Tea Aesthetics in Chapter 2. The second group of medieval artists who are intricately related to the development of tea culture are the men called *dōbōshū*, which literally translates as "companions" (fig. 21). These men were not necessarily actively producing works of arts themselves (although in some cases they were), but rather they held positions as artistic advisors or connoisseurs in the households of the military aristocracy. Often from lower classes, they were able to find access to social groups previously closed to them in part because of their knowledge and in part by taking priestly vows that freed them from the restrictions of class. This can be ascertained in the *ami* suffix, *amidagō*, found after the names of many *dōbōshū*—such as Nōami, Geiami, and Sōami. *Ami* is a religious appellation associated with Pure Land sects of Buddhism that embrace the Amida Buddha. The *dōbōshū* catalogued artwork, advised on authenticity, and, in some cases, worked toward the establishment of new parameters of art.

22. TEA FOR A MILITARY LORD. In the residence of a military lord, men race their horses for the enjoyment of the lord, who sits inside the main room flanked by two young retainers. Behind him is the writing alcove, *shoin*, that gives name to this style of architecture. In the adjoining room, a tea master, *sadō*, prepares bowls of tea for the guests, seated in front of a classic tea shelf, *daisu*, whisking a bowl of tea. The white bowl he is using and the black bowl being carried by an attendant are both Japanese-style, *wamono*, tea bowls typical of rustic tea, revealing the integration of *wabicha* into the cultural life of Edo-period military households. *Chōba Kyūbazu Byōbu*, anonymous, early 17th century. Taga Taisha, Shiga.

Among the *dōbōshū* were men whose role was to make tea. They were called *sadō* or "tea master." This is not to be confused with another word *sadō*, an Edo-period term that means "the Way of Tea."[80] While the lord of the house and his guests sat in the *kaisho* or *shoin*, the *sadō* sat in an adjoining room with a set of utensils for tea. The place where the *sadō* did his work was known as the "tea preparation place," *chatate tokoro*, although this was not the name of a specific room and, at times, might just be the hallway outside the *kaisho*.

An excellent example of the *sadō* performing his task can be seen in the folding screen called *Pictures of Training Horses* (*Chōba Kyūbazu Byōbu*; fig. 22). The painting was done in the early 17th century and resembles a scene described in *Nobunaga Kōki* (*Nobunaga's Public Records*). In 1569, Nobunaga built a residence for the *shōgun* Ashikaga Yoshiaki, about which the *Kōki* relates there was a cherry tree planted in the horse-riding court, much as shown in this painting.[81] The scene in the painting is of a military lord enjoying the view of horses being trained. He sits inside the room, in a white upper garment, with retainers to his left and right. Behind him is the *shoin*, writing alcove, which identifies this room as being the formal, usually south-facing sitting room. In the adjoining room to the right is a man in a black, scarf-like hat, *zukin*, whisking a bowl of tea. He is the *sadō*. In front of him is the black lacquer tea shelf, *daisu*, of which only the bottom shelf can be seen. On the left side of the shelf is the black charcoal brazier, *furo*,[82] on top of which sits the brown iron kettle, *kama*, used for heating water. On the right side of the shelf is the fresh-water container, *mizusashi*, and in the middle is a vase-like vessel (most likely bronze) that would hold the water ladle, *hishaku*, and the iron chopsticks for arranging the charcoal, *hibashi*. In front of that is a waste-water bowl, *kensui*,

with a wiping cloth in it, *chakin*. In front of the *daisu*, set directly on the *tatami*, is a small black container for powdered tea, *cha-ire*, on top of which sits a slim bamboo tea scoop, *cha-shaku*. The whitish bowl that the *sadō* is using is not a formal Chinese-style *tenmoku* bowl but rather an irregular *wamono* bowl in the *wabi* taste, perhaps a Shino bowl. The black bowl in the hands of the servant carrying tea into the main room is most likely a Raku bowl, also in the *wabi* taste. Other than these two bowls, the scene is a classic example of *shoin-cha* or *hare-no-cha*, including the *shoin*-style of architecture, the use of the *daisu* and all of its formal, Chinese-style utensils, and the fact that a servant/tea master is making the tea in a side room separated from those who will have the tea. In rustic *chanoyu*, the host would make the tea himself, usually without a *daisu*, using irregular utensils, sitting together with his guests in a small rustic room.

As important to the development of *chanoyu* as the artisans and artists themselves was the artistic mentality that developed during the medieval period among a broad segment of the populace. In the previous Heian period, the division between those within the aristocratic circle and those outside of it was extremely clear. For all intents and purposes, aristocratic culture—such as *waka* poetry and *shinden*-style palace architecture and gardens—simply did not exist beyond the closed society of the aristocrats themselves. As the military, merchant, and artisan classes developed during the Kamakura period, so did the venues where art was practiced. *Chanoyu* was able to develop among the merchants of Sakai and Kyōto because there were people among those groups who perceived themselves as artists, who saw the world in symbolic and aesthetic terms, and who interacted with other artists and appropriated from them aspects of their art.

4

early development of the *roji*

露地

Before we go on, it would be good to take a quick look again at the various threads that came together to allow for the development of the tea garden in the 15th and 16th centuries. First, you will remember, the custom of tea drinking was introduced to Japan during the Nara period. Subsequently, powdered tea, *matcha,* was introduced during the Kamakura period by Zen priests who, by the end of that period, were including the ritualized drinking of tea, *sarei*, as part of the formal rules of their temple life. During the following Muromachi period, that ritualized manner of drinking tea was incorporated into the culture of the military aristocrats who held tea gatherings known as *cha-yoriai*. The tea service of that time is referred to in three different ways: *daisu-cha*, after the formal tea shelf that was used in tea service; *shoin-cha*, after the style of architecture in which the tea gatherings were held; and *hare-no-cha*, in reference to the gay, boisterous, and lavish quality of the tea service that included tea competitions, *tōcha*, and sometimes even bathing, *rinkan-cha*.

By the mid-15th century, the custom among urban merchants of building small residences, *an*, for retired heads of households, *inkyo*, in the back of their properties had become commonplace. Influenced by the cultural background of literate and artistic hermits who escaped the social and political trappings of urban life by living secluded amid natural or rural surroundings, the retirement residences of urban merchants took on the qualities of a mountain hermitage and were called *sōan*, literally, "thatch-roofed huts."

Within those *sōan*, a new form of tea service was developed based on the philosophy and aesthetics of rusticity, *wabi*, and of refined taste, *suki*. That tea service was known as *chanoyu*, and its rustic form came to be known as *wabi-cha* or *sōan-cha*. Eventually, as part of this new culture, simple entry paths were developed, called *roji*, and with that began the actual creation of tea gardens.

Early Development of the Tea Garden

The evolution of *chanoyu* from the *sarei* of Zen temples and the entertainment of *hare-no-cha* into rustic *chanoyu* happened primarily over the course of the 15th and 16th centuries at the hands of a number of tea masters who gradually re-created the purpose of tea gatherings.

There are many tea masters associated with the development of tea culture through that century and a half, but three stand out as highpoints in the development of *chanoyu*: Murata Shukō (1421–1502), Takeno Jōō (1502–55), and Sen Rikyū (1522–91). They themselves wrote little, if anything, about tea, although there are some documents from the time they lived that record their sayings or activities, and much, much more that has been written about them after their deaths. By the early Edo period (1600–1858), the practice of *chanoyu* they initiated came to be institutionalized, primarily through the auspices of the grand master system.

The grand master is typically the elder male in a family who holds the knowledge specific to a particular "school," be it a school of flower arranging, *chanoyu*, *nō* theater, or any other traditional art. He passes that knowledge on to his sons and apprentices with the understanding that the eldest son will likely take over as grand master when his father goes into retirement.[83] Through this system of exacting repetition of traditional forms, the practice and dogma of *chanoyu* was passed on to future generations of tea practitioners more or less in its original form. As the grand master system developed, identifying the history of tea practice and the lineage of tea masters became ever more important to schools of tea that were establishing their authority, much the way that Buddhist teachings are identified as having passed through a lineage of priests. The private agenda of later-era tea masters who were attempting to elevate their status brings into question the authenticity of the histories and lineages they created.

The isolation of only three historical figures—Shukō, Jōō, and Rikyū—is limiting by the very nature of its exclusionary process. We know of many other people who participated in early *chanoyu*, and surely there were others still who contributed to the development of *chanoyu*—some intentionally, others perhaps through unintentional, incidental acts—but never made it into the mainstream of historical records.

One such figure who comes to mind is a fellow named Hechikan. He hasn't been entirely lost to history; his name shows up briefly in a few historical texts, and most of those, admittedly, date from around the year 1700 although he was a contemporary of Rikyū. What is written about him in those texts was definitely hearsay and perhaps fantasy, but it brings to mind the kind of person referred to here.

In *Chōandōki*, which was written around 1640, there is a record of a Great Tea Party that the hegemon Toyotomi Hideyoshi threw at Kitano Shrine in northern Kyōto in the autumn of 1597. It records that Hechikan sat last among the Kyōto tea masters, in the middle of a pine grove, beneath a huge red garden umbrella—9 feet across, held high on a 7-foot pole—surrounded by a fence made of tall water reeds. The glow of the umbrella in the bright sun caused a stir among the visitors to the shrine. Even Hideyoshi was impressed by the sight, so much so that he absolved Hechikan of the need to perform any duties.[84]

We can only imagine the scene, but it must have been fantastic, that brilliant red disk seeming to hover amid the deep green pines. We see in Hechikan a man of incredible style and panache, the kind who is likely to influence the aesthetic and design sense of those around him.

We'll never know what kind of tea garden Hechikan had for himself, or if he had one at all, but it is easy enough to imagine that he may have done some striking things with the space around his own tea house, something radical enough to have influenced other tea masters about whom historians have been more generous when recording events.

Nevertheless, although giving all credit to Shukō, Jōō, and Rikyū for developing *chanoyu* is oversimplifying things, it is helpful to see these men as being representative of three important stages in the development of *chanoyu* and the very first beginnings of the tea garden or, as it was called then, the *roji*: first, the early movement toward the practice of rustic tea at the time of Shukō (late 15th century); second, the incipient language and forms of *chanoyu* and the *roji* that developed around the time of Jōō (early to mid-16th century); and, third, the full development of both *chanoyu* and the *roji* at the time of Rikyū (late 16th century).

Put another way, Shukō could be said to represent the culture of the urban townsfolk, *machishū*, especially of Kyōto, and their movement away from Chinese-style *karamono-suki* culture to one that incorporated native Japanese things; Jōō can be said to represent the confluence of various cosmopolitan cultures in urban centers such as Sakai and Kyōto; and Rikyū represents the initial integration of *chanoyu* back into mainstream military-class culture, within which it would be developed into the form we know today over the course of the 17th, 18th, and 19th centuries.

Shukō: The Tea of Urban Merchants in the Late 15th Century

Kyōto in the mid- to late 15th century was a place of extreme contrasts. On the one hand, it was a place of devastation. Various military lords who were vying for power through the control of the imperial household were pitched against each other and, even though Kyōto was the imperial capital, it was not spared their ravages. This culminated in the Ōnin War, which lasted from 1467 to 1477 and left Kyōto in ruins. The century following that war is known as the Period of Warring States, *sengoku jidai*, a time when the provinces, and at times the cities, were embroiled in recurrent turmoil as provincial lords sought to secure their hold on their lands, and perhaps their neighbors' as well. Peasant farmers, most often the inadvertent victims of those power struggles, at times also revolted against their overlords in insurrections known as *ikki* or *tsuchi ikki*.

On the other hand, as violent as it was, the same period can also be seen as a tremendously creative time from the perspective of the arts. In part this was because of the aforementioned tally trade through which goods from Ming-dynasty China were imported to Japan. Those foreign goods—and to some degree the social customs, philosophies, and aesthetics associated with them—formed one of the foundations of medieval Japanese urban culture. Another aspect of the era that added to its creative nature was, oddly enough, the social unrest itself because it allowed for a degree of social mobility and a mixing of separated social classes that had theretofore been impossible. As old standards of social structure broke down, cultural traditions shifted to accommodate the new arrangements.

It was also a time of tremendous economic activity. New products were required as the structure of ur-

ban and provincial society changed, resulting in a new distribution of wealth. In particular, the military class and the merchant class, each with its own particular requirements, fueled economic growth. New techniques for making products developed as well—everything from new forms of armor to excellent paper and brushes for drawing ink paintings. It was the merchant class that flourished the most as a result of the new vitality in production and trade. Although merchants were nonexistent as a social class through the aristocratic periods (i.e., until the end of the 12th century), the social changes and mercantile system that developed during the Kamakura and Muromachi periods allowed them to develop into a distinct social class with their own basis of wealth and culture. Significantly, it was the merchants, especially merchants in large urban centers such as Kyōto and Sakai, who created the new manner of serving tea called *chanoyu* (fig. 23).

One of the foundations for the development of *chanoyu* was the creation of a new setting for tea—a small, rustic building, secluded from the flow of everyday life, called an *an* or *sōan*. By the late 15th century, the construction of small "retirement" halls in the back reaches of urban properties had become widespread. The diaries of certain Zen priests also capture glimpses of rustic retreats in the city. According to *Hekizan Nichiroku*, a diary of events kept by the Zen priest Taikyoku, in the third month of 1462 he visited the residence of a wealthy merchant, Fushō Eian, whose name is connected with the construction of the Shijō Ōhashi bridge in Kyōto. Taikyoku writes, "The gate was very narrow, so much so, that one had to turn sideways to enter. Toward the back, there was an arbor, made of splendid materials and wonderful lumber. All four walls were graced by paintings of landscapes."[85]

The narrowness of the entryway and the fact that

23. TOWNSFOLK IN THE CAPITAL. The new vitality of the capital, Miyako (now called Kyōto), was most clearly represented by the Gion festival with its elaborate floats. Initiated in the 9th century, the festival died out during the Ōnin War (1467–77) and was revitalized by the townsfolk, *machishū* (both merchants and artisans), who lived in the city center. Many of the tapestries that decorate the sides of the floats were obtained through trade with foreign merchants, a tangible sign of the cosmopolitan air of the period. *Rakuchū Rakugaizu* (Uesugi-bon), Kanō Eitoku (1543–90), 16th century (depicts Kyōto between 1532 and 1555), lower half of the third panel of the left-hand set of screens. Uesugi Museum, Yonezawa City.

the arbor was situated in the far back portion of the property give the impression that there was an attempt on the part of Eian to create the feeling of a slender path leading to a secluded retreat. And yet, seeing that all four walls were covered with landscape paintings, and that it was made of excellent, noteworthy materials, the building was not in the rustic style of later tea houses that would have been constructed of simple materials and had walls of uncovered clay plaster.

An entry in *Inryōken Nichiroku*—a diary kept by Kikei Shinzui, the resident priest of Inryōken, a subtemple of Shōkokuji—mentions an official visit by *shōgun* Ashikaga Yoshimasa to his *sōan*. It was the ninth day of the third month in 1464. Here again, we find an image of a pavilion surrounded by plants, creating the illusion of the wilds of the mountains within the city.

> Ninth day. An official visit. We climbed up into Musōtei. All was luxuriant with red and white blossoms and the arbor was full with their fragrant scent. What a lovely spot. [The Shōgun said], "In general, when arbors are built within the city, I'm afraid they often lie exposed, but this arbor is surrounded on all four sides with deep, thick groves of bamboo. Thanks to that, it is like being in the mountains." For this [comment], I was truly delighted.[86]

Murata Shukō was one of the urban merchants who were building retreats for themselves and it was he who is attributed with shifting tea gatherings out of the formal rooms at the front of urban properties— the *shoin* and the *kaisho*—and establishing them in the simpler setting of the retreats at the back of the property.[87] Historical records honor him as the greatest tea master of his time; many tea masters in the years following his death credited him with being their teacher, and many texts from later years placed him as the lead figure in the lineage of *chanoyu* tea masters.

That notwithstanding, naturally this shift from *shoin-cha* to *sōan-cha* was not the result of one man's work. There are, for instance, records from the same time of gatherings called *kamado-no-cha*, or "kitchen tea," during which people would gather for tea around the cook-stoves, *kamado*, in the kitchen, an informal setting if ever there was one. *Kamado-no-cha* may well have been one of the cultural predecessors to *chanoyu*, and the many, nameless people who took part in those casual tea gatherings are lost to history. Nevertheless, even though Shukō did not single-handedly initiate that activity of holding tea gatherings in a simple setting, he can be said to represent the general movements of his time.

At the tender age of 11, Shukō entered Shōmyōji, a temple of the Pure Land sect in Nara where he was born. He was sent away from that temple, apparently for unsuitable behavior (including participating in tea contests), and made his way in the world among the merchants of Shimogyō in Kyōto. Shimogyō, the "Lower Capital," was a district where many merchants lived, but few, if any, military lords or aristocrats; and it was in this bustling, "lower class" district that the first inklings of rustic tea can be traced. One of the early terms used in reference to the practice of a new style of rustic tea was *Shimogyō Chanoyu* or the Tea-style of the Lower Capital. The same expression was used to refer to the clique of people who were practicing rustic tea, so another translation could be The Lower Capital Coterie. Specifically it referred to tea gatherings held according to the aesthetics of what would be later termed *wabi* or *wabi-suki*, with an air of affable camaraderie, in simple, somewhat secluded retreats at the back of urban properties, incorporating Japanese articles as part of their aesthetic.

Two aspects of Shukō's legendary life, often repeated, are first, that he studied Zen with Ikkyū, a famously eccentric priest of Daitokuji, and thus came to incorporate aspects of Zen Buddhism into *chanoyu*, and second, that he studied the *shoin*-style of tea (*daisu-cha*) with Nōami (1397–1471),[88] one of the most famous *dōbōshū* who served the *shōgun* Ashikaga Yoshimasa at his Higashiyama Villa. Points can be made to both corroborate and dismiss the specifics of these histories—the former being possible the latter highly unlikely. Whether or not they are true, they neatly symbolize two broader aspects of the development of *chanoyu* at the time Shukō lived and that he can be said to represent. The first is the interest among the merchants of the Shimogyō district of Kyōto in Zen Buddhism and their commingling with Zen priests for both social and religious reasons. Many of the townsfolk, *machishū*, were adherents of the Nichiren sect, but it was the Zen sect, with its cultural connection to China and social/political connection to the ruling military class, that had the most impact on the development of *chanoyu* among the merchants. The second aspect that Shukō represents is the shift that took place at the time he was alive, away from a technologically formal service of tea, epitomized by the *shoin* style of tea practiced in the residences of military lords, toward a more subdued service of tea that incorporated the use of locally made tea utensils (*wamono*) and that was carried out in a rustic tea house (*sōan*).

In developing his own Way of Tea, Shukō seems to have been guided by the characteristics of linked-verse poetry, *renga*. To create a linked-verse poem, a small number of people gathered in a small room and created a long poem according to a strict set of rules. Each participant composed one stanza in turn, "linking" it to the one that came before. Thus, by its very nature, *renga* was a quiet gathering, attended by a small number of people, focused on the subtle aesthetic of words. It was a seated, communal gathering called a *za*, a term meaning "to be seated on the floor." *Chanoyu*, as well, in the shift from *shoin-cha* to *sōan-cha*, became a gathering that involved limited numbers of people and fostered the communal nature of the gathering. Another aspect of *renga* that Shukō is said to have incorporated into *chanoyu* was its aesthetics: chill (*hie*), withered (*kare*), and gaunt (*yase*). For the same reasons that *renga* poets searched for words that would evoke the character of chill, withered, and gaunt in their poetry, Shukō rethought the utensils and physical setting of *chanoyu* to encourage these aesthetics.

A glimpse into the way Shukō thought was captured in the diary of Touemon-no-jō, who recorded the sayings of *nō* master Konparu Zenpō in a diary called *Zenpō Zōtan*. In 1512 after visiting the home of Bandoya, a wealthy merchant in Nara, Touemon-no-jō jotted down something that was said about Shukō at the gathering he attended. "This is what Shukō said. Even the moon is lacking, unless seen between clouds."[89] In other words, the brilliance of the moon fully revealed, like the brilliance of the overt technological perfection found in the practice of *shoin-cha*, is not as appealing or satisfying as the same brilliance when it is partially deflected. It is a small entry in a long diary but has been seized on by students of *chanoyu* history because it reveals aesthetic feelings that are synchronous with what would later be termed *wabi* being expressed by a person who is known to have been instrumental in shaping the development of *chanoyu*.

Shukō captured this core concept of rustic tea in a

letter he wrote to one of his tea disciples, the provincial lord Furuichi Chōnin. The letter, which is very short, is commonly called *Kokoro no Fumi* (*The Letter of the Heart*). In it Shukō admonishes against self-satisfaction and self-attachment, describes briefly his thoughts on what the aesthetic of "withered" is, and makes the following point very clear:

> Critical above all else in this way is the dissolution of the boundary line between native [things] and Chinese [things]. This is vital, truly vital; give it careful attention.[90]

The letter was not dated, but it may have been written about 1488, which places it shortly after the Ōnin War.[91] The relationship between Japan and China was changing in the broadest of terms. The system of tally trade ships, for instance, which had been going to Ming-dynasty China since 1403, was nearing its end. By 1488, sixty-seven of the total eighty-five ships that would travel to China under the tally system had already made their voyage.[92] Shukō's desire to change the focus of tea utensils from Chinese wares to local Japanese wares was representative of larger shifts in the society of his day. It was, on the one hand, a pragmatic reaction to the fact that trade with China was obviously winding down, with imported goods becoming fixed in number and thus difficult to obtain. On the other hand, it was also reflective of the general sentiment of the society that, having focused so strongly on foreign Chinese models, and having digested them, it was time to turn inward and reinvent the imported culture to fit Japanese needs and sentiments.

Shukō's own tea house, like the retirement cottages built behind merchant houses and the urban hermitages of the Zen priests, was a small structure, just four and a half mats in size. Several texts give us glimpses of what Shukō's taste in tea houses was like, the earliest of which is *Yamanoue Sōjiki*, the records of tea master Yamanoue Sōji (1544–90).

Sōji was from the Yamanoue district of Sakai (thus his appellation), and he became one of the closest tea apprentices of Sen Rikyū. He went on to be the tea master, *sadō*, as had Rikyū, first for Oda Nobunaga and then, after Nobunaga's death, for Toyotomi Hideyoshi. He is recorded as having been disheveled or ugly in his personal appearance, and also as having had a very quick tongue. Perhaps for those reasons, he was suspended from the official patronage of the ruler and later, apparently having enraged Hideyoshi, had his ears and nose cut off before being executed. His record of the tea culture of his time, primarily the tea style of Sen Rikyū, was written when he was 45, in 1589, just a year before his death.

Sōji records Shukō's tea house as being north-facing, which means the guests' entry was on the north side (fig. 24). Contrary to this, most tea houses of later eras would primarily be south-facing. Sōji also records the tea house as having been "right-handed," *migi-katte*, which meant that the preparation room (*katte* or *mizuya*) was to the right of where the host sat (*temae-za*), rather than to the left as would become somewhat standard for later tea houses. Sōji continues, describing a tiny walled entry garden, called a *tsubo-no-uchi*, that had one large willow growing within it and a view of a broad pine grove behind it, so that those in the tea house could hear "nothing but the wind in the pines."[93]

Nanbōroku, a later text, states that the four-and-a-half-mat tea room was Shukō's creation. It describes his tea room as being a *shin-no-zashiki*, or a formal sitting room, with its walls covered with white *torinoko* paper, a type of Japanese paper common for interior use, nowadays used primarily not as wall paper but for opaque paper doors called *fusuma*.[94] There was a 1-*ken* (1.818-meter) display alcove, *tokonoma*; the ceiling of the room was made of thin cedar boards and the roof of thin shingles, most likely of *hinoki* cypress, a construction technique now called *kokera-buki*. The roof was a curved hip roof, sloping on all four sides up to a single point, an architectural feature called *hōgyō-zukuri* that was commonly used for small halls in Buddhist temples.[95] The impression given by these descriptions is of a building that has a fairly formal design, harking of *shoin*-style architecture with its clean, white-papered walls, and having a hint of Buddhist architecture in its roof line.

A plan of Shukō's tea house, found in *Chanoyu Shidaisho*,[96] shows the tea house as having, in addition to a single four-and-a-half-mat room and the 1-*ken* *tokonoma*, a veranda made of wooden boards, alongside of which was a slightly lower, slimmer veranda made of half-split bamboo, and beyond that the *tsubo-no-uchi* with the big willow tree. Guests arriving for a tea gathering at this tea house would enter from a side door, step up onto the veranda, and enter the tea room through the paper doors that lined the veranda.[97]

Shukō's tea house, as mentioned above, had a view of a grove of pines, but the area close to the building, the *tsubo-no-uchi*, contained only one large willow. At only four and a half mats, the tea house itself was certainly small, but the *tsubo-no-uchi* was even smaller, perhaps only the size of two *tatami* mats, or about 4 square meters.[98] Enclosed by a low wall, the *tsubo-no-uchi* was a direct extension of the architecture and yet it was unroofed: a mini-courtyard garden attached to the tea house. The purpose of the *tsubo-no-uchi* was to shut the tea house off from the outside world while at

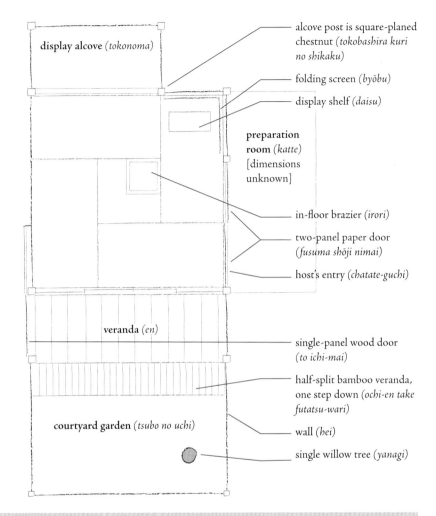

display alcove (*tokonoma*)

alcove post is square-planed chestnut (*tokobashira kuri no shikaku*)

folding screen (*byōbu*)

display shelf (*daisu*)

preparation room (*katte*) [dimensions unknown]

in-floor brazier (*irori*)

two-panel paper door (*fusuma shōji nimai*)

host's entry (*chatate-guchi*)

veranda (*en*)

single-panel wood door (*to ichi-mai*)

half-split bamboo veranda, one step down (*ochi-en take futatsu-wari*)

courtyard garden (*tsubo no uchi*)

wall (*hei*)

single willow tree (*yanagi*)

24. PLAN OF SHUKŌ'S TEA HOUSE. This speculative plan of the tea house belonging to tea master Murata Shukō (1423–1502) was derived from passages in historic tea records. The tea house was very formal by present-day standards, with white-papered walls and a temple-like curved roof. There was no entry garden, but a very small, walled space, known as a *tsubo-no-uchi*, which contained nothing but a single willow tree, was attached to the tea room. The *tsubo-no-uchi* would eventually be expanded into what we now know as a tea garden. Redrawn from a plan in *Chadō Shūkin*, vol. 7, p. 61.

the same time allowing a small "breathing space" for the tea room that offered a glimpse of what lay beyond.

Regarding the garden that might have accompanied the tea houses of Shukō's time, available written records and drawings do not indicate that any well-developed gardens existed at all. There are, however,

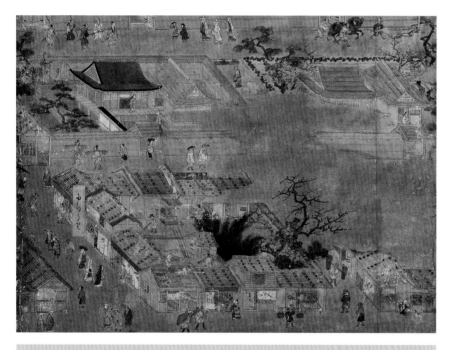

25. MEDIEVAL URBAN RETREATS. The townhouses of urban dwellers formed blocks, *chō*, that enclosed communal open spaces. This example shows, in that space, some tall trees to the right, a grove of bamboo in the middle, and, next to the bamboo, a small building. This structure could be the kind of retreat that was built for the elder man of a family upon his retirement known as an *an* or *iori*. In the 16th century, rustic tea gatherings were first held in *an* like this, although the ideal example would have had a thatched roof. *Rakuchū Rakugaizu* (Rekihaku Kōhon, formerly Machida-bon), 16th century (depicts Kyōto between 1525 and 1536), lower part of the second panel of the right-hand set of screens. National Museum of Japanese History, Tōkyō.

references in contemporary texts to groves of trees or bamboo surrounding the tea houses that may have been planted to create a feeling of seclusion, such as the bamboo grove previously mentioned in the excerpt from the diary *Inryōken Nichiroku*. There are as well some images in paintings from that period that show clusters of trees or bamboo in the rear of urban residences. One such example can be found in *Rakuchū Rakugaizu* (*Sights In and Around the Capital*), a painting from the early 16th century (fig. 25). In one section of the painting, which depicts widesweeping aerial views of Kyōto, we find a rectangular block of simple merchant houses, each facing outward toward the street. The interior of the block has, for the most part, been left undeveloped. In one spot, however, one of the residents has built a small building—a little hut that is certainly crudely built by the standards of present-day tea houses but may well represent a retirement *an*, a small tea house, or some other, similar, secluded building. The building is flanked by a small grove of bamboo and, closer to the nearby houses, by some tall trees.[99]

One of Shukō's followers in this manner of tea service was the merchant Murata Sōshu. Sōshu is the tea master mentioned earlier who had a house called Goshoan, the Arbor of the Noon-day Pine, in the Shimogyō district of Kyōto. Two diaries of Sōshu's contemporaries offer glimpses of Sōshu and his arbor. The first is *Nisuiki*, the diary of aristocrat Washino'o Takayasu. This was mentioned before but, to reiterate, after attending a tea gathering held on an island in the pond of Awataguchi-Shōren'in temple, Takayasu noted that tea was "served by tea master Sōshu, a lower-class lay monk of Shimogyō, greatly skilled at the refinements of *chanoyu*." When he visited Sōshu's tea house some six years later, he noted the following:

On our way home, we stopped by to see [Murata] Sōshu's tea house. It had the appearance of a mountain cottage. It should truly be called an hermitage in the city—a moving thing to see. Sōshu is the leader of contemporary *chanoyu*.[100]

The other journal that captured an image of Goshoan is *Sōchō Nikki*, the diary of the *renga* poet Sōchō (1448–1532). Sōchō traveled a great deal between his home in Suruga (present-day Shizuoka Prefecture) and Kyōto, making notes in his diary of the inns he stayed at and the houses of friends and compatriots he visited. Although Sōchō was not of high birth, he was a renowned poet, a position that gave him an elevated social standing. While in Kyōto, for instance, he would stay as a guest at Shinjuan, a subtemple of the Zen monastery Daitokuji, something not possible for just any wandering minstrel. His fame also gave him access to people of various social classes, such as Zen priests (Ikkyū, for instance, his mentor in Buddhist study), members of the aristocratic class (including Sanjōnishi Sanetaka and Toyohara Muneaki, mentioned above), and merchants of the lower capital. According to Sōchō's diary he visited Sōshu's house on the 15th day of the 8th month of 1526. He writes:

> Tea in the Lower Capital—
> The so-called Lower Capital Tea Coterie practices a style of tea called *suki*, which they hold in four-and-a-half- or six-mat rooms. We stopped by Sōshu's place. There was a large pine tree and some cedars by the gate. Inside the fence, everything was clean and fresh. I noticed four or five fallen ivy leaves, deeply colored, and composed this:

> This morning
> I picked up last night's storm—
> the first colored leaves[101]

A description of what it felt like to walk down the path to a tea house like the one at Sōshu's was captured in a poem about *chanoyu* called *Chōka Chanoyu Monogatari* (*The Chanoyu Epic*), attributed to the *dōbōshū* Sōami (?–1525). This poem tends toward the comic, and is certainly didactic, intending to instruct by presenting an image of what not to do. In any case, it is one of the earliest records of a *roji* in connection with *chanoyu*.

> The large swinging gate
> Is pushed open [by a visitor]
> Please enter, someone calls
> Whereupon
> Down the narrow *roji* path
> He walks briskly
> The sounds of his footsteps loud
> As if stomping
> Passing through the private gate
> And up onto the narrow veranda
> The sight of them entering [the tea house]
> So incompetent and rude
> All the different sandals [that are neatly placed
>   there]
> Getting all kicked about
> [His own sandals] landing here and there
> As he takes them off
> [Holding up] the long hilt and scabbard
> Of his big sword
> At a loss for where to put them
> Not a pleasant sight[102]

The poem offers us a number of revelations, including things that were found in the *roji*, such as swinging gates; the fact that the *roji* was narrow; and that the custom of wearing soft sandals and removing one's sword before entering the tea room had already been established.

To summarize, from the time of Murata Shukō through that of Murata Sōshu and others who engaged in tea in the manner of *Shimogyō Chanoyu*, a number of essential qualities of the practice and setting of *chanoyu* had been established that would eventually lead to the full development of the tea garden. These include the following:

- A blending of Japanese and Chinese aesthetics, including an incorporation of Japanese tea wares with those from China in an integrated fashion.

- Having the host prepare the tea in the room with the guest to enhance the sense of service and camaraderie rather than having a tea master, *sadō*, make the tea in an adjoining room.

- The transfer of the tea gathering away from the formal "front" rooms, *shoin* and *kaisho*, to the simpler retreats, *an* or *sōan*, at the back of urban properties.

- The small size of the rooms used for tea gatherings, at times only four and a half mats in size.

- Setting the tea house in a grove of trees or, through some other means, evoking the feeling of a mountain retreat within the city: *sankyo no tei, shichū no sankyo*, or *shichūin*.

- A gate and/or fences to separate the path to the tea house from the "outer" areas and to augment the sense of "passage" from one place to another.

- A long, narrow path leading back to the *an* referred to as a *roji* though not yet written with the *kanji* that imply the meaning of a "Buddhist path."

- And, of great importance to the development of the tea garden, the *tsubo-no-uchi* that separated the tea room from its surrounding environment, making it "a place apart."

At the time of Murata Shukō, in other words at the end of the 15th century, there was no tea garden. The culture of *chanoyu* being held in a simple tea house had begun, but the only exterior space that had been developed specific to *chanoyu* was this *tsubo-no-uchi*. A very small space holding only the barest of elements that might be considered garden-like (a single tree, a bowl of water), the *tsubo-no-uchi* was the seed that would blossom as a tea garden in the following century.

Jōō: Wabi *and Tea in the Early 16th Century*

Takeno Jōō (1502–55) was born in the very year Shukō died. He grew up in Sakai, a city south of Ōsaka, the son of a merchant. Sakai was a port city and one of the centers of trade between Japan and China. Not only did the foreign trade make Sakai prosperous in general, it also gave the merchants there particularly good access to Chinese tea wares, and the city soon became a center of *chanoyu* practice. Jōō's family traded in leather, perhaps leather for armament, an interesting point because of what it reveals about the social fluidity of the time. Leather workers—butchers, hide strippers, and tanners—were considered among the most "polluted" people in society, and yet here we find that the son of a leather merchant was able to avoid any stigma and associate with people from all levels of society.

Jōō was sent to Kyōto to study when he was 24 and settled somewhere around the intersection of Shijō and Muromachi streets in the merchant quarters. He tried to have his family reinstated to the military status his grandfather had held before dying in the Ōnin War, and was successful in receiving the fifth rank himself. He took the tonsure at age 31, which is when the name Jōō was given to him, and returned at age 36 to Sakai, where he became central in the city's cultural activities (fig. 26). While he was in Kyōto, he socialized with *renga* poets at the salons of Sanjōnishi Sanetaka and with *sōan-cha* tea masters, including Sōshu. Indicative of the social mobility of the times, Jōō crossed all class borders: merchant, military, priest, aristocrat, artist. He is also representative of his times in his movements back and forth between Kyōto and Sakai, reflecting the importance that Sakai played in late-16th-century culture in general, and in the development of *chanoyu* in particular. In short, Jōō epitomizes the merging of classes and cultural flow between urban centers that proved to be fundamental to the coalescing of rustic-style *chanoyu* and to the subsequent creation of the tea garden.

The years from when he took the tonsure until he returned to Sakai were ones of great unrest in Kyōto. It was the time of the Lotus Uprising (Hokke Ikki, 1532–36), during which members of the Hokke sect of Buddhism (Nichiren Buddhism) quarreled with other

26. TEA MASTER JŌŌ'S NEIGHBORHOOD. The tea master Takeno Jōō (1502–55) moved to Kyōto from Sakai when he was 24 and settled near the intersection of Shijō and Muromachi streets, the area depicted in this painting. The communal courtyards enclosed by blocks of *machiya* are shown to be clean, sparsely planted, and containing one simple building each. It is tempting to think these were the urban retreats, *an*, where tea gatherings first took place, but they may have just been communal toilets. In any case, the sparseness of the design is, in part, due to the interpretive eye of the painter. *Rakuchū Rakugaizu* (Rekihaku Kōhon, formerly Machida-bon), 16th century (depicts Kyōto between 1525 and 1536), bottom of the first panel of the left-hand set of screens. National Museum of Japanese History, Tōkyō.

religious groups as well as with the military government. The conflict raged through Kyōto, intensifying until 1536, when twenty-one Hokke temples were burned to the ground and many followers of the religion killed. If Jōō's return to Sakai was not purposefully planned to escape from the turmoil, at least it was done within the context of that social upheaval. Jōō's transfer to Sakai reflects the larger social movements of his time, for he was not the only one to do so. Sakai was a great economic and cultural center, and a relatively safe and protected place. As Rodrigues mentioned, many well-to-do people relocated there and took part in tea gatherings.

> Up to the time of Nobunaga and Taikō, it [Sakai] used to be governed like a republic and for many years did not recognize any outside authority. For it was a very strong place and was like the court of Japan, containing wealthy and well-to-do citizens and noble people who retired there from various places on the account of the vicissitudes of war.[103]

Jōō's family were adherents of the Honganji sect of Pure Land Buddhism, not a Zen sect. Among his high-level associates in Kyōto and Sakai, however, were many Zen Buddhist adherents. Jōō's tea not only furthered the interest in the fusion of Japanese and Chinese things of Shukō's time, but perhaps it also acted as a bridge between Pure Land and Zen thought. Furthermore, in the short letter ascribed to Jōō, called *Jōō Wabi no Fumi* (*Jōō's Letter on Wabi*), we find the following about tea and Shintō—the native religion of Japan.

> The source of the spirit of *wabi* in the land is the

goddess Amaterasu. The great master of Japan, if she desired to construct a shrine hall by inlaying, gold, silver and precious gems, what person could say it should not be so? But, with thatched roof, offerings of unhulled rice, and in everything else down to the least detail profoundly modest and never negligent, the Deity is the finest of tea practitioners.[104]

So perhaps another aspect of Jōō's influence on the development of *chanoyu*, and a way in which he is also reflective of his times, is this fusion of various religious ideals: Pure Land Buddhism, Zen Buddhism, and the native Shintō religion.

Jōō is noted in the history of *chanoyu* for his application of the aesthetic of *wabi* to tea. Although *chanoyu* shifted away from formal tea service at the time of Shukō, it would be proper to say that rustic tea, *wabi-cha*, stems from Jōō's time, primarily the 1530s to the 1550s, also known as the Tenmon era.[105] A number of tea records appear at this time, including records of tea gatherings, *chakaiki*, such as those kept by the Matsuya family of Nara (*Matsuya Kaiki*), the Tsuda family of Sakai (*Tennōjiya Kaiki*), and the Imai family, also of Sakai (*Imai Sōkyū Chanoyu Kakinuki*).[106] These *chakaiki* record in detail the dates and places that tea gatherings were held, who was in attendance, some specific notes about the architecture (i.e., the size of the room, the specific design of the display alcove, etc.), what kind of food was served, and many details about the tea utensils used during the gathering. As such, they are invaluable records for measuring the changes made in the nature of the tea service. Unfortunately, they only rarely make mention of any exterior spaces.

Jōō's tea house was recorded in *Yamanoue Sōjiki* as having been "north-facing, with a *tsubo-no-uchi*, beyond which could be seen a grove of pine trees both large and small" (fig. 27).[107] A plan-view drawing in the same record shows that it was a four-and-a-half-mat room attached to two other four-and-a-half-mat rooms (one of which was a *shoin*) and to a large split-bamboo deck. A narrow veranda separated the tea room from the other two rooms and acted as the means of entry for the host.[108] Also attached to the tea room were two other enclosed spaces: an *omote tsubo-no-uchi* and a *waki tsubo-no-uchi*. Both of the spaces, as with the *tsubo-no-uchi* at Shukō's tea house, were very small. The *omote tsubo-no-uchi* (*omote* means "front") was an attached mini garden while the *waki tsubo-no-uchi* (*waki* means "side") served as an entry space for the tea room.

Although the Sōjiki does not state this precisely, judging from records in other historical texts of similar "backyard parlors," such as the house of Tokuzō, the wine dealer mentioned earlier in the section on *machiya*, the tea house probably lay at the rear of the property and was approached down a narrow path from the street, perhaps something like the *sukiya tōrimichi*, also mentioned in the section on *machiya*, that led to the back of Dōtetsu's property.

At the end of the path, a guest entering would have encountered the tea house and a small entrance door into the *waki tsubo-no-uchi*. A tiny walled room, the *waki tsubo-no-uchi* was attached to the tea room yet was still earthen floored. The plan of Jōō's tea house found in *Yamanoue Sōjiki* is not drawn to scale but, based on other known proportions of a tea house, it shows the *waki tsubo-no-uchi* as being approximately 1.5 meters wide and perhaps 3.5 meters long.[109] In any case, even if the drawing was not accurate, the draftsman intended to show that the space was narrow and long. From there, a guest would step up onto a narrow

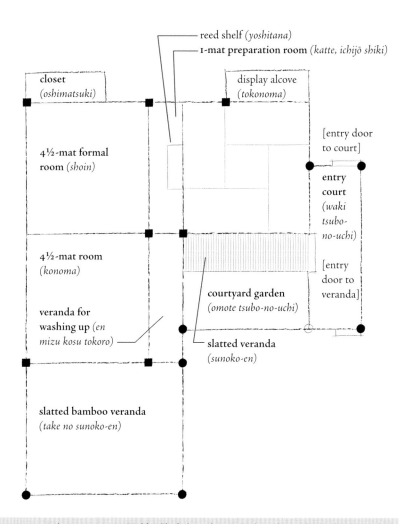

27. PLAN OF JŌŌ'S TEA HOUSE. Unlike Shukō's tea house, Jōō's tea house has a clearly marked side entrance for the use of guests. The small, enclosed space, called a *waki tsubo-no-uchi*, acted as a buffer between the "outside" world and the world inside the tea room. Guests did not, however, enter directly into the tea room through a small crawl-though door, as in later tea houses. Rather, they stepped up onto the veranda and went into the tea room from there. Redrawn from *Chadō Koten Zenshū*, vol. 6, p. 99.

veranda under the eaves of what was most likely a thatched roof[110] and, from the veranda, would have entered through sliding doors into the tea room. During a break midway through the tea gathering, now known as the *naka-dachi*, the guests would withdraw to the veranda again to enjoy the sunlight and the framed glimpse of pines above the enclosing wall (fig. 28).

A tea text that records Jōō's teachings to his disciple Ikenaga Sōsaku, called *Ikenaga Sōsaku e no Sho*, includes a description of the *tsubo-no-uchi*. The plan-view drawing included with the text shows an entry space like the *waki tsubo-no-uchi* recorded in *Yamanoue Sōjiki* but it is much larger and is called an *uchi roji*, or "inner garden path." The space that was called an *omote tsubo-no-uchi* in the *Yamanoue Sōjiki* plan is labeled here as *niwa*, or garden. About this "niwa," it states:

> It is said that there are many ways to make the
> wall of the garden (*niwa*), but a clay wall is by far
> the best. Suitable little stones should be mixed
> into the clay. If they are sprayed with water, they
> will be revealed in a flattering way. The roof of
> this wall should not be extended toward the in-
> side so that rain running off it will be shed only
> outward [away from the garden].[111]

The clay wall mentioned would have been made by erecting a light wooden post-and-beam frame, inserting a substructure of bamboo lath in between the posts and beams, and then plastering the lath with a mixture of clay, sand, and finely chopped straw. It was possible to cover this rough clay with white lime plaster for aesthetic reasons as well as for longevity. The instruction to leave the wall as bare clay, which also extended to the tea house walls at this time, fits well with one of the fundamental characteristics of *cha-*

noyu—eliminating superficial ornament and allowing inner aspects to be revealed. The instruction to wet the wall to reveal the small stones mixed within it is reminiscent of the way Shigaraki and Bizen tea bowls, made of rough earthenware that allows tiny pebbles to break through the surface, are often soaked in water before use to improve their color and sheen.

Jōō's tea house garden was recorded in yet another text, *Usoshū*, which dates from around the end of the 16th or very beginning of the 17th century. It reads:

> The form of the garden is this; there is a four-
> and-a-half-mat room in front of which no grasses
> or trees are planted, no stones are set, no sand
> has been spread, and no small stones are laid out
> as groundcover. In this way, the attention of the
> guest is not distracted and, as they put their spir-
> it into the tea gathering, they will be able to focus
> on the excellent tea wares presented within.[112]

The dry, sparse garden described here seems antithetical to the present-day image of tea gardens, which are so mossy and woods-like. According to this passage, Jōō's *roji* was downright austere: no plants or sand, just a bare earth entryway. What is revealed in this passage is that the intent of the early *roji*—whether it was bare earth or spread with a fine layer of sand or pebbles (as we know from other sources)—was to create a place that was clean and tidy. Extreme cleanliness was, and still is, a fundamental part of *chanoyu* culture because it is a sign of respect and because of the spiritual stillness it elicits.

One other important addition to the tea house Jōō may have initiated was the use of a tiny, low-set sliding door as an entrance. This small door forced guests to bow down and "duck through" as they were entering.

This was done both to require an act of humility upon entering the tea room and as a means of emphasizing the threshold between the inside of the tea room and the outside world. From the time of Rikyū, who is usually credited with the introduction of this device, it has been called a *nijiri-guchi*, or crawl-through door. The plan of Jōō's three-mat tea house in *Yamanoue Sōjiki*, however, shows that it had a *kuguri kido*, or a wooden crawl-through door that was probably a device similar to the later *nijiri-guchi*.[113]

The origin of the small crawl-through door—known variously as a *nijiri-guchi*, *nijiri-agari-guchi*, and *kugurido*—is not known for certain, but several aspects of medieval society are seen as possible models for its use. One possibility is the small doors that acted as entrances to the theaters in urban areas (fig. 29). The performance spaces were surrounded by tall lattice fences that stopped people from entering without paying. One section of the fence had a large wooden panel in which were one or two small doors that customers could crouch through to get inside, a change from the everyday world "on the street" to the magical world of the theater. This feeling of passing through a small portal from an "ordinary" place to a place of heightened experience is very close to the function of the *nijiri-guchi* in the tea house. Another possible inspiration for the *nijiri-guchi* was the small doors that were found on farmhouses on the Korean peninsula. Even though these small doors were used simply to help keep the farmhouses warm in winter, Japanese merchants who visited Korea while looking for pottery might have experienced the enhanced sense of entry they afforded and brought the idea back to Japan. A third possibility is related to the river boats that were the backbone of inter-city travel between Kyōto and Ōsaka/Sakai that merchants such as Jōō and Rikyū would have made

28. THE PROTOTYPICAL TEA HOUSE ENTRYWAY. Shinjuan, Kyōto. This tiny enclosed space is the guest's entry to Teigyokuken, a tea house in Shinjuan, a subtemple of Daitokuji. Purportedly designed by the tea master Kanamori Sōwa (1584–1657), or in the style of his taste, Teigyokuken itself is an extremely small tea room, just two mats plus one partial mat. The enclosed entry, with its stone water basin, is exactly what one imagines the *waki tsubo-no-uchi* of early *sōan* tea rooms would have been like. Photograph from Shinjuan.

29. A MODEL FOR THE CRAWL-THROUGH DOOR. The broad riverbanks (*kawara*) of the Kamo River in Kyōto, near where it crossed Shijō Street, were the setting for all manner of performance venues. Each of the small theaters was enclosed by a tall fence that prevented outsiders from viewing without paying the entry fee. At the entrance, a panel was constructed with one or more small portholes cut into it to strictly control entry, both physical and visual. These small doors would have been well known to the early tea master and are considered to be one possible precursor of the crawl-through door to a tea house. *Shijō-kawara Yūrakuzu Byōbu*, anonymous, Momoyama period, Important Cultural Property. Museum of Fine Arts, Boston.

regular use of. Whether the small door in this case was a hatch on the boat itself or a small door that acted as a wicket to get out to the boats, once you passed through that portal, you would be closed off from the outside world, and, for a time, find yourself in close quarters with a limited number of fellow travelers: an experience not unlike a tea gathering. *Chadō Shiso Densho* states that it was Rikyū who took the idea for the *nijiri* from these river boats. "At the wharfs of Ōsaka and Hirakata, the small doors which were used to go in and out were interesting because they had a feeling of *wabi* about them. It was Rikyū who first used this as a *kuguri* [in a tea house]."[114]

Through the work of Jōō, and undoubtedly other tea masters at this time as well, each adding their own contribution, the practice and physical environment of tea service took on some of the characteristics of what we now know as a rustic *chanoyu*. Those changes included:

+ The introduction of the term *wabi* as the aesthetic theme of the gatherings.

+ The expansion and development of the tiny, walled spaces attached to the tea house, known as *tsubo-no-uchi*, used as entry antechambers to create a physical and spiritual buffer between "inside" and "outside."

+ The simplicity of the design of the entry space that led to the tea house.

+ The use of bare clay walls, *tsuchi-kabe*, for the architecture of the tea room as well as for garden walls.

Rikyū: The Creation of the Tea Garden During the Late 16th Century

The second half of the 16th century was a time of great transformation in Japan. In many ways, the changes that occurred then set the scene for the next two hundred and fifty years and ushered in what is now termed the "modern" era. Of the many changes that took place, three stand out as being most important with regard to the development of *chanoyu* and tea gardens: first, contact with Portuguese, Dutch, and Chinese traders, which fostered an increasingly cosmopolitan air; second, the consolidation of Japan under a single military authority and the consequential restructuring of the military class; and third, the great wealth developed by members of the merchant class and their corresponding influence on society. These are all aspects of society that had been building up progressively over the Muromachi period but reached a critical high point during the last half of the 16th century.

In 1542, three Portuguese men on a Chinese junk that had been blown off course ended up landing on Tanegashima, a small island in the south of Japan. Their accidental visit was followed in subsequent years by many planned ones as Portuguese Jesuit missionaries and merchants began establishing bases in Japan. The most far-reaching impact on the development of the country as a whole from that first contact with Westerners was undoubtedly the introduction of guns, because they revolutionized warfare and allowed for the consolidation of Japan by those military groups that used them.[115] With regard to the development of *chanoyu*, however, it was the cosmopolitan atmosphere the foreigners lent to the era that had the greatest impact. There were new, fanciful imports, not just guns, but also fruits such as melons that began to appear at the meals of military lords and cycad trees that were planted in their gardens. There were new ideas in the air, new ways of seeing the world, which seemed bigger and more complex than it had before. The worldly air fostered an interest in style and, in late-Muromachi society, an interest in style meant an interest in *suki*.

The second half of the 16th century was a cosmopolitan time, but it was also a time of warfare. In retrospect, we can see that these wars consolidated many divergent outlying fiefs and provinces under the strict control of a central military government to an extent that had never before existed in Japan. This happened under the guidance of three hegemons: Oda Nobunaga (1534–82); Nobunaga's lieutenant, Toyotomi Hideyoshi (1537–98), who took over after his assassination; and Tokugawa Ieyasu (1542–1616), whose reign ushered in the Tokugawa period that lasted until 1868. These three men were also greatly interested in *chanoyu*. The reasons for their interest were complex—economic, political, psychological, philosophical, and aesthetic. Significantly, although *sōan-cha* began as an aesthetic movement among urban merchants that ran counter to the traditional aesthetics of the military class, it was under the patronage of these hegemons, and of the military class system they headed, that *chanoyu* was developed into the form that still exists today, including the tea garden.

The late 16th century was also an important time for the merchant class, whose position in society grew as its wealth increased, rising as the importance of interprovincial and, to some degree, international trade grew. There were many cities involved in production and trade—Kyōto, Nara, Hakata, Sakai—but with regard to tea, the burgeoning of Sakai's wealth, its function as an international port, and its relative autonomy from political affairs in Kyōto created just the right socio-economic and cultural environment to support the development of *chanoyu*. The city had protective moats to the north, east, and south, with its western edge facing the Inland Sea. Sakai was called the "Venice of Japan" by Luís Fróis, a Portuguese Jesuit missionary who had landed in Japan in 1563 and wrote of Japan in his *História*. Fróis writes: "It is not only large, wealthy and full of commerce, but is also like a central market for all the other provinces, and people from different regions are continually flocking there."[116] João Rodrigues wrote about the connection between Sakai and *chanoyu* in his *History of the Church in Japan*.

> This new way of *chanoyu*, which is called *suki*, originated in the famous and wealthy city of Sakai, the biggest and busiest trade center of all Japan. . . . Those of the city who had the means devoted themselves to *chanoyu* in a grand manner, and because of the trade that the city conducted all over Japan and even outside the kingdom, the best *chanoyu* pieces, after those of Higashiyama Dono [Ashikaga Yoshimasa], were to be found there. As a result of the continual practice of *chanoyu* among its citizens, Sakai produced the most eminent people versed in this art, and they formed the *suki* now in fashion by changing some of the less essential things of *chanoyu*. For example, they built the hut on a smaller scale than before because they were cramped by the place's straightness, for the city is situated on a hot plain on the seacoast, or rather, in a sandy plain surrounded to the west by a rough seacoast. There are no refreshing fountains and groves of trees nearby, nor lonely and nostalgic places in keeping with *suki*, as there are in the city of Miyako [Kyōto].

Because many people dwell in the moats and near the city, the sites of the houses were for the most part so cramped (formerly, that is, because they have been recently rebuilt after the great fire) that the inhabitants could not have there either gardens or refreshing villas with groves where they could recreate and build houses in which to invite guests to *cha*. As a result of this cramped position it was impossible for all the people who practiced *chanoyu* (and these made up the larger and better part of the city) to build their *chanoyu* house in the fashion laid down by Higashiyama Dono. Also on account of other relevant considerations certain Sakai men versed in *chanoyu* built the *cha* house in another way. It was smaller and set among small trees planted for the purpose, and it represented, as far as the limited site allowed, the style of the lonely houses found in the countryside, or like the cells of the solitaries who dwell in hermitages far removed from people and give themselves over to the contemplation of the things of nature and its First Cause. These are wont to be very nostalgic places for the Japanese and, in keeping with their temperament, not a little attractive, especially for those engaged in the business and bustle of courts and populous cities. In the same way we see that Europeans enjoy the sight of cattle, and the pastoral and rustic life of the countryside on account of its peace and calm. In order that the furnishings might be in keeping with the smaller hut, they did away with many of the utensils and items required by *chanoyu*, together with the order and arrangement of these things, and in everything they did what seemed most fitting and appropriate for their purpose.

So they entertained each other with *cha* in these small huts within the city itself and in this way made up for the lack of refreshing and lonely places around the city. Indeed, to a certain extent this way was better than real solitude because they obtained and enjoyed it in the middle of the city itself. They called this in their language *shichū no sankyo*, meaning a lonely hermitage found in the middle of the public square.[117]

Rodrigues's account clearly points out his observation of Sakai's importance in the development of *chanoyu* into a new form. His record of the nature of the tea house and tea garden and of the language used in reference to them—in particular the term *shichū no sankyo*—reinforces what other Japanese texts from the period were recording about *chanoyu*. His impression, however, that the shift away from *shoin-cha* (which he calls the "fashion laid down by Higashiyama Dono") to *sōan-cha* (which he calls *suki*) began in Sakai shows that he was probably not aware of the earlier development of those tendencies among the *Shimogyō Chanoyu* at the time of Shukō and Sōshu.

Sakai's relative safety may have been one of the reasons tea culture developed there. As noted by Rodrigues, wealthy merchants escaped the vicissitudes of their time by fleeing to Sakai, creating an artificially concentrated population of people who might become, or already were, tea aficionados. As mentioned earlier, Jōō moved back to Sakai—perhaps to escape the turbulence of Kyōto—and became known in that city as one of the "elder" masters of tea. Among those whom he taught were three men who became central figures in the development of tea through the latter decades of the 16th century: Imai Sōkyū (1520–93), Tsuda Sōgyū (?–1591), and Tanaka Sōeki (1522–91). Sōeki would later become known as Sen Rikyū, Japan's most famous tea master.

All three of these men were from wealthy merchant families: Sōkyū's was involved in the wholesaling of general goods (thus his appellation Naya Sōkyū, Warehouse Sōkyū)[118] and Sōeki's in fish wholesaling. Sōkyū in particular became involved in a number of businesses and, having developed a close relationship with Nobunaga, was given, through his influence, protection for river shipments to and from the capital, control of stipended rights from salt production, and a share in silver mines. He also is known to have supplied gunpowder to Nobunaga's campaign.

Obviously, Sōkyū's relationship with Nobunaga was both mercantile and political. Their social exchange, however, was done through the medium of tea gatherings, and their relationship was secured through mutual exchanges of gifts of famous tea wares. Sōkyū had married Jōō's daughter and, upon Jōō's death, had taken possession of his famous tea wares. Here again, his close relationship with Nobunaga is revealed when we learn that Nobunaga arbitrated in favor of Sōkyū receiving the wares instead of Jōō's own son, Shingorō, and some of the most famous of those wares, including a Matsushima *tsubo* (ceramic vessel) and *nasu chaire* (tea caddy) then ended up in Nobunaga's possession.[119]

Sōeki, who from here on will be referred to as Rikyū (even though historical texts often use Sōeki), was also involved in business and also provided weapons for Nobunaga's campaign—in his case 1,000 bullets.[120] He became tea master to Nobunaga around 1573, and to Nobunaga's successor, Hideyoshi, after Nobunaga's assassination. Eventually he rose to a position of Hideyoshi's personal confidant, influential to the degree that a visiting *daimyō*, Ōtomo Sōrin, would

write home that "confidential matters are known by Sōeki [Rikyū] and public matters by the *saishō* [Hidenaga, Hideyoshi's half-brother]."[121] Rikyū was undoubtedly a very talented artist who reshaped *chanoyu* into an increasingly spare and spiritually powerful art form, but it was surely his prestige as a close associate of the ruling military lord that allowed him to exert so much influence on the culture of tea at that time.

Rikyū can be seen as representative of his times in three important ways. First, he reflects the rise of wealthy Sakai merchants to an influential position in society and in the arts. Second, he symbolizes the development of *chanoyu* into its consummate form: the nature of the tea gathering, the types of teas and food served, the utensils used, and the design of the architecture and garden. Third, he represents the movement of *chanoyu*, which was an aesthetic and art form that initially developed among the merchants of cities like Sakai and Kyōto, into the society of the military elite where it became mainstream, upper-class culture. He was not the only person who was involved in these changes, but he serves well as their symbol.

With regard to the tea garden, over the course of the twenty years that Rikyū served as advisor to the military rulers of Japan, almost all of the various elements that are traditionally associated with tea gardens appear in written records, including stepping stones, stone and wooden water basins, stone lanterns, and mossy walks. The tea masters of Rikyū's time based the designs of their tea houses and gardens on Jōō's four-and-a-half-mat tea room but also made certain changes. Rikyū, especially, experimented with making smaller and smaller tea rooms, eventually creating one, called Taian, which was only two mats in size—just enough space for a host and a single guest; no more, no less.[122] The tea masters also did away with or reformed several important parts of the design of tea houses and tea gardens.

The *waki tsubo-no-uchi*, for instance, was given the role of "cleansing antechamber." It was decided that water for the ritual cleansing of hands and mouth should be provided upon entry to the tea room, so a water basin was placed in the entry chamber, as evidenced in a drawing in *Yamanoue Sōjiki* of the three-mat tea room Rikyū built at Ōsaka Castle (fig. 30). Rather than being called the *waki tsubo-no-uchi*, in this case, the entry chamber was called the *waki chōzu-kamae*, or the "side hand-cleansing arrangement."[123]

The same drawing shows a *kuguri-do*, or crawl-through door, like the one on Jōō's three-mat tea room, that led from the entry antechamber directly into the tea room itself, eliminating the need for someone entering to pass across the intermediary veranda. An example of this kind of entry vestibule that has a water basin in it can be found at Teigyokuken, a tea house at Shinjuan, a subtemple of Daitokuji in Kyōto.[124] The next step in the development of the tea garden was to eliminate entirely the *waki tsubo-no-uchi* and incorporate the water basin into the entry garden along the *roji* path that led to the tea house.

The elimination of the *omote tsubo-no-uchi*, the tiny "viewing garden" that was also connected to the tea house, came about naturally as the design of the tea house was reworked to heighten the feeling of an inward-focused "world apart." The addition of a small, crawl-through door (*kuguri-do* or *kuguri kido*) leading directly into the tea room helped to enhance that feeling of separateness, but, having entered the small room, a large opening looking onto an outdoor space would have negated that feeling. Thus, the translucent paper doors (*shōji*) that faced the *omote tsubo-no-uchi* were replaced with a clay wall—punctuated perhaps

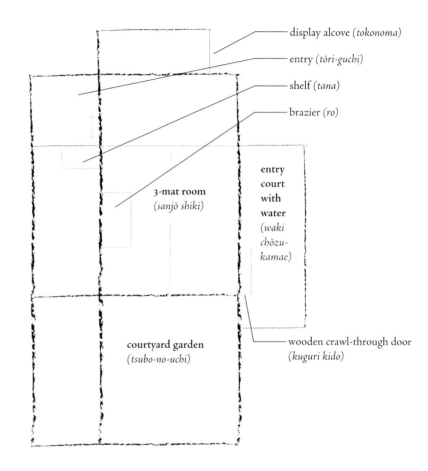

display alcove (*tokonoma*)

entry (*tōri-guchi*)

shelf (*tana*)

brazier (*ro*)

entry court with water (*waki chōzu-kamae*)

3-mat room (*sanjō shiki*)

courtyard garden (*tsubo-no-uchi*)

wooden crawl-through door (*kuguri kido*)

30. WATER FOR HAND-CLEANSING. This three-mat tea house, designed by Rikyū at Ōsaka Castle, had a water basin, or a water bucket, set in the side-entry chamber to allow guests to wash their hands before entering. The space was called the *waki chōzu-kamae*, or "side hand-cleansing arrangement." Redrawn from Sen, *Chadō Koten Zenshū*, vol. 6, p. 102.

by only a small window—and the *omote tsubo-no-uchi* itself, no longer able to be seen from the tea room, lost its meaning and was eliminated.

The *roji* at the time of Rikyū can be surmised from a number of historical texts that afford glimpses of its design. The first thing we sense right off is that the *roji* was not uppermost in the minds of the tea practitioners. Their comments on tea utensils, the decoration of the *tokonoma*, the tea room, and the meals served during a tea gathering are at times painstakingly accurate. Compared to this, comments on the *roji* are mostly occasional, off-hand remarks. Even so, they give us some indication of how the *roji* developed during the decades between the time when Jōō moved back to Sakai and Rikyū ended his life, or roughly the second half of the 16th century.

One of those texts is called *Sōtan Nikki*, the diary of Kamiya Sōtan, a merchant from Hakata who was also an avid tea practitioner. It is interesting that, although Hakata was Sakai's rival in trade, especially international trade, Sōtan associated quite easily with the Sakai merchant/tea masters like Rikyū and Sōgyū, and he recorded his visits to tea gatherings in Kyōto and Sakai in great detail. Another contemporary record that captures images of the *roji* during Rikyū's time is *Matsuya Kaiki*, the diary of three generations of lacquerware dealers from Nara: Hisamasa (?–1598), Hisayoshi (?–1633), and Hisashige (1566–1652).[125] The diary was begun in 1533 but the following entries are from the time of Hisayoshi. In it, and in *Sōtan Nikki*, we find glimpses of the early tea gardens and can witness the various elements that are now familiar parts of tea gardens as they appear one by one. All the comments are from the years 1586 to 1597.

The most prevalent comments related to tea gardens in these records are about water basins, *chōzubachi*. As mentioned above, one of the major changes in the tea house was the addition of the crawl-through door into the tea room and resultant removal of the narrow veranda on which the water basin may have been placed. The water basin was moved into the *waki tsubo-no-uchi* to be used upon entry, and then, after that walled-in space was eliminated, the water basin was moved out into the entry garden along the *roji* path. At times this basin was a wooden bucket, typically placed on a flat-topped stone that served as a pedestal (fig. 31). Sōtan notes, "The water basin was a wooden hot-water bucket, covered in black lacquer and set in the garden (*niwa*)."[126] Occasionally, a basin was carved out of solid wood as recorded during a tea gathering given by Naya Sōkyū in Ōsaka, at which Sōtan noted that the "water basin was boat-shaped, made of pine wood in the Korean fashion, carved long and rounded,"[127] and at Hideyoshi's forward base camp in Hakozaki (where there was a tea house despite the fact that it was a military camp), Sōtan saw "underneath a Box Pine, a water basin carved out of wood, aged and covered with moss."[128]

More often the water basin was made of stone, and set into the ground (fig. 32). In the garden of the Sakai tea master Imai Sōkyū, there was one basin that was made of "stone, about 1 *shaku* 2 *sun* [36 centimeters] tall, wide at the base, covered on the outside with moss,"[129] And at Hideyoshi's lavish Jurakudai Palace in Kyōto, for one of Rikyū's tea gatherings, there was a "water basin made from a large natural stone, carved with a basin."[130] At the tea gathering of Lord Hashiba of Mino, Sōtan finds a "water basin that is made from an ancient, flat, round piece of stone, with a square basin carved halfway through it."[131] This description sounds a lot like a *garan-seki*, a round pedestal stone on top of which rested the massive, round wooden columns of large Buddhist temples. Perhaps not, but the word "ancient" implies that the stone had a former purpose and was being reused.

Another example of a stone that had a former purpose and was being reused as a water basin is described during a tea given by Rikyū himself at Juraku-dai. In this case, "the water basin was made from a large round stone taken from a stone pagoda."[132] A pagoda is a multi-roofed, religious monument that usually indicates a Buddhist temple or grave site. Stone pagodas are made of many separately carved pieces (usually granite) that are stacked one on top of the other to make a tower. Individual sections—a roof section turned upside down or a pedestal section—would be carved anew to create a water basin. The description "large round stone" sounds like it may have been a pedestal section although these are typically square. The technique of reusing old, sometimes discarded, materials in tea gardens or as utensils in a tea gathering became a tradition during the Edo period and is now called *mitate*; objects that are used in that manner are called *mitate-mono*, which would translate as "reused things." The process of *mitate* is to find an object that has a certain use, to see in it a new possible use or new beauty, and then to give it new life by reusing it in a heretofore unthought of way. *Mitate* can also mean "associate," the way a flower basket made from a fisherman's trap would, through association, bring the ambience of the ocean into the room. The reuse of old stone objects of Buddhist origin in tea gardens did both things: the objects found new life and they lent the garden an air of Buddhist piety (fig. 33).

Another of these reused objects that show up in Sōtan's diary is roof tiles. On a visit to Kikuya Sōka in the Kamigyō-tachiuri district of Kyōto he finds that the "water basin was a wooden bucket, with a water ladle laid across the top. In front of it were set some slender, curved roof tiles [perhaps for spilt water to run into] and square tiles laid down as a place to stand on."[133]

An interesting point in the previous comment was the note about the water ladle, *hishaku*, and how it was placed. Many comments about water basins also mention the water ladle and in what manner it was placed: "laid on top,"[134] "laid facing up,"[135] "laid to the right, its handle touching the ground."[136] This detail seems to

31. WOODEN WATER BUCKET. Omote Senke, Kyōto. Stone water basins have become the standard in tea gardens, but in the earliest years of the development of tea gatherings, it was not uncommon for a host to place a wooden bucket, *mizu-oke*, on a flat-topped stone and fill it with cool well water. This example in the tea garden of Omote Senke is in front of the entry to the formal tea room called Zangetsu-tei. Fushin'an Foundation.

32. NATURAL STONE WATER BASIN.
Hakusa Sonsō, Kyōto. Quite often, water basins are made out of natural boulders, in which case they are called *shizen-seki chōzubachi*. Usually the basin itself is carved into the top of the stone by a mason. In some cases, however, river or ocean currents create a boulder that has a natural depression that can be used as the water basin. These are called "water-carved style," *mizubore-gata*. Photograph by Ōhashi Haruzō.

33. BUDDHA WATER BASIN. Ura Senke, Kyōto. Since as early as the late Muromachi period, tea masters have been using in their tea gardens old stone objects that were originally carved for use in Buddhist temples. These objects are called *mitate-mono* or "reused things." This water basin was made from the pedestal stone of a stone stupa, a multi-roofed, pagoda-like stone tower. The four faces of the pedestal were carved with images of Buddha, albeit very worn and difficult to see, thus the name Four-Sided Buddha water basin, *shihōbutsu chōzubachi*. Photograph by Ōhashi Haruzō.

have been of great importance to the tea practitioners of that time. Undoubtedly, they were experimenting to find which way worked best, and were attentive to the solutions of others (fig. 34).

Stone lanterns are a very important addition to gardens that were first used by tea masters at this time (fig. 35). Until then, stone lanterns were used exclusively at Buddhist temples and perhaps also at some of the larger Shintō shrines, either to give light (in which case they would be placed along the entry path, usually in pairs set symmetrically to the right and left of the path) or as votive devices (in which case there would be one large lantern placed in front of the Main Hall on axis with its central entrance). Bringing stone lanterns from temples into the tea gardens provided for several things: light for the path for evening and early morning tea gatherings; a mood of antiquity, because the lanterns had a patina of age; and a hint of a Buddhist atmosphere. The first written record of a lantern in a tea garden is found in *Matsuya Kaiki* for a gathering in 1591 given by Okaya Dōga; it simply states, "There was a lantern (*tōrō*) in the *roji*."[137] An entry in the same diary, five years later, at the gathering of Furuta Oribe, emphasizes the material the lantern was made of, noting, "There was a light in the stone lantern (*ishi-dōrō*),"[138] and again five years after that, at the gathering of Lord Kobori Sakusuke (Kobori Enshū), "There was a lighted stone lantern in the garden and only a hand lantern (*andon*) in the tea room."[139]

Another element to appear in texts is the *kuguri*, crawl-through gate, midway through the garden, that emphasized the sense of "threshold," of passing out of one realm and entering into another. At this point in time, the word *kuguri* was also used for the crawl-through door into the tea room. Eventually the doors into the tea room would be called *nijiri* or *nijiri-guchi* (the "crawl-through" door),[140] as they are today, and the garden gates would be called *soto-kuguri* (outer wicket), *naka-kuguri* (middle wicket), or *chūmon* (middle gate).[141] The term *soto-kuguri* is no longer in common use, but *naka-kuguri* and, more so, *chūmon*, are still used today. The *naka-kuguri* is different from

34. WATER LADLE. Omote Senke, Kyōto. These water ladles are made from finely cut and bent cedar (*sugi*) or cypress (*hinoki*). They are called *hishaku*, but to distinguish them from the ladles used inside the tea room, which are made from bamboo, these ladles are called *chōzu hishaku*. They are laid on top of the water basin with the head of the ladle resting on the stone or on one or two pieces of green bamboo that stretch across the top of the basin. Originally, the direction the ladle faced was not fixed, but nowadays it is common to face the opening of the ladle to the left. Photograph by Ōhashi Haruzō.

35. STONE LANTERN. Rokasensuisō, Ōtsu City. Stone lanterns have been used in many ways in tea gardens. Their function was to give light for early morning and evening tea gatherings, and also to add ambience. One of the most important locations for a lantern was directly behind the water basin, to offer light to guests cleansing their hands. If only one lantern is used in a tea garden, it will be found here. Photograph by Ōhashi Haruzō.

the *chūmon*. The *chūmon* is a roofed gate that, though not large in scale by any means, can be walked through standing up. The *naka-kuguri* is essentially a wall built in the garden with a small, rectangular opening in it that one ducks through (fig. 36; the name comes from the verb *kuguru*, which means to "duck through"). A *naka-kuguri* creates a feeling of threshold and passage in a very clear and dramatic way. They are, however, harder to build and maintain and, being highly abstract, are therefore somewhat unnatural. *Naka-kuguri* are rare in tea gardens these days, and one can surmise they were not very common at the time of Rikyū either. Hideyoshi had one at his Hakozaki camp that was noted by Sōtan.

> At the Hakozaki base camp of the Kanpaku [Hideyoshi]. . . . Upon entering the *roji*, there, in the outer part, was a small crawl-through gate (*kuguri*) through which we passed . . . and in front of the tea house there was a low fence of old bamboo and a swinging gate made of reed screening (*sudo no hanekido*).[142]

The "swinging gate," *hanekido*, that shows up at the end of this passage is another type of midway gate that was found in early tea gardens (fig. 37). It was probably something like the *shiori-do* used in tea gardens these days. *Shiori-do* are lightly built gates made by weaving a lattice of split bamboo over a frame. The *hanekido* in Hideyoshi's tea garden, however, seems to have been made of reed screens, perhaps something like the hanging screens, *sudare*, found under the eaves of Japanese houses today. *Sōtan Nikki* mentions another case: "From four in the morning, Sōtan was waiting by the swinging gate (*hanekido*)."[143]

One of the elements most identifiable with Japanese gardens in general, and the tea garden in particular, is stepping stones, *tobi-ishi* (fig. 38). These, as well, make their first appearance in literature at this time, perhaps for the first time in Sōtan's comment about Hideyoshi's Hakozaki tea garden mentioned above that read, "Upon entering the *roji*, there, in the outer part, was a small crawl-through gate (*kuguri*), through

36. THE MIDDLE WICKET. Omote Senke, Kyōto. When *chanoyu* was first being developed, properties were divided from the street, or were subdivided within, by high walls. At times, to allow entry, those walls had small doors called *kuguri* built into them. The clear sense of threshold and passage felt when going through a *kuguri* must have appealed to tea masters, who then mimicked these walls in the middle of their tea gardens to separate the inner and outer garden. They called them *naka-kuguri*, middle wickets. Photograph by Ōhashi Haruzō.

37. THE SIMPLE GATE. Private Residence. These lightly built, woven bamboo gates, called *shiori-do*, are perhaps the most common gates used in tea gardens. Reminiscent of the gates that might be found on a farm or in a mountain village, they lend an air of rusticity to the garden. Photograph by Ōhashi Haruzō.

38. STEPPING STONES. Nishida-tei, Ishikawa Prefecture. *Tobi-ishi*, literally, "flying stones," were used by the early tea masters for several reasons: they kept the guests' feet from getting wet or muddy as they crossed the mossy garden; they slowed the pace of the person entering, making the garden seem larger; and they created a beautiful pattern on the ground. Historically, older tea gardens tend to have smaller-sized stones than those built from the late 18th century, when large stones came to be in fashion. Photograph by Ōhashi Haruzō.

which we passed." The passage continues with the brief note: "There we found stepping stones."[144] This was written in 1587. In 1600, we find a short passage in *Sōshun'ō Chanoyu Kikigaki* that reads, "In the past, people were asked to walk on the snow [in the *roji*] but as of late, [the host] pours hot water over the stone path (*tatami-ishi*) and stepping stones (*tobi-ishi*) to clear them."[145]

As the passage above shows, along with stepping stones, *tatami-ishi* are another feature of tea gardens that developed at that time (fig. 39). *Tatami-ishi* are sections of paving made up of small flat-topped stones and, at times, pieces of carved granite, that are fit together to form a uniform, rectangular surface. The term derives from the fact that they are shaped somewhat like *tatami* mats, although the width of a *tatami-ishi* is usually narrower and the length often longer. Another term for *tatami-ishi* used nowadays is *nobe-dan*.[146]

Regarding plantings used in the *roji* at this time, there are lists in texts that postdate Rikyū's time that purport to record which plants were favored by which famous tea masters of the past. The texts of Rikyū's era, however, have less to say. Pines are mentioned often, as in this visit by Sōtan to Hideyoshi's Fushimi Castle: "We went through a small gate (*kuguri*) and found ourselves in a pine grove (*matsubara*)."[147] Also, the aged, wooden water basin covered with moss mentioned earlier had been set beneath a pine tree in the *roji*.[148] Of course pine trees were mentioned in connection with the tea houses of Jōō and Shukō as well, so they cannot be said to have been introduced at the time of Rikyū. The species of pines used are not stipulated in the texts but, judging from the tradition of gardening as it exists today and from archeological evidence of historical gardens, the Japanese black pine (Pinus thunbergii, *kuromatsu*) is most likely to have

been used, or possibly the Japanese red pine (Pinus densiflora, *akamatsu*; fig. 40).

Moss was used in the tea gardens of Rikyū's time but, as with the wooden water basin mentioned above, the references seem to be related to moss on aged garden ornaments, not moss as a groundcover *per se*. One case in which the author does describe moss being

39. STONE PAVING. Katsura Detached Palace, Kyōto. Stones of different sizes and shapes can be carefully set together to form a large rectangular section of paving. This is called a *tatami-ishi* because it is reminiscent of a *tatami* mat. This example employs both natural stones as well as chunks of carved granite. Photograph by Ōhashi Haruzō.

used as a groundcover is found in Rodrigues, who, in detailing the roughness and seeming poverty of *suki*, lists "a path paved with rough stones; a basin made of the same material with water for the hands; wild fruit-less tress; and a wood with the ground covered with moss and decrepitude; and many other things, all of them rough with no visible trace of splendor that might delight and please the senses."[149] Rodrigues notes the moss-covered ground but, interestingly, interprets it as a sign of "decrepitude." Also, in *Usoshū* we find a brief note that "the guests went out to the veranda and gazed upon the moss."[150] The passage does not elaborate, but this certainly seems like the guests are looking at an expanse of moss rather than small amounts of moss on a lantern or water basin.

What is important to remember about moss is that, in Japan, with its warm climate and plentiful moisture, things that are not cared for will moss over quite quickly. Moss on a thatched roof, for instance, may have a certain romantic look to some people but, even to this day, for people who live in thatch-roofed

40. COMPARATIVE LIFESTYLES IN THE CAPITAL. The men gathered in the large residence on the left, which belongs to a military-class official, are holding a cockfight. The garden is in the *karesansui* style, featuring large boulders and some plantings of pines and other trees. Across the street, however, the courtyard behind the simple houses of the townsfolk is not so elaborate. No arrangements of boulders, just flat, swept soil and a few trees. Early writings on tea gardens also reflect a very reserved planting palette. *Rakuchū Rakugaizu* (Rekihaku Kōhon, formerly Machida-bon), 16th century (depicts Kyōto between 1525 and 1536), middle of the fourth panel of the left-hand set of screens. National Museum of Japanese History, Tōkyō.

buildings by neccessity and not aesthetic choice (such as farmers), moss on a roof is detested as a sign of, to use Rodrigues's words, "decrepitude." In general, it can be said that, in the 16th century, moss growing over things was perceived by most people in Japan as a sign of poor care, poverty, and decay. Seen in this light, what makes the use of moss in tea gardens so interesting is that it represents a paradigm shift in the minds of people participating in *chanoyu* as to what constitutes beauty.

Chawa Shigetsushū, the first printed and published book of collected writings on tea, released at the very end of the 17th century, mentions three plants with regard to Rikyū: pine, bamboo, and a type of olive tree called *gumi* (Elaeagnus umbellata or E. multiflora).[151] Naturally, the late date of this text means that its information is suspect, but its main point is most likely correct: that at Rikyū's time, and in Rikyū's taste, the tea garden used a very limited palette of plants, including the pine tree (a classic garden plant) and understated plants like *gumi* (an unusual garden plant).

Chafu, a tea treatise from the mid- to late 17th century, records the following about Rikyū's taste in plantings: "large pine trees, large fir trees, and the Japanese cleyera (Ternstroemia gymnanthera, *mokkoku*).[152] Here we see that evergreen trees were prevalent in the tea garden. Pine and fir are, of course, coniferous trees (having needles and seed cones), and the Japanese cleyera is a broadleaf evergreen tree.

Another element of the tea garden that was developed during the time of Rikyū was the *setchin*, or privy, a small shed much like the outhouses of Western countries but more finely built and lacking any pit or vessel inside. The inner floor was spread with sand or fine gravel and had two stones set in it on which to stand, thus elevating the user slightly above the ground.

The *setchin* was installed primarily for decorative purposes and not intended for actual use unless, as João Rodrigues puts it, the guest's "need is so urgent that he cannot wait." *Usoshū*, which dates from around the end of the 16th or very beginning of the 17th century, records the first use of the word *setchin*. It reads, "Outside the corridor there should be a small toilet (*benjo*), and place the privy (*setchin*) somewhat further into the garden. This is essential for times when a nobleman visits and should not be put to daily use so that it will remain feeling clean and fresh" (fig. 41).[153]

Some other elements of tea gardens that were mentioned in texts within five to ten years of Rikyū's death, but that were most likely part of the *roji* at the time he was active, include the following:

41. ORNAMENTAL PRIVY. Ura Senke, Kyōto. There are two types of privy in a tea garden, which outwardly look quite similar: the *shitabara setchin*, intended to be used as a privy, and the *suna setchin*, which is purely ornamental. Inside is a distinctive arrangement of four stones—two long, two small—that form the toilet. The inside would be laid with fresh sand or evergreen boughs to express cleanliness. A flat-topped stone to hold a small kettle of water and a dust-pit are usually included as well. Photograph by Ōhashi Haruzō.

* The *katana-kake*, or sword rack, which was a simple shelf put near the entry to the tea house to allow military men to remove their swords before entering the tea room (fig. 42). Because military men of high rank carried two swords, the *katana-kake* had two shelves, one above the other: the bottom one for long swords and the top one for short ones. The first use of this word shows up in a plan drawing in *Hisashige Chakaiki*.[154] In its present form, the *katana-kake* is placed high off the ground on the wall of the tea house. Just beneath the shelves is a flat-topped stone, 30 to 45 centimeters tall, called the *katana-kake-ishi*, which allows guests to step up and reach the shelves. The stone chosen for this purpose is often two-tiered and stair-like. The first appearance of the *katana-kake-ishi* in literature comes somewhat later than the *katana-kake* itself, which may mean that the rack was moved from a low position to a high one at some point in time or simply that it wasn't recorded before then. We find this first reference in *Furuta Oribe no Kamidono Kikigaki*: "Examining stones that have specific functions [for the *roji*, there are] stones to step up into the crawl-through door (*nijiri-agari-ishi*) and stones to step up to the sword shelf (*katana-kake-ishi*)."[155]

42. SWORD SHELF. Kohōan, Kyōto. Tea gatherings were often attended by men of the military class. Without fail, they would be armed, carrying either one, or at times, two swords: one long, one short. The introduction of weaponry into the tea room was in contradiction to the sentiments of *chanoyu*, leading tea masters to design a shelf outside their tea rooms upon which the swords could be left. The high stone in front of the shelf, *katana-kake-ishi*, allowed guests to step up to the shelf and gracefully place their swords. Photograph by Ōhashi Haruzō.

43. WAITING BENCH. Ura Senke, Kyōto. A waiting bench, called a *koshikake* or *koshikake machiai*, is constructed in the tea garden to provide guests a place to rest while they wait for their host to call them forward. That quiet time allows them to commune with the garden and prepare themselves, physically as well as mentally. The far end of the bench has a bamboo surface and one round stone set beneath it. This marks the place for the lead guest, *shōkyaku*. The green broom, *shuro-bōki*, hanging from the post is made of palm fronds. Photograph by Ōhashi Haruzō.

The *koshikake*, or waiting bench, which is a roofed bench that is placed midway along the *roji* to allow the entering guests to rest and settle themselves while they are waiting to be called forward by their host (fig. 43). Although the length of the whole *roji* may be no more than some tens of meters, the waiting bench creates the atmosphere of a rest stop on a long climb through the mountains to a hermit's hut. It also allows guests a place to ready themselves, physically, by arranging their clothes and such, and, inwardly, by sitting quietly and communing with the garden. The first mention of a *koshikake* comes in *Sōshun'ō Chanoyu Kikigaki* where we find the following notes: "the waiting bench (*koshikake*) was set right where the path came to an end" and "the pathway stones inside the waiting bench (*koshikake*) should be unusual and slightly large. A round stone set between long stones looks wonderful."[156]

♦ The last element of the tea garden that was first used at this time is the *chiri-ana*, or dust-pit, a small tile-lined or stone-lined hole in the ground into which garden debris (*chiri*, literally, "dust") can be placed temporarily when the garden is being cleaned (fig. 44). It was described for the first time in *Sōshun'ō Chanoyu Kikigaki*, which relates that it was "used upon entering the privy (*setchin*), a round hole, 8 *sun* [24 centimeters] in diameter."[157] In the *roji*, the *chiri-ana* is used in a symbolic manner. Before a tea gathering, the host cleans the tea room and *roji*, and then places an evergreen branch and a pair of long, bamboo "chopsticks" called *chiri-bashi* (literally, "dust-chopsticks") in the *chiri-ana* as a sign to the guest that preparations have been made. The *chiri-ana*

is placed in such a way as to be not too obvious but, then again, not completely hidden from view as it would be if it were truly a debris receptacle. Symbolically, it is intended to be a reminder that no "dust of the heart," *kokoro no chiri*, should be carried into the tea room. In other words, worldly affairs are best left outside. In *Chanoyu Ichieshū* (1856) we find the following comments about how the *chiri-ana* should be used:

> In the *chiri-ana*, place some leaves and broken twigs from the *roji* that have been well-soaked in water first. In the autumn, it is possible to mix in some that have fall color. In the *chiri-ana*, leaves and broken twigs should be completely natural, not a forced arrangement of colors. The *chiri-bashi* should be made of fresh, green bamboo, as should the broom, which should be hung on a peg. Under the eaves, if there is no *chiri-ana*, place a *chiri-kago* [dust basket] and put leaves and broken twigs in it in the same way and lay the *chiri-bashi* on top.[158]

The last few images historical texts provide about the *roji* at the time of Rikyū regard not the physical form of the garden but the custom of its use. The first of these is the *mukae-zuke*, or greeting, during which the host appears and silently "greets" his guests. This is presently done somewhere midway in the garden, near the *chōzubachi*. The host places fresh water in the *chōzubachi* in such a way that the guests can see or hear him doing it so that they know the water is fresh and clean. Then the host comes to greet his guests by bowing silently and thereby signaling them to come forward to the tea house. In a record from 1587, Sōtan mentions

44. ORNAMENTAL DUST PIT. Mushanokōji Senke, Kyōto. Fallen leaves and other debris in the garden are swept into a small pit before being collected and disposed of. In tea gardens, these "dust pits," *chiri-ana*, became symbolically formalized. A fresh, evergreen bough is set in the pit just before a tea gathering along with a pair of chopstick-like bamboo debris pickers, *chiri-bashi*. They act as a subtle sign from the host to the guests that all preparations have been completed and the guests are welcome. Photograph by Ōhashi Haruzō.

going to a tea given by Rikyū. He writes, "Arrived in Ōsaka at one or two in the morning. Rikyū was waiting for us in the *roji*. Sōden called out to say we had arrived and Rikyū came out to greet us at the outer gate attended by young men carrying lanterns. Although it was still dark, we went in."[159] Sōtan did not express this with the word *mukae-zuke*, but it would seem that the custom of hosts greeting guests in the *roji* instead of simply waiting for them in the tea house existed by Rikyū's time. Rodrigues mentions the following, which confirms the practice as it is today, except that the host is not silent.

> When someone enters the house and comes along the path, he is alone or with a companion. The host goes to the first small gate to receive them, puts his head outside, thanks them for coming and bids them enter, and then retires straight away by another path leading inside.[160]

Another custom we find revealed in texts from that time is that of *uchi-mizu*, "wetting the garden." Before a tea gathering, the *roji* is sprinkled with water to create a feeling of freshness, as if after a light rain. Regarding a visit to the *yamazato* in Ōsaka Castle in 1587, Sōtan notes, "We entered the *yamazato*. In the *roji*, all the way up to the swinging gate, water had been sprinkled on the ground [in preparation for our arrival]."[161] This description is not as specific as the one in *Nanbōroku*, a later text that mentions the "three wettings" of the *roji* as they exist today, but it does make clear that the custom of wetting down the *roji* before a tea gathering had already begun at the time of Rikyū.

A third custom related to the tea garden regards the footwear used when in the *roji*. Presently, tradition dictates that soft-soled, straw sandals, *roji-zōri*, are to be used. Originally, however, it seems wooden sandals, *geta*, were in favor, and at the time of Rikyū this was beginning to change to soft-soled sandals. Rodrigues mentions a "rough clean stone where the guest changes his sandals"[162] being placed inside the outer gate. Surely this was to change from street sandals to clean sandals for the *roji* but he doesn't mention what kind of sandals would be used in the *roji*: wooden or straw. The clearest record of the fact that wooden *geta* were used at first, and that soft-soled sandals came into fashion after that, is to be found in *Nanbōroku*, which states:

> It was Jōō who determined that both guest and host wear *geta* when entering and leaving through the *roji*—because of the heavy dew on the plants and trees where they pass. It is said that the participants can tell by the sound of the footwear [on the stepping stones] whether the others are accomplished practitioners or not. The person who walks with equanimity and detachment, neither bustling in step nor as though stealing in, you should recognize to be a master. One lacking a genuine grasp of *chanoyu*, however, will be incapable of judging.
>
> Recently, straw sandals with leather soles called *setta* [footwear for snow]—favored by Rikyū and made on order in the Imaichi section of Sakai—have come into use in the *roji*. When I inquired about this, Rikyū replied, "I am not insisting, after *geta* have been so long employed, that it is wrong to use them. But even Jōō, at one of his tea gatherings, said there were no more than three people, including myself, who had mastery of walking in *geta*. At present there are tens of practitioners of tea in Kyōto, Sakai, and Nara, but not five, including yourself, are skilled

in wearing *geta*. . . . As for you, good monk, you have an eccentric fondness for clatter. . . ."[163]

THE TESTIMONY OF RODRIGUES

The last historical material to be presented that represents the nature of the tea garden in the late 16th century is, again, from João Rodrigues. As mentioned earlier, Rodrigues lived in Japan from 1577 to 1610 and did not write his treatise on Japan until the 1620s when he was living in Macao. With regard to which part of the thirty-three years he spent in Japan his memoirs represent, it must be remembered that when he arrived in Japan he was only 15 years old and spoke no Japanese. By the time he was fluent in the language, and old enough to consort with high-society *bushi* and merchants from whom he learned about *chanoyu*, it would have been around the late 1580s. Most of his in-depth experience with tea, therefore, would have been in the decades just before and after Rikyū's death. Surprisingly, although Rodrigues was intimate enough with Hideyoshi to be called to his bedside a week before the ruler's death and Rikyū was Hideyoshi's tea master and confidant, Rodrigues never mentions Rikyū in his memoirs.[164] His writings describe the tea gathering in very much the way it would have existed through Rikyū's time, and, in the things that he stresses, he does not reveal the changes that happen to *chanoyu* and the *roji* after Rikyū, such as the artfulness and artifice of the tea utensils and gardens designed by Furuta Oribe, a tea master whose influence shall be examined in the next chapter.

Rodrigues was an elite guest in Japan—even after the tides turned against Christian missionaries at the end of the 16th century—until 1610 when he was finally deported. As such, he spent time with people who represented the elite of Japanese society. His notions of *chanoyu* should be understood in that light as well. For instance, he had a very negative impression of Kyōto's *wabi-suki*, seeing it as a poor offshoot of the practice rather than essential to the culture as we observe it today. He writes:

> *Suki* is practiced generally throughout the kingdom by all those who devote themselves to it in some way or other, even though poorly. For instead of the rich and expensive items we mentioned, they use the native ones that are similar as regards form but not as regards price and esteem in the genuine *suki*. This way is called *wabizuki*, and it is a poor *suki* that imitates, insofar as possible, the purpose of the genuine *suki*. [165]

Rodrigues's opinions on *chanoyu* seem to be those of a military lord, nobleman, or wealthy merchant, any of whom he was likely to have had dealings with. Those associates of his, being physically and socially separated from the *Shimogyō Chanoyu* tea masters of Kyōto who began the practice of rustic tea a century before and continued to practice it during Rodrigues's time, appear to have looked on the *wabi*-style tea practitioners with disdain. Nevertheless, even though his opinions are biased, because Rodrigues was a foreigner actively trying to record the culture of the country he was living in, his testimony is more thorough and exacting than any by a Japanese person at that early stage in the development of *chanoyu*. Because of that clarity, his writings are worth quoting at length.

> Among this kingdom's social customs, that of meeting to drink *cha* is the chief and most esteemed among the Japanese, and is the one in

which they show the most excellence. So they spare no pains in the construction of the place where they give *cha* to their guests. This is a special building, with a path or an entrance leading to it and with various other things suitable to the purpose of that custom. In general this purpose is the quiet and restful contemplation of the things of nature in the wilderness and desert. Hence all the material of this place is entirely accommodated to this end and to eremitical solitude in the form of rude huts made quite naturally with rough wood and bark from the forest. It is as if they had been formed by Nature or in the usual style of those people who live in the woods or the wilderness. In everything in these houses they imitate nature and its simplicity, but with as much proportion and measurement as Nature herself observes in the things that she naturally creates.

> Thus this *suki*, as they call it, is a sort of rustic creation for the nobles as they entertain a friend with eating and drinking *cha* in their house or hut in the wilderness. [166] They may thus contemplate the path, the wood through which they enter, and everything artlessly formed there by nature with proportion and grace, as well as the house or hut itself and the serving utensils therein, as if it were a recluse's hermitage in the wilderness [fig. 45]. They do not indulge in conversation there apart from what is fitting to the place, but contemplate instead the form, proportion, and quality of all the rustic things to be found there.

> Thus fashionable, finely wrought, and elegant things, such as those belonging to the court and not to mountains and the wilderness, are

45. PATH THROUGH THE WOODS. Tabuchi
Residence, Akō City. Rodrigues described
the *roji* as a path through the woods, entirely
natural in its design as if leading to a recluse's
hermitage in the wilderness. Although the
tea gardens that Rodrigues was detailing featured pine trees, this garden uses cyads and
ferns to create the same effect.

most unsuitable for this building, the eating and drinking utensils therein, and everything else. Instead, they use rough things, twisted artlessly and naturally. As the Japanese lords, nobles, gentry, the wealthy and ordinary people of quality exercise their skill in this, they all almost necessarily have one of these buildings attached to their palace or house, so that they can privately entertain their friends and acquaintances there without any ostentation. However noble he may be, the host generally serves at the table, makes *cha* with his own hands, and offers it to the guest after he has eaten there. This way of entertaining is the greatest honor that can be paid to a guest. Hence a lower-ranking person can also invite lords and nobles to drink *cha* in his own *suki* place. The lord will accept with great courtesy and affability, and behave on this occasion as an equal and not as a superior and noble, even though the host is his own vassal. For this is a rustic relaxation and pleasure.

Various things are considered in the construction. The first is the site, which must be next to the palace or house and within the same compound. The second is the entrance and path where the guests enter on the way to the *sukiya*. As far as the site permits, this entry must be in a solitary and quiet place, set away from the street and the ordinary business of the house. The entrance gate is a small, narrow, and low door, through which a person can enter only by stooping. Inside this entrance or door there are wooden seats like benches[167] at the sides, and here the invited guests sit down and wait while everything is being prepared within. Near this spot to one side there are some toilets,[168] very rough but spotlessly clean, with a pool of water[169] and stepping stones. There is also a certain kind of coarse sand there with a wooden shovel, and everything is freshly sprinkled with water. There is nothing more, such as scented eaglewood or aloes, for there is no filth there as it is merely a formality of the place. Hence nobody goes there unless his need is so urgent that he cannot wait, and then servants are there to clean so that it looks just as it was. These toilets have a rustic gate with a bolt inside and windows of latticework roughly woven from reeds.

Further on there is a wood of trees, partly natural [as] if they were already growing there, partly transplanted thither with great skill. They choose trees that have the best shapes and branches, and the most natural and elegant artlessness. Such trees are mainly pines interspersed with others in such a way that there does not seem to be any artificiality about them, and they appear to have grown there naturally and haphazardly. A long narrow path runs through the middle of this wood, and it is paved with stepping stones over which the guest passes. The path leads to the house or hut where the guest is received. Just before reaching there, he comes to a rough rock erected halfway along the path to the side. This has a pool of clean water in the middle[170] and a container at its base,[171] so that he may draw water there and wash hands. If it is winter, there is warm water inside.

When the guest reaches the house, he finds on one side a small covered cupboard where he leaves his dagger and fan,[172] for they do not enter the house with these things. There are also some hats roughly made of bamboo bark,[173] which the guests use to shelter from the rain or sun when they go to wash their hands at the above-mentioned place or walk through the wood contemplating the form of things therein.[174]

Rodrigues then turns to what goes on inside the tea house but, later on in his record, returns to discuss the "great expense involved in *suki*." He mentions seven items: the utensils (tea caddies, kettles, scrolls, etc.), the tea house, the "special offices" attached to the tea house (such as the kitchen), tableware, the garden, banquets, and the cost of the tea itself. About the garden he notes:

> Fifthly, there is the expense of laying out the wood and the path leading to the hut, for they search in remote areas for a special type of tree of certain fashion and shape to plant there, for any tree whatsoever will not serve. This costs a great deal of money until the trees take root, and the wood looks as if it sprang up there quite naturally. The stones with which they pave the path make up one of the main expenses. They are of a certain special kind and are sought for in distant places. Although rough and unworked, they look as if they appeared there quite naturally and have a certain grace, attractiveness, and simplicity about them. They buy choice stones at a high price, and among them there will be a special one containing a pool of water within a cavity and well in the rough stone for washing the hands.[175] Suitable ones are found only seldom and are worth a great deal. Also to be considered is the construction of the street gate through which they enter the wood, for although it is very small, it is very costly. Also some wooden

benches placed inside where the guests sit down and converse in a low voice after they have entered and closed the street gate. From there they proceed along the path through the wood and contemplate the nostalgic things therein. Then there are some very clean privies made of a reed framework, and these are constructed in a special laborious way at a great expense.[176]

Rodrigues also describes the tea gathering itself and mentions, again, the manner of entering the *roji*. Some points we have heard already, but there is enough new information to warrant quoting the whole passage. The guests are invited by polite letter to a morning, midday, or afternoon tea and respond likewise and, in some cases, in person as well.

> At the appointed hour on the day each guest robes himself neatly and becomingly. Lay people shave a part of the head, while bonzes and those who have performed *inkyo* shave the head and chin. Wearing new stockings, they proceed to the private gate and entrance to the woods. Outside, in front of this gate, there is a swept terrace that, together with the walls, has been recently sprinkled with water for the sake of freshness. The gate is so small and low that a person can enter only by stooping down.[177] In front of the gate there is a rough clean stone where the guest changes his sandals before entering the wood, and puts on new clean ones so as not to soil the path stones for they are sprinkled with water and are very clean.
>
> Up to this point the gate has been locked from within, but now comes the master of the house, opens it, and thrusting his head outside

bids the guests welcome. He closes the gate without locking it and then retires inside his house by another special path, reserved for his use, through the wood; he neither enters nor leaves the little tea house. Once he has withdrawn, the guests open the gate, enter, and then lock it again from the inside. They sit there in the arbour for a short while, relaxing and gazing at the wood. Then as they walk along the path through the wood up to the *cha* house, they quietly contemplate everything there—the wood itself, individual trees in their natural state and setting, the paving stones, and the rough stone trough for washing the hands. There is crystal-clear water there that they take with a vessel and pour it on their hands, and the guests may wash their hands if they so wish.[178] In winter hot water is available there on account of the cold. They now approach the closed door of the small house. This is set somewhat above the ground and is just large enough for a person to pass through provided he stoops. They remove their fans and daggers from their sashes, and deposit them in a kind of a cupboard placed outside for this purpose. They open the door and, leaving their sandals there, they all go inside.[179]

In Rodrigues' perception, there were three principles of *chanoyu* (which he refers to most often as *suki*) that needed to be adhered to, and he states these succinctly. They give a good idea of what was considered important about the practice of *chanoyu* during the time he stayed in Japan.

Suki has three principal and essential features, and all the rest is incidental and variable. The first is the extreme cleanliness in everything, not only in what can be seen outwardly in the *suki* meetings and gatherings, but also in those things that are not seen. . . . The second is the rustic solitude and poverty, and the withdrawal from a multitude of superfluous things of every kind. The third and principal feature is the knowledge and science of natural proportion and suitability, and the hidden and subtle qualities inherent in natural and artificial things, which are in keeping with the purpose of *suki*.[180]

THE FORM OF THE EARLY *ROJI*

To summarize all of this, the tea garden at the time of Rikyū had developed to the point that it was substantially like the tea gardens one can find today in a tea master's house in an urban setting or, more truthfully, could have been found sixty years ago, since so many tea gardens were destroyed during World War II or razed for development over the decades since. These various aspects included:

- The common use of the word *roji* to mean the tea garden.

- The water basin, *chōzubachi*, where the guests could rinse their hands and mouth, made of stone and set in the ground along the *roji*, rather than as a wooden bucket set on the veranda next to the tea room.

- The importance of the water ladle, *hishaku*, including its position on the *chōzubachi*.

- Stone lanterns, *ishi-dōrō*, added to the garden for light and atmosphere.

- The crawl-through gate, *kuguri*, within the garden.

- A swinging gate, *hanekido*, in the garden to divide it into parts.

- Stepping stones, *tobi-ishi*, to allow the guests to walk through the wet garden without getting damp or muddy, to slow their pace so they would better appreciate its subtleties, and to make the short experience of the *roji* path feel longer and more journey-like.

- Rectangular sections of paving known as *tatami-ishi*.

- Simple plantings that evoke the sense of a mountain village or a recluse's hermitage, primarily pines and other evergreen trees, avoiding plants with showy displays of colorful flowers.

- The privy, *setchin*, which was more ornamental than functional.

- The sword rack, *katana-kake*, where guests could leave their swords (and fans) before entering the tea room.

- The waiting bench, *koshikake*, in the *roji* where guests were invited to rest and prepare themselves (outwardly and inwardly) before continuing further into the *roji*.

- The dust-pit, *chiri-ana*, to symbolize the preparedness and cleanliness of the *roji*.

- The custom of greeting guests at the entry of the *roji* or at a gate within the *roji*, now called *mukae-zuke*.

- Wetting the garden before and during a tea gathering, now referred to as *uchi-mizu*.

- Changing footwear to soft sandals within the garden.

- The high cost of making and maintaining a *roji*.

- Three main principles of *roji* design, including cleanliness, an atmosphere of rusticity and poverty, and a sensitivity toward natural subtlety.

Certain refinements and modifications would be made in later years, but the essential practice of *chanoyu* and the fundamental form of the tea garden as it exists today were already defined by this time. The reactionary practice of the Shimogyō merchants, like Shukō and Sōshu, developed a rustic Way of Tea suited to their backyard *an* that was vogue enough to influence the artists and literati of the day. The art then passed through the time of Jōō when the initial application of *wabi* as an aesthetic took place and the small tea house with its incipient entry garden (*tsubo-no-uchi*) was created. It then entered the age of the great merchant/tea masters like Sōkyū, Sōgyū, and Rikyū of Sakai, who fleshed out the practice of *chanoyu*, its architecture, and garden. As masters of the art, they brought it back into the realm of the military class elite, who incorporated *chanoyu* as part of their culture and, by doing so, established it as an upper-class convention.

The tea garden developed through similar stages. It began as a place with a general sense of seclusion

rikyū

113

and wilderness (*shichūin*) in the back of merchants' residences at Shukō's time. The addition of the *tsubo-no-uchi* during Jōō's time strengthened the aspect of the tea room as a "place apart." This function eventually became applied to the wooded entry walk itself during Rikyū's time, so that the entire *roji* took on the original purpose of the *tsubo-no-uchi*. Namely, by offering many subtle points of threshold, purification, and repose—gate, wash basin, waiting bench, and so on—the *roji* was designed to elicit in the guests a sense of traveling out of one world and into another.

Regarding what *chanoyu* meant to its practitioners through that first century of its development, we find that—unlike the writings of later eras such as *Zencharoku* (*Zen Tea Record*, 1828), which overtly and pointedly related *chanoyu* and Zen Buddhism—the historical writings up to the time of Rikyū do not emphasize the philosophic and spiritual aspects of *chanoyu* in such clear terms. Most writings address appropriate social customs (cleanliness, attentiveness, etc.) and aesthetic appreciation (tea utensils are noted especially often). Occasionally, however, there is a note that relates *chanoyu* to Buddhism, such as this reference to the "Buddhist Path" in *Yamanoue Sōjiki* (*Record of Yamanoue Sōji*).

> After being parted from your teacher, the attention given in seeking a new teacher is above all else in importance. As in the Buddhist path, and the way of poetry, or *nō*, dance, and swordsmanship, so in *chanoyu* and the illuminating discernment of utensils, one should take the actions of a renowned master as model, down to the least movement.[181]

There is a brief line in *Yamanoue Sōjiki* that spe-

cifically mentions Zen Buddhism, claiming, "Because *chanoyu* derives from the Zen sect, it is fudamentally the religious practice of priests. Everyone, including Shukō and Jōō, were of the Zen sect."[182] And, of course, there is the work of Rodrigues, which is exceptional in its emphasis on the spiritual aspects of *chanoyu* and its relation to Zen Buddhism.

If asked to what degree did Zen Buddhist thought inform the initial development of *chanoyu* and the *roji*, the answer is that *chanoyu* developed within the context of Zen Buddhism—many of the early creators were Zen practitioners either as priests, lay priests, or laymen—but that context included all the aspects of Zen Buddhism that existed during the Muromachi period, of which three can be clearly seen: Zen as the dominant religion of the military elite, Zen as a vehicle of Chinese culture, and Zen as a religious experience focused on non-attachment and enlightenment through meditation.

In the context of its association with the military elite, *chanoyu* became a vehicle to power, one that Imai Sōkyū, and probably Rikyū, used so noticeably. The great financial cost of the utensils, architecture, and garden and the use of tea wares as tributary gifts to powerful leaders are examples of how this manifested itself. The high cost of the materials used in the tea garden—such as the rare water basins and particular trees—even four hundred years ago when tea gardens were first being commonly built— demonstrates how the tea garden, too, can be understood as having been shaped by its association with wealthy individuals and the powerful elite of the day (fig. 46).

In the context of Zen as a vehicle of broader Chinese civilization—that of the Song, Yuan, and Ming dynasties—clearly we can see how *chanoyu* was influenced by Chinese culture. It began as an offshoot of

46. SPECIAL STONES. Kojima Residence, Kyōto. Rodrigues notes that practicing tea is an expensive proposition. Included in that is the cost of making the garden, and, within the garden, he considered the stones used to pave the path to be a major expense. Here, too, the large, round-shouldered *fumi-ishi* at the entry to the house, the *chōzubachi* made from a large natural stone (see also fig. 79), the particularly broad, *niwa-garan* in the middle, and the more weathered *garan-seki* in the foreground—all of these are expensive stones to use in a garden, now as then.

Chinese Zen temple ceremonial practice and, even in its later development, the interest in *kara-mono* (precious Chinese things) was central to the practice of *chanoyu*. With regard to the tea garden, however, the specific relation to things Chinese is not so clear. As we saw, there were no such narrow, path-like gardens used as settings for tea service in China that would have acted as a direct precedent to the Japanese *roji*. Although the design of the *roji* was intended to evoke the sense of a path to a hermitage, *shichū no sankyo*, and athough the role model for this was as likely to be a Chinese hermit as a Japanese one (if not more so), the imagery on which the design of the *roji* was actually based was drawn from the surrounding natural world, not from images of faraway China, as was the case with other types of gardens in earlier and later eras.[183] It would be safe to say that the tea garden, the *roji*, was not a direct reflection of Chinese culture.

In the context of Zen as a path to non-attachment and enlightenment through meditative practice, one can see how the particulars of the practice of *chanoyu*, and even the design of the *roji*, were intended to foster and nurture Zen Buddhist practice. The paucity of the design, the simplicity of the palette, the integrity of the materials used, the extreme cleanliness—all

these things parallel the characteristics of life in a Zen Buddhist temple. Undoubtedly there were tea masters who practiced *chanoyu* with the intent of fostering a Zen Buddhist mind-set and built their tea gardens in the same spirit; and, also undoubtedly, there were those tea masters who did not. The pertinent point is that if the central concerns of the early designers of the tea house and tea gardens, from Shukō's time right on down, had been exclusively the first two aspects of Muromachi-period Zen culture—its association with the power elite and its role as a vehicle of Chinese culture—the form and practice of *chanoyu* would not have evolved into anything like what it in fact turned out to be.

By the time of Rikyū's death, the experimental phases of tea garden design had been essentially concluded; the basic, overall form of the garden, and the elements contained within it, had been determined. Still, over the course of the following centuries, people continued to modulate and develop their gardens, and this happened in basically two ways. On the one hand the subtleties of the small, inward tea garden, the *roji*, were polished and codified, and, on the other hand, the *roji* was used as a template for the design of large-scale gardens on provincial and urban estates.

5
from *roji* to *chaniwa*: tea gardens in the edo period

茶庭

In 1591, Rikyū was forced to commit suicide. Tsuda Sōgyū died in the same year, and Imai Sōkyū in 1593. With their passing, three of the leading tea masters were gone, and the age in which wealthy merchants defined the form and practice of *chanoyu* had passed. By 1600, the consolidation of Japan under one military/political leader was complete; the military government situated itself in the great city of Edo (present-day Tōkyō), and a new period in Japanese history began.

During the long Edo period (1600–1868), the culture of *chanoyu*, including the tea garden, continued to develop and evolve. On the one hand, practitioners of *wabi-cha* would continue to build narrow, inward-focused *roji* as entries to their tea houses. They would polish and perfect the details of the tea garden, but the form that had been developed by many hands by the time of Rikyū's death would persist. In fact, the *roji* that we find at the residences of long-lineage tea masters (such as the Sen family in Kyōto) are remarkably like the descriptions found in the historical texts mentioned in the previous chapters. So on the one hand, in certain situations, the *roji* continued forward through time in much the same form as in medieval times.

On the other hand, over the course of the Edo period, and then on into the "modern" era that began in the late 19th century, the medieval *roji* served as an inspiration to garden designers who created new forms of gardens. These designers borrowed from the *roji* certain characteristic elements, such as stepping stones, water basins, and stone lanterns, and reused them in a new way.

To the degree that those new gardens were used as settings for tea gatherings they can be called tea gardens, but they typically did not have the inward-focused characteristic and forest-path-like design of their medieval predecessors. In this chapter we will look at how the tea garden was reshaped from the beginning of the 17th century until the present, and how it underlies the design of almost every Japanese garden known today.

The Word Roji

There are several ways to write *roji*, and each has its own interpretation and meaning. Understanding this is important, because the meaning of the word sheds light on the meaning of the gardens—on how they were perceived by the people who designed them and who chronicled their history. The oldest forms of rustic tea houses, as described in previous chapters, did not have an outdoor space or garden designed specifically to be the entry to the tea house other than the tiny, enclosed entry space called the *tsubo-no-uchi*. The path that led to the back of urban properties, however, whether there was a tea house there or not, was called a *roji*, which simply meant "alleyway." We find, for instance, an entry in *Inryōken Nichiroku* in 1485 that says, "tell them to sweep the *roji* and prepare sand for the garden," but the *roji* in this case appears only to be an entrance alleyway, not a tea garden *per se*.[184] Likewise, an entry in *Nisuiki* for 1505 records a visit to the residence of the *shōgun* Ashikaga Yoshizumi (1480–1511, reigned 1494–1508) stating, "29th day. Honorable visit paid to the *shōgun*'s residence. Inside, the participants were gathered as usual in the *roji*."[185] Neither of these references, it should be noted, was regarding a merchant's dwelling—the first was a Zen temple and the second a military-class residence.

The first mention of the word *roji* related specifically to *chanoyu* comes from the end of the 16th century. An entry for 1581 in *Sōkyū Hoka Kaiki* reads, "Morning, accompanied by Koretō, I visited the *roji* of Fukujūin. He had built a tea house with a pool of water into which he had released live fish: *ayu*, *koi*, and *funa*."[186] In all the cases just noted, *roji* was written with the following *kanji*, or Chinese characters: 路次. In the years following, other combinations of *kanji*, all with the original meaning of alleyway, and all pronounced *roji*, were used to refer to the tea garden, including, ろち、路地, 鹵路, and 盧路 (fig. 47). At the end of the 17th century, however, another character set began to be used to write *roji*: 露地. The first usage of this character set was in 1609 in *Nanpō Bunshū Kami*, written in Chinese-style couplets.

> As I look at the garden
> with its thousand wonderful transplanted pines
> and striking stones thickly covered
> with a brocade of verdant moss
> and a bed of wild grasses
> the thought arises of having left the secular world
> and its defilement.
> Although it is said that Zen tranquility is an
> undefiled place
> how can it be superior to this [garden]?
> Heaven and earth [contemplated] in tranquility
> the sun and moon [viewed] at leisure.
> Within the garden there is one *roji*
> watered and swept
> not one speck of dust rises
> no defilement enters.
> Before I can think, I find myself wandering be-
> yond the dusty world [i.e., away from the day to
> day world of human defilement].[187]

Although this new character set has the same pronunciation as the older ones, it translates as "dewy ground," not as "alleyway." This brings a distinctly Buddhist meaning to the garden, since the same usage is found in the Lotus Sutra, known as Saddharma Pundarika Sutra in the original Sanskrit and as Hoke-kyō in Japanese.[188] The Lotus Sutra presents one of the basic doctrines of Mahayana Buddhism—that all peo-

ple can reach enlightenment—unlike Theravada Buddhism, which sees enlightenment as being reserved for scholars and monks.

Within the Lotus Sutra is a passage known as the Parable of the Burning House, in which a wealthy man sees his children caught inside a burning house, but try as he may to get them to come out, they are lost in their games and will not listen to him. Eventually, he resorts to trickery and gets them to come out into the safety that lies outside beyond the gate by offering them gifts. The burning house, *kataku*, is an allegorical image for the Buddhist concept of an unenlightened state of mind also known as the Three

47. THE WORD *ROJI*. There are at least six different ways to write the word *roji*. The example in the bottom right-hand corner is the version used most commonly today with regard to tea gardens.

Worlds, *sangai*—Desire, Form, and Formlessness. The safe area that lies outside the house, at a wide-open crossroads, is an allegorical image for a state of spiritual enlightenment. In the Lotus Sutra this "wide-open crossroads" is expressed using the character set meaning "dewy ground," which leads to the reinterpretation of the "alleyway" *roji* as the "Buddhist" *roji*. This vision of the tea garden as a place of enlightenment, or as a path to enlightenment—even though it was part of the original intent of the garden and can be said to be a fundamental force guiding its design—only became clearly expressed in historical texts from the end of the 17th century onward.

Tea Gardens in the Early Edo Period

The Edo period (1600–1868) marks a time when all of Japan was controlled by a central military government, *bakufu*, in the city of Edo. In order to assert its control, the military government divided the nation into provinces called *han*—some matching pre-existing domains, some made new—and assigned governorship of each to a provincial lord, a *daimyō*. The society was also strictly divided into social classes that formalized preexisting class groupings. This system became known as *shi-nō-kō-shō* in which the military class (*shi*) was the highest ranking, followed by the farmers (*nō*), artisans (*kō*), and merchants (*shō*) at the bottom. In addition to, and separate from, this four-part ranking were several high-ranking classes such as the aristocrats and priests as well as low-ranking "untouchable" classes. The military class, which had held de facto political control of the country since the

late 12th century, now formalized the arrangement on a nationwide basis.

As we have seen, *chanoyu*, which began as a ritualized form of tea drinking among Zen Buddhist priests and a lavish form of entertainment among the early medieval military families, was re-created by the merchant tea masters during the 15th and 16th centuries. This new form was based on new aesthetics and new social patterns encouraging free and equal interaction between people as individuals rather than as class members while embracing the ancient philosophical ideal of the literate hermit. As the military class asserted its full control over society in the Edo period, they incorporated *chanoyu* as part of their own culture, moving away from the *wabi*-style tea of the merchants—Shukō, Jōō, Rikyū, and their associates and disciples—toward a grander style of tea that was, to them, more appropriate to the custom of the ruling class. Two tea masters who began that process of change, and in doing so represent their age, are Furuta Oribe (1543–1615) and Kobori Enshū (1579–1647).

Early 17th Century: Furuta Oribe and the Beginnings of Daimyō-cha

Among Rikyū's apprentices, the person with the most long-lasting impact on tea culture was Furuta Oribe (1543–1615). As with Shukō, Jōō, and Rikyū before him, Oribe can be understood for his personal contributions to the development of *chanoyu* and tea gardens and also as being representative of the era in which he was active. Oribe was born in Mino (present-day Gifu Prefecture) to Furuta Shigesada. His given name was Sasuke (also Shigenari), which often appears in tea records. The name Oribe was a nickname of sorts that he gained when he was awarded the position of Oribe-no-Kami in 1585.[189] He was a minor *daimyō* who served Nobunaga, Hideyoshi, and Ieyasu as a *dōbōshū* and was an apprentice of Rikyū, though only for about nine years. Oribe begins to show up in tea records just after the Yamazaki battle in 1582 and is recorded as the host of a tea gathering for the first time in *Tsuda Sōgyū Chanoyu Nikki* in 1585, the same year he received his position as Oribe-no-Kami.[190]

Oribe is noted as having been one of Rikyū's seven leading disciples, *Rikyū Shichitetsu*. According to *Kōshin Natsugaki*, the memoirs of the 4th-generation grand master of the Omote Senke tea family, the seven disciples were Gamō'u Ujisato, *daimyō*, son-in-law to Nobunaga who worked to reinstate Rikyū's name after his fall from grace and forced suicide; Takayama Ukon, who was known as a Christian *daimyō*; Hosokawa Sansai, *daimyō*, who, with his father Yūsai, was a supporter of Nobunaga; Shibayama Kenmotsu, a military commander under Nobunaga and then Hideyoshi; Seta Kamon, a military commander under Hideyoshi; Makimura Hyōbu, like Ukon, known as a Christian *daimyō*; and Furuta Oribe, who, as mentioned, was also a *daimyō*. Other lists of the famed seven disciples show Sansai, Ukon, and Kenmotsu as requisite members but include the following people as replacements for some just mentioned: Oda Uraku, *daimyō* and younger brother of Oda Nobunaga; Araki Murashige, a military commander; and Sen Dōan (1546–1607), Rikyū's son by his first wife.[191] A quick review of these lists of Rikyū's disciples makes clear the obvious: except for his own son, Dōan, all of Rikyū's disciples were military men—not a merchant among them. This is not to say that Rikyū did not associate with merchants (or nobles, poets, priests, and other literati) or act as their mentor in the study of *chanoyu*. It simply points out that the tradition of *chanoyu*, and its major support group within society, was shifting away from the merchants and to the military class. Merchants would continue to practice *chanoyu*, but the significant changes in *chanoyu* that happened over the decades (and centuries) following Rikyū's death occurred within the context of the military society that was actively supporting and developing the art. In this way, Oribe's time is considered to mark the beginnings of *daimyō-cha*, military lord's tea, which will come to full expression in the time of his disciple, Kobori Enshū.

Oribe was one of the seven leading disciples of Rikyū, but he was not considered to be the one whose style most reflected his master's. That was an honor given to Hosokawa Sansai. Sansai followed Rikyū's *wabi* aesthetic closely, but the patrons of *chanoyu* in the military class (and perhaps among the merchants as well) were seeking a less rigorous practice and were attracted to the boldness of Oribe's taste and the emphasis he placed on beauty over function. The most distinctive aspect of Oribe's style of *chanoyu*, and certainly what every tea practitioner today associates with his name, is his taste in ceramics. The tea bowls he selected or commissioned were irregularly shaped, as were the bowls of Rikyū's time, but they did not have the subtle simplicity of Rikyū's favored black and red *raku* bowls. Quite the contrary. Oribe's bowls were painted with strikingly bold designs that appear "modern" even today. These bowls were described as being "distorted," *hizumi*, more of which will be written later. Oribe's thoughts about the design of the tea garden, as well, differed from his teacher's. This was famously expressed in a passage in the record of tea master Katagiri Sekishū, *Sekishū Sanbyakukajō*.

> With regard to stepping stones, Rikyū is said to have determined that the function of walking weighted six parts of ten, and their attractiveness only four. Oribe, however, felt the opposite; the function merited only four parts of ten and the view six. In the first place, if the purpose of stepping stones is to walk on, then [the ease of] walking should be given primary consideration. However, setting the stones so they are all the same in a straight line is too stiff and one should incorporate some bends and twists. And yet, making things irregular on purpose where it is not called for is not good at all.[192]

There were other points on which they differed as well, for instance, the plantings used in the gardens. Whereas writings about Rikyū's *roji* mention primarily pine trees, under Oribe's direction the *roji* became a place to enjoy; there are some seventeen plants connected with his name, including unusual plants such as hemp palms (*shuro*) and cycads (*sotetsu*).[193] Cycads, also known as Sago palms, are palm-like trees that had been imported from islands further south and lent a distinctly exotic air to the garden—the very antithesis of the *shichū no sankyo*. Their use was not initiated by Oribe, but his use of them does reflect a general interest at that time in "southern barbarian" (*nanban*) imports fostered by the presence of foreign visitors and by Japanese merchants interested in developing external trade. A bold example of the use of cycads was captured by Sōtan on a visit to Hideyoshi's Fushimi Castle in 1597. He notes, "In between [the *kuguri*] and the tea house

(*sukiya*), there was a swinging gate (*hanekido*) made of a reed screen. Passing through that, there was a *roji* planted with nothing but cycads, and from there we went into the tea house" (fig. 48).[194]

An interesting comparison of the planting styles of Rikyū and Oribe can be seen in several historical tea treatises. The first is called *Chafu* (*Tea Notes*), the date of which is unknown but is most likely from the Kanbun era (1661–73). It states that in Rikyū's *roji*, "The plantings were given over to large pines, fir trees, and *mokkoku* (a broadleaf evergreen tree) planted deep and layered one against the next. Behind it all, a glimpse of a thatch-roofed hut and everywhere quiet, the sound of busy men seemingly far away."[195] Given the fact that *Chafu* was probably written in the mid-17th century, its information regarding Rikyū's plantings may be suspect, but the basic oral tradition that Rikyū enjoyed the feeling of a "deep evergreen forest" seems to coincide with what is known about Rikyū from contemporary records.

The second treatise is called *Furuta Oribe no Kamidono Kikigaki* (*Accounts of the Lord Furuta Oribe*). The date of this text is more reliable, the original scroll

48. PALM HILLOCK. Katsura Detached Palace, Kyōto. Just in front of the large *koshikake machiai* at the Katsura Detached Palace, Katsura Rikyū, is this hillock planted with cycads, also known as Sago palms, *sotetsu*. They are only marginally hardy in Kyōto and must be fully wrapped each winter with woven grass mats to protect them against the cold. Sago palms, having been imported from islands further south, were new and exotic to the people of Muromachi-period Japan and, as at Toyotomi Hideyoshi's Fushimi Castle, were planted in the gardens of powerful military lords to indicate their worldliness. Photograph by Ōhashi Haruzō.

having a recorded date of 1612, just three years before Oribe's death. One passage expresses a kind of planned openness to Oribe's design that differs from Rikyū's luxuriant dark woods.

> It was Rikyū's manner to plant many trees close together. Using large trees was also in his style, planted thickly. Ever since Kōshoku [Oribe], though, things have been modified. Any large trees should have their branches pruned within 2 to 3 *shaku* [60 or 90 centimeters] of the ground, or even as much as 1 *ken* [2 meters]. For all trees, they should not be planted too tightly together. Doing this is extremely good with regard to cleaning [the garden]. This [manner of planting] should be employed by all means. Careful attention should be placed when planting trees in both the outer and inner *roji*. Especially in *roji* that are long, trees should be planted in clumps so that they can be seen separately from each other. Planting trees in rows is altogether wrong.[196]

Another passage from *Furuta Oribe no Kamidono Kikigaki* reveals more about Oribe's taste in planting design, including his dislike of the use of plants that flower.

> In both the inner and outer *roji*, absolutely no trees [plants] that flower should be planted. Doing so would negate the meaning of displaying a flower in the tea room (*zashiki*). Likewise, in general one should not plant deciduous trees either. In both the inner and outer *roji*, exotic imported trees (*tōboku* or *karaki*) of any kind can be planted freely. These imported trees can be used even if they are deciduous or bear fruits. If

the flowers of a tree are used in the tea room, and then it bears fruit, even if the tree is an imported tree, it should not be planted [in the *roji*].[197]

The work also mentions that Oribe didn't like having bamboo planted in the *roji* partly because their slender leaves are difficult to sweep up when they fall.

> Regarding the planting of bamboo in the inner *roji*, large bamboo is one step above the rest. In olden days it was used [in gardens] but, ever since Oribe, it has been disliked and avoided because when the leaves fall they are so difficut to sweep up. Low grass-bamboo, however, is planted in the inner *roji*.[198]

Also about plantings, in *Furuta Oribe Densho* (*The Records of Furuta Oribe*), we find a casual assuredness about planting design: "About the arrangement of plantings, it's best to intermix them here and there. Regarding the different heights of plants, it may help to ask an expert but if it looks good, consider it well done. It doesn't really matter if you only studied a little bit."[199]

Regarding the use of stones in the *roji* (fig. 49), *Furuta Oribe Densho* relates that "The space between the edges of the [stepping] stones in the *roji* is the

49. PATTERN OF STEPPING STONES. Shūgakuin Detached Palace, Kyōto. The careful placement of stepping stones, *tobi-ishi*, makes patterns on the ground. The artistic development of those patterns is part of the art of the designer of a tea garden. Mixing stones that are small and large, rounded and squarish, as well as those that have subtle differences of color, is important to create a path that conveys variety and rhythm and that is attractive to the eye. Photograph by Ōhashi Haruzō.

same as the length of a folding fan, from its pivot to its tip."[200] About stones, *Furuta Oribe no Kamidono Kikigaki* states, "Regarding the setting of stones, this must be done skillfully and with great care. Two stepping stones of the same size [placed together] is bad—what is good is using some that are big and small or long and short [mixed together]. Having one long stone then one round one is even better. It's also good to intermix stones of various colors." Further on in the text is the comment: "There is nothing adverse about using natural stones and cut stones together. Cut stones should be set like this [a drawing of two long stones set parallel but staggered accompanies the text], however it's not bad to have, mixed [into the path], one stone like this [an accompanying drawing shows a single long, somewhat wide slab]."[201] Mixing large and small, round and straight, different colors and materials, Oribe was certainly creative in his design of stepping stone paths.

About *tatami-ishi*, the rectangular sections of paving made from various stones roughly in the shape of a *tatami* mat (fig. 50), we find the following in *Furuta Oribe no Kamidono Kikigaki*.

> Regarding the long stones along the edge of the *tatami-ishi*, they can be set either sideways or lengthways. Or, a natural stone that has some slight irregularities in the surface [can be used]. How that long stone should be positioned is not prescribed. Also, one or two large long stones can be used without setting small stones all around them to make a unified surface. A cut [granite] slab would work, as would a large, long, naturally shaped stone that has some small irregularities or just one wide stone. The stones used in a *tatami-ishi-dan* [same as a *tatami-ishi*] are large and

small, mixed randomly and pounded in. Round stones or square stones alike, whatever way they are arranged, whether black, white, or red, there's nothing wrong [with using them]. Arranging stones all in a line is not good. The spacing of stones should be irregular and gravel pounded into the space around the stones. The gravel should be pounded in so that it is flush with the top of the stones—making it lower than the top of the stones is bad."[202]

Although tea gardens nowadays are usually lush green and mossy, in Oribe's time they were still, at times, covered with a layer of small stones, pebbles, or sand as the following entries reveal: "In the outer *roji*, sand shall not be spread. One should spread small stones instead. [In fact,] spread the whole outer *roji* with ocean stones" and, in the same text, "In the inner *roji*, along the whole path, no sand shall be spread. One should pound gravel into the surface."[203]

One aspect of the tea gardens that began to change in Oribe's time was the degree to which the *roji* was considered to be an inward-focused, enclosed space. As provincial lords began to build their estates, they tended to design gardens that would offer sweeping views of the landscape. A question arose whether the *roji* that were built within the gardens should also include those views or be more insular, as was traditional. The following comments recorded in *Sōhokō Koshoku e Otazuneshō* reveal that Oribe was against the trend to open up the *roji* to outside views.

> Concerning seeing a mountain or some other view from the *roji*, is it best if it is seen only partially, between the branches of trees, or is having a distant view of mountains good? [To this ques-

tion Oribe] replied that just a glimpse of mountain ranges and other scenes outside the *roji* is most interesting and that seeing the whole landscape is not in keeping with a *roji*. As an example, he mentioned a starter verse [of a linked verse poem] composed by Sōchō at Mii-dera temple.

On a moonlit night
Only a glimpse of the ocean
Seen through the trees

Gotō Shōzō of Sunpu [present-day Shizuoka City] set up his *roji* to have a great view of Mount Fuji but I hear Oribe said, "Why don't you plant some trees and hide the view?" Not seeing too much of the mountains [outside the *roji*] is praised in both these cases. [204]

Oda Uraku (1547–1621), who was also one of Rikyū's seven disciples, offered a similar opinion. He is recorded in *Shodenshū (Collection of Correct Teachings)*, as having said, "About views from the *roji*, if they are too clear this is not at all a good thing. In that case they might want to be hidden by plantings." Uraku and Oribe were both critiquing designers who had created *roji* within larger gardens that they felt were too open and exposed, revealing simultaneously their dedication to the more insular mode developed up to the time of Rikyū and the trend existing at their time toward open gardens.[205]

Several texts give general images of what Oribe's *roji* was like. A visit to Oribe's Fushimi residence in 1596 by Ōkaya Dōga and Matsuya Hisayoshi was recorded in *Matsuya Kaiki*: "9th day, morning, 6th hour. The entry garden (*roji*) was large. There was a light in the stone lantern and warm water in the water basin. The tea room was a three-mat *daime* style, southern facing, thatch-roofed like a garden arbor. The name

plaque read, "Bōgakuan."[206] A record of the same visit as recorded in another text, *Chadō Shiso Densho*, mentions much the same thing but adds, "the *roji* was made of packed earth (*tataki*)."[207] *Chadō Shiso Densho* also records the following about Oribe's *roji*:

There was no wicket (*kuguri*) in the entry garden (*omote roji*) and so Oribe put a waiting bench (*koshikake*) there. After that, around 1603 or 1604, he made the double-layered entry garden (*nijū-*

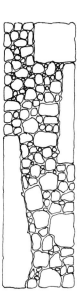

50. STONE PAVING. A group of paving stones set tightly together to form a rectangular section of paving is called a *tatami-ishi* because it resembles a *tatami* mat. This kind of paving is also referred to as *nobedan*. Some *tatami-ishi* are made entirely of small, flat-topped stones, but it is difficult to gather a large quantity of uniform stones and to set them properly, so these are not common. More often, the *tatami-ishi* are made of a mixture of small flat-topped stones and larger pieces of shaped granite.

roji). Oribe was the first to do this. When entering the *roji* for tea, no matter what the time is, for an impromptu tea with sweets, one washes one's hands and enters the tea room. If a meal will be served, one enters the tea room without washing one's hands. From about 1603 or 1604 onward, at tea gatherings in the morning, one would enter the tea room without washing one's hands. After that, at both mid-day and evening tea gatherings, hands would be washed before entering.[208]

In the diary of the priest Sōtan, *Sōtan Nikki*, we find that Oribe's water basin was "dug into the ground, used a large stone, and had the water ladle placed facing to the side."[209] The expression "dug into the ground" reveals that tea masters were beginning to experiment with the technique of setting the water basin in a shallow hollow, or pit, dug into the ground rather than simply setting it on top of flat ground. The hollow would be dug, the bottom flattened, boulders set around the edge to retain the soil, the water basin set in the middle on top of a pedestal stone, and small stones spread on the ground to cover the exposed soil. The hollow gives the water basin an increased sense of placement and also catches any water spilled from the basin. *Furuta Oribe no Kamidono Kikigaki* records more about the details of digging out the hollow for the water basin and also reveals that the arrangement, which originally included only the water basin and a large stepping stone on which to stand when using the water basin, was beginning to include other stones with specific purposes.[210]

Regarding the setting of stones for water basins. It is determined that the water basin shall be a stone—no other vessel should be used. Locate it

along a path. When there is a bend [in the path], or where you enter the wicket (*kuguri*), place it directly ahead or to the right or left of the path. The exact spot is not decided. To begin with, dig out a hole depending on the size of the water basin. The size of the hole is not prescribed. Do not dig the sides straight down. Make the bottom of the hole flat and set a pedestal stone there. For this, use a stone with a flat top. The bottom of the hole need not fit too precisely. The hole should not just fit the size of the pedestal stone, but rather dig the hole so that the shape of the bottom of the hole around the pedestal can be seen. Set the water basin on this pedestal stone. Setting a water basin without a pedestal stone is absolutely not done. The basin should be set in the center of the hole. Or, shift it slightly toward the back and let the front of the hole be a little wide. The amount of the stone that should show above the hole is not determined. Set it so it's just right. About the extra stones (*sute-ishi*), place these at the base of the water basin. Use one or three stones. If just one is used, place it in front of the water basin. If three are used, place one as just mentioned [i.e., in front], and the put the other two on the left as you face the water basin, just on its side. Besides the pedestal stone and these extra stones, one should absolutely never spread small stones about the ground in front of the water basin inside the hole. Nothing else besides the extra stones should be used.

It is good to use a large stone for the water basin. It has been said that small is good but these should not be used. Also, about using a damaged stone, as long as the water does not spill out there is no problem. Similarly, for stones with words carved on them; depending on the appearance there is no problem. Likewise, for basins covered with moss, they should never be washed. However, don't use one that is stained in an ugly way. Use one that is old. It is said that everything in the *roji* should be made to look ancient. Exotic things are disliked.[211]

Another section in the same text describes the stone on which a person stands while using the water basin that is called the *mae-ishi* or "front stone" and some accessory stones that eventually developed into the *tsukubai* arrangement that will be described later on. The stone that acts as a pedestal for the *yuoke*, warm-water bucket, would eventually become codified as the *yuoke-ishi*, warm-water bucket stone.

About setting the front stone of the water basin, make [the top surface of the stone] level and 1 *sun* 7 or 8 *bu* [5 to 5.5 centimeters] higher than the ground. The ground at the base of the stone should be flat too, so that the front surface of the stone shows in the hole. It should be larger than a stepping stone. Also, to the side of the front stone, put one stone that is larger than a stepping stone, also with its top surface level, 1 *sun* 5 *bu* [4.5 centimeters] above the ground. Two stones are not needed. When the weather is cold, place a bucket (*katakuchi*) filled with warm water on this stone to be used to rinse one's hands. Place a small stone so that when a lord or an aristocrat washes his hands, the attendant can stand on it to draw water for them. Place the stone to the side of the hole so that its front face does not show inside the hole itself.[212]

There is also a section in *Furuta Oribe no Kami-dono Kikigaki* that explains how the water basin should be filled with water and some details about the ladle that should be used.

Regarding the manner of putting water in the water basin. In winter, before the guests first enter the *roji*, put plenty of water in the basin. The guests will use this water during the midway break (*naka-dachi*). After this, fill the basin again. In summer, the guests will use the water as they first enter the *roji*. After that, fill up the basin with water for the guests to use at the midway break. When they are done, fill the basin once again. So, in summer, there are three times [when the basin is filled]. It is important to put on a lid that is slightly bigger than the water basin. When the guests first enter the *roji*, the lid should be off the basin. About the ladle, it is bent cedar (*sugi*). The bottom should be cut, and perhaps there are measurements for this. It should be known that, in general, there is no agreement as to the finish, but cypress (*hinoki*) is disliked. About the placement of the ladle when in the inner *roji*, wet it before placing it down, lying it across the basin with the mouth of the ladle resting on the edge of the far side to the left and the handle resting on the edge of the close side to the right. The handle can also be set straight on but, after a guest has used it, they should not place the handle back the same way it was before. By all means, put it a different way. In the summer, even if there are guests who might get thirsty, the amount of water used should be the same.[213]

An interesting development in tea garden design that is accredited to Oribe is the Oribe-style stone lantern, called an *Oribe-dōrō*. It is still a point of debate whether Oribe himself actually designed the first lantern of this type, or whether the naming was apocryphal. Stylistically, it can be said that this "modern" lantern would have suited Oribe's design sense but it is not in fact known if he actually designed the original. The Oribe lantern was designed specifically for use in a tea garden and has many characteristics that facilitate that use. All stone lanterns, previous to their use in tea gardens by Momoyama-period tea masters, were used exclusively in religious settings, primarily at Buddhist temples. More will be written about stone lanterns in the following chapter on garden elements. Suffice it to say here that the designer of the Oribe lantern did away with the specifically religious imagery carved into the stone lantern and also extraneous ornamental aspects, in order to create something that was aesthetically simple and functionally better suited to the tea garden (fig. 51).

Specifically, at the top of a typical Buddhist stone lantern, such as the Kasuga style, is a finial in the shape of a lotus bud (*hoshu*) set atop an abstracted round of lotus petals (*ukebana*). The lotus, of course, is a flower deeply associated with Buddhism. In the Oribe lantern, there is a ball-like finial, but the lotus flower imagery has been abstracted to the point of elimination. The rest of the lantern—roof (*kasa*), fire-box (*hibukuro*), fire-box base (*naka-dai*), post (*sao*), and pedestal (*kiso*)—have had most, if not all, ornamentation removed, for instance the decorative "fiddlehead" ribs (*warabite*) at the corners of a six-sided roof and the lotus petal designs in other locations. Some Oribe-style lanterns are said to have an image of Mary, mother of Jesus, carved into the lower portion of the post, which gives them the name *kirishitan-dōrō*, "Christian lanterns," revealing the interest in Christianity that oc-

curred during the Momoyama period. These images were typically hidden from view because of the military government's anti-Christian stance. Despite this, the Oribe lantern does not represent an overall "Christianizing" of the tea garden.

Another important change made in the Oribe lantern, in comparison to earlier forms, was the removal of the pedestal stone. With the lantern post set directly into the ground, the height of the lantern could be adjusted by burying the post to the desired depth. This is referred to as *iki-ume*, or being buried alive, and was especially important when the lantern was placed just behind a water basin because it was helpful there to have light coming from a low position. Although the Oribe-style lantern was likely not the first to do this (undoubtedly, at first, traditional Buddhist-style lanterns had their pedestal stones removed to allow them to be sunken), it was the first lantern to be *designed* without a pedestal stone at all.

Furuta Oribe no Kamidono Kikigaki states, "To have a pedestal stone beneath the upright post of a lantern is not good. It is best to bury the base of the post directly in the ground. This allows you to set it to exactly the right height. Setting it low feels good but the exact height is not decided. One should make [the lantern] such that it can be buried and then set it into the ground."[214] In the same work we also find the following about lanterns.

> In order to comfortably see the stone steps (*ishidan*), waiting bench (*koshikake*), and tea house entry (*nijiri-agari*), place the lantern with its opening facing the path, so it can be seen as one passes by. It can be set perfectly upright or slightly leaning. If the inner garden (*uchi-roji*) is long, use two lanterns. One should be able to light the

path. Set two, but put one just as mentioned and put the other in the shade of some trees. The light looks interesting there. It is not a bad thing to use two lanterns. They can be set one on each side or both together on the same side; right or left.[215]

Along with the changes in planting style, path design, and the (possible) development of a new style of lantern, the overall nature of the *roji* also began to change under Oribe's influence, as well as that of other contemporary tea masters including the military leader Toyotomi Hideyoshi. As expressed in the quote above from *Matsuya Kaiki*, the *roji* became larger. Part of this expansion outward was the development of a clearly divided, two-part tea garden. Whereas tea gardens up until Rikyū's time were contiguous, elongated along an entry path, a two-part tea garden is purposefully divided into an outer garden, *soto-roji*, and inner garden, *uchi-roji*. Early precedents of this design can be found in the *hanekido* and *kuguri* mentioned earlier, and the full development of the two-part garden would happen at the time of Oribe's disciple in tea, Kobori Enshū, but it is Oribe whom later texts credit with the development of a clearly separated inner and outer *roji*. As just mentioned, *Chadō Shiso Densho* records that this happened around 1603 or 1604. *Genryū Chawa* relates that Rikyū used only a very simple gate, called a *sarudo*, in his *roji* and that Oribe began the practice of using a *naka-kuguri* or middle wicket, and, following him, Enshū used a *chūmon* or middle gate.[216]

A few comments in historical records point to how the use of the *roji* shifted during Oribe's time. One such event was recorded in *Imai Sōkyū Chanoyusho* (*Records of Imai Sōkyū's Tea*), in 1603, which relates that at a certain tea gathering the priest Kuwayama Hōshi and

51. ORIBE-STYLE STONE LANTERN. This style of lantern is named after the famous tea master Furuta Oribe (1543–1615). Of note is that it is carved without the traditional ornamentation, is four-sided, and has no pedestal stone, which allows it to be buried to whatever height the garden designer wishes. In fact, there is no direct evidence that Oribe owned or designed a lantern like this. The expression *Oribe-dōrō* appears in texts well after his lifetime. The small carving on the post is not clear but is often considered to be a Christian image—either Christ or the Virgin Mary.

early 17th century

military lord Takenaka Izu no Kami came in through the *roji* while Sōkyū came in through the thatch-roofed gate, *kaya-mon*. The priest and the military lord were both men of high social standing, while Sōkyū was a merchant tea master and perhaps comrade of Oribe's. So there seems to have been two modes of entry, the use of which depended on one's social status. In 1606, the same *Records* notes that there was a service of food, *kaiseki*, in the parlor, and that a number of guests then entered the tea room through the *roji*. The text uses words such as *omote shoin* (formal parlor), *omote no ma* (front room), and *omote roji* (formal tea garden). The appearance of the word *omote*—which can mean a "forward section" but is often used to refer to something "formal or proper"—implies that the tea gatherings, and the *roji*, were developing to accommodate social activities that were increasingly formal and perhaps somewhat socially stratified.[217] Another word of interest that begins to be used in Oribe's time is *kusari-no-ma*, literally, "connector-room," a room that was positioned between the formal *shoin* parlor and the rustic *sōan* tea room. The development of the *kusari-no-ma* neatly symbolizes the bridging of formal and rustic styles that took place during Oribe's time.

What we can sense in this is that the nature of the tea gathering was being changed to accommodate the needs of the military class. With the establishment of a permanent military government under a single, powerful leader, the members of that class were turning increasingly to social activities that required formal settings. This was the beginning of what become known, in later eras, as *daimyō-cha* or military lord's tea, a form of tea that maintained some of the characteristics of rustic tea, *chanoyu*, but was tailored to suit the aesthetics and social requirements of the established, ruling military class.

To summarize the changes that took place during Oribe's time, as *chanoyu* began to develop into *daimyō-cha*, we find the following:

- A shift away from allowing function to determine form toward a mode of tea service in which artistic sense prevailed.

- Use of a more varied palette of plant materials that followed the rule of avoiding showy, flowering plants but included more deciduous material.

- An artistic sensitivity regarding the use of paving stones in the pathways of the *roji*.

- A water-basin arrangement that comprises more than just the basin stone itself, including other stones that have different and specific functions.

- A new form of stone lantern, specifically designed for the tea garden, that has no base stone, permitting the height to be adjusted by burying more or less of the post into the ground.

- The increased overall size of the *roji*.

- A certain degree of openness to the *roji* and connectedness with the surrounding landscape, created by allowing partial views through the plantings.

- The early development of the two-part *roji*.

- A shift toward a *roji* design that suited the needs

of the formal military-class society that was becoming institutionalized at that time.

Mid-17th Century: Kobori Enshū and the Development of Daimyō-cha

Kobori Enshū (1579–1647) was born in Ōmi province (present-day Shiga Prefecture), the eldest son of a local *daimyō*. Eventually, he became Lord of Tōtōmi province from which position his name derives, the first "Tō" of Tōtōmi being the same character as the "En" of Enshū.[218] Like Oribe, Enshū served the leading military men of his time as an advisor. In Enshū's case his work concerned matters of architecture and gardens as well as tea. He held high-ranking bureaucratic positions such as Magistrate of Fushimi (Fushimi Bugyō; Fushimi was an important district south of Kyōto) and Minister of Construction (Sakuji Bugyō). In his role as Minister of Construction, Enshū oversaw the construction of castles, residences, and gardens for the *shōgun*. Considering the time constraints of his position, including the need for him to travel back and forth between Edo and Kyōto, there is little doubt that he would have been too busy to have worked out the subtle design details for all of the many gardens attributed to him, if any at all.

Enshū's influence on tea, and tea gardens, can best be seen in light of his role within the Tokugawa government. Unlike Rikyū and Oribe, who served the self-made military men Nobunaga and Hideyoshi in a rapidly changing society, Enshū was connected to the early dynastic system of the Tokugawa family, for whom a link to ancient traditions and the development of courtly rituals was of great importance. As a result, Enshu's style of *chanoyu* is noted for its introduction of the mannerisms of the ancient imperial court and for the expansiveness of its setting. His aesthetic taste was historically referred to as *Enshū-gonomi* (Enshū taste) although it is now often referred to by the term *kirei-sabi*, or "beautiful rusticity." *Kirei-sabi*, however, is a rather recent expression, most likely emerging in the postwar era.

Another way to call this newly developing form of tea is *daimyō-cha*, "military lord's tea." The expression *daimyō-cha* is relatively recent in origin, but the description of a specific tea for *daimyō* dates from at least 1612, when it appears in a tea text called *Senrin*, which relates, "In *chanoyu*, there is either the extremely formal type (*gokushin*) or the interplay between formal (*shin*) and informal (*sō*). With the tea for military lords (*daimyō* and *gokamon*),[219] a sense of welcoming and entertainment [is important] and it is appropriate to use such things as fine wooden utensils, gold and silver wrapping paper, and a pedestaled tray."[220] The aesthetic of *daimyō-cha*, or *kirei-sabi*, was based on the older aesthetic of rusticity, *wabi*, which was first developed by the merchants in the Lower Capital, but it was modified by tea masters at the time of Enshū to make it more suitable for the members of the upper-class military society who embraced tea practice through the Tokugawa era.

Perhaps the best way to grasp the shift in the aesthetic sense that took place from the time of Rikyū to the time of Oribe and Enshū is to look at the kind of pottery they selected, or had specially made, for their tea gatherings. The classic Rikyū-taste, *Rikyū-gonomi*, tea bowl is a simple black or red Raku bowl such as the bowl named *Shunkan* (taken after the name of a

Buddhist priest). The shape of this bowl is somewhat irregular and contains slight imperfections, but it is not overtly irregular or rough in its shape. The coloring is subdued and reasonably uniform over the entire surface of the bowl. It is not decorated in any way. All aspects of the bowl—the softly rounded shape, the slight depression at the bottom of the bowl, the specific thickness of the walls of the bowl, the inward curve of the lip, the smooth texture of the surface—were designed to allow the bowl to sit comfortably in the user's hands and to facilitate the drinking of whisked tea. The aesthetic of the bowl flows directly from its function (fig. 52).

Oribe's choice of tea bowls shifts dramatically to those that are markedly "artistic," in other words bowls that clearly show the potter's hand and the designer's desire for decoration. One such bowl is called *Sekiyō* (*Night and Day*). It has an irregular shape, the manner in which the foot of the bowl has been shaped by roughly cutting away at it is purposefully revealed, and the surface is glazed with bold swaths of dark-brown and white glazes. It is clear in looking at this and other bowls chosen by Oribe that he had a distinct, overt aesthetic. A tea gathering given by Oribe at his Fushimi residence was recorded in *Sōtan Nikki*. In the morning of the 8th day of the 2nd month in 1599, Oribe had three guests over for tea, Sōtan among them. He recorded that during the service of thin tea, *usu-cha*, a Seto-style bowl was used that was "distorted and humorous," described with the words *hizumi* and *hyōge-mono*.[221] *Sōjinboku*, a tea record of a slightly later date, also used the expression *hizumi*, stating that Oribe "favors the contemporary ceramics in the distorted fashion that come every year from Seto."[222]

Looking now at Enshū's taste in pottery, we find

that his aesthetic combines a formality and precision that was usually associated with aristocratic court taste rather than with the rusticity of *chanoyu*. The tea bowl called *Takatori Men* reflects this taste. Its overall shape is rather perfect—when compared to the bowls of Rikyū or especially Oribe—and the walls are generally thinner, reflecting the refined clay that the bowl was made from. The foot of the bowl, which is always unglazed and thus reveals the clay body used, makes this clear. In fact, the foot of the bowl is considered to reveal its "heart" and is therefore carefully studied by all those attending a tea gathering after the tea has been partaken of. The perfection of the finishing of the foot stands in contrast to the purposefully unformed quality of Rikyū's bowls or the rough, cut-away nature of Oribe's. The glaze of the bowl is neither somber, like Rikyū's, nor highly decorated like Oribe's. It is subdued, yet elegant, a warm caramel-like color. Although these three tea bowls are obviously stereotypical, and do not represent the entire range of the tea utensils used by these three tea masters or their contemporaries, they do give a general sense of the aesthetic changes that happened over the course of the first half of the 17th century.[223]

As mentioned above, Oribe's taste in tea wares was called *hizumi*, "distorted." This reflects a tendency at the time toward things that were offbeat. Even as the military government, *bakufu*, was consolidating control over the country and beginning to control the cultural trends within their circles, the populace was embracing the odd and unusual. This movement is summed up best by the word *kabuki*, and a brief digression about that subject is in order here because it sheds light on the changes that occurred over the decades in question, in other words, the first fifty years of so of the 17th century.

Kabuki, of course, now refers to a form of theater, but the original meanings of the noun *kabuki*, and the verb *kabuku*, included "to lean or tilt off-balance," "to have a strange personal appearance," and "to act in an uninhibited and free-spirited manner." In the first years of the 17th century, as the Tokugawa military government was establishing itself in Edo, people around the country, especially in Kyōto, were going a bit wild. Perhaps it was a *fin de siècle* reaction to the ending of nationwide warfare and the attitudes that instilled that violence; perhaps it was the opposite, a reaction against the budding establishment. In any case, in 1603, a young woman named Okuni (some records say she was a shrine priestess) gathered together a troupe of women and began performing wild dances and erotic theater at shrines and along the banks of the Kamo River in Kyōto. This would become known as *onna-kabuki* (women's *kabuki*), but its relationship with prostitution caused the military government to crack down, and in 1629 they disallowed the participation of women in these performances in favor of young boys. The resulting cases of homosexual prostitution caused the government to exclude young boys in 1652, since which time *kabuki* has been performed primarily by adult men. The sudden creative burst seen in early *kabuki* in the very first years of the 17th century and its subsequent submission into a more controlled form through the following decades parallel neatly the changes in *chanoyu* that took place at roughly the same time, in particular, Oribe's flamboyant artistry followed by Enshū's conservative traditionalism.

The *daimyō-cha* tea gardens that Enshū devel-

52. THREE GENERATIONS OF TEA BOWLS. To grasp the aesthetic differences between the three tea masters—Rikyū, Oribe, and Enshū—it helps to look at the tea bowls they favored. Of course these are not the only tea bowls they used, but they do capture a certain general taste of each master. *Left:* Rikyū's ideal of a severely restricted tea gathering, creating ever smaller and more sparse tea rooms, while also stressing the humanity of the tea gathering, seems aptly expressed by the black Raku-style tea bowl called *Shunkan* that is utterly reserved and yet not cold, sitting so nicely in the hand. *Center:* Oribe's penchant for the "distorted and humorous"—*hizumi* and *hyōge-mono*—can be sensed in this irregularly shaped and loosely glazed *goshomaru* bowl known as *Sekiyō*. Korean in origin, the generic name *goshomaru* refers to the official ships that sailed between Japan and the Korean kingdoms. *Right:* Enshū's taste, now referred to as *kirei-sabi*, or "beautiful rusticity," is embodied by *Takatori Men*, a simple, light-colored bowl—slimmer than Rikyū's and more conservative than Oribe's. *Left, right:* Mitsui Memorial Museum. *Center:* Fujita Museum of Art.

oped, which reflected military-class tastes, were broader and more open than the narrow *roji* of the urban merchants; the atmosphere of the *roji* suggesting a passage to a hermit's place of reclusion seems to have been dropped entirely in favor of an expression of reserved grandeur. That the *roji* was being reinvented and turned into a pleasure garden is reflected in this passage from *Shōbai Goen*:

> While traveling together [perhaps with Kagahan no Maeda] to the Capital, we stopped in Ōtsu for a tea gathering (*chanoyu*) at the estate of Lord Chūnagon. He ordered the preparation of an artificial mountain (*tsukiyama*) and pond (*sensui*) for the arrival of guests a few days later. Kobori Enshū came to look around the Ōtsu [estate]. Lord Chūnagon was away at the time but Enshū surveyed the garden and thought it was a little small for the taste (*suki*) of a military lord (*daimyō*). Keian Ishiguro Uneme heard Enshū ask, "Why don't you allow that large mountain and lake to be seen?" Learning of this upon his return, Chūnagon laughed. He immediately had the artificial mountain and pond destroyed. He went out abruptly and [even though] it was in the process of being repaired, he had a section of the wall just in front of the sitting room (*shoin*) taken down and a lattice window put in the small [tea] room so that the Lake [Biwa], Mt. Eizan (Hieizan), Karasaki (peninsula), and Mt. Mikamiyama could all be seen in one view. [Having done this] the first thing he did was to request Enshū to visit. Looking [at the result], Enshū clapped his hands and praised the work, "Now this is a tea garden (*roji*) for a military lord. That's a proper pond. That's a proper mountain."

Afterward, [Chūnagon] thought that Enshū was a cut above the rest.[224]

Another aspect of Enshū's garden design that is reflective of garden design during his time is his use of recycled materials, specifically old pieces of carved granite—parts of old lanterns, bridges, and so on. Although there were a few examples of this techinique from earlier periods—such as the ancient stone, pagoda base, and roof tiles discussed previously in the section on Sen Rikyū—the use of old recycled materials became much more prevalent from Enshū's time onward. A passage from *Chōandōki* describes Oribe's use of old stone pieces.

> In the past, one entered a four-and-a-half-mat tea room from the veranda. For a six mat, or four mat room, a water basin was placed in the earth-floored space beneath the roof. It may have been a split-stone carved as a boat, or it could have been carved out of wood, or a wooden bucket could have been set there. At the time of Oribe, there was a stone basin so large it would take fifty to a hundred men to lift it. The long basin with the *giboshi* [a lotus-bud finial] came from Nanbu Hashimoto-chō. I requested it of Chūbō Minamoto Go and then, later, Enshū cut it down to 2 *shaku* 8 *sun* [85 centimeters] and put it in his *roji* at Roku-jizō [in Fushimi, southern part of Kyōto]. After that, he gave it to the Honorable Daitokuin [*shōgun* Tokugawa Hidetada] and it was sent to Edo. Another time, I had possession of the post from a stone lantern with an image of the Buddha carved into it. It had been used as a bollard at the Tenjin Shrine in Kamihate-chō [Nara] but Enshū accepted it and [after using it

at his estate] gave it to the Honorable Daitokuin. From this time on, Buddhist images [on garden ornaments] became quite the fashion.[225]

Enshū was most likely not using the Buddhist imagery in any seriously religious manner—rather it was a stylish affectation that looked nice in the garden. Another case of Enshū using old materials is the stone lantern at Kohōan, a subtemple in the large Zen Buddhist temple Daitokuji. This lantern is not simply an old lantern that was reused; rather all the various carved stone pieces that went into making it were collected from different antique objects—the firebox from an old lantern, the post from an old stupa, etc.—and then put together to make a "new" lantern. This technique is called *yose-dōrō* or a "pieced-together lantern" (fig. 53).

There are many gardens attributed to Enshū, most of which he could have had little if anything to do with. A few that are very likely to express his direct influence are the gardens at Nijōjō Ni-no-maru, Konchi'in, Kohōan, and the Sentō Gosho. Nijōjō Ni-no-maru, the palace area of Nijō Castle, and Konchi'in, a subtemple of the large Buddhist temple Nanzenji, are not tea gardens. The gardens at Nijō Castle center on a pond with dramatic, masculine rockwork and Konchi'in features a dry landscape garden, *karesansui*. The gardens at the subtemple Kohōan include parts that are typical of any Zen temple, such as the open courtyard spread with sand to the south side of the main hall. But there is also a section that is clearly designed as a *roji*, with stepping stone paths, water basins, lanterns, and even a decorative privy. The plantings used in the *roji*, too, are primarily evergreens, which follows the traditional tastes of tea. What is of note at Kohōan, and is often captured in photographs of the garden, are the distinc-

tively modern water basins and their simple, austere placement in the garden.

The Sentō Gosho was built as a retirement villa for Emperor Gomizunoo (r. 1611–1629) and the Empress Dowager, Tōfukumon'in. The property was originally split into northern and southern sections, the north for the empress (her section was called the Join Gosho or Ōmiya Gosho) and the south for the emperor. Most of the buildings that existed at that time have been taken down, but there is at least one tea house remaining at the southern extremity of the garden, Seikatei, and two others were known to have existed, Shiba Ochaya and Kotobukiyama Ochaya.[226] Both north and south have ponds as central features with paths leading through the woods around them. The restrained rockwork that can be found on certain sections of the shoreline and the overall elegantly simple design are indicative of Enshū's taste.

One of the most striking features, however—a long, curved shoreline covered with smooth, black stones—was created around 1815 and is not part of Enshū's influence. Still, the importance of Sentō Gosho lies in how it represents the evolution of the narrow, inward-focused *roji* into a much larger, grander, more open form of garden that included elements of the *roji* but was not used exclusively for tea gatherings. Instead, it was designed to allow people to stroll around a central pond on a meandering path and enjoy various landscape scenes that were woven into the garden along the way. This new type of design developed into what are now called, in modern terminology, *kaiyūshiki teien*, or stroll gardens.

The very form of tea garden that existed during Rikyū's day, which contained no more than a few of the basic elements we now associate with tea gardens—a water basin, a lantern—was enlarged and made more

53. STONE LANTERN. Kohōan, Kyōto. If you look carefully, you will see that the various parts of this lantern are slightly mismatched. The roof is round but the mid-shelf is square; the mid-shelf and finial are deeply pitted and aged, while the post and roof are smooth. This is an example of a *yose-dōrō*, a lantern pieced together from odd parts of old lanterns. Photograph by Ōhashi Haruzō.

complex during the years when Oribe was active. In Enshū's time, many of the aspects of *chanoyu* as they existed during the late 16th century, such as the spatial reduction of the tiny tea rooms, the extreme rusticity of the service of tea, and the narrow, forest-like garden paths that led to the simple tea house, were redesigned to become lighter and brighter, with larger doors and windows that could be opened to allow views. Unlike the self-enclosed medieval *sōan* tea houses, these tea rooms were designed in the formal *shoin* style, with white walls and square-planed posts and beams, harking back to the way tea was served when the Ashikaga family was in power.

To summarize, the changes that occurred in the practice of tea with the development of *daimyō-cha* included:

+ The aesthetic shift from *wabi* to what is now known as *kirei-sabi*.

+ The enlargement of the spaces for tea, in both the tea room and garden.

+ The "formalization" of the tea spaces and service, reverting back to the *shoin*-style room and *daisu*-style tea service.

+ A forwarding of aspects that were considered "traditional" or "aristocratic."

+ A tendency to incorporate elements that show respect for authority.

+ The use of elements of the inward-focused *roji* in the design of large, open stroll gardens.

Late Edo Period: The Codification of Tea Gardens

The practice of *chanoyu* did not completely change over to the *daimyō-cha* style during the Edo period. *Chanoyu* continued to be practiced and developed by some tea masters, and still is practiced to this day. The various styles or schools of *chanoyu*, called *ryū* (literally, "currents"), began to strengthen their own traditions by developing a very clear lineage, dating back to a particular "founder" and continuing through the mechanism of the grand master system, *iemoto-seido*. The grand master is in part archivist (maintaining the large body of knowledge related to the customs and devices of his particular school of tea), in part teacher (passing that knowledge on to other tea masters within his school), and in part artist (adding some modicum of new character to his practice of *chanoyu*). Similar grand master systems developed within many other arts, both cultural and martial. By the late Edo period these arts had become the now-famous "Ways": the Way of the Flower (*kadō*), the Way of Archery (*kyūdō*), and of course, the Way of Tea (*chadō* or *sadō*). An early precedent for this terminology with regard to tea can be seen in a short letter attributed to Enshū known as *Kobori Enshū Kakisute no Fumi* (*A Simple Note from Kobori Enshū*), which begins with the admonition, "As for the Way of Tea, there is no other."[227] In this case, the expression used was *chanoyu no michi* but, eventually, the words *cha* and *michi*, which is also pronounced *dō*, became linked as *chadō*.

The development of the tea garden over the course of the Edo period can be tracked in two ways. First, there were tea gardens that continued to be used as entry spaces to tea houses (*wabi-cha*, *daimyō-cha*, or any other variant) but were developed over the course of time to be more detailed and complex in their design. Second, tea gardens were used as a template or model for the design of other types of gardens that contained elements of tea gardens (such as stone lanterns, stepping stones, or water basins) but were not used exclusively as entry gardens to tea houses. Examples of the latter, such as the stroll gardens of the *daimyō* and the inner courtyard gardens of urban merchants, will be looked at in the next chapter, which introduces extant gardens. Regarding the first type, tea gardens that continued to be used exclusively for *chanoyu*, what we notice immediately in a significant number of the written records of the mid-Edo period is the sheer quantity of comments about tea gardens. Naturally, comments on tea gardens still make up only a fraction of the texts—most comments still concern tea utensils, tea architecture, artwork for the *tokonoma*, and food service—but the degree to which tea gardens are described is infinitely more detailed and well composed than that found in tea records from the late 16th century. Tea gardens, which used to only be mentioned in small, passing glimpses, now have entire chapters devoted to them and, in some cases, are the very first thing to be mentioned in a text. In the minds of tea masters, and other recorders of tea culture during this period, the tea garden begins to take on a significance not seen before.

We will now look at how the Edo-period writings on tea describe four aspects of tea gardens: first, the overall design of the garden; second, various elements of the garden that developed during this time, things that are now considered requisite parts of a tea garden, such as certain named stones with specific, assigned functions; third, some of the customs of use that developed in the Edo period, many of which had earlier precedents but became more developed and codified,

such as the lighting of oil lamps in the stone lanterns and the sprinkling of water on the garden; and, finally, how the philosophic ideals related to the tea garden, such as the relationship of tea gardens to Zen Buddhism, became clearly vocalized over this period of time.

OVERALL DESIGN

The *roji* began as a simple path in the 16th century. As it was developed, however, it was broken into sections separated by symbolic gates. Some gardens remained "single-layered," *ichijū-roji*, meaning they had no middle gate. Most were designed to be double-layered, *nijū-roji*, having an outer part, *soto-roji*, and an inner part, *uchi-roji*.[228] A rare few had three parts: outer, inner, and a middle section (*naka-roji*). These were called "three-layered," *sanjū-roji*. These terms were first recorded around the 1660s. In *Koshokuden* we find, "In the inner *roji*, be even one level more careful, about cobwebs in windows, dust, sprinkling water, and such. The same goes for the middle *roji* but it is not a problem if it is a little unkempt. And, for the [outer] *roji*, if things are out of sorts, it is not a big problem."[229] Cobwebs should be cleaned up, but birds' nests were acceptable, it seems. An entry in *Furuta Oribe no Kamidono Kikigaki* states that "A bird's nest found naturally in a tree in the inner or outer *roji* need not be taken away but can be left just as it is."[230] This sense of naturalism in the *roji* is also reflected in an entry from *Chanoyu Rokusōshō Denki* (1702): "In the plantings around the tea house (*sukiya*), dandelions (*tanpopo no ki*) have been planted. This is a flowering plant. [Oribe] plants these even though flowering plants are disliked in gardens surrounding a tea house. He places wild doves in the [*roji*] plantings and makes them to sing."[231]

Furuta Oribe no Kamidono Kikigaki (1666) mentions the *sanjū-roji* many times, addressing waiting benches, garden privies, water basins, stone lanterns, and so on. A typical passage is: "In a three-layer *roji* there are water basins as well, placed in the same way as in the outer *roji*. However, there is not so much to understand as with the one in the outer *roji*."[232] In the outer portion of a three-layered *roji* would be the outer gate (*roji-mon*), preparation room (*yori-tsuki*), and functional privy (*kafuku setchin*). Passing the middle gate (*chūmon*) into the middle *roji* one would find a waiting bench (*koshikake machiai*) and an ornamental privy (*suna setchin*). The inner *roji* would be entered through a simple gate (*sarudo*) and that is where the water basin (*tsukubai*) could be found.[233]

GARDEN ELEMENTS: STONES AND BASINS

Some of the most familiar elements of the tea garden—stepping stones, stone lanterns, water basins, and such—had already made their appearance by the end of the 16th century or in the first decades of the 17th century. Over the course of the Edo period, however, especially in the gardens of the *daimyō*, these elements tended to become larger and more ornate. At times their original purpose was forgotten as the importance of appearance and style came to take preference over function, as this quote from *Kaiki* (1724–35) illuminates with regard to stone lanterns.

> In today's world, the way stone lanterns are used has become questionable. Enormously large lanterns are placed, just to show off, not for the way they give light. A lantern that is not used to give light is of absolutely no use at all. But there is a reason for this. Having light anywhere and every-

where won't do either. First, place a lantern so it can be seen as one enters the *roji*. When you approach the lantern, then you see another further down the way. All should be decided depending on the size of the *roji*.[234]

Many of the subtle details of the garden, such as the use of specific stones, were developed at this time. Ornamental boulders of unusual shape or color, and stones that are used to evoke a landscape scene, were not used in the *roji* the way they were in other private gardens or in the dry landscape gardens (*karesansui*) found in Zen temples. There were, however, many stones with specific functions, known as *yaku-ishi* (literally, "stones with functions"), that were used in the *roji*. The term *yaku-ishi* was first used in *Genryū Chawa*, a text from the very end of the 17th century, which mentions *yaku-ishi* and *yaku-ju*, or "plants with functions." The term *yaku-ishi* is still commonly used by gardeners these days, but *yaku-ju* has been supplanted by the term *yaku-boku*, which has the identical meaning. *Yaku-ishi* are still an important part of garden design, not just for tea gardens but for Japanese gardens in general. *Yaku-boku*, however, though used, do not play as big a role. More about *yaku-ju* (*yaku-boku*) will be written below in the section on plants.

Most of the *yaku-ishi* mentioned in mid-Edo-period texts are variants of stepping stones or other paving stones used in pathways of the *roji*. *Sekishū Sanbyakukajō* (*Sekishū's 300 Comments*, 1665) mentions a number of such stones. There is a passage, for instance, that describes three flat-topped stepping stones that lie just in front of the small entry door to the tea house, which is called the *kuguri* in this text in the old-fashioned manner. These three, set in a row, act as steps up into the small door that is raised off the ground.

The stone closest to the door, almost against the wall of the tea house, is the *fumi-ishi*, literally, "stepping stone," which has been mentioned before under the name *nijiri-agari-ishi*. It should be set 36 centimeters lower than the floor of the tea house at the entry door and 12 centimeters above the ground. The second is the *otoshi-ishi*, literally, "descending stone," and is supposed to be set 4.5 centimeters lower than the *fumi-ishi*. The third is the *nori-ishi*, literally "mounting stone," and its height is not specified.[235] These measurements are not universally set and would, in fact, depend on the particular situation of each tea house.

Another set of *yaku-ishi* mentioned in *Sekishū*

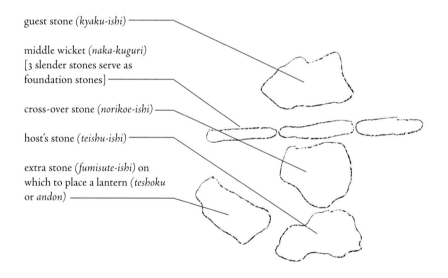

guest stone (*kyaku-ishi*) ——————

middle wicket (*naka-kuguri*) [3 slender stones serve as foundation stones] ——————

cross-over stone (*norikoe-ishi*) ——————

host's stone (*teishu-ishi*) ——————

extra stone (*fumisute-ishi*) on which to place a lantern (*teshoku* or *andon*) ——————

54. STONES FOR THE MIDDLE WICKET. Midway through a tea garden, in a few rare cases, the inner and outer garden are separated by a section of wall with a small, crawl-through door. This is called a *naka-kuguri*, middle wicket. The stepping stones used on either side were given specific names and functions. Redrawn from Sen, *Chadō Koten Zenshū*, vol. II, p. 246.

Sanbyakukajō are those related to the *naka-kuguri*, the middle wicket that separates the inner and outer *roji*. The *naka-kuguri* resembles a free-standing section of clay-plaster wall with a small door, like a *nijiri-guchi*, built into it. A guest approaches the *naka-kuguri* on a stepping stone path, steps up and through the small door, and down onto stones on the other side. The text, as well as a drawing, in *Sekishū Sanbyakukajō* describes the stones used on either side of the *naka-kuguri* (fig. 54). The stone just on the outer side of the *naka-kuguri* is called the *kyaku-ishi*, guest stone. The one just on the inside of the *naka-kuguri* is called the *norikoe-ishi*, cross-over stone. The next one beyond that is the *teishu-ishi*, host's stone. Just to the side of the *norikoe-ishi* and *teishu-ishi* is a stone called the *fumisute-ishi*, literally, "step and throw-away stone." Unlike a *sute-ishi*, which is a small stone placed along the side of a stepping stone path to break up the visual pattern of the stepping stones, this *fumisute-ishi* is specifically noted on the drawing as being a pedestal for a hand-held candle, *teshoku*, or lantern, *andon*. The name of the stone, however, and its alternate name, *fumichigae-ishi*, implies that it is a "waiting stone" placed to allow someone to step aside and wait. The text goes on to state that the *kyaku-ishi* and *norikoe-ishi* should be set higher than stones normally are. The *kyaku-ishi* may be set with a little space around it, around 14 centimeters (from the *naka-kuguri*) but the *norikoe-ishi* should be closer, about 9 centimeters. If the *kyaku-ishi* is granite then the *norikoe-ishi* should be some other, miscellaneous kind of stone. Likewise, if the outer stone is squarish, then the inner stone should be rounded.

Another specialized stepping stone appears in *Teiyōshū* (1710) called the *gakumi-ishi*, the tablet-viewing stone.[236] Tea houses were given poetic names by the owner, or by an honored guest, and that name was carved into a wooden tablet that was displayed outside the tea house. The *gakumi-ishi* was a fairly large, flat-topped stepping stone, placed somewhere along the entry path, that was positioned to allow an initial view of the tablet.

Two other stones that are also considered to be *yaku-ishi* and also first appear in *Teiyōshū* are the *yuoke-ishi* and the *teshoku-ishi*—the warm-water bucket stone and the candle-holder stone. In the last section we saw that at the time of Oribe certain accessory stones were beginning to be placed near the water basin, such as the stone recorded in *Furuta Oribe no Kamidono Kikigaki* that was used as a pedestal for a warm-water bucket. Now, some decades later in the Edo period, we see that the use of these accessory stones has been formalized and they have been given proper names. What was called simply a stone in the above example, for instance, now has the specific name *yuoke-ishi*. The purpose of setting out a bucket of warm water was to allow people to warm their hands after using the frigid water in the *chōzubachi* as described in *Chanoyu Rokusōshō Denki* (1702), although this passage doesn't mention a dedicated pedestal stone for the bucket.

> On the occasion of an Honorable Visit (*onari*)
> from a lord or person of high rank, if it is winter-
> time or a cold season, put some warm water in
> a bucket. The host carries this out and sets it on
> top of the water basin. Or, [the lord's] attendant
> can hold the bucket and pour from it.[237]

The *teshoku* is a metal candle holder with three legs: two beneath the holder itself and one extended outward to act as a carrying handle. Historically, tea gatherings were often held at night or in the early morning. Depending on the phase of the moon and the cloud cover, and remembering that this was a time well before electric lights, the *roji* may well have been pitch black. A stone lantern set by the water basin provided some light there, but the *teshoku* was needed to be able to make one's way down the *roji* from outer gate to tea house. The *teshoku-ishi* provided a place to set the *teshoku* down while using the *chōzubachi* and allow it to cast light on the water. The following passage from *Kaiki* (1724–35) makes it clear that the *teshoku-ishi* had become a requisite part of *chanoyu* by that time:

> The candle-holder stone is for the purpose of
> setting down the candle holder. In a modern *roji*,
> if there is no candle holder, the garden would be
> dark and dangerous. I implore you to keep this
> in mind.[238]

The design of the water basin and the accessory stones around it became increasingly formalized through the Edo period, eventually being developed into a circular arrangement referred to as a *tsukubai*. This will be described in more detail in Chapter 7. The stones included the water basin, *chōzubachi*; the front stone, *mae-ishi*; the candle-holder stone, *teshoku-ishi*; and the warm-water bucket stone, *yuoke-ishi*. The *chōzubachi* is mentioned in texts from very early on in the development of the *roji*, as is the *mae-ishi*, which appears in 1587 in *Rikyū Kyaku no Shidai*, but the others only come into use later and were recorded in tea records in the late Edo period. The all-encompassing term *tsukubai* appears for the first time at the very end of the Edo period in a text called *Chanoyu Ichieshū* that is dated 1860.[239]

Another stone that appears in *Chanoyu Ichieshū* for the first time is the *seki-ishi*, barrier stone, typically called the *sekimori-ishi* these days. The *seki-ishi* is a small stone, usually tied with a black, palm-fiber twine in a cross pattern, that is placed on top of a stepping stone to designate that that particular path, in a multi-path garden, is closed to entry. The same text also mentions a *seki-chiku*, barrier bamboo, that serves the same purpose.

GARDEN ELEMENTS: PLANTS

Regarding the use of plants in the *roji* through the mid-Edo period, we find, as with earlier tea gardens, that there is very little specific information given in the texts. Certainly when compared to notes on others aspects of the gardens, such as water basins, the information about plants seems very scant. In part this may be because the tea gardens were sparsely planted. Descriptions of small, walled tea gardens from the late 16th and early 17th century, as mentioned before, often note only a single pine, maple, or willow tree. And, rather than having a luxuriant mossy groundcover, the ground was often spread with gravel, *kuri-ishi*, which refers to small stones ranging from chestnut size (*kuri* means chestnut) to fist size.

Most plans that note anything for a groundcover, note *kuri-ishi*. There are some exceptions, however. For instance, one plan of a tea garden belonging to Matsuya Hisayoshi (?–1633) shows the ground covered with moss (fig. 55); another belonging to Kobori Enshū describes the area around the entry gate as being heavily planted but the area beyond that as being covered with lawn-grass, *shibafu*. Another plan for an Enshū garden (fig. 56) notes that "everything was [covered with] *kuri-ishi*" but also that "there are many plantings: *momi* [Abies], *mokkoku* [Ternstroemia], and *akushiba* [Vaccinium japonicum]." This garden is shown as being surrounded by wild thickets (*yabu*)

but separated from them with fences made of bamboo branches (*take no e gaki*, usually called a *chikushi-gaki* these days). Another section of the same plan (fig. 57) shows no details for planting but simply notes in two locations, "everything, everything is heavily planted (*mina mina uekomi*)."[240]

So, it would seem there are two variants of tea gardens from the late 15th century on that were at times separated and at times combined. One was a dry, clean *roji* spread with gravel or small stones, and the other a green, planted *roji*, at times heavily planted, shady, and mossy.

Moss grows easily in central Japan, especially in humid Kyōto, and its ubiquitousness may have meant that tea masters didn't see it as striking enough to note. Also, moss was seen as a sign of degeneration and decomposition, and struck some tea masters as being unclean. Remember Rodrigues commenting on the ground being "covered with moss and decrepitude." There is a passage in *Sugiki Fusai Densho*, a text dated 1690, that advises caution with the use of moss. "In order to create a sense of quiet loneliness (*sabishiki tei*), the *roji* must be kept very clean. If the stone lanterns and water basins become thick with moss of their own accord [that is one thing], but to purposely apply moss to stone lanterns and such to create a sense of age is absolutely wrong."[241] Likewise, in *Chanoyu Ichieshū*, which dates from 1856, we find a passage related to moss and the water basin that reads, "Keeping the water basin clean is a fundamental thing; the part where the water collects must be cleaned regularly, and one should pay attention to how it ages. It is not a problem if the outer edges get a slight bit of aging, but getting a lot of moss or too much aging is definitely unwanted."[242] The same text continues, listing plants that can be used in a *roji*:

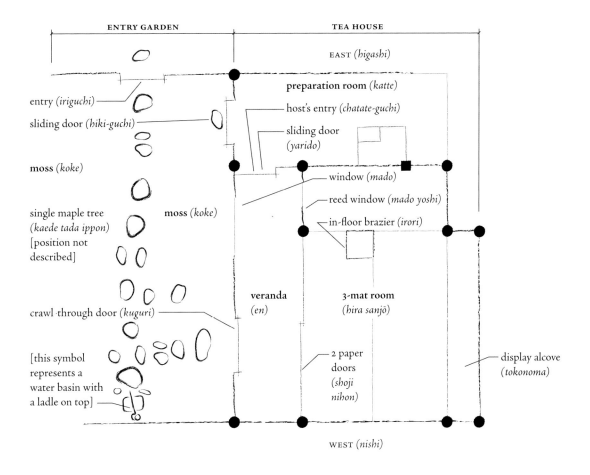

ENTRY GARDEN | TEA HOUSE

EAST (*higashi*)

preparation room (*katte*)

entry (*iriguchi*)

host's entry (*chatate-guchi*)

sliding door (*hiki-guchi*)

sliding door
(*yarido*)

moss (*koke*)

window (*mado*)

reed window (*mado yoshi*)

moss (*koke*)

single maple tree
(*kaede tada ippon*)
[position not
described]

in-floor brazier (*irori*)

veranda
(*en*)

3-mat room
(*hira sanjō*)

crawl-through door (*kuguri*)

2 paper
doors
(*shoji
nihon*)

display alcove
(*tokonoma*)

[this symbol
represents a
water basin with
a ladle on top]

WEST (*nishi*)

55. MOSS AS GROUNDCOVER. The earliest records of moss in tea gardens only refer to it as an artifact, clinging to water basins or lanterns. As a groundcover, one of the first mentions is in this drawing of a tea house that belonged to Matsuya Hisayoshi (?–1633). Redrawn from *Chanoyu Hishō*, p. 205.

late edo period

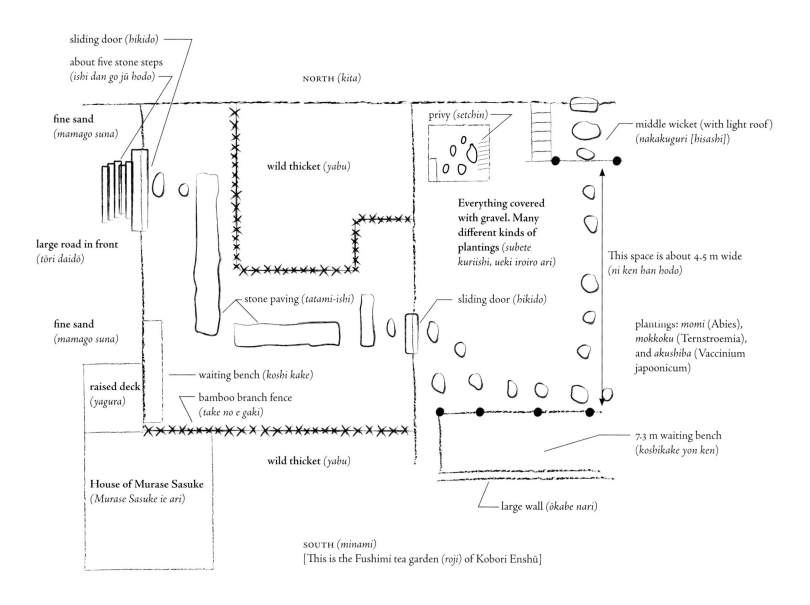

sliding door (*hikido*)

about five stone steps
(*ishi dan go jū hodo*)

NORTH (*kita*)

fine sand
(*mamago suna*)

privy (*setchin*)

middle wicket (with light roof)
(*nakakuguri [hisashi]*)

wild thicket (*yabu*)

large road in front
(*tōri daidō*)

Everything covered
with gravel. Many
different kinds of
plantings (*subete
kuriishi, ueki iroiro ari*)

This space is about 4.5 m wide
(*ni ken han hodo*)

stone paving (*tatami-ishi*)

sliding door (*hikido*)

fine sand
(*mamago suna*)

plantings: *momi* (Abies),
mokkoku (Ternstroemia),
and *akushiba* (Vaccinium
japoonicum)

waiting bench (*koshi kake*)

raised deck
(*yagura*)

bamboo branch fence
(*take no e gaki*)

7.3 m waiting bench
(*koshikake yon ken*)

wild thicket (*yabu*)

large wall (*ōkabe nari*)

House of Murase Sasuke
(*Murase Sasuke ie ari*)

SOUTH (*minami*)
[This is the Fushimi tea garden (*roji*) of Kobori Enshū]

56. PLANTS IN THE ROJI. The garden path to this tea house, owned by Kobori Enshū (1579–1647), winds its way through a wild thicket in the outer garden, but the inner garden is clean—spread with gravel—and planted with a variety of plants, mostly evergreens. Redrawn from *Chanoyu Hishō*, pp. 217–18.

Matsu [Pinus sp.], *momiji* [Acer sp.], *shirakashi* [Quercus myrsinaefolia], *shii* [Castanopsis sp.], *gumi* [Elaeagnus sp.], *kuri* [Castanea crenata], *yama-gaki* [Diospyros kaki var. sylvestris], *kōboku* [Magnolia officinalis], *kuchinashi* [Gardenia jasminoides], *aoki* [Aucuba japonica], *nishikigi* [Euonymus alatus], *haze* [Rhus succedanea], and *take* [bamboo] are all fine to use. *Nanten* [Nandina domestica], *umemodoki* [Ilex serrata], *ichigo* [perhaps Rubus hirsutus], and other fruiting plants are not particularly preferred. For grasses, *susuki* [Miscanthus sinensis], *hagi* [Lespedeza bicolor], *fuki* [perhaps Ligularia dentata or Adenocaulon himalaicum], *shida* [fern, variety unknown], *asagao* [morning glory, variety unknown], and other herbaceous plants should be given consideration. The beauty of the *roji* must be given careful consideration, and it is best to make things so they do not seem too artificial. Trees pruned into shapes or exotic plantings should not be employed. Discern the taste of the garden very carefully, and choose the plantings to create an atmosphere of *sabi* [rustic yet elegant refinement]. Doing that will attain a feeling of graciousness.[243]

Genryū Chawa, a tea text from the very end of the 17th century, mentions two plants that are important, not simply because of their genus and species but because of their particular function in the *roji*; they are called *yaku-ju* as mentioned above. They are the *gaku no matsu*, tablet pine, and the *sode-suri no rui*, sleeve-brushing plants. The *gaku no matsu*, which is also called the *gakumi-matsu*, is a pine tree artfully placed in the *roji* so as to frame the view of the tablet that is inscribed with the name of the tea house and usually

hangs high above the tea-house entry near the ridge. As a guest stands on the *gakumi-ishi*, tablet-viewing stone, he would see the tablet framed beautifully by the branches and trunk of the pine. This is part of the initiation into the poetic meaning of the tea gathering. In *Hosokawa Chanoyu no Sho*, we find a passage that admonishes the first-time guest: "When you enter the *roji* for the first time, even if you look carefully around you, when it is dark you cannot see well, so study the

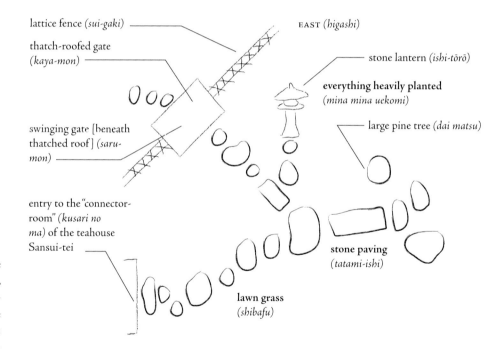

lattice fence *(sui-gaki)*

thatch-roofed gate *(kaya-mon)*

swinging gate [beneath thatched roof] *(saru-mon)*

entry to the "connector-room" *(kusari no ma)* of the teahouse Sansui-tei

EAST *(higashi)*

stone lantern *(ishi-tōrō)*

everything heavily planted *(mina mina uekomi)*

large pine tree *(dai matsu)*

stone paving *(tatami-ishi)*

lawn grass *(shibafu)*

57. GRASS IN THE ROJI. The plan for this tea house owned by Kobori Enshū (1579–1647) notes that the *roji* had grass, an uncommon feature. Written *shibafu*, it refers to grass as a groundcover rather than an ornamental plant. Redrawn from *Chanoyu Koten Sōsho*, vol. I, p. 275.

tablet carefully. However, do not read the words out loud or praise the tablet in a loud voice. You may be reading it wrong."[244]

The *sode-suri no rui* is a sleeve-brushing plant,

58. SLEEVE-BRUSHING PINE. The path in this *roji* was made to pass so close to the old pine tree, a person's kimono might brush against it. The tree was thus referred to as a "sleeve-brushing pine," *sode-suri matsu.* This wood-block print is of Myōkian, a temple of the Rinzai Zen sect founded around the year 1500, where Rikyū built his two-mat tearoom, Taian. *Miyako Rinsen Meishō Zue.* International Research Center for Japanese Studies, Kyōto.

in other words, a large tree situated in the *roji* close enough to the path that a guest's sleeve would brush up against it as he passed. *Sode* is the sleeve of a *kimono*, *suri* means "to brush against," and *rui* means "categories." The most typical of these trees is the *sode-suri matsu* or sleeve-brushing pine tree, but the use of the word *rui* here reveals that there were a variety of different trees that served this purpose. An interesting aspect of these sleeve-brushing trees is that they were large, thus, very old trees that predated the *roji* itself. The designer of a *roji* did not plant the tree so it would become a sleeve-brushing tree, rather he designed the path to pass an existing tree in such a manner that it would work as one and then named it accordingly (fig. 58).

CUSTOMS OF USE: WETTING THE GARDEN

As mentioned above, through the 1600s and into the 1700s, many of the elements of tea gardens that are now considered requisite made their first appearance in texts, although they may have been used in tea gardens, unrecorded, before then. Some of the customs related to tea gardens, too, were recorded in those texts for the first time, for instance the custom of sprinkling water on the garden in preparation for a tea gathering, known as *uchi-mizu.* In fact, wetting down the garden is recorded in earlier texts at the time of Rikyū, as was mentioned above, but the highly developed system of wetting the garden in a very specific manner is indicative of the development of tea through the 1600s and 1700s. The custom of wetting the garden three times, for instance, which is still in use today during a long tea gathering, a *chaji*, is mentioned in *Nanbōroku*: "As a rule, the *roji* is watered before the guests enter, before the mid-gathering respite (*naka-dachi*), and at the conclusion of the gathering when the guests are about to depart: a total of three times. Knowing that, diversely for the morning, noon, and evening gathering, each of these three wettings has a deep significance."[245]

To give a sense of what some other texts from about the same period say, we find in *Hosokawa Chanoyu no Sho*: "Regarding the wetting of the *roji*, in winter it should be sprinkled ever so lightly on top of the stepping stones, and around the vicinity of the water basin and the waiting bench. In summer, all the plants should be sprinkled liberally."[246] In *Sugiki Fusai Densho*, in a section on morning tea gatherings, we find: "About the wetting down of the *roji*, it is fine to sprinkle from above. Around the privy and the underplantings near the waiting bench should be thoroughly wetted. Also, it goes without saying, that hot days and cold days should be treated differently. In the morning, before the guests arrive, it is good to change the water in the water basin, and the wetting of the *roji* should be done as above three times. Before the guests take their midway break, just as the tea gathering is ending, and just before the guests leave."[247]

CUSTOMS OF USE: LIGHTING THE GARDEN

As with the wetting down of the garden, another custom that existed from the late 16th century but became more developed through the 17th century is the use of lights in the tea garden for evening or early morning tea gatherings. Stone lanterns were used before, as were hand-held lighting devices such as wooden lanterns (*andon*) and candle holders (*teshoku*), but the degree to which these were described in detail increased greatly in the later texts.

An *andon* is a wood-framed lantern that has papered sides. Often there is an extended handle on top by which the *andon* may be held. *Andon* may be carried

into the tea garden but were usually left along the path by the host at strategic points to provide light. According to *Sekishū Sanbyakukajō* (1665), the *andon* that were used in the tea room should be made of cedar (*sugi*) while those for use in the *roji* should be made of cypress (*hinoki*). In general, cypress is more resistant to rot and a better choice for external applications.[248]

It seems that the tea master Oribe preferred the *andon* to the *teshoku*, or at least thought it captured the spirit of *wabi* better. In *Furuta Oribe Densho* (1612), regarding light inside the tea house, we find: "In terms of *wabi*, use no *teshoku* and just one *andon*." And following that: "For an evening tea gathering (*yobanashi*) it goes against the spirit of *wabi* to have an *andon* in the *roji*. However, the *andon* that is in the tea house can be carried out into the *roji*."[249] We can assume that the *andon* captured the spirit of *wabi* better because the light of its oil lamp was softer or mellower than the bright, flickering light of the thick candles used in the *teshoku*, but no specific explanation was given. *Hosokawa Chanoyu no Sho* (1641) states, "About hand-held, wooden garden lanterns (*roji andon*), whether in the morning or at night, if it is dark they should be set out."[250]

Similar to the *andon* is the *kidōrō*, literally, "wooden lantern," favored by the school of tea following Katagiri Sekishū. The *kidōrō* is a wooden firebox with papered windows and a wooden roof. It could be set low to the ground (on a stone or stump), on top of a wooden post that was temporarily situated in the *roji*, or hung from the eaves of the tea house by a hook affixed to its roof ridge. *Sekishū Sanbyakukajō* (1665) records the following thoughts:

The Honorable Sakon [Kuwayama Sakon] asked of Sekishū, "Stone lanterns are for use at night but are left out during the day. When it is done that way, they add to the scenery of the *roji*. Why not leave wooden lanterns (*kidōrō*) out during the day, too?" Although this is what the Honorable Sakon suggested, Sekishū said, "You are right. Indeed it is acceptable to do it that way. I never asked this point of Rikyū, but he did say that it is fine to place them on top of an old tree stump or a stone." From that time on, Sekishū left the wooden lantern as it is and since Sekishū left it out during the day, it is considered to be his personal statement.[251]

59. PORTABLE LANTERNS. A variety of lanterns were carried into the tea garden during nighttime tea gatherings by guests, or were placed along the *roji* path by the host. The metal *teshoku* (top left) was commonly carried, while the wooden *oki-andon* (top right) was more typically placed at key points in the garden. The two lanterns at the bottom are of a more modern design.

The *teshoku*, as mentioned above, is a metal candle holder. The candle itself may be exposed or protected by a conical paper enclosure that is open at the top but still works to prevent the wind from blowing out the candle. The tea records of Hosokawa Sansai, *Hosokawa Chanoyu no Sho* (1641), give a detailed description of how to use the *teshoku*.

For evening tea gatherings, or those in the morning, the host should go out to receive his guests carrying a candle holder (*teshoku*). After opening the middle wicket and making a bow, the gate should be closed but left slightly open and the *teshoku* should by all means be placed on the waiting stone (*fumichigae-ishi*), if there is one, lying between the cross-over stone (*norikoe-ishi*) and the host's stone (*teishu-ishi*).[252] Set it so that it lights the other stones as well; a closer stone is best. If the head guest is a peer [of his companions], he should lift the candle holder so those behind can see as well and then place it near the water basin. When an important guest [military lord, noble, etc.] is using the water, the second guest should hold it up. If the host is important enough a person that he sends [an assistant] into the *roji*, leave the candle holder right where it is next to the sword shelf. If he is so humble (*wabi*) that he will not send an assistant to the *roji*, then the flame should be put out and the wick trimmed. When the gathering is at night, if the host is humble, the guest puts out the flame and carries [the candle holder] into the tea room (*sukiya*) and places it at the entry to the preparation room (*katteguchi*) or somewhere else that is convenient for the host to take. For a morning gathering or at dawn when a light is no longer needed, [the candle holder] can be brought inside during the first sitting. Paying close attention to the time of day is crucial.[253]

The physical form of the lamps and lanterns themselves developed over the Edo period but so did the manner in which they were lit and used; for instance, the choice of how bright a light to use depended on conditions (fig. 59). The light source in a stone lantern was an oil lamp, not a candle. These oil lamps were very rudimentary, consisting of a ceramic plate, or shallow bowl, sometimes double layered, into which a long, cord-like wick was inserted. The following entry from *Hosokawa Chanoyu no Sho* (1641) records details about how many wicks should be used and when: "About lighting a light in a stone lantern, there should be three wicks. On a moonlit night, use four wicks but if [the lantern] is still too dark, add one more wick."[254] Similarly, in *Hosokawa Chanoyu no Sho*, we find, "Regarding the light in a (stone) lantern, it is said that in the morning it should be strong, and in the evening weak. On a moonlit night, make it strong. However [Sanasai thought] that making them faint in the morning and strong in the evening is better."[255] *Kaiki* (1724–35) relates something similar: "For an evening tea gathering, [if?] there are several stone lanterns, then they all should have lights lit in them. On a moonlit night, wherever the light of the moon reaches put no light [in the lantern]. Where the moonlight does not reach and the lantern is in the dark, shadow, then put a light in it."[256]

The culture of lighting the *roji* was becoming elaborate and exacting. In *Nanbōroku*, for instance, there is a comment on lanterns and snow.

For night gatherings when the snow has fallen, you should generally not light the stone lanterns in the *roji*. Overwhelmed by the whiteness of the snow, they afford nothing worth noticing, their light wan. There may be exceptions, however, depending on the conditions or the presence of trees; it is impossible to speak absolutely.[257]

Sekishū Sanbyakukajō goes into some detail about how many lanterns should be placed in the garden, where they should be set, and which should be lit (fig. 60):

There is no standard regarding the height of a stone lantern. [Of five important spots in the *roji*] there should be two spots where lanterns are used and three where they are not. A stone lantern is set [in the *roji*] for its light. [Set one in a] spot from which it lights the middle wicket (*naka-kuguri*), a spot to light the waiting bench (*koshikake*), a spot to light the water basin (*chōzu-ishi*), and a spot from which light will reach through to the sword shelf (*katana-kake*). [Lanterns] are used to give light to these five places. That said, if you light them all it is not good and will look like lights at road crossings. For that reason, lanterns should be used at only two of the spots and not at the other three. For instance, if one lights the crawl-through door (*nijiri-agari*) and the sword shelf, then the waiting bench, water basin, and middle wicket should not have lanterns. Or, when the middle wicket and water basin are lit, then the crawl-through door, sword shelf, and privy (*setchin*) are not. Depending on the *roji*, it is not necessarily done just this way. One should use one's own discretion, depending on the feeling of the stone [lanterns]. Even if they are set as has just been written, it is not good for the stone lanterns themselves to be too prominent. Small plants should be planted in front of, and behind them, so that they fit in better.[258]

By the 19th century, sprinkling water on stone lanterns seems to have become an important effect; perhaps it was because the lamp light looked fresh and sparkly, radiating on the lantern when it was wet,

or perhaps it was just to keep the lantern clean. *Chanoyu Ichieshū* (1856) records the following: "For stone lanterns, when day breaks, the paper covering (*shōji*) should be removed. Place a ceramic or bamboo vessel inside and spray mist all the way into the firebox. By doing that, you will keep it clean and oil [soot] will not build up inside the firebox."[259] And a little further in the text, "For stone lanterns, from the roof to post, one should spray [water] until it is completely wet, enough so that water pools in the firebox and drips."[260]

60. POSITION OF STONE LANTERNS. Tabuchi Residence, Akō City. Much thought is given to the placement of stone lanterns within the *roji*, as well as to how and when to light them during evening and early morning tea gatherings. The person who set this one in the Tabuchi Residence *roji* might have read *Sekishū Sanbyakukajō*, written in 1665, which states, "[Set a lantern in a] spot from which it lights the middle wicket (*naka-kuguri*)," just as this lantern does. Placed near the lattice window, the lantern light shines on both the inner and outer *roji*.

PHILOSOPHIC INTERPRETATIONS

The various elements found in the tea garden became more complex through the 17th and 18th centuries as did the many subtle customs associated with the tea garden that are now considered to be integral to the art. Another important aspect of *chanoyu* that became expressed clearly and abundantly for the first time during the 17th century was the idea that *chanoyu* is a spiritual or religious practice, primarily a Zen Buddhist practice.[261] As has been discussed earlier, there are many ways that Zen Buddhism can be seen as having had a formative influence on *chanoyu*. However, other than the writings of Rodrigues—the Portuguese Jesuit missionary who so clearly stated that "those who practice *chanoyu* try to imitate these solitary philosophers [of the Zen sect] and hence all pagan followers of this art belong to the Zenshū sect"[262]—the references to Zen Buddhism in early writings on *chanoyu* are occasional at best. Certainly with regard to the written record of *chanoyu*, the references linking Zen Buddhism and *chanoyu* become increasingly pronounced with time, culminating in such texts as *Nanbōroku* (1690), *Chawa Shigetsu Shū* (1701), and *Zencharoku* (1828). This trend continues to this day in the form of popular press publications on *chanoyu* that stress Zen Buddhism as a pillar of *chanoyu*.[263] We have already taken a look at how some of these texts relate Zen Buddhism to *chanoyu* in general terms. What follows is a look at how those same texts relate Zen to the tea garden in particular. The opening lines of *Nanbōroku*, for instance, contain the following:

> [In the voice of the narrator Nanbō] Whenever I go to have tea with Rikyū, he unfailingly brings water to fill the stone basin in a bucket and pours it in himself. I once asked the significance of this. He replied, "In the *roji*, the host's first act is to bring water; the guest's first act is to use this water to rinse his hands. This is the very foundation underlying the use of the *roji* and thatched hut. It is precisely so that the person who calls and the person called on can together wash off the stains of worldly dust in the *roji* that the stone basin is placed there.[264]

It is unclear whether *Nanbōroku* is the actual recording of Rikyū's teachings by his companion, the priest Nanbō, or a complete fabrication by Tachibana Jitsuzan, or a compilation of Rikyū's teachings that were transmitted within the select circle of tea practitioners and then presented through the fictional voice of Nanbō by Jitsuzan or others (which is this author's belief). What is clear is that by the mid-17th century, some tea practitioners believed strongly that Zen Buddhism was the fundamental underpinning of *chanoyu*. Men such as Jitsuzan wanted to remind their contemporaries of that fact. The writings in texts such as *Nanbōroku* and *Zencharoku* seemed particularly intent on this mission.

In texts of this period, notes about the *roji* are often introduced toward the beginning of the work (if not at the very beginning) and at times the *roji* is described in great detail. This indicates its growing importance in the minds of the texts' authors. Also, many of these descriptions begin to suggest that the *roji* is not just a simple entry space, or a forest-like path, but rather a place of spiritual cleansing or a passageway from the sordid, work-a-day world into a world of spiritual enlightenment. Again, from *Nanbōroku*:

> [In the voice of Rikyū] There are a hundred thousand rules and regulations governing the *daisu* and other aspects of tea. Men of the past left off with these and appear to have understood them to be the whole of *chanoyu*; they recorded and transmitted in secret writings only that we should regard each rule of form as important. But taking these prescribed forms as footholds, I was possessed of the aspiration to climb slightly higher and eagerly made inquiries of the masters of Daitokuji and Nanshūji. Day and night, with the monastic rules of the Zen temples as my basis, I simplified the measurements regulating the highly refined manner of the *shoin* room; I unfolded the world of the Pure Land in the locus of the *roji*, brought the spirit of *wabi* to its culmination in a thatched hut of two mats, endeavored in practice through gathering firewood and drawing water, and at last realized, though faintly, that there is the taste of the real in a bowl of tea.[265]

Here we find the *roji* described in specifically Buddhist terms, with the author likening it to the Pure Land, *jōdo sekai*. The expression "Pure Land" is a Buddhist term but not one particular to the Zen sect, which shows the admixture of philosophies from various Buddhist sects that had an influence on the development of *chanoyu*.[266] The idea that the *roji* is a "locus of the Pure Land" or, seen another way, as the passageway through to the Pure Land, is summed up in a short passage from *Nanbōroku*.

> You may boil water a hundred times over
> but it is best when both guest and host cleanse
>   their spirits together
> the *roji* is simply a path beyond this transient
>   world
> how then does it scatter all the dust from the
>   spirit?
> It must be understood that the essence of *cha-noyu* is nothing more than
> boiling water, whisking tea, and partaking of the
>   drink.
> In the *roji* or tea house [*sukiya*], guest and host
>   sharing tea
> in harmony, their spirits linked as one.[267]

The "transient world," *ukiyo*, is an expression for the mortal world we live in with all its faults and illusions that trouble the mind. Those troubles are referred to as the "dust of the spirit," *kokoro no chiri*. Clearly the author of *Nanbōroku* wished his readers to perceive the *roji* as an essential part of the spiritual path that he felt *chanoyu* was capable of being. This idea of the *roji* as a spiritual path is also described in a short supplemental text to *Nanbōroku* called *Kochū Rodan*.

> *Roji* is the name given to that boundary place [that acts as the entry to] the quiet and lonely thatch-roofed arbor. A parable in the Lotus Sutra describes how the many children of a wealthy man escape the Burning House and can be seen sitting out in the *roji*. Also, the *roji* is called the white bull or the white *roji*, [where one] detaches oneself from the toil and soil of the world to be wholly pure and free of possessions; hence the bold appellation of white *roji*. Thus, it refers to the original human mentality, and the external representation of the mentality is a singular garden of natural trees and stones. It is an excellent realm where not a single bird sings and clouds envelop ancient trees.

> That being the case, because spectacular natural landscapes are rare within residential districts of a city, one plants trees, grows clusters of bamboo, admires the dew both morning and evening, strolls on snowy, moonlit nights. Even a garden that is not so thickly wooded can recall the enchanting scenes of Yoshino and Katsuragi. Attending groups of arriving guests, enjoying the flowerless stands of trees or waiting on a friend who feels the same way, brushing away the snow from beneath the eaves. It is not easy to detail all these sensibilities. Just take the *roji* of Shū'un'an, the Arbor of Gathering Clouds, or the simple brushwood gate of Shōkadō, the Hall Beneath the Pine, as your place to meet, and hang a single wooden sign there, that says the following:

> - When the guests have all assembled at the waiting bench, the sounding board should be struck.
> - Concerning the water in the stone basin, it is wholly the cleansing of the heart and mind that is crucial to the way.
> - The host will emerge to invite the guests in. He is poor; the utensils for tea and rice, irregular; the food, lacking any refinement in flavor. The trees

and rocks in the garden are simply as in nature. Any who find this incomprehensible should leave forthwith.

- When the water heating in the kettle produces the soft sound of wind in the pines, the gong will be struck. The guests should then reenter. To be out of timing with the boiling water and the burning charcoal would be a terrible mistake.
- Idle conversation about worldly matters in and around the tea room has been prohibited by long tradition.
- There is to be a direct and straightforward encounter of guest and host, without reliance on deftness of speech or ornamentation.
- A gathering should not exceed four hours from start to finish. Exception to this rule is made for speaking of Buddhist Teachings (*dharma*) and other undefiled conversation (*seidan*)."[268]

Chawa Shigetsu Shū, a text from 1701 that purports to be an anthology of the words and deeds of Sen Rikyū as observed by his grandson Sōtan, has a brief passage that also makes a clear connection between *chanoyu* and Zen Buddhism.

In response to someone who happened to ask about the Way of Tea, [Rikyū] said, "Since it was originally formulated on the basis of Zen, there is no 'way' that need be further specified. If you simply take the tea stories of our predecessors that I often recount as a pointer to the moon, you will naturally come to understand." Although the art may be different, the principle is the same as that found in the words of the poet, Fujiwara Teika, who stated, "In *waka*, there is no teacher. Simply take the poems of old as your teacher."[269]

The last text to be introduced here that clearly expresses *chanoyu* and the tea garden in Zen Buddhism terms is *Zencharoku* (*The Zen Tea Record*). The content of this text is not intended to be the recorded sayings of a past master, as *Nanbōroku* and *Chawa Shigetsu* were. Instead, it was written by someone (purportedly the Zen priest Jakuan Sōtaku, but this cannot be confirmed) who was intent on reminding the people of his day that the fundamental pillar of tea was, and is, Zen Buddhism. The *roji* is mentioned in the very first lines (again showing its importance to the author),

61. MOSSY GROUND. Yoshida Residence, Kyōto. In the earliest *roji*, tea masters created a feeling of purity and cleanliness by spreading the ground with pebbles. Later, in keeping with the interpretation of a *roji* as a "dewy ground," they used moss as a groundcover more often. Swept clean and sprinkled with water, the deep green moss carpet lends the *roji* an air of peace and serenity.

and there is also an entire section devoted to the *roji* in which the author goes so far as to equate the *roji* with the tea room itself (fig. 61).

In secular society at present, the terms "inner *roji*" or "outer *roji*" are used to refer to [sections of] the garden. The fundamental meaning of *roji*, however, is entirely different: *ro* means "to be disclosed," "to appear," and *ji* refers to the heart and mind.[270] Thus, the term actually means "to disclose self-nature." Eradicating all blind passions one manifests one's original nature.

The term "white roji" (*haku roji*) has the same meaning. "White" signifies purity. Since the tea room is the site of enlightenment (*dōjō*) where original nature becomes manifest, it has been termed the *roji*. Thus, the *roji* is an alternate term for the tea room itself.

Roji also refers to the vastness and immaculateness of the red earth without trees and grasses. Again, this is an image for original nature. A commentary from the Lotus Sutra states:

[Concerning the phrase, "open space (*roji*) at the crossroads":] "Crossroads" is an image for the Four Noble Truths, the four branches representing the differences among their contemplations. When the contemplations of each of the Four Truths are grasped as the same and one perceives truth, they are like [the open space of] the wayside. Hence the expression, "crossroads."

Even if confusion in seeing is eliminated, as long as thought remains, we cannot speak of "open space." "Open space" is a term for the exhaustive abolition of thought concerning the three realms of existence.

Further, the term, "site of enlightenment" (*dōjō*), has the same meaning as *roji*. *The Treatise of Great Stillness and Discernment* states:

"Site of enlightenment" (*dōjō*) refers to the realm of purity. The chaff—blind passions that are the five abodes—is washed away and the grain of reality is revealed.

Eradication of thought concerning the three realms is therefore termed "open space" (*roji*).

By disposing of the chaff—blind passions that are the five abodes—one manifests the kernel of original nature that is reality or purity; this is called *roji* or "site of enlightenment." These terms are completely synonymous.

Moreover, it is said that the tea room is a "different world." This is also an expression for one's own mind. The *Diamond Sutra* states: "The world is not the world; therefore, it is the world." One must, "without any abode, give rise to this mind."[271]

In some ways the above passages are clear—the author describes the *roji* as being a purified place as well as an open and exposed place. He likens that to the open and exposed state of mind of a person who is enlightened. But the text is also rather abstruse, as is the case with many religious texts. It is important to see that this kind of highly developed language and philosophy related to *chanoyu* and the tea garden comes only after several hundred years of development of the art.

6

extant tea gardens
and gardens influenced by tea

The classic tea gardens of the late 16th and 17th centuries, which were designed to be used as entry spaces to tea houses, continued to be built through the Edo period and even until this day. Extant examples can be found at the homes of the grand masters of various lineages of tea, teachers of tea, and avid amateur aficionados. They also can be found in Buddhist temples and secular locations such as elegant restaurants, inns, and hotels. A few examples from the residences of grand masters will be presented first in this chapter because these represent some of the clearest examples of classic *roji*. There are, however, many other extant gardens from the Edo period or later that were influenced by the design of the *roji* but are not strictly *roji* themselves either in their use or form. These gardens can be found in many different situations—such as the residences of provincial lords, aristocratic families, merchant families, and others—and several examples of each will also be presented. Some of these gardens were used, in part, as passages to tea houses or as settings for tea gatherings and, in as much, could possibly be called tea gardens, even though they weren't entirely dedicated to the practice of *chanoyu*.

In most cases, however, tea gatherings were not the major aesthetic, philosophic, or functional intent of these gardens. In fact, the term "tea garden" doesn't seem appropriate at all, and yet, by the end of the 17th century, the expression tea garden, *chatei* or *chaniwa*, was applied to many types of gardens, some of which have little or no connection to tea whatsoever. *Shokoku Chatei Meiseki Zue* (*Illustrations of Famous Tea Gardens Throughout the Country*),[272] a book of black-and-white woodblock prints of gardens published in 1694, for instance, has images of gardens that are very "*roji*-like"—with stepping stones, small gates, water basins, and tea houses—alongside gardens that seem very unlike tea gardens, containing elements such as raked sand, elaborately pruned pine trees, and scenes of complex rockery where each stone has been given a specific name (as in the medieval gardening text *Sansui Narabini Nogata no Zu*). Despite the obvious incongruity, all these gardens are presented together under the title *Chatei* (*Tea Gardens*), because by the mid-Edo period the expression "tea garden" had taken on a certain panache and was applied to gardens that were not at all connected with tea culture, simply because it was in vogue.

Chatei and *chaniwa* are merely different pronunciations of the same set of two characters. Through the 18th century, the pronunciation *chatei* seems to have been favored but nowadays *chaniwa* is far more common, especially in the popular press. In the following descriptions of extant gardens there are some that would readily be described as being *chaniwa*, such as the classic *roji* of tea grand masters. Others, such as the large estate gardens mentioned further on, would not typically be called *chaniwa*. They are, however, very much derivative of earlier tea gardens, and it is for that reason they are included here.

The Roji of Tea Grand Masters

After the military leader Toyotomi Hideyoshi forced Rikyū to commit suicide in 1591, Rikyū's sons, Dōan (1546–1607) and Shōan (1546–1614), escaped Hideyoshi's wrath by seeking refuge outside the capital. Dōan went to Hida (in present-day Gifu Prefecture), and Shōan went to stay with Gamō Ujisato of Aizu-Wakamatsu (in present-day Fukushima Prefecture). Ujisato was later instrumental in intervening with the

62. OMOTE SENKE ROJI PLAN VIEW. Redrawn from plans included in Shigemori and Shigemori, *Nihon Teien-shi Taikei*.

extant tea gardens and gardens influenced by tea

158

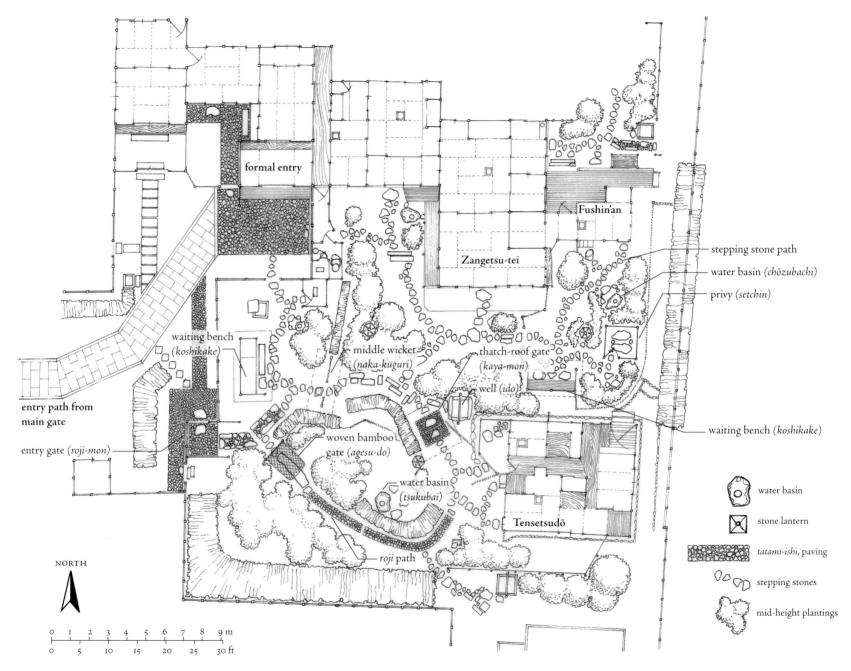

formal entry

Fushin'an

Zangetsu-tei

stepping stone path

water basin (*chōzubachi*)

privy (*setchin*)

waiting bench (*koshikake*)

waiting bench
(*koshikake*)

middle wicket
(*naka-kuguri*)

thatch-roof gate
(*kaya-mon*)

well (*ido*)

entry path from
main gate

woven bamboo
gate (*agesu-do*)

entry gate (*roji-mon*)

water basin
(*tsukubai*)

Tensetsudō

roji path

NORTH

0 1 2 3 4 5 6 7 8 9 m

0   5   10   15   20   25   30 ft

water basin

stone lantern

tatami-ishi, paving

stepping stones

mid-height plantings

159

63. THATCH-ROOFED GATE. Omote Senke, Kyōto. The *roji* at Omote Senke offers the guest two main routes to enter. One leads to the *koshikake* and from there through the middle wicket; the other passes through a woven bamboo gate, *agesu-do*. Both paths, however, eventually lead to this thatch-roofed middle gate, *kaya-mon*. Photograph by Ōhashi Haruzō.

shōgun Tokugawa Ieyasu and having the Sen family reinstated. Shōan returned to Kyōto and, although not the eldest son, became head of the Sen family lineage. Shōan's son, Sōtan, had four sons, but the first two left home at an early age. When the time came to split up the family property, he gave the southern portion to his third son, Sōsa (1593–1675), and retired to the northern portion with his fourth son, Sōshitsu (1622–97), who, in time, inherited the property.

The portion of the property given to Sōsa included the tea house Fushin'an, and because the southern side of a property was considered the "front," or *omote*, the lineage of tea masters that have lived on that property are known as the Omote Senke or Omote Sen Family. On the portion of the property Sōtan retired to, he built a tea house called Konnichian, and, it being the northern or "rear," *ura*, portion of the property, the lineage of tea masters who have lived there ever since are known as the Ura Senke or Ura Sen Family. Shōan's second oldest son, Sōshu (1593–1675), returned at a later date and was given property on Mushanokōji Street where he built his tea house, Kankyūan. The lineage of tea masters who have lived there since then are known as Mushanokōji Senke. Fushin'an, Konnichian, and Kankyūan are very small tea houses, ranging from one and three-quarters to three and three-quarters mats in size. Naturally, the owners and their families did not live in these small rooms; they had other residential buildings on the property. The names of the tea houses, however, have become appellations for the residences as a whole and for the lineages of *chanoyu* as well. Thus, Fushin'an, Konnichian, and Kankyūan can refer to the small tea houses, the residential properties around those tea houses, or the complete lineage of tea associated with them, depending on the situation.

OMOTE SENKE ♦ FUSHIN'AN [273]

There are several important tea houses at the residence of Omote Senke: Fushin'an, a three-and-three-quarters-mat (*sanjō daime*) tea house in the *wabi* style; Zangetsu-tei, a twelve-mat tea room in the formal *shoin* style; and Tensetsudō, a three-and-three-quarters-mat tea room also known as the *sōdō*, or Ancestor's Hall, where the founders of the family lineage are enshrined. In addition to those tea houses there are many other, larger buildings that make up the bulk of the property. An intricately designed and heavily planted *roji* acts as an entryway to all the tea houses. Fushin'an was originally built in the mid-17th century but it, along with the other structures that were built later, has been lost to fire and rebuilt at least twice since then: once in 1788 and again in 1906. The present-day Fushin'an tea house was rebuilt in 1914. Despite these renovations, it is thought that the various tea houses more or less represent their original forms. With regard to the *roji*, however, drawings do not exist from the earliest period, and the degree to which it has been changed over the years is not well recorded. A bird's-eye drawing and a plan view map from the late 1700s show a few familiar features, such as the *agesu-do* gate, but many aspects are different as well. All that can be said is the present garden stems from some time after that (figs. 62, 63).

Entering the property from the street one passes through an imposing two-story gate, across an open courtyard to the main entry of the residence. The courtyard is formal, hard surfaced, and basically unplanted. Just to the right of the main entry, is a tall clay-plaster wall behind which lies the *roji*. The wall is punctuated only by a simple, wood-panel door. This is the *roji-mon*, or tea garden gate. The panel can be opened fully for maintenance or partially to evoke a *wabi* feeling for a tea gathering. Entering the *roji*, the change is startling. Outside the *roji-mon* it is dry and bright; inside is shaded and green. The carefully pruned yet dense plantings, in combination with some fences, divide the *roji* into various sections that are not clearly seen one from the other. The result is that the *roji*, which is only about 15 by 15 meters in overall size, appears to be much larger.

One of the striking features of this *roji* is its gates, of which three are often noted: the *agesu-do*, the *naka-kuguri*, and the *kaya-mon*. The *agesu-do* is similar to the swinging gate mentioned earlier, called a *sudo no hanekido*. A large panel of loosely woven bamboo slats has been hung on an overhead bar. When the panel is swung up and held aloft with a pole, guests can pass underneath. The *naka-kuguri*, already mentioned many times, resembles a section of clay-plaster wall that has been set in the garden. This is the most artificial, and in some ways the most magical, of the *roji* gates. It requires the guest to step up on a tall stepping stone, duck down through a small door, and then step back down on the other side. The only purpose in this extreme form of gateway is to increase the sense of threshold—the feeling of passing from one world into another. The *kaya-mon* is a thatch-roofed gate probably similar to the gate described in *Imai Sōkyū Chanoyusho* as the one that Sōkyū entered while the priest Kuwayama Hōshi and military lord Takenaka Izu no Kami went directly through the *roji*.

All three of these gates have old historical precedences, so either they were all part of the original design (although the old drawings do not show this clearly) or they were purposefully introduced at a later date to create an atmosphere of antiquity and tradition.

The story of the Ura Senke residence is similar to that of Omote Senke—the property is primarily occupied by various large residence buildings with the tea houses of note gathered on the southern side and the *roji* that connects them forming a 7- to 8-meter-wide strip along the outside of these buildings (fig. 64). Although the property was first developed in the mid-17th century, it too was destroyed by fire in 1788, so the tea houses that exist today are not original even though they are likely to be accurate reproductions. As for the *roji*, it too experienced changes over the years due to damage as well as architectural additions, such as happened in 1691 when the tea house/ancestor hall, Rikyūdō, was added to the rear of the residence.

The tea houses include Mushikiken, a five-mat room with a one-mat wooden entry floor that is used as a waiting room, *machiai*; Kan'untei, an eight-mat room noted for its three types of ceiling finishes that express three areas of the room: formal (*shin*), middle (*gyō*), and informal (*sō*); Konnichian, the one-and-three-quarters-mat (*ichijō daime*) *wabi*-style tea room that gives name to the whole residence; Yūin, a classic four-and-a-half-mat (*yojōhan*) tea room; and Rikyūdō, which is three and three-quarters mats (*sanjō daime*), the three-quarters-mat section being made of wood boards (*nakaita daime*).

What differentiates the *roji* of Ura Senke from that of Omote Senke is the expression of the details—Ura Senke being somewhat more rustic. Whereas the main entry walk of Omote Senke, for instance, is made

64. URA SENKE ROJI PLAN VIEW. Redrawn from plans included in Shigemori and Shigemori, *Nihon Teienshi Taikei*.

*extant tea gardens
and gardens
influenced by tea*

162

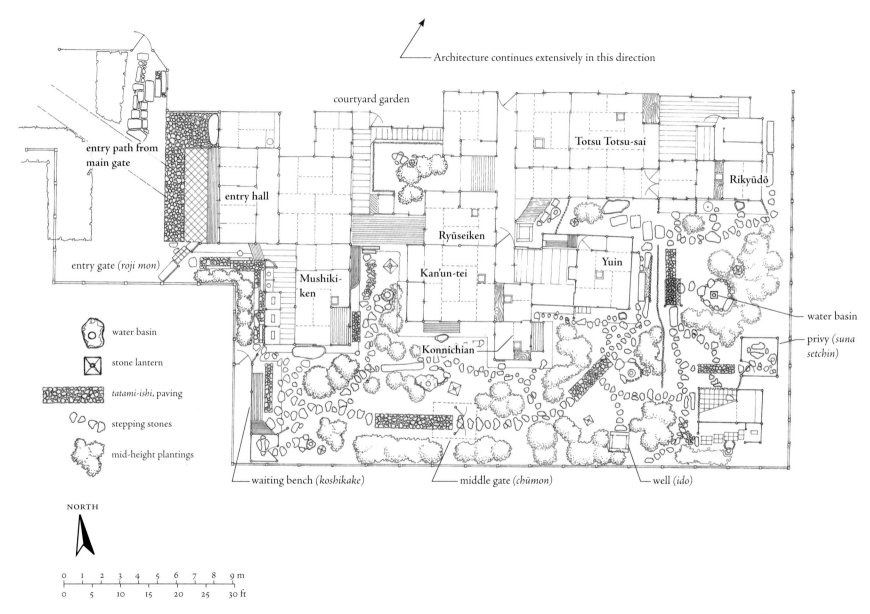

Architecture continues extensively in this direction

entry path from
main gate

courtyard garden

Totsu Totsu-sai

Rikyūdō

entry hall

Ryūseiken

Yuin

entry gate (roji mon)

Mushiki-
ken

Kan'un-tei

water basin

privy (suna
setchin)

Konnichian

water basin

stone lantern

tatami-ishi, paving

stepping stones

mid-height plantings

waiting bench (koshikake)

middle gate (chūmon)

well (ido)

NORTH

0 1 2 3 4 5 6 7 8 9 m

0   5   10   15   20   25   30 ft

163

65. YŪIN TEA HOUSE. Ura Senke, Kyōto. The *roji* at Ura Senke leads past the *koshi-kake*, through a bamboo-roofed middle gate, past the tiny two-mat tea room, Konnichian, to the four-and-a-half-mat tea house with a thatch roof, Yūin—the classic rustic tea house, *sōan chashitsu*. Photograph by Ōhashi Haruzō.

of cut-granite paving stones, that of Ura Senke is made of small, flat-topped stones that have a simpler more naturalistic feeling. The Omote Senke entry, as mentioned, is bright, open, and basically unplanted. Ura Senke's entry walk passes between two clipped hedges, each much taller than a person, and tall overhanging trees that make the path shaded and green. Both entry walks are straight and formal, but the Ura Senke entry feels much more like one is walking into a forest. Similarly, the waiting bench (koshikake) of Omote Senke has a tatami bench whereas that of Ura Senke is made of wooden boards and bamboo decking. The various gates in the roji, too, are different. The naka-kuguri and kaya-mon of Omote Senke, although rustic, are striking in their design and construction when compared to the simply designed middle gate of Ura Senke with its plain round posts and split bamboo roof.

There are interesting elements in the roji at Ura Senke that echo some of the historical points we have covered in previous chapters. The squarish stone water basin, for instance, that sits to the east of Yūin, is made from a block of carved granite that was originally the pedestal stone of a stupa. Perhaps this is similar to the one that was mentioned in the description of Rikyū's tea gathering at Jurakudai, although that one was round. The old pedestal stone at Ura Senke was turned into a water basin by carving a deep hollow on its upper surface, transforming it into what is called a shihōbutsu-gata chōzubachi, which translates literally as "four-sided Buddha-style water basin." Each of the four faces of the pedestal stone has a Buddha image carved into it, although the original carving was not detailed and years of weathering have further eroded the image so that only the barest of forms can be made out (see fig. 33). Another interesting element of the roji is the pine tree that grows to the south of the entry to

Yūin, which is a good example of the gaku no matsu, "tablet pine," mentioned in Genryū Chawa (also called a gakumi-matsu). The curved trunk of the pine artfully frames the name tablet of the tea house that hangs under the thatch beneath the ridge (fig. 65).

One interesting connection between the garden and the architecture is found in a large tea room called Tairyūken. Built in the taste of the 13th grand master, Tetchū Sōshitsu (1872–1924, also known as Ennosai), the main post (tokobashira) of the display alcove (tokonoma) is a natural red pine post of rather large girth that was taken from a tree which had grown in the roji just in front of the Yūin tea house. Of course this is an extremely rare case in which materials from the roji have been used directly in construction of the tea house, but it does reflect the general sentiment that the design of the roji was intended in many ways to be integral to the design of the tea house.

Estate Gardens of Provincial Lords

The beginning of the Edo period (1600–1868) was marked by the consolidation of most of Japan's territory by a single hegemon, Tokugawa Ieyasu (1542–1616), who arranged the seat of his military government in the city of Edo, now known as Tōkyō. Because his descendants continued after him to occupy the role of chief military lord, shōgun, the era is also known as the Tokugawa period. All of the provinces, han, in Japan during this period were divided among various provincial lords, daimyō. Ieyasu's victory over his competitors for control of Japan had come in a decisive battle at Sekigahara (1600), and the structure of

Japan thereafter followed the lines drawn at that battle. Those *daimyō* who were loyal to Ieyasu at the time of Sekigahara were labeled *fudai daimyō*, "lineage" *daimyō*, and, since they were considered to be trustworthy, either they were given positions close to or within the central government in Edo, and consequently lived in Edo, or they were given strategic positions to occupy throughout the country along trade routes or in areas surrounding Edo itself. A second group consisted of those *daimyō* who opposed Ieyasu at Sekigahara; these became known as the *tozama daimyō*, "outsider" *daimyō*. They either were allowed to hold on to their historic domains or were shifted elsewhere to another to suit the needs of the central government. A third, smaller group, called *shinpan*, was made up of families who were related by birth to the Tokugawa family. There were many retainers and wealthy families, but the appellation *daimyō* was given to those men who were in control of lands that produced 10,000 *koku* of rice or more, a *koku* being the amount required to feed a person for one year, or about 180 liters. On average, the domains of *tozama daimyō* produced about twice the amount of rice as those of *fudai daimyō*. In each

of the three groups there were members with only 10,000 *koku* as well as those with more than 100,000 *koku*. About two thirds of all the *daimyō* held estates of 50,000 *koku* or less; those very large estates producing 100,000 *koku* or more amounted to only about fifteen percent of the total. The large estate gardens that will be discussed here were constructed by *daimyō* of the latter group with very large holdings and can be

66. RITSURIN PARK. Takamatsu City. This garden has been part of the estate of the Matsudaira family, lords of Sanuki province (present-day Kagawa Prefecture) since 1642. Many generations of that family have added to the garden's design since then; and taken away from it, too. In 1850 Lord Yoritane cut down all the chestnut trees that gave name to the estate (Ritsurin means Chestnut Grove) to improve his duck hunting. The cluster of wide roofs seen across the lake is a group of pavilions called Kikugetsutei, the architecture of which, *sukiya* style, is an outgrowth of *sōan* tea architecture. Photograph by Ōhashi Haruzō.

67. KŌRAKUEN PARK. Okayama Prefecture. The garden was initiated in the late 17th century as part of the estate of the Ikeda family, lords of Okayama province. The garden mixed elements of a stroll garden, such as the central pond and long, meandering paths that wind around and through the water (as seen here). On an island in the pond sits the Shima Chaya, Island Tea House. Although the estate has been called Kōrakuen since 1871, before that it was known by many names including Chaya Yashiki—the Tea House Villa. Photograph by Ōhashi Haruzō.

68. KOISHIKAWA KŌRAKUEN. Tōkyō. Begun in 1629 by Tokugawa Yorifusa (1603–61), first lord of Mito province, the property was one of his estates in Edo (now Tōkyō). The garden features many abstracted scenic images of Japan and China, famous scenes that were widely known through literature and painting, including this plank bridge cutting through a bed of irises that evokes the standard image of Yatsuhashi, a scenic spot in Aichi Prefecture known for its *kakitsubata*, Iris laevigata. The name Kōraku comes from a Northern Song–dynasty text: "A true Lord takes his pleasure (*raku*) after (*kō*) the nation (or emperor)." Photograph by Ōhashi Haruzō.

69. KENROKUEN. Kanazawa City. This garden was the estate of the Maeda family, lords of Kaga province (now Kanazawa Prefecture). It is thought that the early design and implementation of the garden may have been influenced by Kobori Enshū, who was tea advisor to the Maeda family, and by Kentei (a well-known gardener), who is known to have visited Kenrokuen from 1630 to 1632. The Harp-Stand Lantern (Kotoji-dōrō), photographed here in front of Misty Lake, Kasumigaike, has become the symbol of Kenrokuen. Lanterns were first used in gardens by the tea masters of the late 16th century, who took them from Buddhist temples. Two hundred years later, the garden lantern had become sculpture, as attested to by this beautiful example. Photograph by Ōhashi Haruzō.

found both in their home provinces as well as in Edo. In modern parlance these are called *daimyō* gardens (because of who built them) or stroll gardens (because of the way they were used).

A means of controlling provincial *daimyō* employed by the central government was the system of "alternate attendance," *sankin kōtai*, by which *daimyō* were required to be in attendance in Edo personally every other year, and to leave core members of their personal families in Edo in their stead when they were not there themselves. This was a thinly veiled system of hostage taking, but, more importantly to the issue of gardens, the *daimyō* were thereby required to maintain, in addition to an estate in their home province (usually with a castle, too), as many as three additional residences in Edo. These Edo residences—upper (*kami-yashiki*), middle (*naka-yashiki*), and lower (*shimo-yashiki*)—and the ones in their home province all had gardens, and the design of all of these gardens was based, to some degree, on tea gardens. Observing the historical flow, one can see that the narrow, introverted *roji* of the *wabi*-style of tea, which developed primarily within the merchant class in the late 1500s, was re-created into a lighter, more open, and grand style of tea by Oribe, Enshū, Katagiri Sekishū, and others in the first half of the 1600s as they were developing the *daimyō-cha* style of tea. It was this *daimyō-cha* tea garden that influenced the development of large estate gardens in the late 1600s and after.

At the commencement of the Meiji period, in 1869, the social system that supported the *daimyō* was dissolved, and the provinces were restructured as prefectures under the new government. At that time, or soon afterward, many of the large estates of *daimyō* were turned into prefectural parks, and some of those that have not since succumbed to the pressures of development still exist in more or less the same form they had been in at the end of the 19th century. Among these are Ritsurin Kōen in Kagawa Prefecture, Kōrakuen in Okayama Prefecture, Koishikawa Kōrakuen and Rikugien in Tōkyō, and Kenrokuen in Kanazawa Prefecture (figs. 66–68).[275] The gardens at all of these residence-turned-parks have similar designs. They feature a large central pond that instills a broad-sweeping, open atmosphere. The ponds are circumambulated by meandering paths that alternately hide and reveal sections of the garden and distant views, a technique now called *mie-gakure*. These large gardens were specifically designed to allow people to wander about them, thus the name "stroll garden," *kaiyū-shiki teien*, a modern term that was only recently applied by garden scholars.

A *daimyō*'s residence was in part his private estate and in part a pleasure garden used to entertain upper-echelon visitors who came on business related to the province. The gardens contained various artistically re-created landscape vistas within which were situated various buildings, including tea houses. The tea houses were typically known as *chaya* and were different in atmosphere from the tea houses used for *chanoyu*. These *chaya*, like the tea pavilion mentioned in *Kissa Ōrai*, *kissa no tei*, were primarily viewing platforms from which to enjoy the garden. Unlike the rustic tea houses, they were not small, dark, and introverted but, quite the opposite, would normally be open to the outside and more suited for the service of *daimyō-cha* than *wabi-cha*. At times the entries to these tea houses were separated from the larger stroll garden by a fence, and the entry garden designed as a *roji*, but more often than not the *chaya* was simply situated in the garden to take advantage of a certain view and did not have its own, rustic entry path.

The simplest way in which the design of the *roji* can be seen to have influenced the design of stroll gardens is in the appearance of certain elements that were used for the first time in early-era *roji* and then went on to be also used in the larger-scale stroll gardens. The most common of these are stepping stones, water basins, and stone lanterns. The design of these elements, however, often changed as a result. Understatedly diminutive in the *roji* of urban merchants, these elements often became grandiose in the gardens of provincial lords.

Due to the vastly larger scale of the gardens of provincial lords, and also due to the lords' predilection for things that expressed authority and power, the materials used to make the gardens increased in scale as well. The perception of these elements, or their appreciation, changed too. To begin with, the use of elements such as stepping stones, water basins, and stone lanterns was new—if not radical—during the 1500s. This was not so by the 17th and 18th centuries when the provincial lords began to build their grand estate gardens. Stone lanterns, for instance, had only been used at religious sites before the advent of their use in *roji* at the end of the 1500s. Small bonfires in iron baskets had been used to provide light in nighttime gardens since the Heian period if not before, but stone lanterns were exclusively a religious artifact. Their use, therefore, in the *roji* was absolutely novel and lent the garden an atmosphere of antiquity and solemnity. By the early 1600s, however, their use in gardens was typical and, by the end of that century, stereotypic. The appreciation of the lanterns shifted to an entirely aesthetic one, and they became viewed as sculptures of a sort. The quintessential example is the lantern at Kenrokuen called Kotoji-dōrō, or "Harp-Stand Lantern," which is so well known that it has come to symbolize the garden (fig. 69). This lantern has lost all of the features of older lanterns that reflect Buddhist iconography and instead is designed exclusively to be visually stunning, which, of course, it is.

The nature and purpose of the urban *roji* was to provide a space within which guests could prepare themselves, inwardly and outwardly, for the tea gathering to come. The gathering was a quiet, inward affair—a temporary separation from daily cares and perceptions—and the *roji* was designed to evoke in the guests entering it the appropriate mental state.

It can be argued that the stroll gardens had a similar task on a grander scale: that the paths through woods and along the great ponds, the various bridges and gates, and the subdued plantings of mostly evergreen trees, were intended as an elaborate, extended *roji*. In as much as the point of the stroll garden was to allow a visitor to escape from personal reality into a fantasy landscape, and also because that experience might have included a stop at a tea house for a bowl of tea, the stroll garden can be seen as a tea garden. However, it is obvious that the estate gardens were designed to impress, and the mood they induced in a person traveling through them was utterly different from that achieved by passing through the compressed urban *roji*.

Another indicator that the practice of tea was perceived separately from the gardens surrounding the tea house in *daimyō* gardens, or said another way, an indicator that the stroll garden was not perceived as a tea *roji*, is that in tea records from tea gatherings at *daimyō* estates, detailed lists of the tea utensils are recorded but the garden (*roji*) and familiar elements of the garden such as the water basin, stepping stones, stone lanterns, and garden gates, do not show up at all.[276]

Imperial Gardens

The aristocratic families of Japan, those who had a connection through bloodline or marriage to the imperial family, lost direct control over the administration of the country at the end of the Heian period (794–1185). Their position of power was usurped by military families, many of whom, in fact, ended up imitating "aristocratic" customs of behavior after they had established themselves for a number of generations. Even though aristocratic families lost direct control, and although the financial position of those families varied greatly depending on the vagaries of the age they lived in, they did not cease to exist. They maintained old court customs, such as annual festivals (*nenjū gyōji*), court music (*gagaku*), and court dance (*bugaku*), wore clothes of a different style, did not personally bear arms, and had their homes built in their own style. If they could afford it, they had gardens too.

As with the *daimyō*, the wealthiest of whom built the very large stroll gardens that exist today, so, too, the very largest of the aristocratic gardens were built by those members who were at the very top of the aristocratic lineage—emperors, their immediate family, and most powerful supporters. Four such examples are the Katsura Detached Palace, Shūgakuin Detached Palace, Sentō Imperial Palace, and Shūsuitei, all in Kyōto. As with the *daimyō* gardens, the design of these gardens was based on that of tea gardens. In fact, the four gardens we will look at are much closer to the *roji* of the early 1600s in their overall feeling, subtlety of detailing, and manner of use than are the gardens of the *daimyō*.

KATSURA RIKYŪ[277]

Katsura Detached Palace, or Katsura Rikyū, was begun by Prince Toshihito (1579–1629), son of Emperor Goyōzei (1571–1617), around 1620. He had been adopted as heir to the childless ruler Toyotomi Hideyoshi, but was then disowned when Hideyoshi's wife finally bore him a son. In compensation, he received new titles and a new name, becoming the founder of the Hachijō no Miya family. His new financial independence gave him the wherewithal to develop a country estate. The fact that tea culture was an important aspect of the design of that estate—which would later be called Katsura Rikyū—can be seen in its early, self-effacing name: the Simple Tea House in the Melon Fields (Uribatake no Karoki Chaya).[278] The garden fell into disrepair after Toshihito's death until his son, Toshitada (1619–62), married the daughter of the lord of Kaga province and the garden was refurbished, around 1642. Although some changes to the garden were made by descendants in the years following, the garden we see today is primarily the work of the first two generations of Hachijō princes (fig. 70).

Katsura is a stroll garden, in that the main function of the garden is to allow people to meander about

70. KATSURA DETACHED PALACE. Kyōto. This garden is an excellent example of an Edo-period aristocratic villa garden. Prince Toshihito (1579–1629) began construction around 1620, followed by his son, Toshitada (1619–62). In its early days, the garden was called the Simple Tea House in the Melon Fields (Uribatake no Karoki Chaya), a name that reveals its fundamental connection to tea culture. In fact, it can be said that the complex and brilliantly designed pathway that circumambulates the central pond is in many ways an elongated *roji*. Photograph by Ōhashi Haruzō.

*extant tea gardens
and gardens
influenced by tea*

the complexly shaped ponds with their many inlets and traverse between hillocks that provide a constantly changing sequence of views. Included among these views are abstracted images of famous scenes (*meisho*) such as Amanohashidate, a spit of land on the Japan Sea coast of Kyōto Prefecture. That particular design feature was not derived from the *roji* of the late 16th and early 17th centuries, but many other aspects of the design are very much in the tea garden mode. In fact, Katsura can be said to be a *roji* that has been elongated out into space, spread across a park-like setting. The design aesthetic seems to straddle the boundary between *daimyō-cha* and *wabi-cha*. There is for instance a rustic waiting bench (*soto koshikake*) not far from the main formal entry to the garden. This is clearly a waiting bench for *chanoyu* (not simply a resting spot in the garden), and although the thatched roof, natural timbers used for posts and beams, and simple clay walls are in the *wabi* style, the structure is much grander than *koshikake* found in older *roji*: more of a small building than just a roofed bench. Also, it faces onto a hillock planted with exotic Sago palm trees (*sotetsu-yama*), a species that had been used in tea gardens from the end of the 1500s, but only by military lords. The water basin near the waiting bench, too, is rather formal in its design and placement. The stone is an exact square, shaped overall like a flattened cube, and is positioned just at the end of a very long straight *tatami-ishi* path, at the other end of which is a small stone lantern. This precise axial alignment is unusual for Japanese design but could be said to be more in keeping with the grandeur of *daimyō-cha* than the natural subtlety of *wabi-cha*.

The design of the architecture as well incorporates aspects of both the *shoin* style (*daimyō* style) and *sukiya* style. The main residence, for instance—with its white plaster exterior walls, white-papered interior walls, and formal arrangement of *tokonoma* and display shelving—is in the *shoin* style, while some of the smaller arbors, like Gepparō and Shōkintei, which have clay-plastered walls and exposed roof rafters (no ceiling), are designed in the manner of a *sukiya*. Shōkintei even contains a *wabi*-style three-mat tea room.

Another aspect of the garden at Katsura that derives from earlier tea gardens is the design of the paths, which has been taken to an unusual level of artistic expression. In the aforementioned comparison of the pathway designs of Rikyū and Oribe, in which Rikyū favored function over design six parts to four, and Oribe the opposite, favoring style, the pathways at Katsura seem to go Oribe one better, being preeminently stylish. One example of this is the series of stepping stones that traverse the edge of Onrindō, a private Buddhist hall. Each stone is a square of cut granite, each the same size, and yet the layout of all the stones is irregular, following a meandering pattern typical of stepping stone paths made with natural stones. As the stepping stones meander, they cut into and out of a band of flat-topped pebbles that surrounds Onrindō as a drip-edge. The pattern made by the seemingly

71. SHŪGAKUIN DETACHED PALACE. Kyōto. This estate was originally the country villa of abdicated Emperor Gomizunoo (1596–1680, r. 1611–29), who began working on it in 1655. The emperor's passion for the arts of flower arranging and tea ceremony strongly influenced the design of the gardens. Divided into three sections along a path that winds up a hillside, the architecture of the upper and lower sections is *sukiya* style and the garden details are clearly based on those of a *roji*. Photograph by Ōhashi Haruzō.

random interaction of these very precise elements is "modern" still, hundreds of years later.

SHŪGAKUIN RIKYŪ[279]

Shūgakuin Detached Palace, or Shūgakuin Rikyū, was built by retired Emperor Gomizunoo (1596–1680, r. 1611–29) as a country villa after a prolonged search for the perfect spot (fig. 71). In 1655, he found what he was looking for on the slopes of Mount Hiei in the northeast of Kyōto and began his project. Eventually the site was developed with upper, lower, and middle sections. The first two sections were made by Gomizunoo, while the middle section was the private villa of the emperor's daughter Akenomiya. After the emperor's death, the middle section became a temple, Rinkyūji, and was incorporated as part of the Rikyū in the Meiji period (1868–1912).

The upper and lower sections in particular are, like Katsura, very much influenced by the aesthetics of tea: in part *wabi-cha* and in part *daimyō-cha*. The architecture of buildings such as Jūgetsu-kan, in the lower section, and Rin'untei, in the upper section, have low-pitched cypress-shingle roofs and bare clay walls, which evoke the elegant rusticity of *wabi* aesthetic. They also have devices, however, such as the *jōdan*, a slightly raised section of the *tatami* floor that elevates persons of important rank, in this case the emperor himself. In addition, the inclusion of stepping stone paths in places (most of the paths are presently earthen or gravel) and many varieties of stone lanterns is also derived from their initial use in tea gardens.

SENTŌ GOSHO[280]

Sentō Gosho is a retirement villa built just to the southeast of the Imperial Palace, located in the Imperial Palace Park, in Kyōto (fig. 72). It was built in several stages during the Edo period, initially by Emperor Gomizunoo upon his abdication. The garden was originally divided in two with the emperor occupying the southern portion of the site and the empress dowager, Tōfukumon'in, in the northern section, known as the Ōmiya Gosho. The dividing wall is no longer extant but one can still feel the separation of the two sections created by a series of low hills between the two ponds. Most of the pavilions and halls that were built in the garden are no longer extant, so it presently has a much less "developed" feeling than it would have had when it was actively lived in by retired emperors; and any portions of the garden that may have been specifically designed as tea *roji* are no longer extant. Still, the remaining pavilion, Seikatei, at the very southern end of the property is in the *sukiya* style, although its deep-red clay walls seem to suit the aesthetics of *daimyō-cha* better than those of *wabi-cha*.

72. SENTŌ GOSHO. Kyōto. Just to the southeast of the Imperial Palace within the Imperial Palace Park, Kyōto Gyoen, is this estate developed in 1629 for the abdicated Emperor Gomizunoo. The garden has two main sections: the southern half was for the emperor and the northern for the empress dowager, Tōfukumon'in. All of the tea houses that previously existed have been razed, save one on the southern end. Perhaps the most striking feature of the garden is a 100-meter-long, 10-meter-wide curved beach (*suhama*) that is covered with uniformly fist-sized, smooth, black stones. The stones were a gift to Emperor Kōkaku in 1815 from Ōkubo Tadamasa, Lord of Odawara (present-day Kanagawa Prefecture). Photograph by Ōhashi Haruzō.

Shūsuitei is a garden of the former Kujō family residence within the Imperial Palace in Kyōto. It is on a much smaller scale than the three gardens previously mentioned, but it is also the one that is most like a classic *roji* in its design and function (fig. 73). The areas of the Imperial Palace Park that are outside the Imperial Palace and Sentō Gosho are now designated as a public park and are fairly open, composed of large expanses of gravel and wooded areas. In the past, however, the same area was crowded with the houses of aristocratic families, *kuge*, the size of which varied greatly depending on the owner's position in the imperial hierarchy. The Kujō family were one of the five families, *gosekke*, that were traditionally entrusted with the position of regent, *sesshō*, and chief advisor to the emperor, *kanpaku*. In comparison to the other *kuge* residences within the Imperial Palace grounds, they had a rather large property in the southwest corner. What still exists today is the pond, part of the garden, and one refurbished building. The building is two storied, with a distant view across the pond to the eastern mountains from the second floor, and a closer view across the pond from the first floor. There is a small *wabi*-style tea room attached to the building on the

north side. A path leads from the main entry, around the building to the northeast corner where there is a water basin and an entry to the tea room. The basin, interestingly, is not low to the ground as is typical for those in *wabi*-style tea *roji*. Rather, it is a standing basin, *tachi-chōzubachi*, indicative of the aristocratic class of its owners and, like the use of flowering trees such as the crape myrtle, representative of a garden design that favors scenic beauty over the desire to create the atmosphere of a hermit's retreat.

73. SHŪSUITEI. Kyōto. In the southwest corner of the Imperial Palace Park is one of the few remaining properties from the time when the vast park was crowded with the residences of aristocratic families. Called Shūsuitei, it was built as the residence of the Kujō family. The water basins in the *roji* are all tall, *tachi-chōzubachi*, precluding the need to crouch to use them, typical of an aristocratic setting. The tea house itself, however, is in the *wabi*-style, being internally focused, dimly lit, and having a *nijiri-guchi*.

Gardens of Merchant Residences

As described in some detail in the previous section on the townhouses of the merchant class, *machiya*, the plan of a merchant residence in central Kyōto from the mid- to late Edo period on typically consisted of three architectural units: shop, residence, and storehouse. This is, of course, a classic description of the form. and in reality many variations existed. Although most townhouses have been destroyed by the urban development that has taken place in recent decades, the remaining townhouses still follow this pattern.

The plots that the residences are built on are generally deep and narrow, having a slim frontage and going far back into the block. That unique shape developed during the Edo period, in part, as a means to avoid taxes that were based on the width of street frontage. The shop, called the *omoteya* or *mise*, is situated adjoining the street, as might be expected. The next structure going back into the property is the residence, or *omoya*, and the last structure, furthest back into the property, is the storehouse, or *kura*. In between these three units are two small open spaces, the sizes of which depend on the overall size of the property and, thus, on the wealth of the owner. The space between the shop and the residence is typically rather small, sometimes no more than a few meters square. It is usually called a *tsubo niwa* these days, though not every household uses this same standardized term. Some call the space simply *niwa* (garden/court) or *naka niwa* (inner garden/court). The space between

the residence and the storehouse is usually larger than the *tsubo niwa* and is often called a *senzai* or, again, simply *niwa*.

The expressions *tsubo niwa* and *senzai* have roots in Heian-period court culture and aristocratic architecture. At that time, the *tsubo* was a small courtyard, enclosed between various halls in an extensive aristocratic residence. Each *tsubo* usually contained only one species of plant, from which it gained its name, i.e., Paulownia Court (*kiritsubo*) and Wisteria Court (*fujitsubo*). The courtiers who lived in rooms adjacent to a particular *tsubo* were referred to by that courtyard's name, so we find in the Heian-period classic *The Tale of Genji* characters called Kiritsubo no Mikado, the emperor and Genji's father; Kiritsubo no Kōi, the emperor's Intimate and Genji's mother; and Fujitsubo, the empress. *Senzai*, which translates literally as "forward plantings," referred to a part of the garden that was close to the residence or simply to a part planted with grasses and shrubs (which were also called *senzai*). Finding the terms *tsubo* and *senzai* used by the merchant class to refer to their own residences may have been the result of their desire to affect a certain air of culture.

Returning to the gardens of the *machiya*, the

74. YOSHIDA RESIDENCE. Kyōto. The Yoshida Residence is a classic example of *omoteya-zukuri*, a style of architecture typical of Kyōto townhouses. Classically, there are three parts: a shop fronting the street (*omoteya*), a residence a little further back on the property (*omoya*), and one or two storehouses (*kura*) further back still. In the spaces between these buildings are small gardens. The one between shop and residence (shown here) is often called a *tsubo niwa*, and the one further back, *senzai*. The water basin and lantern, of course, have their roots in the design of the *roji*.

75. HATA RESIDENCE. Kyōto. The rear garden of the Hata Residence, *senzai*, adds a great visual depth to the main room. The meandering path and carefully placed plantings create an effect of a path leading off into the distant woods—all this in the middle of the city. The stepping stones, water basin, lantern, mossy ground, and naturalistic plantings all derive from the design of the *roji*. The water basin is a sunken type, *ori-tsukubai*, and the large stepping stone with a disk shape carved into it is a *niwa-garan*.

76. SUGIMOTO RESIDENCE. Kyōto. The Sugimoto Residence is larger and more complexly laid out than the classic *omoteya-zukuri* townhouse. Along the sides and at the rear of the main residence are garden spaces reflecting the design sentiments of *chanoyu*—mossy ground, naturalistic plantings, and so on. The small courtyard holds a water basin, a tall lantern, and the well, which can be seen behind the trees with a bamboo cover on top of it. Photograph property of Naraya Hozon Kai.

77. KOJIMA RESIDENCE. Kyōto. The garden at the Kojima Residence gives the impression of being much bigger than it is, with its stepping stone path leading back into the trees. Of note here are the dramatically large stones in the garden, such as the water-carved river boulder used as the water basin and the large circular stepping stone, *niwa-garan*, in the garden path. The white-walled building in the background is the storehouse, *kura*, where valuable objects, or those that are out of season, are kept.

walls of the rooms facing these outdoor spaces consist primarily of translucent paper doors, *shōji*, which, when slid open, allow a completely unobstructed view of the gardens. The *tsubo niwa* is thus shared by the shop and the front room of the residence, while the *senzai* is primarily meant to be seen from the back room of the residence, which is considered the main room—the room for entertaining important guests and for the head of the household to use when there are no guests. This room will always have a display alcove (*tokonoma*), display shelves (*chigai-dana*), and sometimes a hearth (*ro*) cut into the floor, all of which are accoutrements of a tea room. Similarly, the design of both the *tsubo niwa* and the *senzai* are based on that of the *roji*, and they often contain many of the components of a tea garden: a water basin, one or two stone lanterns, a stepping stone path, moss as a groundcover, and sparse plantings of mainly broadleaf evergreens. Even if the gardens are not actually used as *roji*, they are designed in the *roji* motif. Four examples of *machiya* with inner courtyard gardens are Yoshida-ke, Hata-ke, Sugimoto-ke, and Kojima-ke (figs. 74–77).[282] The suffix -*ke*, as with Senke, means "family" or "home," so Yoshida-ke would be the Yoshida Residence and so on. All of these structures date from some time after 1864, when the central part of Kyōto burned in a huge conflagration.

20th-Century Private Estates

extant tea gardens and gardens influenced by tea

Throughout the Edo period, the wealth of the merchant class continued to grow as the national mercantile system developed and as merchants began to perform profitable services for the military government, such as exchanging rice collected as tax into coinage. Specific laws governing social structure, however, prevented them from obtaining a high order of social status and power throughout that time. After the Meiji Restoration, however, through which Emperor Meiji was reinstated as head of state and the dominant position of the military class was dissolved, the merchants were able to prosper in a manner theretofore disallowed them. More to the point, they could express that prosperity in public ways that were previously prohibited, and one form of that expression was the construction of large residences and gardens. Two such estates are Sankeien and Tairyūsansō.

SANKEIEN[283]

Sankeien, in Yokohama City, is a very large country estate garden encompassing several hills and valleys (fig. 78). The original owner and initiator of the garden was Hara Tomitarō (1868–1939), who used the pseudonym Sankei. The adopted son of a wealthy silk merchant, Hara Zenzaburō (1824–99), Sankei took over the business upon Zenzaburō's death and established himself at the family estate three years later in 1902. Sankei began sponsoring artists and collecting artwork with the enormous wealth that resulted from his business success, becoming one of the great patrons of his age. He also set about to collect beautiful and historically important wooden buildings and stone garden ornaments, the artful placement of which became a key element in the design of his garden; for instance, a Muromachi-period (1333–1568) pagoda set on top of a hill in the garden has become the symbol of Sankeien.

The overall design of the garden is in the stroll garden motif, with a large central pond and a long, meandering path that offers changing views of the natural landscape and the buildings placed within it. In a narrow valley that leads up from the pond into the surrounding hills are several structures that are designed specifically as tea houses. A quick stream runs down the center of the valley with the tea houses set staggered on both sides, half hidden from each other by thick vegetation. These are Gekkaden, a beautiful *shoin*-style building and its attached tea house, Kinmōkutsu; an unusual two-story building called Chōshūkaku that resembles the prow and raised bridge of a ship; and Shunsōro, a tea house that contains a three-and-three-quarters-mat tea room.

Kinmōkutsu and Shunsōro both have many elements of *wabi*-style tea houses, such as crawl-through entries, *nijiri-guchi*, and also have stepping stones and waterbasins set in their entry gardens that act as a *roji* during a tea gathering. These areas are directly modeled after tea gardens—both in their function and aesthetics—although the rest of the estate feels more like a pleasure park than a roji.

TAIRYŪSANSŌ[284]

Tairyūsansō is one of several private gardens to be found in the historic part of Kyōto called the Nanzenji district, named after the large Zen monastery found there. The gardens have several aspects in common, the first of which being that they all were designed in a partnership between the owner and a particular family of gardeners named Ogawa. As is typical of artisan families in Japan, the person who took over the head of the family (usually the eldest son but not always) also took the given name of the former family head, which in the case of the Ogawa family was Jihei. There have been eleven generations of garden-ers named Ogawa Jihei, also known by the appellation Ueji, but it was the seventh (1860–1933) and eighth (1882–1926) generations who were involved with the gardens presented here.

Another similarity between the gardens is that they all draw water from the same canal. Known as the Biwako Sosui, the canal connects Kyōto to Lake Biwa, in neighboring Shiga Prefecture, via a tunnel through the low mountains that separate them. It was built primarily to allow small barges to ferry goods back and forth but also served to bring drinking water to Kyōto and to generate hydroelectric power. Many of the estates that were built in the Nanzenji district, which is located just where the canal leaves the mountain tunnel and enters Kyōto, have historical rights to use some of the canal water to feed their garden streams and ponds.

A third aspect the gardens share in common is a strong influence of *chanoyu* in their design. The buildings in the gardens are primarily built in the *sukiya* style and the gardens feature stepping stone paths, stone lanterns, water basins, subdued forest-like plantings, and other aspects of tea garden design.

Tairyūsansō was originally built in 1896 by entrepreneur Ijūin Kanetsune, but was developed much further by the second owner, Ichida Yaichirō, in partnership with Ogawa Jihei from 1902 to 1905 (fig. 79). There are several small rooms for tea at Tairyūsansō: a four-and-a-half-mat tea room (*yojōhan*), a three-and-three-quarters-mat tea room (*sanjō daime*), and a three-mat waiting room (*sanjō yoritsuki*). At the entry to the waiting room, there is a water basin, *tsukubai*, built into the ground as is traditional; but for the tea rooms themselves, there is instead a rather unusual water basin called a *nagare-tsukubai* that is situated directly in the middle of a small stream. Large stepping stones allow the guests to step out into the stream, well

78. SANKEIEN. Yokohama. Hara Tomitarō (1868–1939), a well-known supporter of the arts, developed his huge estate as a strolling park and as a setting for his collection of historic buildings. The grounds range over three hills, thus the name, Sankeien, the Garden of Three Valleys. One of those valleys contains a collection of tea houses including this one, Chōshūkaku, which was originally commissioned by the third Tokugawa *shōgun*, Iemitsu (1604–51), for the Nijō Castle in Kyōto. Photograph by Tabata Minao.

79. TAIRYŪSANSŌ. Kyōto. Developed into its present form as the estate of the Ichida family, the residence is an excellent example of *sukiya*-style architecture. The gardens are loosely divided into an upper and lower section. The brook that runs between the two flows quite near one of the tea rooms in the middle of the residence. The water basin, *chōzubachi*, has been situated directly in that stream, a so-called *nagare-tsukubai*. To use the water, a guest steps between two large clusters of Equisetum hyemale, *tokusa*, and onto the stepping stones while the brook runs along beneath their feet. Photograph by Tabata Minao.

above the water surface, and use the water in the basin while the stream water flows beneath them. The feeling is at once exhilarating and refreshing.

Other Private Residences

TABUCHI RESIDENCE

The Tabuchi family residence presently lies in Akō City in Hyōgo Prefecture (fig. 80).[285] When the family moved there in 1673, the region was called Akō-han, or Akō province, and was governed by the *daimyō* family Asano. The Asano family was replaced by the Nagai family in 1701 and then by the Mori family in 1706, who governed the province thereafter for twelve generations. The value of the province was only 20,000 *koku*, so it was definitely not one of the large and powerful provinces mentioned before, the lords of which created sumptuous stroll gardens. The Tabuchi family were involved in the production of salt in oceanside paddies, for which the region was famous, as well as in the wholesaling of salt and coal. As such they were of the merchant class, and yet they also held positions in the bureaucracy of the province and often received official visits, *onari*, from the lords of the province. So,

80. TABUCHI RESIDENCE. Akō City. At the residence of the Tabuchi family, the property is divided into an upper section and a middle section, each with a tea house, and a lower section with the main residence. The entry to the smaller of the two tea houses is defined by this middle wicket, *naka-kuguri*, a clay-plastered fence with a small door through which the guests bow to enter. There are very few tea gardens that still have a *naka-kuguri*.

although their property should be looked at as the country estate of a wealthy merchant family, in some ways it also is representative of the residence of a minor *daimyō*.

Although the Tabuchi family moved to the present location in 1673, the condition of the original residence is not precisely recorded. The fourth generation, Tabuchi Ichibei (1703–60), was named to be the *kuramoto* of Akō-han, or essentially the provincial bank. On the occasion of a visit by Mori Tadahiro, some time between 1751 and 1764, the Tabuchi family built a tea house called Meienrō at the upper end of the property. The two-story, thatch-roofed pavilion sits at the top of a steep slope; from the second floor there is an open view to the sea and, in the past, to the salt paddies. Tabuchi Kyūbei (1712–96), who was the fifth household head in the family line, is reputed to have been particularly fond of *chanoyu* and to have studied under the Kyōto tea master Hisada Sōsan. In 1764, Sōsan requested of Kyūbei that a tea house be built on the property, and it was at that time that Shun'insai was built and the *roji* that leads to it as well.[286]

The result of this development is that the Tabuchi property is divided into three sections that descend down the steep slope: an upper area around the tea house Meienrō, a middle section with an enclosed inner *roji* that leads to Shun'insai, and a lower section around the large, *shoin*-style residence. The gardens that link these three sections are an interesting weave of two styles: viewing garden design and *roji*. In the lower section, for instance, as part of the residence, there are two rooms that were specifically intended as places to receive important guests, the local *daimyō* undoubtedly top among them. One is called the *onari no ma*, "room for official receptions," and the other the *jōdan no ma*, the "raised room," a four-and-a-half-mat

81. HAKUSA SONSŌ. Kyōto. The residence of painter and tea aficionado Hashimoto Kansetsu (1883–1945) has, in its garden's southern half, an arbor and two adjoined tea houses facing across a small pond. In fact, the design of the entire garden—the fences, gates, pathways, and so on—is drawn from the precepts of the tea *roji*. The stepping stones moving off to the left lead to the *nijiri-guchi* of the four-and-a-half-mat tea room, Keijakuan, and those leading off into the distance to the entry of the eight-mat tea room, Isuitei. Photograph by Ōhashi Haruzō.

space that is slightly elevated above the surrounding rooms as a sign of respect toward those who use it. It is in this second room that the most important visitor would sit, while others in attendance, guests or hosts, would be in the *onari no ma*. Both of these rooms face outward toward a pond garden immediately behind which is the steep embankment that leads up to the tea houses. There is an elegant moon-viewing deck made of fine bamboo off to the side and a cluster of exotic Sago palms on the embankment, giving the whole arrangement a feeling of grandeur as might be expected in the garden of a *daimyō*. One can step off the moon-viewing deck onto a garden path that leads up the slope, through the palms and a small gate in the fence that surrounds the lower garden, and enter the part of the garden that was designed specifically as a *roji*. Having ascended the slope and passed the gate, one finds oneself on a stepping stone path that leads directly to Meienrō or, if one turns left and ducks through a clay-plaster wall designed as a *naka-kuguri*, to the inner *roji* of Shun'insai with its waiting bench and water basin.

HAKUSA SONSŌ[287]

Hakusa Sonsō, Villa of the White Sands, was not built by a merchant family or a *daimyō*; rather, it was the private residence of a successful painter named Hashimoto Kansetsu (1883–1945; fig. 81). The villa's name derives from the fact that the river that flows by the estate—the Shirakawa, or White River—carries a granitic white sand down from the neighboring hills. Kansetsu, who was a great aficionado of tea and things Chinese, worked on his garden in stages over the first three decades of the 20th century. The main residence and a large painting studio/exhibition hall were built in 1916. The tea houses in the lower garden were built in 1932. There are two that are internally connected. One is a six-mat room called Isuitei (Arbor of Mellow Respite) and the other a four-and-a-half-mat room, Keijakuan (translated loosely as Arbor for Idling Amid Nature). The gardens that surround and link the architecture are the result of Kansetsu's continual work over those three decades. He was an avid collector, and the garden contains many unusual, carved stone objects (lanterns and stupas), prized natural stones (such as the long *kurama-ishi* slabs that are used as entry stones), and exotic plants (lacebark pine, Pinus bungeana).

There are two entries to the property, both in the northeast corner. Entering from the main gate, the path immediately crosses an old stone bridge and approaches the main entry hall. The stream beneath the bridge is quick, the land is formed into small hillocks, and the plantings are given over to cryptomeria trees and grass bamboo, all of which are intended to evoke the sense of the mountains north of Kyōto. Two paths off to the left lead down to a pond garden that is overlooked by the residence and studio. Further on in the garden are the lower pond and tea houses. Although all of the garden can be said to reflect tea garden features to some degree—the evergreen plantings, delicate fences, and thatch-roofed or bark-roofed gates—it is this lower section that was clearly designed as a *roji*. The thatch-roofed arbor that overhangs the east side of the lower pond, Mongyotei (Arbor for Talking with the Fishes), acts as a *machiai*, a waiting pavilion, on the way to the tea house. Originally it was a simple arbor that Kansetsu used for working on sketches, but it was remodeled in 1932, when the tea houses were built, to be used as a *machiai*.

Leaving the arbor and passing through a small

middle gate and across a narrow bridge brings one to the two connected tea houses. Here the path turns to stepping stones in the style of a classic *roji*, and water basins are provided at the entries to the tea houses. Keijakuan is designed in the *wabi* style—it is entered through a *nijiri-guchi* and, once entered, is rather dark and introverted. Isuitei, however, is an open-sided building and is designed to look out across the lower pond to Mongyotei and beyond to Mount Daimonji and the eastern mountains. In fact, the tufted shape of the roof of Mongyotei perfectly echoes the shape of Mount Daimonji, so, originally, it must have been an excellent example of *shakkei*, borrowed scenery. Unfortunately, recent development outside the garden has forced the owners to allow the trees on the property line to grow up, and that borrowed view has been almost entirely obscured.

Traditional Inns (Ryokan) [288]

During the Edo period, travel throughout the country greatly increased among citizens from a wide range of classes. In part this was due to the development of social systems such as the system of "alternate attendance," *sankin kōtai*, that was described in the section on the tea gardens of provincial lords. Also, individual and group pilgrimages became popular, appealing to both the strict religious adherent and the tourist. Likewise, the increasing strength of the mercantile economy required travel for business both for sales and for delivery of goods. The result of all this was an increase in the need for lodgings for travelers, along the roadways and in the cities as well. At the upper end of these inns were the *honjin*, which were set up for the use of *daimyō*, government officials, and members of aristocratic families, and the *waki-honjin*, which were used by the retainers of the former. In urban areas and resort areas, such as where hot springs were abundant, inns known as *ryokan* developed and still exist to the present day. In as much as *chanoyu* culture had become the epitome of fine etiquette, many of the rooms in a *ryokan* feature the accoutrements of a tea room, such as a display alcove, and there may even be a dedicated, *wabi*-style tea room in the inn as well. The gardens of the inns, much like those of the merchants' residences just described, were modeled after tea gardens, including elements such as stone lanterns, rustic fences, stepping stone paths, and a mossy covering to the ground (figs. 82–85).

*extant tea gardens
and gardens
influenced by tea*

82. SUMIYA INN. Kyōto. As with traditional townhouses, inns also often have small gardens built into the spaces left open between buildings to allow for light and air. The design of these gardens—for instance, the lantern, water basin, naturalistic plantings, and mossy ground shown here—is more often than not derived from that of the tea *roji*. Photograph by Ōhashi Haruzō.

83. KAWABUN INN. Kyōto. Although the guests of this inn are in the middle of a large city, looking at the garden with its rustic fences and natural planting makes them feel as if they are staying far out of town at a mountain inn. Photograph by Ōhashi Haruzō.

84. TAWARAYA INN. Kyōto. This tiny garden distills the tea garden down to its most basic elements: a basin to hold water, a lantern for light, and one evergreen plant to suggest all of nature. Photograph by Ōhashi Haruzō.

(overleaf)

85. TORIIWARŌ INN. Kyōto. The design of this small garden creates a sense of depth, contrarily, by subdividing the space with plantings and fences that conceal the rear of the garden. The curved bridge leads the eye back and suggests the beginning of a path that would take you to what lies hidden beyond. Photograph by Ōhashi Haruzō.

7

parts of a tea garden

There is no single prescribed design for a tea garden, but among the tea gardens that are used exclusively for *chanoyu*—in other words, as entry gardens to a rustic tea house—those with the double-section configuration (*nijū-roji*) that developed in the early 1600s have what can be considered the classic form. In this design, guests first enter the outer garden, *soto-roji*, and then pass a middle gate into the inner garden, *uchi-roji*. Some tea gardens are simpler, having no inner and outer sections, and are called accordingly *ichijū-roji*, single-section tea gardens. Those that are more complex—with outer, middle, and inner sections—are considered to be three-section gardens, *sanjū-roji*, but these are not common. What follows is a description of the various elements used in a stereotypical two-section garden. The order in which they are described is more or less the order in which they would be encountered when entering the *roji* (fig. 86).

Outer Gate: Soto-mon *or* Roji-mon

The outer gate, called a *soto-mon* or *roji-mon*, marks the point of entry to the *roji* (fig. 87). The gate may face onto a street that runs by a residence, onto an entry walk that leads to the front entrance of the residence, or onto a larger ornamental garden that is part of the residence. Of course the tea garden may also be found on temple grounds, a public park, or elsewhere but, the function of the outer gate is still the same. The street, entry walk, or ornamental garden onto which the outer gate faces represents, in the mind of the guest entering, the outside world—the world of ordinary business and social life. By entering the outer gate, and closing and locking it, the guests make a point of separating themselves, at least for the time of the tea gathering, from the activities of that world and state of mind that accompanies it.

The outer gate may be a free-standing, roofed structure or simply a sliding door set within a tall wall, but the doors of the gate are always solid panels of wood that visually close off the garden when the gate is shut. It is not a defensive gate, so its construction is not overly solid, but the symbolic effect of closing the gate is still clear. On the inside of the gate, if the doors swing open rather than slide, there is a horizontal wooden bar, *kannuki*, that can be slid into place to lock the door. It is the role of the last guest, *makkyaku* or *otsume*, to close and lock the door, and the sound of the gate being locked is the first signal to the host that the guests have arrived. An early record of the custom of locking the gate upon entry was given by Rodrigues (see pages 111–12) and another can be found in *Sukiyadō Shidai*.

For guests, there are manners for them to consider upon entering. The person in the lead role (*kamiza*) enters at the appointed time. [He should] open the gate (*te-kuguri*) with the left hand, place a hand on the threshold, and, first, take a look around at the garden inside the gate. Then, it is said, one should enter slowly and leisurely, and someone who enters afterward should close the gate and lock the gate.[289]

The earliest term for the entrance gate was not

86. TYPICAL *NIJŪ-ROJI* PLAN VIEW. During the Edo period, the *roji* developed into its classic two-part form called a *nijū-roji*, or double-layered tea garden. The first part to be entered is called the outer garden, *soto-roji*, and the portion closer to the tea house is known as the inner garden, *uchi-roji*. This plan nicely presents all of the classic elements of a tea garden, not all of which exist, in fact, in every tea garden depending on its size and the taste (and/or wealth) of the owner. Based on the garden of Joan—redrawn from Kitao, *Chaniwa*, p. 120.

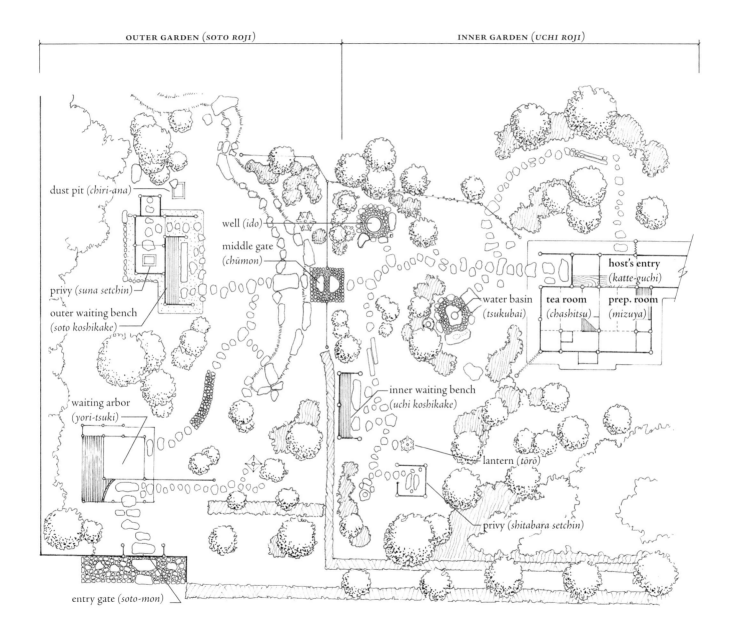

dust pit (*chiri-ana*)

well (*ido*)

middle gate
(*chūmon*)

privy (*suna setchin*)

outer waiting bench
(*soto koshikake*)

host's entry
(*katte-guchi*)

tea room
(*chashitsu*)

prep. room
(*mizuya*)

water basin
(*tsukubai*)

waiting arbor
(*yori-tsuki*)

inner waiting bench
(*uchi koshikake*)

lantern (*tōrō*)

privy (*shitabara setchin*)

entry gate (*soto-mon*)

87. OUTER GATE. Mushanokōji Senke, Kyōto. The designs of the *roji-mon*, the gates that lead into a *roji* from an adjoining part of a property, are not prescribed but tend to be simple. This gate, for instance, is no more than a wooden door in a tall clay-plaster wall that slides away to allow entry. The gate makes no grand statement about entering; it simply and effectively marks the boundary between the "outer" world and the world of the tea gathering. Photograph by Ōhashi Haruzō.

roji-mon but *roji-guchi*, literally "the mouth of the *roji*," as recorded in *Oribe Chakaiki* in 1603: "Midday. The tea masters from Sakai met at the entrance to the tea garden (*roji-guchi*)."[290] As described earlier, Rodrigues recorded that "The entrance gate is a small, narrow, and low door, through which a person can enter only by stooping."[291] Folding screens from the early Edo period, such as *Rakuchū Rakugaizu*, show scenes of *machiya* in Kyōto and Sakai. Townhouses line the street shoulder to shoulder. Now and again, one can see the entrance to an alleyway in between two townhouses. Typically, the entry has a gate and the gate has a full-sized door. Whether these lead to a tea house in the back or just to the backyard or some other location cannot be told from the painting. There are, however, a few images of gates that have a small door, like a *nijiri-guchi*, built into a roofed fence that closes off the entrance to the alleyway. Usually, a man is shown poking his head out of this small door, greeting guests who have come to pay a visit (fig. 88). In these cases, it is obvious that this is not simply a gate to an ordinary alleyway but that it is the entry to a tea house path—in other words that the gate is a *roji-guchi*.

Tea Path: Roji no Michi

Even as the etymology of the word *roji* reveals (see page 119), the tea garden is essentially just a path. The design of that path became one of the most important aspects of creating a tea garden. Take, for instance, the design of the stepping stones, *tobi-ishi*, that meander through the *roji*. Although stones or pieces of wood have been used to cross muddy ground from ancient times, the purposeful use of stepping stones to make a path stems from the early development of tea gardens at the time of Rikyū. The stepping stones had several objectives, but the main function was to elevate the guest from the ground. In part this was practical. The *roji* had developed to resemble a forest path, shaded and mossy. This stood in contrast to the entry courts of upper-echelon residences and temples that were open, dry spaces often spread with sand or fine gravel to keep them clean. So that their guests would not get their feet and the edges of their robes dirty and wet as they entered the *roji*, tea masters employed stepping stones. As the *roji* evolved through the Edo period, the design and layout of the stepping stones—their size, shape, number, and layout—became a highly developed art.

The size of the stones has changed somewhat over time. The earliest gardens, as evidenced by the extant gardens of the Sen family, used stepping stones that were generally quite small and placed fairly together. Large stones, and the great labor required to move them into place, were not in keeping with the philosophic attitude of creating a "hermitage in the city." By the end of the Edo period, however, with the influence of *daimyo-cha* aesthetics on the design of the *roji*, stepping stones became much larger. Also, with the increased use of *mitate-mono*, or reused objects, in the garden, many large and unusual objects came to be used as stepping stones.

The best example is the *garan-seki*, the large circular pedestal stones, carved out of granite, on which rested the massive wooden columns of Buddhist temples (fig. 89).[292] These stones are wonderful design features, making a striking visual point along the flow of the path. Also, having been taken from old temples, they added an atmosphere of antiquity and Buddhist sanctity. But true *garan-seki* are very big and heavy, many

88. GREETING GUESTS AT THE OUTER GATE. This painting shows the entry to a *roji* on a street; in this case the entry itself is a small crawl-through gate. The man inside the gate is undoubtedly the host, having come to greet his guests. Of the two guests outside the gate (who appear to be exchanging greetings), the man on the left is a *samurai*, as can be told by his clothes, hair style, and sword. An attendant with a sword sits to his left. The man to the right has a shaven head, like a priest, but since he is attended by a man with a sword and wears green, patterned robes, he is more likely an *inkyo*, a retired man who has taken the outer countenance of a priest. *Rakuchū Rakugaizu Byōbu* (formerly Wakimura-bon), dates unknown. Tanabe City Museum of Art, Wakayama Prefecture.

being at least a meter in diameter. Moreover, in order to withstand the weight of a temple column, the stones are made very thick, usually with a roughly pointed underside. The rarity of these stones, and the cost and labor involved in moving them, means that there are few true *garan-seki* in gardens. In the late Edo period, stone carvers began producing an imitation *garan-seki* for the gardening trade. These are called *niwa-garan*, "garden pedestal stones," and have a similar look on the top surface but are much thinner than the originals, making them easier to transport. In addition to *garan-seki*, some other unusual materials used as stepping stones in the *roji* path include blocks of granite that were foundation stones or stairs, old mill-stones, and old granite bridge piers.

Regarding the shape of the stones used for stepping stones, the primary considerations for natural stones is that they have a relatively flat top surface for ease of walking and that they be thick enough so they can be buried into the ground for stability and still stick out of the ground about 2 centimeters. The difficulty in finding just the right stones for this purpose lies behind Rodrigues's comment on the high cost of stepping stones and how they were brought from afar for the purpose. In fact, the stepping stones in older *roji* are not always particularly flat-topped, sometimes having a slight curve or a dimpled surface. The desire to have easy-to-walk-on stones has gone to the extreme in recent years as people have become more and more used to smooth walking surfaces such as concrete and asphalt sidewalks. Perfectly uniform flat-topped stones are now manufactured for the gardening trade and used to make paths that are easy to walk on but artificial in feeling (fig. 90).

These days, the color of the stones used for stepping stones is usually limited to understated browns and grays, avoiding stones with striking striations or markings. This wasn't always so, as the previously mentioned passage from *Furuta Oribe no Kamidono Kikigaki* stated: "whether black, white, or red, there's nothing wrong [with using them]."[293] But Oribe's aesthetic in this case did not become mainstream and, as a rule, it can be said that the colors of stones used in the *roji* are subdued.

THE IMPORTANCE OF PLACEMENT

The placement of stepping stones is one of the critical aspects of designing a *roji*—they are not just casually or randomly laid out, although they may seem that way at first. To begin with, the stones are not laid in a single line; there is always, or almost always, a slightly staggered placement so that as guests walk, their left and right steps fall on certain stones, and, if they began with the wrong foot, they would find themselves walking cross-legged. The stones are also not set in an endless run from entry gate to tea house; rather they are laid out in discrete segments, often of three, five, seven, or nine stones. This predilection for uneven numbers is usually, though not strictly, observed. At the end of each section of stones, the path will change direction slightly or be divided from the next section by a larger stone, such as a *garan-seki*, though not necessarily something that large or distinctive. If this larger stone falls at a place where paths meet, such as at the point where a small path leads off the main path to the water basin or waiting bench, that larger stone is called the *fumiwake ishi*, or junction stone. In *Sukiyadō Shidai* (1602), we find an early mention of that expression: "The guests who enter first should stand waiting on the junction stone (*fumiwake no ishi*) in front of the waiting bench and take careful note of what is around them."[294]

tea path

203

tea room (*chashitsu*)

crawl-through gate
(*nijiri-guchi*)

entry stone (*fumi-ishi*)

descending stone (*otoshi-ishi*)

swordshelf stone (*katanakake-ishi*)

outer garden (*soto roji*)

middle gate (*chūmon*)

inner garden (*uchi roji*)

guest's stone (*kyaku-ishi*)

cross-over stone
(*norikoe-ishi*)

host's stone (*teishu-ishi*)

water basin (*tsukubai*)

tablet-viewing stone
(*gakumi-ishi*)

stone lantern (*ishidōrō*)

front stone (*mae-ishi*)

89. PEDESTAL STONE. Mushanokōji Senke, Kyōto. A stone of larger proportions often punctuates certain points along the *roji* path, such as where several paths meet. The round stone shown here is a *niwa-garan*, a stone that mimics, in its superficial appearance, the stones that were used as pedestals for the large wooden columns of Buddhist temples. Photograph by Ōhashi Haruzō.

90. VARIOUS STEPPING STONES. The various types of stones used in a stepping stone path are given specific names depending on their function.

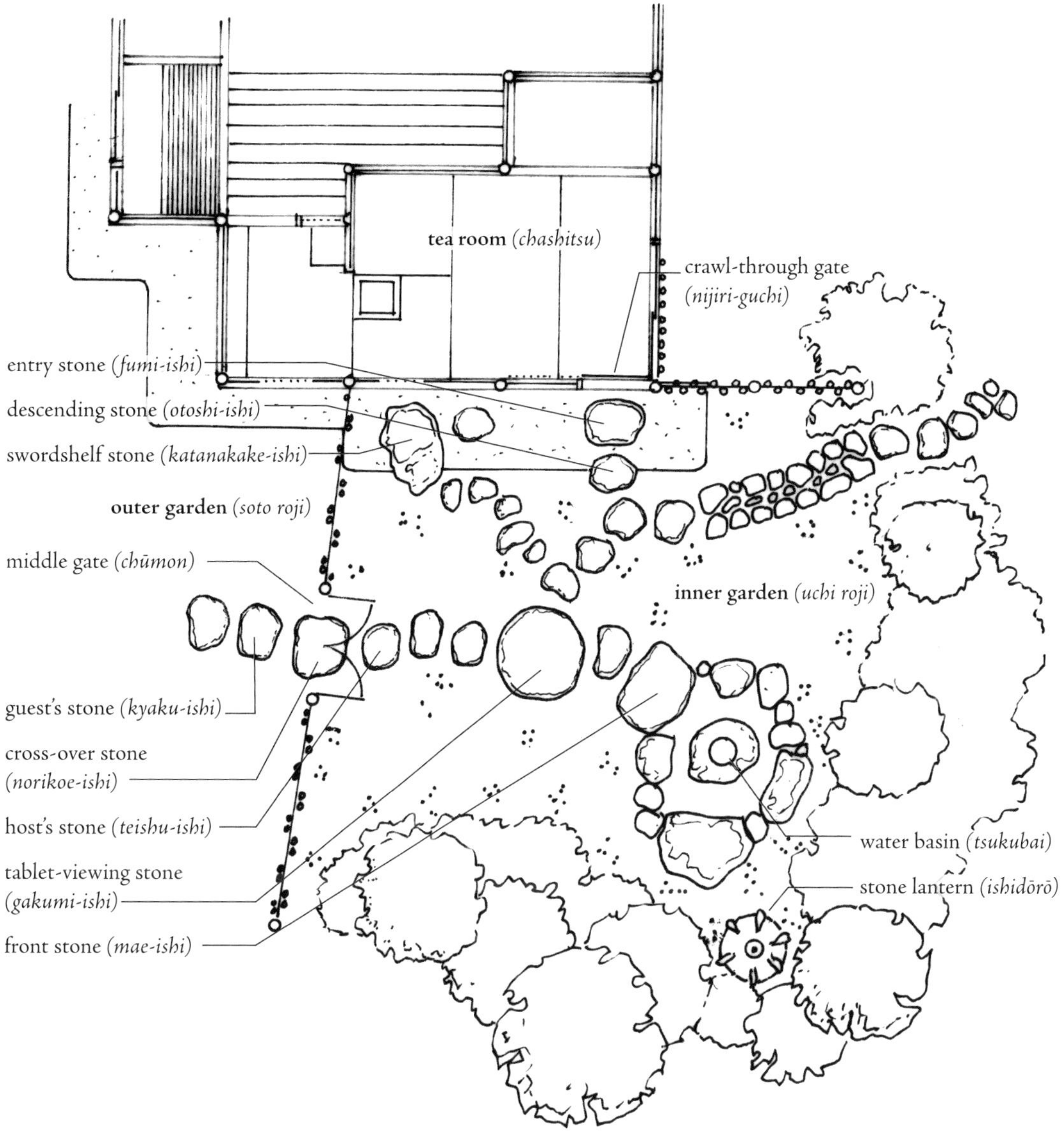

91. A BARRIER STONE. Shōkadō, Kyōto. The barrier stone, *sekimori-ishi*, marks a path that is not to be used during a tea gathering. The simple device of placing a stone wrapped in black twine is enough to signal to any guest that the path is off-limits for that day. Photograph by Ōhashi Haruzō.

Another kind of paving used in the *roji*, usually used in combination with stepping stones, is the *tatami-ishi*, or *nobe-dan*, as it is also called. As mentioned earlier, *tatami-ishi* are sections of paving made up of small flat-topped stones and, at times, pieces of leftover cut granite that are fitted together to create a uniform surface. The result is a slab of paving that is rectangular like *tatami* mats though somewhat narrower and often longer than a *tatami*. Single sections of *tatami-ishi* are introduced at certain points along the *roji* path by the designer in order to affect the flow of movement through the *roji*.

Walking on stepping stones, one's pace slows naturally because of the uneven surface. A slower pace allows time to sense the subtle qualities of the garden and also causes the heart rate and breathing to slow, which is conducive to a contemplative mood. So, one aspect of movement that is controlled is speed; another is related to vision. The difficulty in walking across stepping stones causes a person's attention to drop toward his feet as a precaution against stumbling. The larger context of his physical environment falls away from his consciousness. At points along the path, however, larger path surfaces are introduced, like the *fumiwake ishi* or a *tatami-ishi*. At that point the person can lift his head and look around again. Through careful planning, the designer of a *roji* can dictate places along the path where a guest's head will drop and where it will lift—where attention will be introverted and where it will be outward focused. This, combined with the slower pace of walking, makes the experience of moving through the *roji* a longer and more complex one, thus evoking in the persons entering a feeling that they have traveled much further than they actually have.

As another possibility, there may be a stone set away from the path to the left or right to allow the walker to temporarily step off the path and pause. These are called *monomi-ishi*, viewing stones, and are placed at a point along the *roji* to reveal a certain view. Typically this was an excellent view of some part of the *roji* or something within it—not a view from the garden, but within it—but not always, as this passage from *Chanoyu Ichieshū* records:

> There is a very large and flat stone called the viewing stone. From [the vantage point of] that stone, any of these things would be good to look at: a tea house plaque, a stone lantern, the garden well, a large tree, some stepping stones or, a distant view. Never do without [this stone]. When looking at something, one should always be still and look. It is wrong to offer compliments in a loud voice, rather, simply appear to be moved.[295]

STONES WITH SPECIFIC FUNCTIONS

Some other stepping stones worthy of mention are the host's stone (*teishu-ishi* or *shujin-seki*), the guest stone (*kyaku-ishi* or *kyakujin-seki*), and the cross-over stone (*norikoe-ishi*) all three of which are related to the middle gate (*chūmon*). The host's stone is placed on the inner side (the *uchi-roji* side) of the middle gate; the guest stone on the outer side; and the cross-over stone directly beneath the gate itself or just inside the gate on the host's side. When the host comes forward to silently greet his guests at the beginning of a tea gathering, he will go only as far as the host's stone at the inside limit of the inner *roji*. Likewise, the head guest (*shōkyaku*) will approach the guest's stone. The cross-over stone marks the threshold from outer to inner *roji*.

Also among the pathway stones that have specific functions are the *nijiri-agari-ishi* and the *katana-kake-*

ishi. The former, which is also called simply a *fumi-ishi* (as are the entry stones to any traditional Japanese building), is used to step up into the crawl-through door, *nijiri-guchi*, of the tea house. Typically, the stone needs to rise 10 to 20 centimeters off the ground, though be not too big around and have a clean, flat top surface. In some cases there may be only this one stone, but there can also be two or three stones in line that progressively rise up from the ground. In this latter case, the second down from the *nijiri-agari-ishi* is known as the "descending stone" (*otoshi-ishi*) and the third is called the "mounting stone" (*nori-ishi*), the direct translations of which are not very informative but imply that they are secondary stones for stepping up into, or down out of, a room.

The *katana-kake-ishi*, like the *nijiri-agari-ishi*, is used as a step, in this case to reach up to a sword shelf (*katana-kake*) that is affixed to the outer wall of the tea house. One of the revolutionary aspects of early *wabi-cha* was its "democratic" character. Men of the aristocratic, military, and merchant classes would freely gather in the confines of a small tea room to share a bowl of tea. One of the important steps in the "leveling" of the social status of men from these different classes was for the military men to remove their swords upon entering the tea room. To this end, a simple wooden shelf was affixed to the outer wall of the tea house, just near the *nijiri-guchi* entrance. The reasons for elevating the sword shelf are unclear, but the fact that it is raised requires a stepping stone with some height to get up to the shelf. The stone used for this purpose is often unusually shaped, having two flat places in a double rise somewhat like a short stepladder.

The last stone to be mentioned is the "barrier stone" (*sekimori-ishi*). This is a fist-sized, round stone that is tied in a cross-pattern with black palm-fiber twine and set on top of a stepping stone as a signal that the path beyond that point is closed off (fig. 91). Some tea gardens have several choices of routes that can be taken through the garden, either because there are several tea houses on the property or because several routes to one tea house have been developed. The *sekimori-ishi* lets the guests know which paths to take and which to avoid.

The Waiting Bench: Koshikake

The *koshikake*, or *koshikake machiai* as it is also called,[296] is a roofed bench that is placed in the *roji* to allow guests to sit while waiting for the host to call them forward into the tea house (figs. 92, 93). A drawing in *Chanoyu Hishō* shows a simple unroofed bench, *shōgi*, in the garden, just outside the four-and-a-half-mat tea house owned by Matsuya Hisamasa.[297] This may have been how the custom began: first with a simple, uncovered bench and, later, with a roofed bench. The *koshikake* allows the guests a moment to prepare themselves both outwardly (straightening their clothes) and inwardly (calming themselves and arranging their thoughts). In a *nijū-roji*, there may be two *koshikake*, one in the inner *roji* (*uchi koshikake*) and one in the outer *roji* (*soto koshikake*), but it is the one in the outer garden, within sight of the middle gate, where the guests wait for the host. During a long tea gathering, there is a midway break, *naka-dachi*, during which guests can return to the *roji* to relax. It is then that the waiting bench in the inner *roji* comes into use.

Although there are many variations of its form, the *koshikake* is made of simple natural materials like the tea house itself. The frame is a lightly built post and beam structure, the walls are of clay-plaster, and the roof is typically of thin wood shingles or bark shingles from the Japanese cypress, *hinoki*. The bench itself may be straight or L-shaped but it will always have a place at one end reserved for the head guest, *shōkyaku*. This may be denoted by a change in the material used to surface the bench, but it can always be identified by the slightly raised stepping stone that is placed on the ground in front of it. Called the *shōkyaku-seki* or *kinin-seki*, it is raised only about 12 to 15 centimeters above the ground; the elevation is intended as a sign of respect. In front of the rest of the bench are simply low-set stepping stones or a *tatami-ishi*. Many other stepping stones are placed in front of the *koshikake* in such a manner that allows the guests to enter and leave without bunching up against each other.

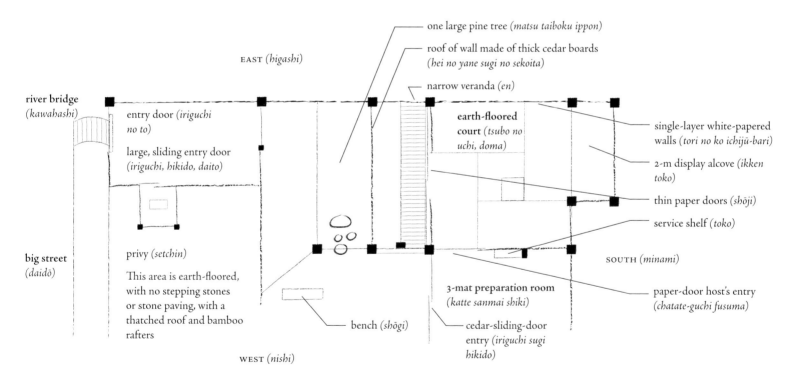

one large pine tree (*matsu taiboku ippon*)

roof of wall made of thick cedar boards (*hei no yane sugi no sekoita*)

narrow veranda (*en*)

EAST (*higashi*)

river bridge (*kawahashi*)

entry door (*iriguchi no to*)

large, sliding entry door (*iriguchi, hikido, daito*)

earth-floored court (*tsubo no uchi, doma*)

single-layer white-papered walls (*tori no ko ichijū-bari*)

2-m display alcove (*ikken toko*)

thin paper doors (*shōji*)

service shelf (*toko*)

big street (*daidō*)

privy (*setchin*)

This area is earth-floored, with no stepping stones or stone paving, with a thatched roof and bamboo rafters

SOUTH (*minami*)

paper-door host's entry (*chatate-guchi fusuma*)

3-mat preparation room (*katte sanmai shiki*)

bench (*shōgi*)

cedar-sliding-door entry (*iriguchi sugi hikido*)

WEST (*nishi*)

92. SIMPLE WAITING BENCH. The placement in a tea garden of a *shōgi*, a simple unroofed bench, may have been the first mechanism for allowing guests to rest partway through the *roji*. Later, roofed benches called *koshikake machiai* became more typical. Redrawn from *Chanoyu Hishō*, pp. 202–3.

93. ROOFED WAITING BENCH. Ura Senke, Kyōto. The waiting bench, *koshikake*, is typically a simple structure, no more than a bench enclosed with clay-plaster walls and covered by a bark or bamboo roof. By tradition, a spot for the head guest is denoted by the placement of a stepping stone that is slightly higher than any others. Also by tradition, a box with tobacco is set at one end of the waiting bench, although this is mostly decorative these days. Photograph by Ōhashi Haruzō.

The Middle Gate: Chūmon

The division between the inner and outer *roji* is defined by a gate of some sort, most commonly called *chūmon* or middle gate. The gate may be designed in any number of ways, but middle gates are typically lightly built and do not have any sort of protective quality—even when the gate is closed, it is still possible to walk around it to the left or right. Some of the gates are roofless, some have roofs of thatch, bamboo, bark, or wood shingles, and some are wall-like structures.

UNROOFED GATES

These are the simplest forms, usually consisting of no more than two upright posts and a simple lattice door set between them. Because they are far less expensive to construct than a roofed gate, they are also far more common.

Shiori-do: Perhaps the simplest form of middle gate, the *shiori-do* is a lightly woven panel of split bamboo attached between two posts: hinged on one post and latching closed onto to the other. The gate itself offers no visual blockage and only the slightest suggestion of separation when it is shut (fig. 94).

Agesu-do: A variant of the *shiori-do*, the *agesu-do* is made with a large panel of woven, split bamboo that is attached at the top to a horizontal bar that runs between two upright posts. When the panel is pushed from the bottom, it swings upward and can be held in that upward position by a long bamboo pole, which is the way it is set during a tea gathering (fig. 95).

ROOFED GATES

These gates are usually found in larger *roji* and, due to the cost of their construction, in the *roji* of wealthier owners. The structural framework of roofed gates is made of wooden posts and cross-braces, usually of Japanese cypress, *hinoki*, which has been debarked but left in its natural state showing slight variations in size and protrusions where branches have been cut off. Some few rare gates use posts that have the bark on them still, such as the gate for visiting dignitaries at Katsura Rikyū, the *miyuki-mon*. The size and proportion of these gates can vary, but unless they are made for official visits, as the *miyuki-mon* was, they are just large enough for a person to pass through without stooping. Normally there are two door panels, each attached to a post, that swing outward to both sides.

Takebuki-mon: The roof of this gate is made of half-split bamboo that is applied in interlocking layers; the bottom layer split-side up, overlapped by the top layer set split-side down.

Hiwadabuki-mon, kokerabuki-mon: The roofs of both of these gates are made from Japanese cypress, *hinoki* (or possibly the Sawara cypress); the *hiwadabuki-mon* is made of finely prepared strips of the bark, and the *kokerabuki-mon* is made of very thin shingles of the wood.[298] Both of these materials, and the techniques used to apply them, are highly refined, allowing for the creation of elegant shapes, such as the subtly curved *amigasa-mon* in the *roji* of Mushanokōji Senke. An *amigasa* is a traditional rain hat made from woven reeds and has a curved, downward-sloping shape that the roof of the gate mimics (fig. 96).

Sugikawa-mon: This gate is roofed with the bark of the Japanese cedar, *sugi*. The bark is somewhat thicker than that of *hinoki* and is usually used in larger sheets, laid facing down the slope of the roof and held in place by thin bamboo rods that are nailed down on top of the bark.

Kaya-mon: The *kaya-mon* is an elegant variant of the middle gate that has a roof made of thatch. *Kaya* is the generic name for grasses commonly used for roofing, which might include *susuki* (Miscanthus sinensis), *chigaya* (Imperata cylindrica var. major), and *yoshi* (Phragmites of various species). The ideal for the rustic tea house at the beginning of the development of *chanoyu* culture (if not still today) was the "thatch-roofed hermitage," *sōan*, a building that was thatched with some variety of *kaya*. The *kaya-mon* also has this idealized rustic feeling, as, originally, *kaya* was a relatively inexpensive building material that was used on the roof of every farmhouse in Japan. The situation today is quite different, with the sources of *kaya* and the craftsmen who can do the work becoming increasingly scarce. The *miyuki-mon* mentioned above and the *kaya-mon* at Omote Senke are good examples of this type, as is the garden gate at Hakusa Sansō (fig. 97).

WALL-LIKE GATES

Naka-kuguri: The *naka-kuguri* is an unusual gate that looks like a short section of a clay-plastered wall set in the middle of the *roji*. It has a narrow roof to protect the wall from rain damage and a small sliding door inset in it that is similar to, but a bit larger than, the *nijiri-guchi* that leads into the tea house. *Naka-kuguri* often have, in addition to the small door, a small, latticed window (*shitaji mado*) that allows a carefully positioned glimpse of the inner *roji* from outside. The door is set at chest height in the wall and has high stepping stones set next to it on the inner and outer sides. The entering guest approaches the door, steps up on the stone, crouches through the opening, and steps back down on the inside. Of all the gates, the *naka-kuguri* is the clearest, and most striking, expression of threshold.

There were many situations in the society of the late 1500s through the 1600s in which people were required to "crawl through" a hatch-like door in order to enter a property. As mentioned earlier there were the hatch-like entries on the wharves where river boats docked and at the entrances to theaters in the entertainment quarters. Also, large properties, such as those of a *daimyō*, were divided into individual courtyards by high clay-plaster walls. In places, the walls had sliding doors built into them that allowed access from one court to another. What is interesting about the *naka-kuguri*, as it exists in most extant gardens, is that it

94. SIMPLE BAMBOO GATE. Kōtōin, Kyōto. The most common form of middle gate, *chūmon*—which divides a two-part tea garden into its inner and outer sections—is the simple *shiori-do* made of woven strips of bamboo. Photograph by Ōhashi Haruzō.

95. SWINGING BAMBOO GATE. Omote Senke, Kyōto. An unusual gate, which feels like something that might be found in a rustic farm setting, the *agesu-do* accentuates the sense of passage by requiring the persons who enter to duck slightly as they pass through the gate. Photograph by Ōhashi Haruzō.

96. UMBRELLA GATE. Mushanokōji Senke, Kyōto. This beautiful gate, with its curved cedar-bark roof, is a remarkable piece of craftsmanship. It is called an *amigasa-mon*, or woven-umbrella gate. Even if this gate were closed, a person could easily walk around either side. The gate, in fact, is not there for any defensive purpose; rather it is exclusively a symbolic expression of passage—of moving from the outside world, into an inner one. Photograph by Ōhashi Haruzō.

97. THATCH-ROOFED GATE. Hakusa Sonsō, Kyōto. This thatch-roofed gate, *kaya-mon*, has a feeling of great rusticity. Although this garden is in the city, elements like this lead visitors to feel that they are walking into a mountain village. Photograph by Ōhashi Haruzō.

has been taken out of its original context of being a functional gate intended to separate different outdoor spaces. It no longer connects to a building or stretches across an alleyway to bar entry. It simply stands in the garden, disassociated from any architecture, and the guests are asked to walk up to this wall and step through it to the other side. It is precisely this artificiality that accentuates the feeling of passage—that reminds the guests as they enter that they are passing into a different place (fig. 98).

98. MIDDLE WICKET. Tabuchi Residence, Akō City. The middle wicket, *naka-kuguri*, is in fact a clay-plaster wall that has a small door built into it, much like the *nijiri-guchi* of a tea house. The guest must duck through the entry, like entering the porthole to a ship. The opening frames the view of the garden beyond, offering only a glimpse of what lies inside to the guests as they arrive.

The Water Basin: Tsukubai

The water basin is the most important element of the *roji*. Remember the quote from *Nanbōroku* mentioned earlier: "In the *roji*, the host's first act is to bring water; the guest's first act is to use this water to rinse his hands. This is the very foundation underlying the use of the *roji* and thatched hut" (see note 264). It is the oldest element—in fact, its use in *chanoyu* predates the development of the *roji*—and its function, that of ritual cleansing, is of primary importance. One can design a *roji* without many of the other elements—the middle gate or dust pit, for instance—but not without a place where water for cleansing can be used.

There are some cases where this water is provided in a freshly made wooden bucket or a ceramic bowl. In that case, a flat-topped stone is set in the *roji* at some point as a pedestal and the bowl or bucket is placed on top of it. The pedestal stone fixes the location of the water basin in the garden, but the vessel holding the water is placed on the stone only at the time of the tea gathering. Using a wooden bucket harks back to the oldest form of rustic tea in which a water bucket was placed on the tea house veranda for the use of the guests, and then later in the *waki tsubo-no-uchi*.

By far the most common arrangement for using water in the *roji*, however, is a stone water basin arrangement called a *tsukubai* (figs. 99, 100). The word *tsukubai* is a noun derived from the verb *tsukubau* that means to crouch down. Unlike the taller *tachi-chōzubachi* water basin that is hip-high, the *tsukubai* is set low and requires the user to crouch down to touch the water, thus the name. This is an intentional design, forcing the guests to humble themselves by bowing down as they use the water. Properly speaking, *tsukubai* is not the name of the water basin but rather the name for an arrangement of several stones that are set in a loosely circular arrangement that includes the water basin and others as described below. At first, only the water basin, *chōzubachi*, was used during a tea gathering. This word shows up in records from the 16th century, the first mention being the passage related earlier about a "basin that was made of stone, about 1 *shaku* 2 *sun* [36 centimeters] tall . . ." from *Sōtan Nikki* in 1586 (see note 129).

Through the 17th and 18th centuries, the various special stones that make up the *tsukubai* arrangement were experimented with by tea masters and, after they came to be used regularly, were given formal names that appear in texts thereafter. The expressions *teshoku-ishi* and *yuoke-ishi*, for instance, first appear in *Teiyōshū* in 1710, so we can assume their use began some time before that. Exactly when the entire arrangement now known as a *tsukubai* was completely developed is not clear, but it is likely to have been by the mid- to late 18th century. The word *tsukubai*, however, does not appear until 1860 in *Chanoyu Ichieshū*, which mentions a "*tsukubai chōzubachi*." A typical *tsukubai* arrangement consists of the water basin (*chōzubachi*), the front stone (*mae-ishi*), the candle-holder stone (*teshoku-ishi*), the hot-water bucket stone (*yuoke-ishi*), and, in some cases, several other, unnamed small boulders that are used to complete the circular arrangement.

BASIN DESIGNS AND MATERIALS

The *chōzubachi*, or water basin, is, as the name implies, the stone that has a depression that holds the water. Within the *tsukubai* arrangement, the *chōzubachi* can either be set in the direct center, in which case it is called a *naka-bachi*, middle basin, or it can be set in the rear center, in which case it is referred to as a *mukō-bachi*,

opposite-side basin (being on the opposite side of the arrangement from the user). There are three types of stone *chōzubachi*: those made from naturally shaped boulders (*shizenseki chōzubachi*), those made from blocks of stone that are carved specifically to be water basins (*sōsaku-mono chōzubachi*), and those carved

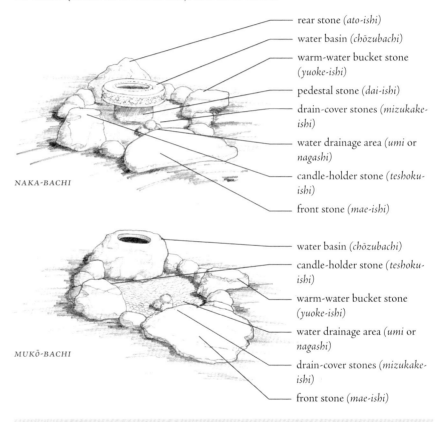

rear stone (*ato-ishi*)
water basin (*chōzubachi*)
warm-water bucket stone (*yuoke-ishi*)
pedestal stone (*dai-ishi*)
drain-cover stones (*mizukake-ishi*)
water drainage area (*umi* or *nagashi*)
candle-holder stone (*teshoku-ishi*)
front stone (*mae-ishi*)

NAKA-BACHI

MUKŌ-BACHI

water basin (*chōzubachi*)
candle-holder stone (*teshoku-ishi*)
warm-water bucket stone (*yuoke-ishi*)
water drainage area (*umi* or *nagashi*)
drain-cover stones (*mizukake-ishi*)
front stone (*mae-ishi*)

99. STANDARD TYPES OF WATER BASIN ARRANGEMENTS. The arrangement of stones used for the water purification ritual in the roji is called a *tsukubai*. The two most common variants include the *naka-bachi* (top), in which the water basin is set in the center of the arrangement, and the *mukō-bachi*, in which it is placed on the opposite side of the arrangement from where the guest approaches.

from pieces of old stone objects that were previously used for other purposes (*mitate-mono chōzubachi*).

In the case of natural boulders, the stone may be an ocean stone or river stone that has a basin-like depression that was carved by natural erosion over the years, but these are rare. More typically, a natural boulder has a basin carved into it by hand and, at times, the top portion flattened to make a uniform surface area. The rest of the stone, however, is left in its natural state, and it is the particular beauty of each individual stone—its shape, surface texture, and coloring—that is sought after. The carved shape of the basin itself varies depending on the overall shape of the stone and the degree of formality desired. The opening might be rectangular or circular, ovate or irregular, or even shaped to fit the irregularities of the stone. The lip of the basin might be a simple corner, or it might have a narrow shelf or groove carved into it to accentuate the edge. The basin may be more or less straight-sided but almost always has some slope to it, usually widening toward the bottom. In some cases the sides are rounded and swelled outward, giving the water a deeper, darker appearance. This is called *mikan-gata*, "tangerine-style," because the overall shape resembles that fruit. Like the sides, the bottom of the basin may be flat or somewhat concave. All these features—the opening, sides, and bottom— are taken into account when a mason carves the stone. Some shapes are easier to accomplish, thus cheaper, but the decision of which shape to use for which stone is, in the end, an aesthetic one.[299]

When a block of stone is carved for the purpose of use as a *chōzubachi*, it is called a *sōsaku-mono*, a "created thing." Granite is the most common stone used for this purpose. An intrusive igneous rock, granite is fairly hard, thus durable, and yet reasonably easy to carve with iron or steel chisels. In these cases the entire stone—not just the basin—is carved into the shape, and with a surface pattern, desired by the designer. Some examples of *sōsaku-mono* are the strikingly geometric-patterned *Ginkakuji-gata* and the *Ryōanji-gata*, which is one of the most reproduced forms in Japan. The *Ryōanji-gata*, named after the Zen temple Ryōanji where the original is found, is a variety of the *zeni-gata* or "coin-style," which mimics the square-hole-inside-a-circle shape of an old coin called a *zeni*.

Water basins that are recarved from old stone objects are called *mitate-mono*, or "reused things." These include those made from old stone bridge piers (*hashigui-gata*), the cube-shaped pedestal stones of stone stupas (*shihōbutsu-gata*), the roofs of stupas turned upside down (*kasa-gata*), the pedestal stones of stone lanterns (*kiso-gata*), and the pedestal stones of wooden pillars (*soseki-gata*).

FRONT STONE

The *mae-ishi*, or front stone, is a relatively large, flat-topped stone that is set so that the lead edge of the stone is about 50 to 70 centimeters from the center of the *chōzubachi*. The guests crouch down on the *mae-ishi* in order to use the *tsukubai*, reaching out to take hold of the water ladle that has been placed on top of the water basin. Because of the way the *tsukubai* is used, the distance between the *mae-ishi* and the *chōzubachi*, and the height from the top surface of the *mae-ishi* to the top of the *chōzubachi*, must be subtly controlled so that the guests do not feel like they are reaching awkwardly to use the water. Since the front of the *mae-ishi* faces the hollow that the water basin is set in, the stone used for the *mae-ishi* must be thick enough so that its front edge can be revealed, around 10 to 20 centimeters.

CANDLE-HOLDER STONE

The *teshoku-ishi*, or candle-holder stone, is a flat-topped stone placed to one side of the *chōzubachi*. Typically, it is placed on the left side, but the Ura Senke style of tea uses the right side. During evening tea gatherings, or gatherings in the early morning when it is still dark, a candle is carried by the head guest in an iron candle holder, *teshoku*, and placed on the *teshoku-ishi* while the guests are using the *chōzubachi*. There are times when a

hand-held wooden lantern, called an *andon*, is used instead of a *teshoku*, although, typically, if *andon* are used, they are set out on the ground along the path, whereas *teshoku* are carried in by the guests. While a stone lantern near the *chōzubachi* provides enough light for the water basin, the *teshoku* is needed for walking along the dark paths. By tradition the *teshoku-ishi* is usually placed to the left side as one faces the *chōzubachi*. The height of the *teshoku-ishi* is not fixed, but it will

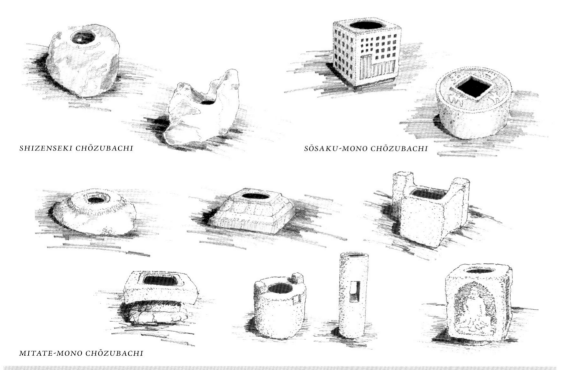

SHIZENSEKI CHŌZUBACHI

SŌSAKU-MONO CHŌZUBACHI

MITATE-MONO CHŌZUBACHI

100. VARIOUS TYPES OF STONE WATER BASINS. There are many, many variants of stone water basins, but they all fall into three main groups: those made from naturally-shaped boulders (*shizenseki chōzubachi*), those made from blocks of stone that are carved specifically to be water basins (*sōsaku-mono chōzubachi*), and those that are carved from pieces of old stone objects that were previously used for other purposes (*mitate-mono chōzubachi*).

the water basin

be lower than the *chōzubachi* and higher than the *mae-ishi*. Its relationship to the *yuoke-ishi*, which is set to the other side, is not predetermined—sometimes it is higher, sometimes lower.

WARM-WATER BUCKET STONE

The *yuoke-ishi*, or warm-water bucket stone, like the *teshoku-ishi*, is a flat-topped stone that is placed to one side of the *chōzubachi*. Again, typically, it is placed on the right side, but the Ura Senke style of tea uses the left side. During winter tea gatherings, or if an elderly guest has been invited and the weather is particularly

101. SUNKEN WATER BASIN. Kōtōin, Kyōto. A set of stepping stone stairs leads down to the water basin of this *ori-tsukubai*. Sunken below ground level, surrounded by plants, and in the shadow of overhanging trees, this *ori-tsukubai* has a cool freshness even in summer.

cold, a wooden bucket filled with warm water, *yuoke*, is placed on the *yuoke-ishi* so the guests can warm their hands after using the frigid water in the *chōzubachi*. As with the *teshoku-ishi*, the height will be higher than the *mae-ishi* but lower than the *chōzubachi*.

SUNKEN AREA

The *umi* is the sunken area that lies in between the four stones mentioned above. *Umi* is written with the character for "ocean"; often there is a layer of river pebbles covering the bottom, onto which any spilled water falls and percolates into the ground. Another name for this area is *nagashi* or, literally, drain. In modern gardens, there may be a mortar layer beneath the gravel and a drainpipe at the lowest point in the middle to carry away the waste water. At times, a pile of fist-sized stones is carefully placed over the pipe entry to disguise it. Those are called the *mizukake-ishi* and also have the function of absorbing the flow of the falling water so it doesn't splash about. The amount of water used during a tea gathering, however, is so small that a drainpipe is really not needed unless the *tsukubai* has been built indoors or on a rooftop or some other location not directly on soil.

* * *

These five parts—*chōzubachi, mae-ishi, teshoku-ishi, yuoke-ishi,* and *umi*—are the basic components of a *tsukubai*. Completing the circle that surrounds the *umi*, smaller stones are placed in between the four major stones to fill in the gaps, or, alternatively, a shallow basin is created around the central water basin out of mortar. A lantern is often placed diagonally behind the *chōzubachi* to provide light for evening tea gatherings, and plantings of understory plants, such as ferns or *senryō* (Sarcandra glaber), and evergreen shrubs are set around the back of the arrangement to encircle it and give it a sense of privacy and enclosure.

Some unusual *tsukubai* that were developed in later years include the *ori-tsukubai* (fig. 101; see also fig. 75) and the *nagare-tsukubai* (see fig. 79). In the case of the *ori-tsukubai* or "sunken water basin," the *chōzubachi* is set into a sunken area that is accessed via a set of stone steps. The depth of the depression is not great, usually only knee height or hip height, but because it is often covered with a canopy of overhanging tree branches, the *ori-tsukubai* has a cool and refreshing feeling even on a hot summer day. The *nagare-tsukubai*, or "stream water basin," is one in which a water basin is placed directly in a running brook, usually without any ancillary stones other than the *mae-ishi*. Stepping stones lead out to the basin so that as a person bends to use the water the stream flows by underneath. This too has a particularly cool and refreshing feeling.

WATER SCOOP

The *hishaku*, water scoop, is not a part of the *tsukubai*, per se, but without it the *tsukubai* cannot function as intended (fig. 102). The *hishaku* is made out of a short section of hollow bamboo pipe that is cut to form the cup of the ladle, and a long thin piece of bamboo that forms the handle. The section that forms the cup is cut so that the node of the bamboo (a diaphragm of wood inside the otherwise hollow bamboo stem) forms the base of the cup. It is set on top of the water basin, usually resting on one or two pieces of fine bamboo that are laid across the opening of the water basin. The custom of using the *hishaku* is slightly different in the various schools of tea, but, in general, the guest crouches

down on the *mae-ishi*, picks up the *hishaku* with the right hand, and pours some water over the left hand to rinse it and symbolically cleanse it. The *hishaku* is then switched to the left hand in order to pour some water over the right hand to rinse it. Next, a little water is poured into the cup of a palm and taken up to rinse the mouth. Finally, the remaining water is allowed to fall over the stem of the *hishaku* so that it is rinsed for the next person in line. A similar practice is followed by people entering Shintō shrines, suggesting that Shintō ritual may have been the role model for the use of water as a cleansing element in *chanoyu*.

BAMBOO WATER PIPE

The *kakehi*, bamboo water pipe, is often found at *tsukubai* in public settings—parks and restaurants—and also at some private homes (fig. 103). There are many ways to build a *kakehi*, but the basic component is a bamboo (or a wooden or even a stone conduit) that guides a steady stream of water to the *chōzubachi*, allowing it to fall into the basin from above to create the burbling sound of running water. The use of bamboo pipes to guide water to where it is needed in the garden, and to let water flow up out of underground water systems as a well-spring, is an ancient technique. It even appears in the 11th-century gardening manual *Sakuteiki*.[300] During a tea gathering, however, the water that is put in the *chōzubachi* is supposed to be the same water that will be used to make tea. The guests hear the host pour fresh water into the *chōzubachi* as they wait at the waiting bench, and then taste that water as *water* before they taste it as tea. A *kakehi*, although it provides a pleasant soothing sound in a garden, is not typically used in *roji* that is being actively used for tea gatherings.

102. WATER LADLE. Matsuo Residence, Nagoya. The standard placement of the water ladle, *hishaku*—on top of the water basin and facing to the left—was not fixed in the early days of *chanoyu*, when records show it facing up, facing down, or even set next to the water basin. Photograph by Ōhashi Haruzō.

103. BAMBOO WATER SPIGOT. Chadō Gakkai, Tōkyō. Although the water running from the bamboo *kakehi* into the water basin makes a cool and refreshing sound, during a tea gathering, *kakehi* are not typically used. Rather, the same water that will be used to make tea is drawn—from a well or from a faucet—and poured into the water basin from a wooden bucket. Photograph by Ōhashi Haruzō.

Stone Lanterns: Ishi-dōrō

Stone lanterns were originally used only at religious sites—Buddhist temples and, later, Shintō shrines—where they were used in one of two ways (and still are today). The oldest usage was as votive lanterns, in which case a single lantern, or a pair of lanterns, would

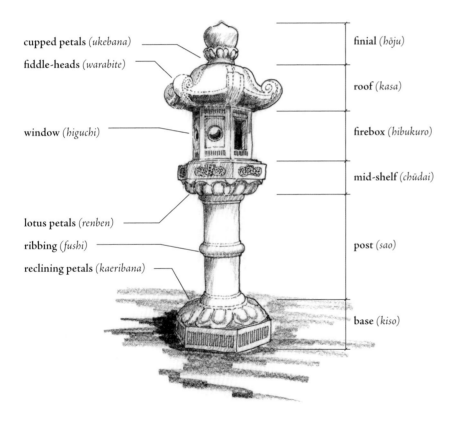

cupped petals *(ukebana)*
fiddle-heads *(warabite)*

window *(higuchi)*

lotus petals *(renben)*
ribbing *(fushi)*
reclining petals *(kaeribana)*

finial *(hōju)*

roof *(kasa)*

firebox *(hibukuro)*

mid-shelf *(chūdai)*

post *(sao)*

base *(kiso)*

104. PARTS OF A STONE LANTERN. A typical stone lantern has six main sections that are separately carved—finial, roof, firebox, mid-shelf, post, and base.

be placed directly in front of the center of a Buddhist Hall, the main hall of a temple where an image of a Buddha is enshrined. Lighting a candle or oil lamp in a votive lantern is an honorific gesture to the deity enshrined within the hall. As temples grew in size and wealth, lanterns were also used for illumination, placed in pairs along the entry walks to the temple halls. These lanterns offer some meager light to illuminate the path; more recently, they represent the devotion of the person or group that donated the lantern and whose name is carved on the back of the support post. The first record of a lantern in a *roji* is from 1591 in *Matsuya Kaiki* at a tea gathering given by Ōkaya Dōga. Although this entry does not necessarily mark the time that a lantern was first used in a *roji*, it suggests that stone lanterns were used in tea gardens for the first time in the very last decades of the 16th century.

The oldest, traditional forms of stone lanterns are composed of six parts: *hōju, kasa, hibukuro, chūdai, sao,* and *kiso* (fig. 104).[301] At the top is the *hōju* or sacred gem. It is a teardrop-shaped ball that sits inside a lotus-flower-shaped receptacle, *ukebana*. Beneath the *hōju* is the roof of the lantern called the *kasa*, literally, "rain hat." The *kasa* is usually six sided but can be square, eight sided, or round, as well as some other rare and unusual shapes. In some designs, ridges divide the sections of the roof. These ridges usually end in curled extensions called *warabite*, literally, "fiddle-heads." Beneath the *kasa* is the firebox, *hibukuro*, that holds the candle or oil lamp. The firebox can be enclosed by small paper panels, *shōji*, that fit over the openings to prevent the wind from blowing out the flame inside. When lanterns are used as lights, *shōji* are usually inserted, and when the lanterns are placed in the garden simply for their sculptural effect, the *shōji* are left off. It was important for a tea master to pay attention to the number of wicks placed in the oil lamp, and thus the strength of light. Beneath the *hibukuro* is a base stone, *chūdai*, that balances aesthetically with the *kasa*, framing the *hibukuro* on the top and bottom. Beneath the *chūdai* is the post or shaft of the lantern, *sao*. Finally, beneath the *sao* is the pedestal stone or foundation stone, *kiso*. At times, beneath the *kiso*, is a secondary pedestal stone called the *kidan*. One of the radical changes tea masters made to stone lantern design (or to the use of antique lanterns) was to not use the pedestal stone at all. Rather, they sank the lantern post directly into the ground, allowing them to adjust the height of the lantern to the degree they wanted. This was especially helpful when it was placed behind the water basin, where the light needs to come from a low position, and it may well have been experimentation with the height of the lantern at the water basin that initiated the custom of burying the lantern post in the first place (see figs. 51, 53).

Dust Pit: Chiri-ana

Extreme cleanliness being one of the pillars of *chanoyu*, the *roji* is cleaned just before the guests arrive and sprinkled with water to evoke the feeling of morning dew, or the moist cleanliness after a rain. To clean the garden a broom and dust-box (*chiri-bako*) are used, and during the Edo period the dust pit became a permanent fixture in the *roji*. In an ordinary garden, a dust pit would be made as a place where collected debris (fallen leaves, twigs, and such) could be temporarily stored before disposing of them. In the *roji*, the dust pit takes on a symbolic function: that of reminding the guests

of the preparations made by the host on their behalf. Just before the guests arrive, after the tea house and garden have been completely cleaned and prepared, a small evergreen branch is placed in the dust pit with a set of long, freshly cut bamboo debris pickers, *chiri-bashi*, that resemble oversized chopsticks, to symbolize the preparations of the host (fig. 105). In autumn, some leaves in fall color can be placed in addition to

105. ORNAMENTAL DUST PIT. Mushanokōji Senke, Kyōto. This small hole is a decorative waste pit, ostensibly used for garden debris such as fallen leaves but in fact used symbolically to express the preparations that the host has made for the guests. During a tea gathering, an evergreen bough and freshly cut bamboo "twig pickers," *chiri-bashi*, are placed in the hole. Photograph by Ōhashi Haruzō.

106. ORNAMENTAL PRIVY. Katsura Rikyū, Kyōto. This privy is intended only as a decorative element in the *roji*. Like the *chiri-ana*, its purpose is to symbolically represent the host's effort at cleanliness and state of preparation. Guests peek into the *suna-setchin* as they enter for a tea gathering to get a sense of how the host cares for his garden. Photograph by Ōhashi Haruzō.

the evergreen branch. The dust pit is usually situated somewhere near the entry to the tea house so that guests will notice it just before entering. There may be another near the waiting bench, *koshikake*. The rules regarding this are not fixed, but, in general, the dust pit next to the *koshikake* for a tea house larger than four and a half mats in size (*hiroma*) is rectangular in design, while a dust pit set near a small tea room (*koma*) is circular in design.

Privy: Setchin

There are two kinds of privy used in tea gardens: the *suna-setchin* (fig. 106), also called a *kazari-setchin* (or sometimes simply *setchin*), and the *shitabara-setchin*. The *suna-setchin* is meant for show only; its tidiness and cleanliness are a way for the host to display to the guests entering the *roji*, who will inspect the *setchin* for this purpose, the care with which he has made his preparations, a symbolic function similar to that of the *chiri-ana*. The placement of the stepping stones within the privy, the way the gravelly white sand is spread inside, the manner in which water is sprinkled on the sand before the tea gathering—all these symbolize the spirit of the host concerning cleanliness and pure thought. Conversely, the *shitabara-setchin* is intended as a functional toilet. In a larger *roji*, the *shitabara-setchin* will be in the outer part and the *suna-setchin* in the inner. In fact, these days, with indoor plumbing readily available, it is not common for *roji* to have a *shitabara-setchin* at all, and the *suna-setchin* is installed only by those who can afford the additional expense.

Fences: Kakine

The compact size of tea gardens and the desire of the designers to further subdivide that space to emphasize the feeling of threshold and passage within the garden have given rise to the use of a number of elegantly designed fences. There is no record that these fences were used in the earliest tea gardens; rather it appears that as the culture of *chanoyu* developed over time so too did their design.

Bamboo fences are perhaps the most common, bamboo having been, until recently, the least expensive material one could work with. That inexpensiveness gave it, in the eyes of medieval and early modern tea practitioners, the feeling of being a peasant's material, and its use in the tea garden gave the garden an air of a peasant village or a mountain hamlet (*yamazato*). It is hard to imagine what the reaction must have been among people participating in the very earliest tea gatherings as tea masters began to make utensils out of bamboo. Remember, at that time a person who had any status in society at all would use flower vases made of porcelain or bronze. For tea masters to use a simple, cut piece of bamboo instead was unthinkable; to do so when their guests included military lords or aristocrats was tantamount to impertinence. At that time, the use of bamboo in *chanoyu* was new and radical and, like the vases, using bamboo fences to evoke a rustic feeling must have had a similar effect on the people taking part in tea gatherings. By the late Edo period, however, when the more complex styles of fencing developed, the culture of rustic tea was mainstream and the feeling toward garden elements such as bamboo fences would have changed.

Yotsume-gaki is the simplest form of bamboo fence, requiring no more than a few horizontal pieces

107. SIMPLE BAMBOO FENCE. Ozawa Residence, Sendai City. The simplest fence, one that lends only a suggestion of division both physically and visually, is the bamboo *yotsume gaki*. It is the kind of simple fence that has its origins in agricultural settings but has become a standard element of Japanese gardens. Photograph by Ōhashi Haruzō.

108. BAMBOO POST FENCE. Yabunouchike, Kyōto. This fence is called a *taimatsu-gaki*. A *taimatsu* is a torch made by bundling together many slim sticks or slivers of split wood. Likewise, the upright posts of this fence are made by bundling many slim pieces of split bamboo. The purposeful misalignment of the nodes on the outer layer makes for a decorative pattern. The finished fence is similar in appearance to a *teppō-gaki* in which rows of unsplit bamboo are tied to a frame, resembling a row of shotguns standing at the ready (a *teppō* is a long-barreled shotgun). Photograph by Ōhashi Haruzō.

109. BAMBOO TWIG FENCE. Kibune, Kyōto. In traditional Japanese society, bamboo was grown and harvested in huge quantities. Accordingly, vast quantities of cut branches remained after the harvest. These were used to make all manner of fences, from rough agricultural barriers to refined bundle fences like this downward-facing *takeho-gaki*. Photograph by Ōhashi Haruzō.

of slender bamboo attached between upright cedar posts and a series of upright pieces of slender bamboo tied to the horizontal bamboo with black palm-fiber twine (*shuro-nawa*).[302] The *yotsume-gaki* forms a low physical barrier but not a visual barrier and may be used, for instance, on either side of the middle gate to suggest a separation between inner and outer *roji* without creating an overbearing division (fig. 107).

Teppō-gaki uses bamboo that is somewhat thicker than that used for a *yotsume-gaki*; it is tied in upright rows that mimic rows of rifles (*teppō*) stood on end for ready access (fig. 108). While this fence has some visual transparency (especially when seen on the diagonal), it is much taller and more of a visual barrier than the *yotsume-gaki*.

Twig fences use collected natural materials and lend the garden a pastoral or rural feeling. The fences in tea gardens, of course, are designed and built to a far more exacting standard than the fences that one actually finds on country farms. Twigs are collected and tied together into long bundles, and then the bundles are tied to a frame, much the way a *teppō-gaki* is built. Some of the materials commonly used to make these fences are bush clover stems (*hagi*, Lespedeza sp.), spice bush stems (*kuromoji*, Lindera sp.), and bamboo twigs. Fences made from bamboo twigs are called broom fences, *takeho-gaki* (fig. 109), and are usually made from either *mōsō-chiku* (Phyllostachys pubescens) or *ma-dake* (Phyllostachys bambusoides).

Sode-gaki, or sleeve fences, are short rectangular sections of fence, perhaps 1 to 2 meters long at most, the shape of which recalls the rectangular shape of a draping *kimono* sleeve, thus the name (fig. 110). They can be made out of any of the above-mentioned materials; what is important is not the material but the function. *Sode-gaki* are attached at one end to a building—a tea

house or a main residence—and extend out into the garden a short way, usually a meter or two. Acting as screens, their skillful placement blocks the view of one section of the garden from another as seen from the vantage of the room or veranda next to the fence.

110. SLEEVE FENCE. Kojimake, Kyōto. These decorative "sleeve fences," *sode-gaki*, so named because they resemble a draped kimono sleeve, are placed alongside the architecture at various key spots to subdivide the area and to deflect views of one place from another. Photograph by Ōhashi Haruzō.

fences

Walls: Kabe

As mentioned in *Yamanoue Sōjiki*, clay walls were the preferred method for strongly dividing spaces in tea gardens (fig. III). In ancient times, solid, thick, rammed-earth walls, called *tsuiji-bei*, were used on the perimeters of residences because of their defensive strength. Inner walls, however, and certainly the walls used within tea gardens, were not thick rammed-earth walls, but rather were light, thin, clay-plaster walls. To make a clay-plaster wall, a wooden frame of posts and cross-pieces is constructed, then infilled with bamboo lattice-work, which in turn is plastered with a mixture of clay, sand, and chopped straw, making the base coat called *ara-kabe*. This rough clay base is then covered with two more layers of clay plaster—first, *naka-nuri*, a middle layer that has finely cut plant fibers in it, and then a final outer coat, *uwa-nuri*, that normally does not contain fibers for strength. The final plaster coat, however, may have material mixed into it for decorative purposes, including long pieces of straw placed to make an artful pattern, granular pieces of sand, or small bits of iron that eventually rust and spall the surface in a decorative, pock-marked pattern. Most clay-plaster walls have a wooden baseboard near the ground where the clay plaster would receive the most damage from weathering, and in some this baseboard is extended upward as a wainscoting so that the clay plaster is applied only at the very top of the wall.

III. EARTHEN WALLS. Shinnyodō-mae, Kyōto. Solid earthen walls and plastered-clay walls are used to surround and subdivide properties. *Yamanoue Sōjiki* mentions that "suitable little stones should be mixed into the clay" for the visual effect they have. The stones in this wall were probably added for strength but have much the same quality after the wall has had a chance to weather some.

Garden Well: Ido

Since *chanoyu* is, at its heart, simply the boiling of water and making tea for guests, the source of that water is of great importance. Most historical tea gardens had wells on their property. In fact, many residences had several wells, some inside the buildings and some outside. In recent years, many of those wells have become purely decorative. In urban areas, the water level has dropped considerably, causing wells to dry up, and in many cases the water quality has dropped to the point that wells that still provide water cannot be used safely. Traditionally, however, the water for tea was drawn from the well early in the morning of the tea gathering when it was most cool, undisturbed, and fresh. The water used in the *chōzubachi* and that used for making tea were from the same source, so that the guest first tasted the water cold in its natural state, then hot as tea. In some rare cases, water for tea was imported from a historically famous well—perhaps one at a temple or shrine—but in most cases, the garden well provided the water (fig. 112).

The Plantings: Ueki

By and large, tea gardens these days use a simple palette of evergreen plants (figs. 113–16). The rarefied *roji* from the late Muromachi period that contained little in the way of planting—one willow, a maple, or just a grove of pines—and the exotic tea gardens of the Momo-yama and Edo periods, which featured Sago palms and other semitropical imports, are no longer common. The intent of the tea garden is to mimic the feeling of a forest path—shady, mossy, unobtrusive, and seemingly unplanned. To this end, showy flowering plants are generally shunned because they would lessen the tranquil feeling created by a simple, green environment. Likewise, because tea gardens are relatively small and the enclosure of overhead leaves provides them with the feeling of being in a world apart, evergreen plants are favored over deciduous ones for the year-round cover they provide. The plants preferred for use in tea gardens vary depending on the school of tea and the individual taste of the tea master or gardener who is designing the garden; some of the most commonly used plants are shown in the accompanying chart.

In its classic form, a *wabi-cha roji* is planted with a

112. GARDEN WELL. Kōtōin, Kyōto. Traditionally, urban properties of any size would have had several wells—some outside, some inside the residence. Symbolic of the water to be used in the tea, the well in the *roji* was neatly tended and, at times, given a decorative roof and glazed-ceramic pulley wheel.

forest-like cover of small evergreen trees, tightly spaced and annually pruned to keep them from growing too tall and lanky. The pruning is also intended to thin the leaf cover so that enough light reaches the understory to support the shrubs and groundcover plants. Beneath this forest canopy, shrubs as tall as head-height are planted to further enclose the *roji* path, controlling views through the garden. This visual division of the *roji* path allows the guests to gradually experience many points of discovery in the garden as they walk down the path to the tea house. Beneath the shrubs, there are occasional clumps of ferns or other low herbaceous plants, but rarely are they expansive sweeps of those plants. The ground is covered with moss or left bare, but in most parts of central Japan (around Kyōto and Ōsaka) where tea gardens developed, moss will grow of its own accord on bare ground that is shaded and kept free of other weeds. Bare soil, however, is not con-sidered an eyesore and is left exposed in parts of many gardens. Wood chips, bark mulch, or other forms of organic groundcovering are never used to cover up sec-tions of bare ground.

One material that is traditionally applied as a groundcover—though its use is extremely time con-suming and so not very common—is newly fallen pine needles. These are not used to cover bare ground but rather to protect moss during the winter months. As autumn comes to an end, fallen pine needles are col-lected and carefully laid out on areas of the tea garden where there is a moss cover. The intent is functional but also decorative, and in some cases the needles are selected so that only unbroken needles are used. The needles are not simply cast about on the ground, but are carefully laid out, and the edges of the covered areas are tended with a broom to make a clean edge to the needle bedding (see fig. 114).

Tea Garden Plants

CONIFEROUS EVERGREEN TREES

Akamatsu	Japanese red pine	Pinus densiflora	赤松
Kuromatsu	Japanese black pine	Pinus thunbergii	黒松
Sugi	Japanese cedar	Cryptomeria japonica	杉
Hinoki	Japanese cypress	Chamaecyparis obtusa	檜
Inumaki	Japanese yew	Podocarpus macrophyllus	犬槙
Momi	Fir	Abies	樅

BROADLEAF EVERGREEN TREES

Isunoki	none	Distylium racemosum	柞の木
Kaname-mochi	Japanese photinia	Photinia glabra	要縗
Kurogane-mochi	Dwarf Chinese holly	Ilex rotunda	鉄縗

Kusu	Camphor	Cinnamomum camphora	楠
Nezumi-mochi	Japanese privet	Ligustrum japonicum	鼠黐
Shii	Japanese chinquapin	Castanopsis cuspidata	椎

BROADLEAF EVERGREEN SMALL TREES/LARGE SHRUBS

Arakashi	none	Quercus glauca	粗樫
Masaki	Japanese spindle tree	Euonymus japonicus	柾
Mokkoku	none	Ternstroemia gymnanthera	木斛
Mokusei	Fragrant olive	Osmanthus fragrans	木犀
Shirakashi	none	Quercus myrsinaefolia	白樫

DECIDUOUS TREES

Gumi	none	Elaeagnus sp.	茱萸
Haze no ki	Wax tree	Rhus succedanea	黄櫨の木
Iroha-momiji	Japanese maple	Acer palmatum	いろは紅葉
Kōboku	Japanese bigleaf magnolia	Magnolia officinalis	厚朴
Konara	none	Quercus serrata	木楢
Kuri	Chestnut	Castanea crenata	栗
Yama-momiji	Matsumurae maple	Acer amoenum var. matsumurae	山紅葉
Yama-gaki	none	Diospyros kaki var.sylvestris	山柿

BROADLEAF EVERGREEN SHRUBS

Aoki	Japanese aucuba	Aucuba japonica	青木
Asebi	Japanese andromeda	Pieris japonica	馬酔木
Hiiragi-nanten	Japanese mahonia	Mahonia japonica	柊南天
Hisakaki	Eurya	Eurya japonica	姫榊
Inutsuge	Japanese holly	Ilex crenata	犬柘植
Kakuremino	none	Dendropanax trifidus	隠蓑
Kuchinashi	Gardenia	Gardenia jasminoides	梔子
Nanten	Nandina	Nandina domestica	南天
Sazanka	Camellia	Camellia sasanqua	山茶花
Tobera	Tobira	Pittosporum tobira	扉・海桐
Tsubaki	Camellia	Camellia japonica	椿
Tsutsuji	Azalea	Rhodoendron (various)	躑躅
Ubamegashi	none	Quercus phillyraeoides	姥目樫・馬目樫
Yatsude	Fatsia	Fatsia japonica	八手

CONIFEROUS SHRUBS

Kyara	Dwarf Japanese yew	Taxus cuspidata var. nana	伽羅

DECIDUOUS SHRUBS

Dōdan-tsutsuji	Japanese enkianthus	Enkianthus perulatus	灯台躑躅
Hagi	Bush clover	Lespedeza bicolor	萩
Nishikigi	Burningbush	Euonymus alatus	錦木
Umemodoki	Japanese winterberry	Ilex serrata	梅擬
Utsugi	Deutzia	Deutzia crenata	空木

GROUNDCOVERS, LOW HERBACEOUS PLANTS, VINES

Asagao	Morning glory	Ipomoea nil	朝顔
Beni-shida	Autumn fern	Dryopteris erythrosora	紅羊歯
Fuki	none	Ligularia or Adenocaulon	蕗
Fukkisō	Japanese pachysandra	Pachysandra terminalis	富貴草
Haran	Iron plant	Aspidistra elatior	葉蘭
Manryō	none	Ardisia crenata	万両
Senryō	none	Sarcandra glaber (Chloranthus glaber)	千両
Susuki	Japanese silver grass	Miscanthus sinensis	薄
Tsuwabuki	Japanese silver leaf	Farfugium japonicum	石蕗
Yabukōji	Japanese ardisia	Ardisia japonica	藪柑子

BAMBOO

Kuro-chiku	Black bamboo	Phyllostachys nigra	黒竹
Tō-chiku	Tootsik bamboo	Sinobambusa tootsik	唐竹

MOSS

Edatsuya-goke	none	Entodon rubicundus	枝艶苔
Sugi-goke	none	Pogonatum inflexum	杉苔

*parts of a
tea garden*

113. EVERGREEN PLANTINGS. Nishida Gyokusen, Kanazawa City. The planting palette for the *roji* is based on evergreen plants, both broadleaf and coniferous. Here we see, in addition to a carpet of moss, *inumaki* (Japanese yew), *tsutsuji* (azalea), *mokkoku* (Ternstroemia), and *akamatsu* (red pine). Photograph by Ōhashi Haruzō.

114. PINE NEEDLE GROUNDCOVER. Ume-zawa-tei, Tokyō. As winter protection for the carpet of moss, pine needles are collected and spread carefully over the surface. They stay in place surprisingly well, unless a very strong wind blows; the edges along the paths are defined by a curbing of thick rice-straw bundles. Photograph by Ōhashi Haruzō.

115. PLANTINGS BY WATER BASINS. Musha-nokōji Senke, Kyōto. In addition to broadleaf evergreen shrubs, the plantings around this water basin include *beni-shida* fern and the round-leafed *tsuwabuki* (Japanese silver leaf). Plants like *tsuwabuki* and *fukkisō* (Japanese pachysandra) are used near water basins but only as small accents—a sprig here or there. Photograph by Ōhashi Haruzō.

(overleaf)

116. FOREST-LIKE PLANTINGS. Omote Senke, Kyōto. The ideal image for the *roji* was a narrow path through a mountain forest, leading the guests back to a simple hut of a hermit, far away from the cares and callings of the world. The naturalistic plantings here include *tsubaki* (camellia) of various types, *beni-shida* fern, and *nanten* (nandina), the leaves of which are tinged with red. Photograph by Ōhashi Haruzō.

附録

Notes

Every care was taken in transcribing the Japanese text for these notes. Readers whose purpose is either detailed research or publication should refer back to the original sources.

1. Sen, *Chadō Koten Zenshū*, vol. 4, p. 319:『南方録』「露地ハ只ウ キ世ノ外ノ道ナルニ、心ノ塵ヲ何チラスラン。」

2. A few English books that introduce tea culture include: Plutschow, *Historical Chanoyu*; Sen, *Japanese Way of Tea: From Its Origins in China to Sen Rikyū*; and Varley and Kumakura, *Tea in Japan: Essays on the History of Chanoyu*.

3. The term "aristocrat" is used with emphasis on the hereditary and hierarchical nature of that system of social control. "Civil aristocrat" refers to those families that exercise control through political, economic, and cultural means but were not personally armed or trained in military arts. "Military aristocrat" refers to those families that exercised control through military force and were personally armed and trained in military arts. The imperial family and subject families such as the Fujiwara, Reizei, and Tachibana are examples of the former. The Ashikaga, Hosokawa, and Toyotomi families are examples of the latter.

4. There are illustrations of this process in an exhibition catalogue from the National Palace Museum, Taiwan: *Empty Vessels, Replenished Minds: The Culture, Practice, and Art of Tea*, pp. 7–8 (Chinese with English captions). Also in this catalogue are all the images from the collection of the National Palace Museum that are mentioned on these pages, as well as many others.

5. For a full English translation of the text see Lu, *The Classic of Tea*.『茶経』「茶者南方之嘉木也。」

6. Eichū (永忠 743–816), Saichō (最澄 767–822), and Kūkai (空海 774–835).

7. The text mentioning the *chagi* 茶儀 is called *Ōgishō* 奥儀抄 and the archeological dig was at the Toro Iseki 登呂遺跡.

8. In Japanese the Four Accomplishments are referred to as *kin-ki shoga* 琴棋書画. They include the lute (Ch: *qin* 琴 Jp: *kin*); Chinese chess (Ch: *qi* 棋 Jp: *ki*); calligraphy (Ch: *shu* 書, Jp: *sho*); and painting (Ch: *hua* 画, Jp: *ga*). The paintings mentioned in the text but not depicted—*Reading in an Open Hall, Eighteen Scholars of Tang*, and *Preparing Tea*—can be seen in the museum catalog *Empty Vessels, Replenished Minds: The Culture, Practice, and Art of Tea*.

9. The mountain retreat Longmian (WG = Lung-mien 龍眠) is in Shuzhou (WG = Shu-chou 舒州).

10. In Japanese, military families are known as *bushi* 武士, Zen priests as *zensō* 禅僧, merchants as *shōnin* 商人, and artists and artisans as *geinōsha* 芸能者 and *shokunin* 職人, respectively.

11. Eisai's full name is Myōan Eisai 明庵栄西, which can also be pronounced Myōan Yōsai. Myōe is written 明恵.

12. *Daisu-cha* is also referred to as *denchū no cha* or "tea served within palaces," after the architecture where the tea gatherings were held.

13. *Kara* 唐 is the character that represents the Tang dynasty and, by default, was used in Japan from ancient times to refer to China in general. Even though the Tang dynasty had fallen by the time of the Kamakura period, and was replaced by the Song and then Yuan dynasties, the Japanese still often referred to China as *Kara*.

14. The careful reader will notice a ten-year gap between the Nara and Heian periods. This is the brief period when the capital was situated at Nagaoka; the period holds little information of merit regarding gardens.

15. For a detailed account of Heian-period gardens, see Takei and Keane, *Sakuteiki*. The reference to Mountain Village Style is on p. 161.

16. See W. G. Aston, *Nihongi: Chronicles of Japan from the Earli-*

est Times to A.D. 697 (Rutland, VT: Charles E. Tuttle Company), vol. 2, 1972, p. 144. The entry is for Empress Suiko, A.D. 612.

17. *Chadō Bunka Kenkyū Dai'isshū*, p. 108.『烏鼠集』「石たてす
・・・・そのゆへハ客のめ(目)不移良、御茶に精を入れ、名物に心を
つけしめんため也。」

18. See map of 16th-century Kyōto in Horiguchi, *Zusetsu Chadō Taikei*, vol. 4, p. 153.

19. A *jō* was about 3.03 meters, so the lots were about 30.3 by 15.15 meters or 28.0 by 15.15 for the smaller, inner lots. Nakamura, *Machiya no Chashitsu*, p. 63. How the word for alleyway, *ainomachi* 間の町, was actually pronounced is unknown.

20. The central location of Manjūya-chō was expressed as *Kyōto no heso*, "Kyōto's navel." *Teien Gaku Kōza 2*, p. 17.

21. *Kiwari* 木割, also called *kikudaki* 木砕, was a method of processing wood into uniform shapes as well as determining their size according to the span they were related to. The thickness of a post, for instance, would be determined by making it a certain percentage of the span between posts. The oldest written record of this process, *kiwarisho*, dates to 1489. Itoh, "*Sōanfū Chashitsu no Genryū: Part 1*," *Nihon Rekishi*, vol. 101, p. 26.

22. Itoh, "*Sōanfū Chashitsu no Genryū: Part 1*" *Nihon Rekishi*, vol. 101, p. 22.

23. Rodrigues, *João Rodrigues's Account of Sixteenth-Century Japan*, pp. 283–84.

24. English translation after Kuitert, p. 146. *Inryōken Nichiroku* 蔭涼軒日録 is the official diary of Inryōken, a residence within the Rokuon'in subtemple of Sōkokuji temple. The diary was kept by Kikei Shinzui 季瓊真蘂 from 1435 to 1466 and by Kisen Shūshō 亀泉集証 from 1484 to 1493. Inryōken 蔭涼軒 can also be pronounced Onryōken. The entry from 1492 regarding Tokuzō's *zashiki* reads:「就德藏酒屋借宿。後園有座敷。華美過洛中。有爐有厠安便至也。」(返点省略). Takeuchi, *Inryōken Nichiroku*, vol. 5, p. 14.

25. Laozi and *Daodejing* are often romanized in the Wade-Giles manner as Lao Tzu and *Tao Te Ching*. In Japanese, Laozi 老子 is pronounced Rōshi and *Daodejing* 道德経 is *Dōtokukyō*.

26. Translation from Hall, *Japan in the Muromachi Age*, p. 209. In Japanese, Tao Yuanming (陶淵明 365–427) is pronounced Tō Enmei.

27. In the *Four Admirers*, Tao Yuanming 陶淵明 is the chrysanthemum (Jp: Tō Enmei, 365–427); Huang Shangu 黄山谷 the orchid (Jp: Kō Sankoku, 1045–1105); Lin Hejing 林和靖 the plum (Jp: Rin Nasei, 967–1028), and Zhou Maoshu 周茂叔 the lotus (Jp: Shū Moshuku, 1017–73). For more on these paintings, and on the role of the recluse in Momoyama-period Japan in general, see Brown, *The Politics of Reclusion*, p. 4, and elsewhere in that text.

The figures in the *Three Laughers of the Tiger Glen* and the *Three Sages Tasting Vinegar* are Tao Yuanming 陶淵明, a Confucianist; Buddhist priest Huiyuan 慧遠 (Jp: E On, 334–416); and Taoist Lu Xiujing 陸修静 (Jp: Riku Shūsei, 406–77). The *Three Sages Tasting Vinegar* does not always use these three figures; there are other groupings that are employed. For more detailed information on both paintings see "The Unity of the Three Creeds: A Theme in Japanese Ink Painting of the Fifteenth Century" in Hall, *Japan in the Muromachi Age*, pp. 205–25

28. In Japanese, Hanshan 寒山 is pronounced Kanzan and Shide 拾得 is pronounced Jittoku.

29. *Nihon Koten Bungaku Taikei*, vol. 29, p. 167:「とふ人もおもひ絶えたる山里の淋しさなくば住み憂からまし」and p. 71:「あばれたる草の庵にもる月を袖にうつして眺めつるかな。」

30. *Nihon Koten Bungaku Taikei*, vol. 29, p. 71.「木の間渡る有明の月をながむれば淋しさ添ふる嶺の松風。」

31. Translation from Watson, *Japanese Literature in Chinese*, vol. 1, p. 63.

32. One *jō* 丈 is equal to ten *shaku* 尺. One *shaku* is 30.3 centimeters, so a *jō* is 3.03 meters or 9.94 feet.

33. The *Essentials of Salvation* (*Ōjōyōshū* 往生要集), a compilation of three sutras by the monk Genshin 源信 (942–1017), was intended to aid in the study of Amida Buddhism. The sutras describe *mappō*, the Degenerate Age of Buddhism that was purported to have begun in 1052. Chōmei's descriptions of his own world reflect this *mappō* mindset—that the world is a degenerate place.

34. "*Masaki* vines" may refer to *teika kazura* 定家葛, Trachelospermum asiaticum.

35. Matsushita, *Kokubun Taikan*, vol. 7, pp. 549–50. Also online at http://etext.virginia.edu/japanese/hojoki/.『方丈記』「こゝに六十の露消えがたに及びて、さらに末葉のやどりを結べる

ことあり。いはゞ狩人のひとよの宿をつくり、老いたるかひこのまゆを
いとなむがごとし。これを中ごろのすみかになずらふれば、また百分
が一にだもおよばず。とかくいふ程に、よはひは年々にかたぶき、すみ
かはをりをりにせばし。

　その家のありさまよのつねにも似ず。廣さはわづかに方丈、高さ
は七尺が内なり。所をおもひ定めざるがゆゑに、地をしめて造らず。
土居をくみ、うちおほひをふきて、つぎめごとにかけがねをかけたり。
もし心にかなはぬことあらば、やすく外へうつさむがためなり。その
あらため造るとき、いくばくのわづらひかある。積むところわづかに二
輌なり。車の力をむくゆるほかは、更に他の用途いらず。

　いま日野山の奥にあとをかくして後、南にかりの日がくしをさし
出して、竹のすのこを敷き、その西に閼伽棚を作り、うちには西の垣
に添へて、阿彌陀の畫像を安置したてまつりて、落日をうけて、眉間
のひかりとす。かの帳のとびらに、普賢ならびに不動の像をかけた
り。北の障子の上に、ちひさき棚をかまへて、黒き皮篭三四合を置
く。すなはち和歌、管絃、往生要集ごときの抄物を入れたり。傍にこ
と、琵琶、おのおの一張をたつ。いはゆるをりごと、つき琵琶これな
り。東にそへて、わらびのほどろを敷き、つかなみを敷きて夜の床と
す。東の垣に窓をあけて、こゝにふづゑを出せり。枕の方にすびつ
あり。これを柴折りくぶるよすがとす。庵の北に少地をしめ、あばらな
るひめ垣をかこひて園とす。すなはちもろもろの藥草をうゑたり。かり
の庵のありさまかくのごとし。

　その所のさまをいはゞ、南にかけひあり、岩をたゝみて水をため
たり。林軒近ければ、つま木を拾ふにともしからず。名を外山といふ。
まさきのかづらあとをうづめり。谷しげゝれど、にしは晴れたり。觀念
のたよりなきにしもあらず。」

36. English translation from Keene, *Essays in Idleness*, p. 11 and
pp. 120–21. Original in *Nihon Koten Bungaku Taikei*, vol 30,
p. 98–99：『徒然草』第十一段。「神無月の比、栗栖野といふ所を
過ぎて、ある山里にたづね入る事侍りしに、遙なる苔の細道をふみ
わけて、心細くすみなしたる庵あり。木の葉に埋もるゝ懸樋の雫なら
では、露おとなふものなし。閼伽棚に菊・紅葉など折りちらしたる、さ
すがにすむ人のあればなるべし。」See also p. 205：『徒然草』第
百三十七段。「兵の軍に出づるは、死に近きことを知りて、家をも忘
れ、身をも忘る。世を背ける草の庵には、閑かに水石をもてあそび
て、これを余所に聞くと思へるはいとはかなし。しづかなる山の奥、
無常のかたき、競ひ來らざらんや。其の死に臨める事、軍の陣に進
めるに同じ。」

37. The poem was written by the *renga* poet Sōchō 宗長
(1448–1532) about Yamazatoan 山里庵, the urban retreat
of Toyohara Muneaki 豊原統秋 (1450–1525). Muneaki can
also be pronounced Sumiaki. Sōchō's poem is found in
the *Sekirekishū* 磧礫集. The Japanese original is in Moriya,

Nihon Chūsei e no Shiza, p. 74.「山にても憂からむときの隠家や
都のうちの松の下庵。」

38. Washino'o, *Nisuiki*, vol. 3, p. 79.『二水記』「午時参青連院、万
里小路(中略)於池中嶋有御茶(中略)數奇宗珠祗候、下京地下入
道也、數奇之上手也。」

39. The first recorded use of the term *chaya* comes from 1421
in *Kanmon Gyoki* 看聞御記 the diary of Prince Fushimi no
Miya Sadafusa 伏見宮貞成親王(1372-1456). Sen, *Chadōgaku
Taikei*, vol. 6, p. 347.

40. Washino'o, *Nisuiki*, vol. 4, p. 92.『二水記』「御歸(かえり)路之
次(村田)宗珠茶屋御見物、山居之躰尤有感、誠可謂市中隠、當時
數奇之張本也。」

41. In modern Japanese, the *kanji* for marketplace, 市 (pronounced *ichi* when written separately), also means "city" as
in Kyōto-shi 京都市 or Kyōto City. But this usage stems
from the late 1800s, after the Meiji Restoration installed
Western-style governmental bureaucracies.

42. For a more detailed discussion of the "hermit in the city"
ideal, see Parker, *Zen Buddhist Landscape Arts of Early
Muromachi Period Japan*.

43. Rodrigues, *João Rodrigues's Account of Sixteenth-Century Japan*, p. 291. In the original text, which is in Portuguese, Rodrigues romanized the expression *shichū no sankyo* as *xichu
no sankio*, so that spelling shows up in many Japanese texts.

44. Rodrigues, *João Rodrigues's Account of Sixteenth-Century
Japan*, p. 291, footnote 2.

45. Many of the comments on aesthetic terms presented here,
and the poetry related to them, were drawn from entries
in the dictionary of tea culture edited by Hayashiya,
Kadokawa Chadō Daijiten Hon Hen. A good source for
information in English is the website JAANUS: Japanese
Architecture and Art Net Users System (http://www.aisf.
or.jp/~jaanus/).

46. Both of these terms—*hie-yase* and *hie-kare*—were written
by Shukō in his one-page letter known as *Kokoro no Fumi*
(*Letter of the Heart*)：『心の文』「又、當時、ひゑかるゝと申て」
「後まてひへやせてこそ面白くあるへき也。」In Shukō's letter,
hie-kare is written *hie-karuru* ひゑかるゝ. Sen, *Chadō Koten
Zenshū*, vol. 3, p. 3. For an in-depth description of the aesthetics of Shinkei's *renga* poetry and their effect on *chanoyu*,
see Hirota, *Wind in the Pines*, pp. 37–63.

47. *Shin Nihon Koten Bungaku Taikei*, vol. 1, p. 170. 万葉集 3026
「君は来ず我れは故なみ立つ波のしくしくわびしかくて来じとや。」

48. *Shin Nihon Koten Bungaku Taikei*, vol. 5, p. 84. 古今和歌集・
242・題しらず・平貞文「今よりは植へ(うゑ)てだに見じ花すすきほ
にいづる秋はわびしかりけり。」

49. *Nihon Koten Bungaku Taikei*, vol. 26, p. 133. 新古今和歌集・
363・藤原定家朝臣・西行法師すゝめて百首哥よませ侍りけるに「見
わたせば花も紅葉もなかりけり浦のとまやの秋のゆふぐれ。」

50. Sen, *Chadô Koten Zenshū*, vol. 4, pp. 16, 421, 449.『南方録』「
花をのみまつらん人に山ざとの雪まの草のはるをみせばや。」The
poem is mentioned in *Nanbōroku* as having been written by
Fujiwara Ietaka and included in *Shin Kokinshū*, but in fact
no such poem is found in that collection.

51. Sen, *Chadô Koten Zenshū*, vol. 6, p. 97.『山上宗二記』「古人の
云、茶湯名人ニ成テ後ハ、道具一種サヘアレハ、侘数寄スルカ専一
也。心敬法師連歌ノ語曰、連歌ハ枯カシケテ寒カレト云、茶湯ノ果
モ其如ク成タキト紹鷗常ニ云ト、辻玄哉云レシ也。」

52. The English translation is from Levy, *Man'yōshū*, p. 55.
Nihon Koten Bungaku Taikei, vol. 4, *Manyōshū*, vol. 1, p. 29.
ささなみの國つ御神の心さびて荒れたる京見れば悲しも。

53. Rodrigues, *João Rodrigues's Account of Sixteenth-Century
Japan*, p. 288.

54. The first written use of the word *wabi* in relation to *chanoyu*
may be in *Ikenaga Sōsaku e no Sho* (*Tea Writings of Ikenaga
Sōsaku*), a short record from 1555 purported to be the teachings of Takeno Jōō as recorded by Ikenaga Sōsaku. The
passage reads, "In the vicinity of the City of Sakai, of those
who follow the rustic tea style (*wabi-suki*), there are many
who have open clay-hearth braziers (*kudo-kamae*) and by
all means follow Jōō's methods of tea." Sen, *Chadô Koten
Zenshū*, vol 3, p. 80.『池永宗作への書』「境(堺)ノ邊(あたり)ニ
ハ、ワビ數奇トシテ、クドカマエバカリシテ持ツ人ヲヲシ、是ヲバ常翁
(紹鷗のことか)ガマエトモ伝也。」

55. For more detailed information on *shinden* layout and design
see, Takei, *Sakuteiki*, p. 11.

56. The residential architecture of the military aristocracy
was influenced by that of Zen temples. The *shoin* 書院, or
reading alcove, was a sign of literacy and was included in
Zen temple architecture before it was incorporated into
residences. Buildings of this style—both Zen temples and
residences—are called *shoin-zukuri* 書院造り or "*shoin* style."

A more specific term for the residences of the military class
is *buke-yashiki* 武家屋敷, literally, "military family residence."

57. For more information on the development of *shoin*-style
architecture, see "The Development of Shoin Architecture"
in Hall, *Japan in the Muromachi Age*.

58. A record in *Chanoyu Hishō*, which was published in 1738,
states that "In olden days, outside the tea house (*zashiki*)
or private gate (*tsumado*), three or four nails would be set
in order to hang swords or folding fans. The sword rack
(*katana-kake*) was first used by Rikyū," implying that before
there was a sword rack, simple nails were used. Given the
date of this record, however, the veracity cannot be guaranteed. *Chanoyu Bunkagaku* (Kyōto), March 1999, p. 188.『茶
湯秘抄』「昔ハ座敷ノ縁か妻戸ノ外ニ釘三ツ四ツ打置、是ニ脇指
扇モ掛置、刀掛ハ利休仕初し也。」

59. Nakamura, *Machiya no Chashitsu*, pp. 13–14.

60. The famous expanse of white sand that covers much of the
garden at Ginkakuji and the tall conical pile of sand that
stands next to it are additions of the Edo period and were
not part of the garden at the time Yoshimasa was alive.

61. Sen, *Chadô Koten Zenshū*, vol. 2, pp. 176–77.『喫茶往來』漢文
の解題:「昨日の茶會には光臨(おいで)下さらないので、無念(ざん
ねん)のあまり大へんくち惜しく、滿堂(いちどう)の失望もはなはだし
い、御故障(さしさわり)はどういうことか。さてさてかの會所(おやし
き)の有様は、内の客殿(ひろま)には、美しい簾(みす)をかけ、前方の
ひろい庭にはきれいな砂(原文:大庭鋪玉沙)をしき、軒(のき)の幕
をひきまわし、窓に帷(たれぎぬ)を垂れている。同好の人々(原文:好
士)がだんだんと來て、會衆がより集つた後、はじめに水織酒(せい
しゅ)三獻の儀禮がありついで、索麺(さくめん・そうめん)・茶を一度い
ただき、その後、山海の珍味で食事ををすすめ、よく茂つた園のみご
とな果物で味いたのしみ、その後、座をたつて席を退き、あるものは
北窓の築山にむかい、緑樹の陰(原文:松柏之陰)に暑さをさけ、ある
ものは南の軒先の瀧をながめて、襟をひらいて水しぶきの涼しい風
をいれる。このところに奇殿(立派な書院)があつて、棧敷(さじき)を
二階にたかく時てて、眺望(ながめ)のよいように四方が開いている。
これが喫茶の亭で(あずまや(原文:喫茶之亭))、月見をする砌(ばし
ょ)である。左側には思恭(しきょう・張思恭という謎の書家)の書い
た彩色の繪で釋迦の靈山(りょうぜん)説化(靈鷲山というインドの
やまで釋迦が説法したということ)のようすが巍々(おごそか)である。
右側は牧溪(宋元時代の書家)の書いた墨繪で、普陀落山(ふだらく
せん・南インドである八角形の觀音が住む山である)に現われた觀
音像が蕩々(のびのび)としている。」

62. Dairin Sōtō (大林宗套 1480–1568). Translation from Hirota, *Wind in the Pines*, p. 81. Hayashiya, *Nihon no Chasho*, vol. 1, p. 148.「曾結弥陀無碍因、宗門更転活機輪、料知茶味同禅味、汲尽松風意未塵。」

63. Rodrigues, João. *João Rodrigues's Account of Sixteenth-Century Japan*, p. 289.

64. For more insights into *Nanbōroku*, see Dennis Hirota's excellent work on Buddhism and tea, *Wind in the Pines*.

65. Hirota, *Wind in the Pines*, p. 237. Daitokuji and Nanshūji are both temples of Rinzai Zen. Daitokuji is in Kyōto and Nanshūji is in Sakai, Ōsaka. Both temples have many connections with the development of tea culture. Sen, *Chadō Koten Zenshū*, vol. 4, p. 265.「大徳(大徳寺)、南宗〔南宗寺〕ナトノ和尚タチニ一向間取シ、旦夕、禪林ノ清規(しんぎ)ヲ本トシ、カノ書院結構ノ式ヨリカネヲヤツシ、露地ノ一境、浄土世界ヲ打開キ、一宇ノ草菴二疊敷ニワビスマシテ、薪水ノタメニ修行シ、一碗ノ茶二眞味アルコトヲヤヽヤウホノカニヲボヘ候ヘトモ。」

66. Sen Sōtan (千 宗旦 1578–1658), Fujimura Yōken (藤村庸軒 1613–99), Kusumi Soan (久須美疎安 1636–1728).

67. Hirota, *Wind in the Pines*, p. 249. Sen, *Chadō Koten Zenshū*, vol. 10, p. 199.『茶話指月集』「本來禪によるかゆへに、更に示(しめす)へき道もなし、但(たん)わか平生かたり傳ふ古人の茶話を以(もって)指月とせハ、をのつから得ることあらんと。」

68. Rodrigues, *João Rodrigues's Account of Sixteenth-Century Japan*, p. 288.

69. Translation from Hirota, *Wind in the Pines*, p. 245. "One-Page Testament of Rikyū (*Rikyū Ichimai Kishōmon* 利休一枚起請文), *Chanoyu Quarterly*, no. 33, 1983, p. 44 (based on version in *Sukido Shidai*).『一枚起請文』「御当世の茶湯とは、もろこし本朝にもろもろの茶のみ達の沙汰し申さるヽ茶湯にあらず。唯学問をして茶の湯の心をさとりてのめる茶湯にもあらず。只のどかはくをやめん為に何となく湯を沸しぬれば、うたがひなくやむぞとおもひのめる外にはべつの子細無しと見えたり。」

70. English from Hirota, *Wind in the Pines*, p. 217. Sen, *Chadō Koten Zenshū*, vol. 4, p. 3.『南方録』「小座敷の茶湯は、第一佛法を以て修行得道する事也、家居の結構、食事の珍味を楽とするは俗世の事也、家ハもらぬほど、食事ハ飢ぬほど、にてたる事也、是佛の教、茶の湯の本意也、水を運び、薪をとり、湯をわかし、茶をたてヽ、佛にそなえ、人にもほどこし、吾ものむ、花をたて香をたく、みなみな佛祖の行ひのあとお學ぶ也、なを委(くわ)しくハわ僧(吾僧)の明めにあるべしとの給ふ。」Also see endnote 130 in Hirota, p.

363. The image of "drawing water and gathering firewood" comes from the Tang-dynasty layman, Pang Yun (Japanese, Bō Un 彪蘊, 740–803). An English translation can be found on p. 46 of Pang Yun, *The Recorded Sayings of Layman Pang: A Ninth-Century Zen Classic*, trans. Ruth Sasaki, Yoshitaka Iriya, and Dana Fraser (New York: Weatherhill, 1971): "My daily activities are not unusual, I'm just naturally in harmony with them. Grasping nothing, discarding nothing, in every place there is no hindrance, nor conflict. Who assigns the rank of vermilion and purple?—The hills' and mountains' last speck of dust is extinguished. [My] supernatural power and marvelous activity—drawing water and carrying firewood."

71. Hirota, *Wind in the Pines*, p. 217. Sen, *Chadō Koten Zenshū*, vol. 4, p. 3.『南方録』「家居の結構、食事の珍味を樂とするは俗世の事也、家ハもらぬほど、食事ハ飢ぬほどにてたる事也。」

72. *Roji Seicha Kikaku* 露地清茶規格 is part of *Kochū Rodan* 壺中炉談. Hirota, *Wind in the Pines*, p. 240. Sen, *Chadō Koten Zenshū*, vol. 4, pp. 415–16.「庵主出請して、客庵に入るべし、庵主、貧にして、茶飯の諸具不偶、美味も又なし、露地の樹石、天然の趣、其こゝろを得ざる輩ハ、これより速に歸られ。」

73. Sen, *Chadō Koten Zenshū*, vol. 6, p. 93.「一期二一度ノ會。」

74. Alvarez-Taladriz, J. L., "Caceria de Refranes en el 'Vocabulario da Lingoa de Japam,'" *Monumenta Nipponica*, vol. 10, 1954, p. 172. In the original it reads, "Biôbuto, Aqiūdotoua sugunareba miga tatanu. 屏風と商人とは直なれば身が立たぬ."

75 Hideyoshi's father, Kinoshita Yaemon 弥右衛門, was a low-ranking *samurai* who turned to farming, making his living as a farmer and joining in battle only as situations required.

76. This dish, called *namasu* in the diary, comprises thinly sliced meat, fish, mollusks, or vegetables, served with vinegar.

77. Sen, *Chadō Koten Zenshū*, vol. 9, p. 186.『松屋会記・久好茶会記』「七日朝。一中坊源五殿へ、書院二而飯アリ、御茶ハ四条〔ママ〕半ニテ。床二大筒ニキク・水仙花、棚二肩衝、白地金欄袋二入、壁二柄杓、セト水指、亀ノフタ、ヤキ茶ワン、茶巾、茶杓。
　一番・ヲカヤ道か、キヌヤ壽閑、クスリヤ宗方、久政、クレヤ〔宗甫〕、源次フツシヤ、六人。二番・ハントウヤ常勘、ナヘヤ宗立、コヤ宗有、イモノヤ久恰、キタノハシ御佐、三テウ布ヤ、六人。三番・大ヒカシ紹九、タ・ミヤ善右衛門、ハルタ叉左衛門、久好、ウシロイヤ五郎左衛門、コキヤ善四郎、六人。以上。」

サケヤキ物、汁トリフ入、引テ、カウノ物〔香の物・漬け物〕・ヤキ鳥。ナマス(タイ、スヽキ)。飯。スイモノ(タコ・サクラ入・クヽタチ)。サケ三返、クワシ(イモ・コンニヤク)。」

78. For the English of *Shōtetsu Monogatari*, see Brower, *Conversations with Shōtetsu*, p. 158. The original can be found in *Nihon Koten Bungaku Taikei*, vol. 65, p. 230.

79. Kogaku Sōkō 古岳宗亘 (1465–1548), Jūshiya Sōgo 十四屋宗伍 (dates unkown), Fujita Sōri 藤田宗理 (dates unknown).

80. While *sadō* is pronounced the same in both cases, the *kanji* for the two are different. The *kanji* for *sadō* as tea master is 茶頭 (literally, "tea head"), while those for the Way of Tea are 茶道 (literally, "tea path").

81 Ashikaga Yoshimitsu (1537–97) was *shōgun* from 1568 to 1573. The painting *Pictures of Training Horses* (*Chōba Kyūbazu Byōbu* 調馬図屏風) was described in Tsutsui, *Chanoyu Kaiga Shiryō Shūsei*, pp. 50–51.

82. The brazier, called a *furo* 風炉, is not to be confused with a bath, also called a *furo* 風呂.

83. There are cases in which a son other than the eldest takes over the family lineage and even cases, such as when there were no male children, in which a child from outside the family is adopted for the purpose of taking over the role of grand master.

84. Sen, *Chadō Koten Zenshū*, vol. 3, p. 360.『長闇堂記』「京都衆のするにあたりて、へちくわん(ノ貫)と云し者、一間半の大傘を朱ぬりにし、柄を七尺計、二尺程間をおき、よしかきにてかこひし、照日にかの朱傘かゝやきわたり、人の目をおとろかせり、是も一入興に入せ給ひて則、諸役御免をくだされ、八すきにハ皆/\御暇くだされ、それより互に棧敷分散して、そのひに又、本の松原おなせり、ない/\(内々)にハ諸方の名物をもめしあけるへきとの取さたあれとも、」

85. Takeuchi, *Hekizan Nichiroku*, p. 137.『碧山日録』「其門甚隘、側身以容、及至其奥房舎、皆良木壽材之所構、四壁図山水之境。」

86. For a more detailed description of Inryōken 蔭涼軒, see note 24. The red and white flowers were most likely plums. *Shōgun* Ashikaga Yoshimasa 足利義政 was invited by the head priest of Inryōken, Kikei Shinzui 季瓊真蘂, to visit his temple. The comment about "groves of bamboo" could also be interpreted as "bamboo and trees." Takeuchi, *Inryōken Nichiroku*, vol. 1『蔭涼軒日録』, p. 457.「九日(中略)御成(中略)無双御登覧。紅白花滋。馨香満亭。此亭在所恰好。凡京中構亭。則有憚其露頭也。此亭者。四面竹樹深密。而(考・恐脱如字)山

87. Whether Murata's given name was pronounced Shukō or Jukō is not known. Most dictionaries of tea culture use Shukō. The case for using Jukō comes from a passage in *Matsuya Kaiki* that states he is also called *Jūnikō*. Sen, *Chadō Koten Zenshū*, vol. 9, p. 372.『松屋会記』「タトイ珠光成共、十二光ナリ共、御ナヲシ候テ。」

88. Nōami 能阿弥, also at times known as Shinnō 真能, is known as a *renga* poet, a painter, and the founder of the Ami-ha school of painting. Originally employed in the court of the Asakura family of Echizen, Nōami became a *dōbōshū* (art connoisseur) in the court of Ashikaga Yoshimasa, taking responsibilities for art curation, tea, incense, and more. He is the father of Geiami and grandfather of Sōami.

89. *Zenpō Zōtan*, 禅鳳雑談, *Zenpō's Idle Chatter* (or, literally, *Zenpō's Miscellaneous Talks*), is a compilation of various comments made by Konparu Zenpō (金春禅鳳, 1454–1532) to his apprentices over the years 1504–21. Konparu was a *nō* theater playwright and actor, and his compiler was a man named Tōemon 藤右衛門. The original entry about Shukō and the moon can be found in Hayashiya, *Nihon Shisō Taikei*, p. 480, 1512.11.11.「珠光の物語とて、月も雲間のなきは嫌にて候。これ面白く候。」

90. Personal letters, of course, do not have formal titles. The name *Kokoro no Fumi* is an appellation of a later era and, in fact, the letter is referred to in several different ways. *Chadō Koten Zenshū* refers to it as *Shukō Furuichi Harima Hōshi Ate Isshi* 珠光古市播磨法師宛一紙, and it is also called *Kokoro no Shi no Fumi* 心の師の文 and *Kokoro no Shi no Isshi* 心の師の一紙. Dennis Hirota translates the title as "Letter on Heart's Mastery." For a translation of the entire letter, see Hirota, *Wind in the Pines*, pp. 195–98. Sen, *Chadō Koten Zenshū*, vol. 3, p. 3. 此道の一大事ハ、和漢そさかい(境)をまき(紛)らかす事、肝要/\、ようしん(用心)あるへき事也。」

91. Varley, *Tea in Japan*, p. 21.

92. Figures on the tally trade are taken from Kobata, *Chūsei Nisshi Tsūkō Bōekishi no Kenkyū*, pp. 303–6.

93. Sen, *Chadō Koten Zenshū*, vol. 6, p. 100. The entry in *Chadō Koten* has a minor but important typographical error here, mentioning Jōō 紹鷗 rather than Shukō 珠光. The entry

reads,「紹鷗カ丶リハ北向右勝手、坪ノ内ニ大ナル柳一本在リ、ウシロニ松ノ林在リ、ヒロシ、松風計聞」but should read,「珠光カ丶リハ・・・」.

94. *Torinoko*, or *torinoko-gami* 鳥の子紙, is a paper made primarily from the inner bark of a shrub called *ganpi* 雁皮, Lychnis coronata.

95. Sen, *Chadō Koten Zenshū*, vol. 4, p. 52.『南方録』「四畳半座敷ハ、珠光の作事也、眞座敷とて鳥子紙の白張付、杉板のふちなし天井、小板ぶき、寶形造、一間床也。」

96. The plan from *Chanoyu Shidaisho* 茶湯次第書 can be found in Nakamura, *Chadō Shūkin*, vol. 7, 1984, p. 61.

97. *Yamanoue Sōjiki*, *Nanbōroku*, and *Chanoyu Shidaisho* are all texts written after Shukō's death. They are records of oral tradition or of other written texts that are no longer extant and, therefore, may not provide accurate information with regard to Shukō's life and tea practice.

98. Presently, a standard *tatami* mat measures 1.818 meters by 0.909 meters, or 1.65 square meters.

99. This scene comes from the *Kyū Machida Bon* version of *Rakuchū Rakugaizu* 洛中洛外図・旧町田本 now held by the National Museum of Japanese History, Kokuritsu Rekishi Minzoku Hakubutsukan 国立歴史民俗博物館. The painting is in a folding-screen format comprising two, six-panel sets. This image is at the bottom of the second panel of the "left" set. Images can be found in three books: Hayashiya, *Kadokawa Chadō Daijiten Shiryō-Sakuin Hen*, p. 27 (clearest image); *Kinsei Fūzoku Zufu*, vol. 3: *Rakuchū Rakugai*, part 1, p. 10 (bottom left, small) and p. 17 (large but partial); and *Rakuchū Rakugaizu: Miyako no Keishō*. p. 12 (bottom left, small).

100. For original Japanese text, see note 40.

101. English translation based on Mack Horton's work. See Sōchō, *The Journal of Sōchō*, p. 109. Shimazu, *Sōchō Nikki*, p. 92.『宗長日記』大永6年8月「下京茶湯・下京茶湯とて、此比数寄などいひて、四畳半敷・六畳敷をの(中略)興行。宗殊さし入、門に大なる松有、杉あり。垣のうち清く、蔦落葉五葉六葉いろきを見て。　今朝や夜の風をひろふはつ紅葉。」

102. *Chadō Bunka Kenkyū Dai'isshū*, pp. 92–93.『長歌茶湯物語』「大戸ひらき戸、をしひらき(押開)、こなたへとほぶ、そのときに、路ち(地)ほそ(細)道を、あらけなく、足をと(音)高く、ふみ(踏)ならし、つま(妻)戸の内に、ほそえん(細縁)に、たち(立)入すがた(姿)に、ふつかに、しきれ(尻切)ハしなか(足半)、ふみ(踏)ちらし、ここ

103. Nobunga is, of course, Oda Nobunaga and Taikō is Toyotomi Hideyoshi. For this and more comments on Sakai see Rodrigues, pp. 290–91.

104. English translation from Hirota, *Wind in the Pines*, p. 209. Hirota doubts the letter was written by Jōō himself but finds it likely to be representative of an oral traditional of Jōō's thought. Yabe, *Shinshū Chadō Zenshū*, vol. 8, p. 18.『紹鷗侘びに文』「天下の侘の根元は、天照御神にて、日國の大主にて、金銀珠玉をちりばめ殿作り候へばとて誰あつてしかるもの無の候に、かやぶき・黒米の御供、其外、何から何までもつゝしみふかくおこたり給はぬ御事、世に勝れたる茶人にて御入候。」

105. The Tenmon era 天文時代, also called the Tenbun era, was the period under Emperor Gonara (1532.7.29–1555.10.23).

106. *Matsuya Kaiki* 松屋会記 covers the years 1533 to 1650; *Tennōjiya Kaiki* 天王寺屋会記 from 1548 to 1616; and *Imai Sōkyū Chanoyu Kakinuki* 今井宗久茶湯書抜 from 1554 to 1614. Dates from Hayashiya, *Kadokawa Chadō Daijiten*.

107. Sen, *Chadō Koten Zenshū*, vol. 6, p. 100.『山上宗二記』「右ハ紹鷗座敷ノ指圖也、但、北向、坪の内、又ハ見越ニ松大小多シ。」

108. The host of a tea gathering makes preparations in a side room, *mizuya* 水屋, and enters the tea room from there to greet his guests and serve tea. The guests, meanwhile, enter the tea room from another door, usually on the opposite side of the tea room from the *mizuya*.

109. The plan of Jōō's tea house can be found in Sen, *Chadō Koten Zenshū*, vol. 6, p. 99. The in-floor hearth, *ro*, appears in the upper right-hand corner of the central, half-sized *tatami* but should be in the upper left.

110. The roof may have been made of wooden boards weighted down with a grid of bamboo poles and stones as seen in the image on pp. 14–18 (and many other places) in *Rakuchū Rakugaizu: Miyako no Keishō*.

111. Clay walls were either slim walls made of clay plastered on a wooden frame or thick walls made of rammed earth or adobe-like construction. This quote refers to the former, slim walls, *kaki* 垣, rather than the latter, heavy walls, *hei* 塀. The text, called variously *Ikenaga Sōsaku e no Sho*, *Ikenaga Sōsaku Chasho*, and *Jōō Oyobi Ikenaga Sōsaku Chasho*, dates from 1555. Sen, *Chadō Koten Zenshū*, vol. 3, p. 69.『池永宗作

への書」「庭ノ垣ハ、色々ニスルト云トモ、土カベ尤モヨモシ、ヨイコロ(比)ノ小石ヲソエテスルナリ、水ヲ打テハ幽ニ石アラワレテコヒル也、ヲ、イヲバ内へ出スシテ、外へ、計水ノシタタル様にするへシ。」

112. *Chadō Bunka Kenkyū Dai'isshū*, p. 108.『烏鼠集』「庭の様躰、四疊半敷にハ草木不植、石たてす、砂まかす、栗石ならへす、そのゆへは客のめ(目)不移良、御茶に精を入れ、名物に心をつけしめんため也。」

113. The inscription *kuguri kido* is found on a plan in Kuwata, *Yamanoue no Sōji ki no Kenkyū*, p. 280, but not on the same plan in Sen, *Chadō Koten Zenshū*, vol. 6, p. 100. The latter is an omission. The verb *kuguru* means to "duck under and slip through" but in the case of the tea house door, "crawl-through" gives an apt impression of what the guest does.

114. Matsuyama, *Chanoyu Koten Sōsho*, vol. 1, p. 54.「大阪ひらかたノ船付ニ、くゞりにて出(入)を佗て面白とて小座(シキ)をくゞりニ易仕始るなり。」

115. For many years following that first contact, guns in Japan were called Tanegashima after the island where they were first encountered and, subsequently, manufactured.

116. This quote is from Luis Fróis, *História de Japam* [sic], Biblioteca Nacional, Lisbon, 1976–83, 1, p. 234, as cited in Watsky, "Commerce, Politics, and Tea: The Career of Imai Sōkyū," p. 53.

117. Rodrigues, *João Rodrigues's Account of Sixteenth-Century Japan*, pp. 290–91.

118. The appellation Naya was common among tea masters from Sakai, so much so that they were referred to as the Naya-shū 納屋衆 or the Warehouse Fellows. In fact, those given the appellation Naya were normally involved in some sort of wholesale business rather than in the warehouse business specifically. In *Sōtan Nikki*, along with Naya Sōkyū ナヤ宗久, we find Naya Sōkun ナヤ宗薰(薰カ), Naya Sōshun ナヤ宗春, Naya Yotarō ナヤ與太郎, and Naya Ryōchō ナヤ了鳥.

119. A detailed description of Imai Sōkyū's career, and the politics of tea during this period, can be found in Watsky, "Commerce." For the episode with Shingorō see p. 54.

120. The remark about Rikyū's bullets is from Okuno, *Zōtei Oda Nobunaga Monjo no Kenkyū*, p. 82, as cited in Watsky, "Commerce," p. 62.

121. Beatrice Bodart, "Tea and Counsel: The Political Role of

122. Taian 待庵, "The Arbor of Biding Time," which is listed as a national treasure in Japan, is found at Myōkian, a branch temple of Tōfukuji in the Yamazaki area east of Kyōto. Taian was either built there by Rikyū at the order of Hideyoshi, or moved there from Rikyū's own house in Yamazaki.

123. The plan of the *chōzu-kamae* can be found in Sen, *Chadō Koten Zenshū*. vol. 6, p. 102.

124. The tea house Teigyokuken 庭玉軒 is found at Shinjuan 真珠庵, a subtemple of the large Zen monastery Daitokuji 大徳寺 in Kyōto.

125. The names of the three generations of Matsuya-family tea masters are Hisamasa 久政 (?–1598), Hisayoshi 久好 (?–1633), and Hisashige 久重 (1566–1652). Dates from Hayashiya, *Kadokawa Chadō Daijiten*.

126. Sen, *Chadō Koten Zenshū*, vol. 6, p. 300.『宗湛日記』1594.3.29「手水ハ、黒ヌリノ大ユトウ(湯桶)ニ入、庭ニアリ。」

127. Sen, *Chadō Koten Zenshū*, vol. 6, p. 222.『宗湛日記』1587.3.20「手水鉢、松ノ木ノ船也、高麗物ノ様也、丸ク長ク切テ。」

128. The "Box Pine" (*hakomatsu*), if like the one in Ritsurin Park called by that name, is a Japanese black pine that has been shaped through pruning into a box-like form. Sen, *Chadō Koten Zenshū*, vol. 6, p. 229.『宗湛日記』1587.6.19「箱松ノ下ニ手水鉢有、木ヲクリタル也、古シテコケ(苔)ムス。」

129. "Wide at the base, covered on the outside with moss" could also be interpreted as "covered richly at the base with soft moss." Sen, *Chadō Koten Zenshū*, vol. 6, p. 145.『宗湛日記』1586.12.19「手水鉢ハ石(高一尺二寸ホト)下フクラニ苔ムス。」

130. Sen, *Chadō Koten Zenshū*, vol. 6, p. 258.『宗湛日記』1590.9.20「聚楽第ニテ、利休老、御會(中略)手水鉢、自然ナル大石ヲクリテ。」

131. Sen, *Chadō Koten Zenshū*, vol. 6, p. 174.『宗湛日記』1587.1.11「手水鉢ハ、古平丸キ石ヲ内角半分ニ切テナリ。」

132. Sen, *Chadō Koten Zenshū*, vol. 6, p. 257.『宗湛日記』1590.10.11「手水鉢ハ、大キナル丸キ石堂(塔カ)也。」

133. Sen, *Chadō Koten Zenshū*, vol. 6, p. 187.『宗湛日記』1587.2.1「手水鉢ハ、桶ナリ、ヒシャクフセテ、前ニハ瓦細ニシテクボク(窪133)、フミ石に角ノ瓦置テ也133。」

134. Sen, *Chadō Koten Zenshū*, vol. 6, p. 229.『宗湛日記』

1587.6.19「ヒシャクハ上ニフセテ。」

135. Sen, *Chadō Koten Zenshū*, vol. 6, p. 257.『宗湛日記』
1590.2.10「ヒシャク、アヲノケテ也。」

136. Sen, *Chadō Koten Zenshū*, vol. 6, p. 145.『宗湛日記』
1586.12.19「ヒシャク(柄杓)ハ右ノ方ニフセテ、エ(柄)ハ土ニシク
也。」

137. Sen, *Chadō Koten Zenshū*, vol. 9, p. 179.『松屋会記』
1591.10.14「ヲカヤ道賀ヘ、路地ニ灯籠アリ。」

138. Sen, *Chadō Koten Zenshū*, vol. 9, p. 187.『松屋会記』1596.3.9
「石灯籠ニ火アリ。」

139. Sen, *Chadō Koten Zenshū*, vol. 9, p. 204.『松屋会記』
1601.11.21「伏見小堀作介殿ヘ(中略)石灯籠ニ火アリ、座敷ニア
ントン斗。」

140. According to Sen, *Chadōgaku Taikei*, vol. 6, p. 373, the
first mention of a *nijiri*—in reference to the crawl-through
door of the tea house—comes in 1608 in the form of the
word *nijiri-agari-kuguri* ニシリ上リクヽリ, written on a plan in
Hisashige Chakaiki 久重茶会記, which can be found in Sen,
Chadō Koten Zenshū, vol. 9, pp. 233–34. There is, however,
in 1600, a reference to a stone used to step up into a crawl-
through door, *nijiri-agari no ishi* にじり上りの石 in *Sōshun'ō
Chanoyu Kikigaki* 宗春翁茶湯聞書 (1600), which indicates
that the crawl-through door to the tea house was already
called a *nijiri* at that earlier date.

141. According to Sen, *Chadōgaku Taikei*, vol. 6, pp. 371–72,
the first mention of a *soto-kuguri* (outer wicket) is in 1601
in *Oribe Chakaiki* 織部茶会記; of a *naka-kuguri* (middle
wicket), in 1626 in *Sansaikō yori Shōgen Kikigaki* 三斎公より
将監聞書; and of a *chūmon* (middle gate), in 1697 in *Fusai
Densho* 普斎伝書.

142. Sen, *Chadō Koten Zenshū*, vol. 6, p. 229.『宗湛日記』
1587.6.19「箱崎御陣所ニテ、關白様ニ(中略)此路地ノ入ハ、外ニ
クヽリ(潜り)ヲハイ入テ(中略)數奇屋ノ前ニ古竹ニテ腰垣アリ、ソ
コニス(簾)戸ノハネキト(撥木戸)有。」

143. Sen, *Chadō Koten Zenshū*, vol. 6, p. 207.『宗湛日記』
1587.2.25「宗湛ハ七ツ時分ヨリ参上ソロテ、ハネキト(撥木戸)ノ本
ニ罷居候得。」

144. Sen, *Chadō Koten Zenshū*, vol. 6, p. 229.『宗湛日記』
1587.6.19「此路地ノ入ハ、外ニクヽリ(潜り)ヲハイ入テ、トヒ石ア
リ。」

145. Sen, *Chadōgaku Taikei*, vol. 6, p. 373.『宗春翁茶湯聞書』
1600「昔ハ雪ヲふませ候中比ハタヽミ石飛石湯ニテ洗候テ通シ
候。」*Chadōgaku Taikei* lists this passage as a first usage of
the word *tobi-ishi*, but clearly the passage in *Sōtan Nikki*
predates it. The issue of first written usage of the word
aside, it is clear that stepping stones were used in tea gardens by the time of Rikyū.

146. Sen, *Chadōgaku Taikei*, vol. 6, p. 373, lists the term *nobe-
dan* but does not list a date of first appearance. According to
Sen, also p. 373, the first record of *tatami-ishi* is from 1600 in
Sōshun'ō Chanoyu Kikigaki 宗春翁茶湯聞書, but it is believed
that the use of *tatami-ishi* stems from Rikyū's time.

147. Sen, *Chadō Koten Zenshū*, vol. 6, p. 317.『宗湛日記』1597.1.24
「先ク、リヲハイ入テ松原有。」

148. See note 128.

149. Rodrigues, *João Rodrigues's Account of Sixteenth-Century
Japan*, p. 292.

150. *Chadō Bunka Kenkyū Dai'isshū*, p. 199.「終日の會にハ、中程
に繪(絵)・字かけたあり、船かさり花いたり、大壺なとさハ、客は縁
ヘ出て庭の苔をなかめ、其間に仕廻(仕舞)をさせよ、一禮して入
て詠よ。」

151. Sen, *Chadō Koten Zenshū*, vol. 10, p. 204.『茶話指月集』「
宗易 [利休] 露地の樹ハ、凡松竹、した木にハ茱萸(グミ)をうへ
たり。」

152. From *Chafu* 茶譜 (*Tea Notes*, 1661–73), as cited in Nakamura, *Machiya no Chashitsu*, p. 154.「樹木ハ、大松、大樅 [モ
ミ]、木殼 [モッコク] 。」*Mokkoku*, written here as 木殼 is usually written 木斛.

153. *Setchin* can also be spelled *secchin* or *setsuin*. As cited in Sen,
Chadōgaku Taikei, vol. 6, p. 373.『烏鼠集』「廊下の外に小便
所、其奥に雪隠ありてよし、貴人の来儀にはなくて不叶、平生の用
をかなへす、さわやかに持也。」

154. As cited in Sen, *Chadōgaku Taikei*, vol. 6, p. 374.『久好茶会
記』1596.

155. Ichino, *Chanoyu Koten Sōsho*, vol. 2, p. 85.『古田織部正殿聞
書』「能ヲ吟味シテ居ル石ノ事。ニシリ上リノ石、刀掛之石。」

156. Kuwata, *Shinshū Chadō Zenshū*, vol. 9, p. 244.『宗春翁茶湯
聞書』「つきとめ腰掛の方ニテすぐニつき留ル也。」「腰掛の内路石、
いかにもいふう(異風)なる少大キ成石すえ候。長ミの有石ニ、間ニ
丸石すえ見事なり。」

157. Kuwata, *Shinshū Chadō Zenshū*, vol. 9, p. 245.『宗春翁茶湯聞書』1600「雪隠の塵穴、雪隠へはいりて用也。寸法さし渡し八寸丸き穴也。」

158. Sen, *Chadō Koten Zenshū*, vol. 10, p. 343.『茶湯一會集』「塵穴(ちりあたな)の内、露地の落葉・折枝を水にひたして入る、紅葉の節ハ、紅葉をも取交せて入置事ありハ、塵穴之内ニ、天然の落葉・折枝を入る事ニて、態(わざ)と氣色ニ入るニあらさる事を可知、塵箸、青竹ニ改め立かけ置、箒も青竹ニ仕替、箒かけの釘に懸くへし。塵穴なき軒下ニハ、塵籠を出し、落葉・折枝同様ニ入れ、塵箸立かけ置く。」

159. Sen, *Chadō Koten Zenshū*, vol. 6, p. 174.『宗湛日記』1587.1.11「大阪ニ八ツ時分(午前1時〜2時)ニ着、利休路地ノ口ニ待、宗傳内意トシテ案内被申候へハ、則コノ方ヘトテ、外ノ久ノリマテ、小性(姓)衆ニアントンヲモタセ御出候ホト、夜不明ニハイ入候也、両人乗物ハ一間ヲ置テ、マタセ候也。」

160. Rodrigues, *João Rodrigues's Account of Sixteenth-Century Japan*, p. 157.

161. Sen, *Chadō Koten Zenshū*, vol. 6, p. 208.『宗湛日記』1587.2.25「山里ニハイ入申也、此路地ニハ、ハネキドマテモ水ヲ打立置候事。」

162. Rodrigues, *João Rodrigues's Account of Sixteenth-Century Japan*, p. 301.

163. English translation from Hirota, *Wind in the Pines*, p. 222. Sen, *Chadō Koten Zenshū*, vol. 4 pp. 6–7.『南方録』「露地の出入ハ、客も亭主もゲタ(下駄)ヲハクコト、紹鴎ノ定メ也、草木の露フカキ所往來スルユエ、如是、互ニクツノ音、功名(者カ)不功者、ヲキヽシルト云々、カシガマシク(喧しく)ナキヤウニ、又サシアシスルヤウニモナクテ、ヲダヤカニ無心ナルガ、功者トシルベシ、得心ノ人ナラデ批判シガタシ、宗易コノミニテ、コノ比(頃)、草履ノウラニ革ヲアテ、セキダ(雪駄)トテ、當津(堺)今市町ニテツクラセ、露地ニ用スル、此事ヲ一間申タレハ、易ノ云、ゲタハクコト今更アシキニハアラズ候ヘトモ、鴎(紹鴎)ノ茶ニモ、易トモニ三人ナラバ、ゲタヲ踏得タルモノナシト鴎モイハレシ也、今、京・堺・奈良ニカケテ、數十人ノスキ者(數奇者)アレトモ、ゲタヲハク功者、ワ僧トモニ五人ナラデナシ(中略)亭坊別而カシマシサノ物ズキナリト。」

164. In fact, Rodrigues does not mention any tea masters by name, except Higashiyama Dono (*Shōgun* Ashikaga Yoshimasa), who he, mistakenly, implies is the patriarch of rustic tea. Rodrigues, *João Rodrigues's Account of Sixteenth-Century Japan*, pp. 284–85.

165. Rodrigues, *João Rodrigues's Account of Sixteenth-Century*

Japan, pp. 292–93.

166. Rodrigues later notes that the tea house was actually called *sukiya*, not *suki*, in which -*ya* means "building."

167. The benches are called *koshi-kake*. Typically, nowadays, the *koshi-kake* is a small, roofed bench, but Rodrigues does not mention a "roof" over the benches. It may be that the earliest form was a simple, unroofed bench (*shōgi*) or that the roof was too obvious to warrant mention.

168. These toilets are the *setchin* described on page 227.

169. This "pool of water" was, of course, not a large pool but a small device like the present-day *chōzubachi*, or "hand-washing basin."

170. As above, this "stone with a pool of water in it" is the *chōzubachi*.

171. This "container at the base" could have been one of two things. Either it was a small container used as a water ladle, as the *hishaku* is used, or it was what is presently called a *yuoke*, a "warm-water bucket." The *yuoke* is a small wooden bucket used in winter to hold warm water so that guests may warm their hands after using the frigid well water provided in the *chozubachi*.

172. This cupboard is somewhat different in form from the *katana-kake* that developed in the early Edo period but had the same function. The note about the fan is interesting because nowadays a fan is a requisite part of the guest's accoutrements. Presumably, the reason the fan was left behind with the sword in this case was that a fan could conceal a small dagger, or could itself be made of iron, and was therefore considered a potential weapon.

173. These are similar to what are called *roji-gasa* nowadays.

174. Rodrigues, *João Rodrigues's Account of Sixteenth-Century Japan*, pp. 155–57.

175. The "stone with a cavity" is a natural river stone, or perhaps ocean stone, that has a depression within it and could be used as a *chōzubachi*. The other texts mentioned previously record carving a basin into stone, but this is the first mention of a naturally shaped *chōzubachi* being used.

176. Rodrigues, *João Rodrigues's Account of Sixteenth-Century Japan*, pp. 293–94.

177. The outer gate of the *roji* nowadays, called the *soto-mon* or

roji-mon, is not the stoop-through device described by Rodrigues but neither is it typically a grand gate.

178. It is interesting that Rodrigues notes that the guests may wash their hands. These days, the custom of rinsing one's hands is only a formality, or perhaps a sign of spiritual cleansing—no one actually *washes* his hands.

179. Rodrigues, *João Rodrigues's Account of Sixteenth-Century Japan*, p. 301.

180. Rodrigues, *João Rodrigues's Account of Sixteenth-Century Japan*, p. 307.

181. *Wind in the Pines* pp. 206–7, Sen, *Chadō Koten Zenshū*, vol. 6, p. 94.『山上宗二記』「茶湯ノ師ニ別テ後、師ニ用ル覺悟ハ、一切ノ上、佛法、歌道能并、亂舞、刀ノ上、尤又、下々ノ所作マテモ、名人ノ仕事ヲ茶湯ト目明ノ手本ニスル也。」

182. Sen, *Chadō Koten Zenshū*, vol. 6, p. 95.『山上宗二記』「茶湯ハ禪宗ヨリ出タルニ依テ、僧ノ行ヲ專ニスル也、珠光・紹鷗・皆禪宗也。」

183. An example of a Chinese influence on the design of earlier garden forms is the *karesansui*—dry landscape gardens made of stone and raked sand that appear in Zen temples and the residences of the military lords. The design of these gardens was based in part on the images of Chinese landscapes revealed in black-and-white ink landscape paintings imported from China.

184. Takeuchi, *Zōho Zoku Shiryō Taisei: Inryōken Nichiroku*, vol. 2, p. 241.『蔭涼軒日録』1485.9.4「路次掃地寺邊普請庭沙等可被申付。」

185. *Dainihon Kokiroku: Nisuiki*, vol. 1, p. 51.『二水記』1505.3.29「廿九日、武家御參、内、路次參會衆如例。」

186. The reference to *roji* is found in *Sōkyū Hoka Kaiki* as cited in Sen, *Chadōgaku Taikei*, vol. 6, p. 371.『宗及他会記』1581.4.11「朝、惟任殿供申候、路次にて福寿院振舞、茶屋ヲ立テ、生鮎 [あゆ, sweetfish]・生鯉 [こい, carp]・鮒 [ふな, crucian carp] せんすひを俄用意にて、魚共をはなされ候。」Although *Chadōgaku Taikei* lists 1581 as the first instance of the use of the word *roji* in connection with *chanoyu*, it also shows up in the form 路ぢ (pronounced *roji*) in *Chōka Chanoyu Monogatari*, a poem supposedly written sometime before 1525. There is much about *Chōka Chanoyu Monogatari*, however, that is prescient; either that, or the actual date of the poem is much later than believed.

187. According to Sen, *Chadōgaku Taikei*, vol. 6, p. 370, the first use of the "dewy ground" *kanji* was in 1609 in *Nanpō Bunshū Kami: Chakaiki*:『南浦文集上・茶会記』「眄其庭際、移千株之珍松、種数片之怪石、青苔之堆其錦、野草之鋪其茵、即有抜俗出塵之想矣、雖曰禪寂無塵之地、豈復若之哉、所謂静裏乾坤、閑中日月也、中有一露地、灑之掃之、不立一塵、不容一芥、不覚令人逍遥於風塵之外。」

188. The full title of the sutra known as *Hoke-kyō*, or *Hokke-kyō*, is *Myōhō Renge Kyō* 妙法蓮華経. The passage that contains the "Buddhist" *kanji* for *roji* is in Takakusu, *Taishō Shinshū Daizōkyō*, vol. 9, p. 12, bottom. A modern Japanese version of the same text reads as follows:「爾の時に諸子、父の所説の珍玩の物を聞くに、其の願に適えるが故に、心各勇鋭して互に相推排し、競うて共に馳走し争うて火宅を出ず。是の時に長者、諸子等の安穏に出ずることを得て、皆四衢道の中の露地に於て坐して復障碍無く、其の心泰然として歓喜踊躍するを見る。」. http://www.sattva.jp/data/h-kun.html.

189. Oribe-no-Kami 織部正 was the title of the chief of the Oribe-no-Tsukasa 織部司, a government agency affiliated with the treasury that was in charge of textiles and dyed goods. Furuta Oribe was also known as Koshoku 古織, a moniker made up of the first *kanji* of his family name, 古田, and of his appellation, 織部.

190. Oribe's first tea was recorded in *Tsuda Sōgyū Chanoyu Nikki* 津田宗及茶湯日記, which is another name for *Tennōjiya Kaiki* 天王寺屋会記 1585.2.13 (天正十三年二月十三日朝). As cited in Ichino, *Chanoyu Koten Sōsho*, vol. 3, p. 398.

191. The Seven Disciples of Rikyū 利休七哲 mentioned in *Kōshin Natsugaki*『江岑夏書』were Gamo'u Ujisato 蒲生氏郷, Takayama Ukon 高山右近, Hosokawa Sansai 細川三斎, Shibayama Kenmotsu 芝山監物, Seta Kamon 瀬田掃部, Makimura Hyōbu 牧村兵部, and Furuta Oribe 古田織部. In addition there were Oda Uraku 織田有楽, Araki Murashige 荒木村重, and Sen Dōan 千道安.

192. Sen, *Chadō Koten Zenshū*, vol. 11, p. 236–37.『石州三百ケ条』「飛石は利休は渡を六ふん景気四ふんに据へ申候よし、織部は渡を四景気を六ふんにすへ申候、先、飛石ハ渡りのためなれは、わたりを第一とす、然共、まつすくに同じやうについつけてハかたく候、それゆえひつみを取也、しかれとも無用の所にて、わさとひつませ候ハ作物にてあしき也。」

193. *Teien Gaku Kōza 2*, p. 22.

194. Sen, *Chadō Koten Zenshū*, vol. 6, p. 317.『宗湛日記』1597.1.24「廿四日朝、大閤様、御会會、御城、御座敷、五疊敷、此入ノ次第ハ、先ヘリヤハイ入テ松原有、御スキヤ[ト]ノ中ノ間ニ、ス戸ノハネキト有、是ヲ通テツテツ斗ノ路地アリ、是ヨリ御數寄屋ニハイ入候也。」

195. Nakamura, *Machiya no Chashitsu*. p. 154.『茶譜』「樹木ハ、大松、大樅［もみ］、木殼［モッコク］、加様ノ類ヲ深植也、其奥ニ、茅［かや］屋有ヤウニ、成ホト静ニ人音遠躰也。」

196. Ichino, *Chanoyu Koten Sōsho*, vol. 2, p. 94.『古田織部正殿聞書』「木ヲ多植込事利休代之儀也。大成木ヲ本之枝茂リシテ植也。古織以来是ヲ改テ大成木ハ地ヨリ二・三尺又ハ一間余モヲロシテ植也。惣テ多ク不植込也。掃除之為ニモ尤吉。是モ可用也。内外之路次之木植心得之事。長路ハ一村一村ニ別々ニ見ユル様ニ可植、並木ニ植ル心得悪シ。」The title of this text is given as *Furuta Oribe no Kamidono no Chanoyu no Kikigaki*『古田織部正殿茶湯聞書』in *Kadokawa Chadō Daijiten*.

197. "Exotic, imported plants" (*tōboku* or *karaki*) refers to Southeast Asian plants such as rosewood (*shitan*, 紫檀, Diospyros ebenum), ebony (*kokutan*, 黒檀, Dalbergia cochinchinensis), and kilet (also called Bombay black wood, *tagayasan* 鉄刀木, Cassia siamea). Ichino, *Chanoyu Koten Sōsho*, vol. 2, p. 95.『古田織部正殿聞書』「内外之路次ニ花之咲木惣テ不可植也。座鋪ニ花ヲ生候無詮故也。同葉落ル木モ大方植間敷也。内外路次ニ唐木ハ何モ植ル也。葉ノヲツル木成トモ何植、唐木ニハ実生候モ植。花咲テ此花数奇ニ出シテ其後之生木ナラハ唐木成共不可植也。」

198. Ichino, *Chanoyu Koten Sōsho*, vol. 2, p. 96.『古田織部正殿聞書』「内路地ニ竹ヲ植ル事、大竹杯ハ一段見事成故、古ハ植ル由ニ候。古織以来不好、嫌也。葉落テ掃除難成故也。根篠ハ内路地ニ植候也。」

199. Hayashiya, *Nihon no Chasho 1*, p. 357.『古田織部伝書』「植木の取り合わせ、其の時どき相替ら候。長旦（短）の木の様子之事は、時の公（巧）者（この方面での熟達者）にもたずね、人のめ（目）によく候えば、上手にて候。少習にかからわず候（学習の不足は関係がない）。」

200. Hayashiya, *Nihon no Chasho 1*, p. 357.『古田織部伝書』「路次石の間、おうぎ（扇）のかなめ（要）より先、石と石のかど（角）の事也。」

201. Ichino, *Chanoyu Koten Sōsho*, vol. 2. p. 80:『古田織部正殿聞書』「石品様之事。此石ハ克ヲ吟味シテ可居、踏石二つ同シ大サ悪シ。大小長短有之吉、壱ッ長ク一ツハ丸クナト猶面白シ。石之

202. Ichino, *Chanoyu Koten Sōsho*, vol. 2, pp. 86-87.『古田織部正殿聞書』「又畳石之縁ニ居ル長石、切石之向脇共直クニシテモ居、又自然石之少出入有之モ可居、長石何方ニ畳ト所不定、又畳石ニ大成長石ヲ一ツニシテ余之小石不交一面ニ居候事不苦、是ハ切石ニシテモ自然形之少出入在之長石大成モ用居ル、広長石一ツヲモ可居、畳石旦之内之石ハ大小ヲ交ゼ乱ニ間〳〵ニ打込也。丸石・角石如何様成モ又黒・白・赤色何モ不苦、并テ立打込ハ悪シ、石之間〳〵ヘ乱ニ可打込、此打込タル右［石カ］之廻之間〳〵ニシヤリヲ打、石之面ト上ヲ同面ニ打、石面ヨリシヤリヲ低ク打事悪ク候。」

203. Ichino, *Chanoyu Koten Sōsho*, vol. 2.『古田織部正殿聞書』, p. 100:「外路地ニ砂ヲ蒔事無之儀也。小石ヲ可蒔」「外路次惣庭ニ海石ヲ敷也」; p. 90:「内路地道通惣テ砂ヲ蒔事無之儀也。ジヤリ（砂利）ヲ打テ可叩付也。」One of the difficult aspects of texts such as *Furuta Oribe no Kamidono Kikigaki*, which list random assorted teachings of a master, is that they tend to contradict themselves from time to time. Right beside the admonition not to spread the *roji* with ocean stones is another passage that supports the use of ocean stones—"using black ocean stones is good" (p. 100, 何モ海石之黒ヲ用テ吉)—but earlier in the text we find that Oribe "didn't like ocean stones" (p. 85, 海石ハ不好).

204. Ichino, *Chanoyu Koten Sōsho*, vol. 2, p. 33.「慶長十四年正月（1609.1）・・・織部殿へ。露地より、山又ハ何れのけい［景］を見候事、木々の間よりすこし見申候かよく候や、山なとおほく見へ候か能候やと尋へハ、山其外景ハ木の間より少シ見たるか面白由、山なとおほく見候へハぶしほなる（景しきならさる）よし。是ニ付て引事に、三井寺にて宗長之発句に　夕月夜　海すこしある　木の間かな駿府［すんぷ］にて、後（藤）庄三路次よりせんけんの山［浅間山・富士山カ］をほく見へ候を道也（道巴）に、木にて植かくし候へと被申候由。いづれも山多く見えざるをほめ候へるよし。」The poem about the moon by Sōchō (1448–1532) seems to make reference to a longer poem by his predecessor, Saigyō (1118–90): "If you gaze at the moon at dawn leaking through the trees . . ." *Nihon Koten Bungaku Taikei*, vol. 29, p. 71.「木の間もる有明の月をながむればさびしさ添ふるみねの松風。」

205. Nakamura, *Machiya no Chashitsu*, p. 154.『正伝集』「路地の景は、あまりよきは一向不好事なり、其時は景を植えかくすことあり。」

206. Sen, *Chadō Koten Zenshū*, vol. 9, p. 187.『松屋会記』「伏見ニ
而古田織部殿へ参ル。大カヤ道か、久好二人。九日朝、六時分、御
茶湯。路地ヒロシ、石灯籠ニ火アリ、手水湯出ル、座敷三条大 [三
畳台目か] 、南向也、カヤヽ(茅屋)、アツマヤ(四阿)、ガクハ望覚
庵トアリ。」

207. Matsuyama, *Chanoyu Koten Sōsho*, vol. 1, pp. 74–75.『茶
道四祖伝書』「九日(朝)古織部殿へ。路地広シ、夕、キ路地ナリ、
(石)灯籠ニ火アリ。手水、湯出ル、額ハ望覚庵。」*Chadō Shiso
Densho* is a compilation of extracts from *Matsuya Kaiki* and
other sources produced by Matsuya Hisashige sometime
around 1650.

208 Matsuyama, *Chanoyu Koten Sōsho*, vol. 1, pp. 102–3.『茶道四
祖伝書』「路次表ニクゞリナク(リ)、是ニ腰掛を(テ)織部(殿)メサ
ルヽニ、其以後、慶長八九ノ比(頃)ニ二重路地ニ成候。織部殿ゞソメ
給ふ。路次入(ヲ)、何時ニテモ菓子不時ノ茶湯ニハ手(洗)を遣て
入座す。飯ノ時ニハ手洗を不遣入座するを、慶長八九ノ頃ヨリハ、
朝会斗ニ手洗不遣入座す。其已後ハヒルモ晩モ会ニて行とも手洗
遣て入候なり。」

209. Sen, *Chadō Koten Zenshū*, vol. 6, p. 336.『宗湛日記』
1599.2.28「手水所、掘テ、大石ヒ、ヒシャクヨコニ也。」

210. As cited in Yabe, *Furuta Oribe* p. 285.

211. Ichino, *Chanoyu Koten Sōsho*, vol. 2, p. 83.「一・手水鉢之石居
様之事。手水鉢ハ石ニ定也。余ノ器ハ不用也。所ハ道通、曲目ナト
有時ハクヽリヲ入テ、真向ニモ又道之左右ニモ可有。所不定。先穴
ヲ上広手水鉢之大小長ニ随テ可堀。穴ノ広サ不定、廻リ下へ真切
[異筆・本ノマヽ] ニモ可堀、穴ノ底真直也。底ニ台石ヲ居ル。此石
平面直ニ成ヲ用、穴之底ニ不定成 [異筆・イカヽ不分]、不苦。穴ハ
台石之大サニ不構、台之脇ヨリ穴底地形之見ユル程ニ堀也。此台
石ニ手水鉢ヲ居置也。台石ナク手水鉢斗居事無之儀也。手水鉢
穴ノ真中也。又向之方へ少寄テ前ノ少広クモ居、高サ穴ヨリ上へ
出ル不定、克程タルヘシ。捨石之事。手水鉢之根ニ置也。数ハ一ツ
モ三ツ置一。一ツモ置時ハ手水鉢之前之方ニ可置。三ツ置時ハ一
ツハ如右ニ、二ツハ手水鉢ニ向テ左之方、脇之方ニ置。台石・捨
石之外ニ手水鉢之根穴之中ニ小石杯蒔置事、夢々無之。惣テ捨
石之外ハ不可有之。

一・手水鉢之石大成吉也。チイサキヲ克トスルト云事有、不用也。又欠
損シ事、水之コボレサル程ナラハ不苦。同文字杯彫付有之、様子ニ
ヨリ不苦。同青苔付候事ナトハ洗ヲトシ申マシキ也。但ムサクヨコ
レタルヲ用ニ非ス。古ク持成候也、惣テ路次中万古ク見ル事専一
也。異風成事嫌也。

一・手水鉢ヒクク居ル事。公方之御路次ニヒクク居ル也。是ハ御数寄

屋近ク侯ニ立テ手水遣候儀如何成故ト人ニヨリ時宜ニヨリ、ケ様
ノ事一篇ニハ可有之。」

Sute-ishi, which is translated "extra stones" here, is a term
usually used to refer to a few extra stepping stones, small in
size, that are added on the edges of a stepping stone path
to diffuse the design. In this case, *sute-ishi* seems to refer to
what are normally called *waki-ishi*, side stones, or *yaku-ishi*,
stones that have a given function.

212. Ichino, *Chanoyu Koten Sōsho*, vol. 2, p. 89.「手水鉢前石居様
之事。地形ロクニシテ高サ一寸七・八分也、石之根モ地形直クニテ
穴之内へ石ツラ見ユル能石ヲ可居。飛石ヨリハ大成ヲ居。又此前
石之脇ニ、踏石ヨリ大成ヲ一ツ石之根地形ロクニシテ、高サ壱寸五
分程居置也。二つ居事ハ不可有之。是ハ寒天之時ニ片口ニ湯ヲ入
テ此石之上ニ置、手水遣候故ニ置也。主人・貴人御手水被成時ニ
御供之者、此石ニ居テ御手水ヲクミ掛ル為、此小石ヲ居ル也。穴之
際ニ石之面穴ノ内へ見ヘサル様ニ可置也。」

213. Ichino, *Chanoyu Koten Sōsho*, vol. 2, p. 215.「手水鉢ニ水入置
様之事。冬ハ初路次入之時前方ヨリ水十分ニ入置、中立ニ客此水
ヲ遣也。此跡ニ水十分ニ入置也。夏ハ初路次入之時客遣テ入、此
跡水十分ニ入置、此水中立ニ遣也。此跡へ又入置、此水上(迄)夏
ハ以上三度也。手水鉢水余リ廻リ蓋ハ不掛候様入事専用也。客初
路次入之時手水鉢ニ蓋ハ不可有之。同柄杓之事。杉ノ曲物也。底
ハ切入底ニ、寸方有之歟。其仕手可心得不承知、檜ハ嫌也。内路
次水手鉢ニ柄杓置様之事。シメシテ可置、口ヲ左之方へシテカブ
せ横ニ手水鉢之向之縁ニ持せ、柄先右之方へ直違前縁ニ持せテ
置也。又柄先前へ直ニモ可置、客手水遣候テハ柄先最前之様ニ
ハ不可置、必置替テ吉。夏ナトハ客人内ニカワキ候事有トモ其分
ニテ置ヘシ。」

214. *Teien Gaku Kōza 2*, p. 20.『織部聞書』「灯籠直柱ノ本台石ノ
有ハ悪シ、柱ノ本ヲ、直ニ地掘リ入テ吉、トウト惣ノ高サ見合能程
也、低ク居ルハ心持吉、高サハ不定、掘入地形ニシテ掘居ルベ
キ也。」

215. Nakamura, *Chadō Shūkin vol 7*, p. 170, note 12.『古田織部正
殿聞書』「石旦 [石段か] 腰掛ニジリ上リ見ユル心持、灯籠ノ口
ヲ道ノ方へシテ道通ヨリ見ニ、形直ナル様ニモ又少斜コレアリテモ
居ル。内路次長ニハ灯籠ニ二ツモ居ル。一ツモ道通ノ見ユル様ニ二
ツ居候テ、一ツ右ノ通又一ツハ木陰ニ居エルベシ。火ノ影面白キ物
也。道ノ両方ニモ又左右一方ニ成トモ二ツ居ルモ苦シカラズ。」

216. As cited in Yabe, *Furuta Oribe*, p. 277.

217. As cited in Yabe, *Furuta Oribe*, p. 276. The dates of the text
Imai Sōkyū Chanoyusho, vol. 2 今井宗久茶湯書(下巻), from
which this is taken, reveal that the work is not of Sōkyū's

hand but more likely of one of his grandsons.

218. Tōtōmi is written 遠江, and Enshū is 遠州.

219. *Daimyō* 大名 was a general term to refer to military lords. *Gokamon* 御家門 referred to certain families of *daimyō* related to the Tokugawa lineage.

220. Sen, *Chadō Koten Zenshū*, vol. 11, p. 380.『僊林』「それ茶湯に極眞力、眞ト草との差異あり。或ハ、大名、或ハ御家門なとの御茶湯、もてなしもけつかうに、木具上器、金銀のきそく（亀足）、ふちたか（縁高）なと可然候。」

221. Sen, *Chadō Koten Zenshū*, vol. 6, p. 336.『宗湛日記』1599.2.28「ウス茶ノ時、セト茶碗、ヒツミ候也、ヘウケモノ也。」

222. Sen, *Chadō Koten Zenshū*, vol. 3, pp. 234–35.『草人木』「茶碗は年々瀬戸よりのほりたる今焼のひつみたる也。」

223. Rikyū's bowl was named after the Shingon priest Shunkan (俊寛 1143–79), who appears in *The Tale of The Heike* conspiring against the Taira. The name of Oribe's bowl, *Sekiyō* 夕陽, means *Evening Sun* or *Setting Sun* and refers to the pattern of its glaze. The name of Enshū's bowl, *Takatori Men* 高取面, is descriptive in nature, referring to the *mentori*, or beveling, that was applied to the base of the bowl.

224. *Shōbai Goen* 松梅語園 is found in *Kagahan Shiryō* 加賀藩資料. As cited in Mori, *Kobori Enshū*, p. 197.「御上洛御供に中納言様大津御屋敷に而御茶湯被成とて、築山、泉水被仰付、近日後客之御用意也、然処小堀遠州大津御見廻に被参、留守なれども御庭一覧被成、御大名之物数奇には小さき事、あの大山と湖水御目に不見かと被申、慶安石黒采会聞、御帰とひとしく御耳に入、中納言様御聞被成御笑、至極とて泉水、築山御崩し、不斗御出、御書院の向塀御懸直し中を御切抜、格子小間に仰付、湖水・叡山・唐崎・三上山一目に見ゆる様に被成、先遠州を御招請、宗甫見て手を打、是こそ大名の御露地なれ、如形泉水、如形山被仰付たりとてほめ被申退出也。跡に扨も、和尚に成者の器量は別の事と御意也。」

225. The "earth-floored space beneath the roof" referred to here was probably the *tsubo-no-uchi*. Sen, *Chadō Koten Zenshū*, vol. 3, pp. 372–73.『長闇堂記』「昔ハ四帖半（四畳半）、ゑん（椽）上口にして、六帖・四帖・土間屋ねの下有、手水それにすわり、ぬけ石の石船すへ、又ハ、木をもほり、桶をもすへし也、織部殿の時、大石の五十人百人して持石船となれり、長鉢は南部橋本町きほふし（擬宝珠）有けるを、中坊源五殿（井上高清・奈良中坊氏の家臣）へ某申請て持しを、遠州（小堀）殿とり結ひて、長二尺八寸にきり、六地蔵（伏見六地蔵の遠州屋敷）の路次にすへ結ひしを、後、大徳院

様 [徳川秀忠・ひでただ・1579～1632・在職1605～1623] へ上りて、江戸へ下りし也、又、石燈籠の柱に佛の有し石、京ばて町（奈良の京終町）天神の車よけに掘こみ有しを、某もらいおしし、是も遠州殿取ありてすへ結ひて後、大徳院様へ上りし也、それより其世に佛はりつけはやりし也。」

226. Seikatei 醒花亭 (Arbor of the Flower of Awakening), Shiba Ochaya 芝御茶屋 (The Grass Tea house), and Kotobukiyama Ochaya 壽山御茶屋 (Arbor of the Immortal Mountain).

227. Sen, *Chadō Koten Zenshū*, vol. 11, p. 137.『小堀遠州書捨書』「それ茶の湯の道とて外にはなし。」

228. *Ichijū-roji* can also be pronounced *hitoe-roji*, and *nijū-roji* can be pronounced *futae-roji*.

229. Ichino, *Chanoyu Koten Sōsho*, vol. 3, p. 291.「内路地ハ、一段念を入、窓などにもくもの家塵ほこり水打事能々念を入、中路地も同前なれ共、少はくるしからす候、拗路地ハそさうにしてもくるしからす候。」

230. Ichino, *Chanoyu Koten Sōsho*, vol. 2, p. 97.「内外之路次之木ニ自然鳥之巣ヲ喰候事不取捨、其儘置て不苦カルマシキ也。」

231. Ichino, *Chanoyu Koten Sōsho*, vol. 3, p. 320.「数寄屋の植込の内に、たんほうの木を植て有、是ハ花有木也、惣て数寄屋かこひの庭にハ花有木をきらへとも植給ふ、山鳩をうえこみの内に置、なかせ給ふ。」The reference to dandelions, written *tanhoho no ki* in the original text, may in fact refer not to dandelions but rather to two species of exotic flowering trees: *tan* and *hoo*. In that case, *tan* refers to varieties of trees such as as *shitan* and *kokutan* (see footnote 194), and *hoho* refers to *hoo no ki* (朴の木, *Magnolia obovata*).

232. Ichino, *Chanoyu Koten Sōsho*, vol. 2, p. 101.「三重路次ニモ手水鉢可居置、居様外路次ニ同シ。但外程ニ略スル心得能也。」

233. This description of the three-layered *roji* is based on Uehara, *Zōen Jiten*, p. 344.

234. Sen, *Chadō Koten Zenshū*,vol. 5, p. 408. *Kaiki*『槐記』(1724–35):「今ノ世ノ石灯籠ヲ置クコトイブカシ、夥シキ大灯籠ヲ据ヘテ、見聞ノ爲ニシテ(トス)、明リノ爲ニ非ズ、灯籠ハ明リノ爲ニアラズシテハ、何ノ役ニモ立タヌモノナリ、併シ夫ニ又譯アリ、唯ドコモカモ明リキヤウニハナラヌコトナリ、先ヅ路次ヘ入ルト、向フニ向テ火ノ見ユルヤウニ据ヘ、其灯籠ノ本マデ行クト、又行ク先ノ向フニ當リ、ドコマデモ路次ノ廣狭ニ因ルベシ。」

235. As cited in Sen, *Chadōgaku Taikei*, vol. 6, p. 373.「くゝりの敷

居よりふみ石まて一尺二寸に居る時ハ、(中略)くゞりの石高さ四
寸と心得、其次の石を居る也、是をおとし石といふ、此石ハくゞり
の石面より一寸五分斗下る也、此おとし石の次に居る石を、のり
石と云。」

236. The passages from *Teiyōshū* 貞要集 are cited in Sen,
Chadōgaku Taikei, vol. 6, p. 374. *Teiyōshū* is dated 1710.

237. Ichino, *Chanoyu Koten Sōsho*, vol. 3, p. 320. 「「御成、又ハ貴人
高位を申入而ハ、冬寒気の時分ハ片口に湯を入、てい主持出手水
鉢の上に置、又御近習に為持て、出しかけさする事あり。」

238. Sen, *Chadō Koten Zenshū*, vol. 5, p. 44. 「手燭石ハ、手燭ヲ置
ク爲ナレバ、今様ノ路次ノ手燭ナケレバ、庭暗クシテ危キヤウニ覺
へ候ハ如何ガト伺フ。」

239. The passages from *Chanoyu Ichieshū* 茶湯一會集 are cited in
Sen, *Chadōgaku Taikei*, vol. 6, p. 374. The term *tsukubai*, or
tsukubai chōzubachi as it is most often expressed in *Chanoyu
Ichieshū*, was written つくはい. The *kanji* used for the name
these days, 蹲踞, appears at a later date.

240. The Matsuya plan and the Enshū plan with the thicket
appear in "*Chanoyu Hishō*," *Chanoyu Bunkagaku*, March
1999, p. 205 and pp. 217–18, respectively. *Chanoyu Hishō* is
purportedly a collection of old writings on tea, but since it
is dated 1738, over a hundred years after the death of Hisayoshi, the information is uncertain. The plan of the Enshū
tea house noting *shibafu* appears in Matsuyama, *Chanoyu
Koten Sōsho*, vol. 1, p. 275.

241. Sen, *Chadō Koten Zenshū*, vol. 10, p. 163. 『杉木普斎傳書』
「サヒシキテイニ、ロチハキレイニアリタキ事也、石灯籠・手水ハチ・
ヲノツカラ苔厚シテワサト苔ヲ付石灯籠ナトヘツケ、フルメカシテイ
(体)ニモテナスサマ、一向悪敷候。」

242. Sen, *Chadō Koten Zenshū*, vol. 10, p. 344. 『茶湯一會集』「つ
くはひ手水鉢ハ、清浄なる事本體なれハ、水溜を常々あらひ清め、
さひ付さる様に懸くへし、外まわりハ、少々のさひあるもくるしから
す、苔つたなとの付まとひて、さひ多きハ不好事也。」

243. Sen, *Chadō Koten Zenshū*, vol. 10, p. 163. 『杉木普斎傳書』
「蘆地ノ植木、松・紅葉・白カシ・椎・クミ(グミ).栗・山カキ・厚朴・ク
チナシ・青木・ニシキ・はぢ(ハゼ)・竹、イツレノヤウナルヲヨロシトス、
南天・梅モトキ・苺(イチゴ)・ミノナルモノハアマリ不好、クサニハ薄・
萩・フキ・シタ(羊歯)・アサカオ・ソノホカ草木見合有へし、蘆地ノ佳
居ヲ能々分別シテ、ワサトナラス作リナシタルサマヨロシ作り木、カラ
メイタル木草ハ用捨有へシ、ヨク〜〜味ワキマエシリテ、サシキキ
テイニ植ナシタルコソ、オカシキモノナリ。」

244. Sen, *Chadō Koten Zenshū*, vol. 11, p. 118. 『細川茶湯之書』「は
じめ蘆路へ入にも、能見れとも、くらき時は見えず、がく(額)を念を
入見る物也、但、高よミ、たかくほむべからず、よミちがふ。」

245. English translation from Hirota, *Wind in the Pines*, pp.
220–21. Sen, *Chadō Koten Zenshū*, vol. 4, p. 5. 『南方録』「大
概をいはゞ、客露地入の前一度、中立の前一度、會すみて客たゝる
ゝ時分一度、都合三度也、朝、昼、夜、三度の水すべて意味ふかき
事と心得べし。」

246. Sen, *Chadō Koten Zenshū*, vol. 11, p. 96. 『細川茶湯之書』「路
次の水うつ事、冬ハ飛石の上、石鉢・腰かけのあたりに、かすかにう
つ也、夏ハ草木にもたくさんにうつ也。」

247. Sen, *Chadō Koten Zenshū*, vol. 10, p. 153. 『杉木普斎傳書』
「露チ(地)ノウチ水モ、霄ヨリウチテヨシ、雪隠ノウチ戸、腰カケノ
下木草いつれもクマクマ(隅々)マテ水ヲウツヘシ、又、暑天ノ時分、
寒天ノ折節、見合勿論有へし、朝ハ客入來ル前ニ、手水鉢ノ水入カ
エテヨロシ、蘆路ノウチ水ハ以上三度也、客中立ノ前。茶湯ミテ、歸
申さるゝ前なり。」

248. Sen, *Chadō Koten Zenshū*, vol. 11, p. 166. 『石州三百ケ条』
「数寄屋ノ行燈ハ杉ノ木にて木地なり、路次暗鈍(行燈)ハ檜に
てつくる也。」

249. Hayashiya, *Nihon no Chasho*, vol. 1, pp. 353–54. 『古田織部
伝書』「一・佗は、手そく(燭)なしに、あんどん(行燈)を一つにて用
い候。一・夜咄(よばなし)の時は、あんどん、路地に置く事は、佗(佗
び茶ノ湯)には無く候。座中のあんどん、路地へ出し候。」

250. Sen, *Chadō Koten Zenshū*, vol. 11, p. 97. 「蘆路行燈、朝にても
夜にても、くらくハをくべきなり。」

251. Sen, *Chadō Koten Zenshū*, vol. 11, p. 244. 「木燈籠口伝有、私
の申分有。木籠ハ夜中用て、晝ハ路次に可置候、左近殿(桑山左
近大夫重長)へ石灯籠も夜の爲なれとも、晝も差置て、左候〔近カ〕へハ路次の景にも成まゝ、木燈籠晝も
置候てもいかゝと尋被申候、左近殿被申とも、成程置候ても然候、
利休へハ終に尋不申候得共、ぼく〔杢カ〕の上又は石なとの上
にのせ置候てもよく候はんと申され候、それより石州ハ木灯籠其儘
〔ママ〕差置被申候也、石州より(も)晝も差置候故、私の申分とか
ゝれ候。」

252. The *fumichigae-ishi* is also called the *fumisute-ishi*. See page
142.

253. Sen, *Chadō Koten Zenshū*, vol. 11, pp. 147–48. 『石州三百ケ
條』「夜會又ハ朝會の時、亭主迎に手燭を持て出、中潜(なかくゞ
り)を明て一礼畢而(おわつて)くゝりを差シ、少シ明ヶかけて置也、
手燭ハのりこへ石・亭主石の間にふみ違の石あれハ、是に置也、其

外の石も見合様子能處に置也、先の石に置をよしとする也、上客同
輩なれハ、手燭を持、跡もミへ候様にして、手水鉢の邊に置也、貴
人杯ハ次の人持也、拟(さて)、路(次)の者も出し候程の亭主なれ
ハ、手燭を其儘(そのまま)刀掛の脇に差置、亭主わひて路次の者
も出さぬなれハ、火を消、はな紙にて火口(ほぐち)をつミ切置也、
夜會にて後の時ハ、亭主わひなれは客火をそのまま。」「刀掛の脇
に差置、亭主わひて路次の者も出さぬなれハ、火を消して、数奇屋
の内へ持入、亭主の取能勝手口にも置也、朝會杯にハ、夜明て
火も不入時分になれハ、初座の時、持て入もよし、ケ様の事ハ時
節の見合肝要也。」

254. Sen, *Chadō Koten Zenshū*, vol. 11, p. 22. 『細川茶湯之書』「石
どうろうに火をともすハ、とうしん三筋なり、月の夜には四すぢ也、ひ
かりうすきゆへに一筋ますなり。」

255. Sen, *Chadō Koten Zenshū*, vol. 11, p. 97. 『細川茶湯之書』
「灯籠の火、朝ハ火つよく、夜るはよはくともし申由也、月の夜にハ
つよくと申候、又、朝ハかすかに、夜ハつよくともし申よし、これかよ
く候よし。」

256. Sen, *Chadō Koten Zenshū*, vol. 5, p. 453. 『槐記』「夜ノ茶湯
ニ、石灯籠幾ツアリトモ、皆火ヲ入ルヽコトハ候ヤ、月夜ナドニテ、月
光ノ明リノ及ブ處ニハ、火ヲ入ルズ、月光ノ及バザル處ニテ、暗キ陰
ノ灯籠ニハ、火ヲ入ルヽトモ申シ。」

257. Translation from Hirota, *Wind in the Pines*, p. 225. Sen,
Chadō Koten Zenshū, vol. 4, p. 9. 『南方録』「雪の夜會にハ、
露地の燈籠ハ凡(およそ)、とぼすべからず、雪の白きにうばハれて見
所(見どころ)なく光るうすし、但露地の木だち・様子によりて一向にも
云がたし。」

258. Sen, *Chadō Koten Zenshū*, vol. 11, pp. 243–44. 『石州三百ヶ
條』「石とうろう高さ、ほとらいなし、置所ニッを用、三ッを捨へし、石
とうろうハあかりの用に立候爲也、中くゝりのみゆる所、腰かけのミ
ゆる処、手水石のみゆる處、刀かけの見通し、此五所のあかりのた
め也、しかれ共、不殘用に立候様に居てハ、辻とうろうの様にて惡
敷也、それゆへ二ッの用に立、三ッ捨てよきなり、縱ハにしり上り刀
懸の見通しのあかりの用に立候へハ、腰かけ・手水石・中くゝりの三
つハ捨る也、又中くゝり・手水鉢之之の用に立候時ハ、にぢり上り・
刀かけ・雪隱なとの方にすゆ(つ)る物也、路次つきより、必如此に
ハならぬもの也、先、石の心持にて了簡すへし、右の通りにすへ候と
も、あらハに灯籠はかり出候へあしく候、前後に小き木なと植候て
あいしらい候てよき也。」The text says five places but lists only
four. The crawl-through door (*nijiri-agari*) seems to have
been forgotten.

259. Sen, *Chadō Koten Zenshū*, vol. 10, p. 343. 『茶湯一會集』「石
灯籠ハ、夜あくると障子をはつし、土器・竹輪とも取入、火袋の内ま

て、露をよく打込へし、依て火袋の内、常々油のかゝらさる様、奇麗
に致置事肝要也。」

260. Sen, *Chadō Koten Zenshū*, vol. 10, p. 351. 『茶湯一會集』「石
灯籠ハ、笠より竿まて、能々しめり候ほと打かけ、火袋ハ、水たまり
雫落るまて打込へし。」

261. The influence of Shintō and certain sects of Buddhism
other than Zen can be detected to a slight degree, but
primarily the spiritual/religious context associated with
chanoyu has been related to Zen Buddhism.

262. See note 63.

263. As a small indicator of how common the connection has
become, a Google search in Japanese for the words Zen 禅
and *chanoyu* 茶の湯 gets nearly 320,000 results.

264. Translation from Hirota, *Wind in the Pines*, pp. 217, 219.
Sen, *Chadō Koten Zenshū*, vol. 4, pp. 3–4. 「宗易へ茶に参れ
ば、必手水鉢の水を自身手桶にてはこび入らるゝほどに、子細を問
候へば、易(宗易)のいわく、露地にて亭主の初の所作に水を運び、
客も初の所作に手水をつかふ、これ露地・草庵の大本也、此露地
に問ひ入るゝ人、たがひに世塵のけがれ(穢れ)をすゝぐ爲の手
水ばち也。」

265. Translation from Hirota, *Wind in the Pines*, pp. 236–37.
Sen, *Chadō Koten Zenshū*, vol. 4, p. 265. 『南方録』「臺子ヲハ
ジメ、諸事ノノリ(規矩)法度ハ百千万也、古人モコヽニ止ツテ、コレ
ヲ茶ノ湯ト心得ラレタルト見ヘテ、ヲノヲノ方式ヲ大切ニスルコトノミ
ヲ必書ニシルシヲカレタリ、易ハ其方式ヲ階子ニシテ、今少高キ所
ニモ登リタキ志有テ、大德(大德寺)南宗(南宗寺)ナトノ和尚タチニ
一向問取シ、旦夕、禪林ノ清規(しんぎ)ヲ本トシ、カノ書院結構ノ式
ヨリカネヲヤツシ、露地の一境、浄土世界ヲ打開キ、一字ノ草庵二
疊敷ニワビスマシテ、薪水ノタメニ修行シ、一椀ノ茶ニ眞味アルコト
ヲヤウヤウホノカニヲボへ候。」

266. The Pure Land is a paradisiacal concept described in
various Buddhist texts and sutras and promulgated most
strongly by the Pure Land sects such as Jōdo-shū and Jōdoshinshū. There are various Pure Lands, such as the Pure
Land of the Amida Buddha, known as the Western Para-
dise, Saihō Gokuraku Jōdo, and the Pure Land of Yakushi
Nyorai, known as the Lapis Lazuli Pure Land, Jōruri Sekai.
The Pure Land sects of Buddhism are referred to as relying on *tariki*, "external power," in other words relying on
prayers made to higher deities to extract the petitioner from
the mortal world and bring him or her to a Pure Land that

lies beyond this world. The Zen sect, on the other hand, is referred to as relying on *jiriki*, "internal power," in other words relying on meditation and other ascetic practices to attain enlightenment. It could be said that a Pure Land is an external state of bliss and Zen enlightenment is an internal state of bliss.

267. Sen, *Chadō Koten Zenshū*, vol. 4, pp. 319–20.『南方録』「客アルジ其直(眞力)心ヲス、グコソ、百沸湯ノ湯アヒ也ケレ、露地ハ只ウキ世ノ外ノ道ナルニ、心ノ塵ヲ何チラスラン、茶ノ湯トハ只湯ヲワカシ茶ヲ立テ、ノムバカリナル本ヲ知ベシ、露地スキヤ客モアルシモヲ茶トモニ、フリヤハラゲテ隔心モナシ。」

268. The Burning House, *Sangai no Kataku*, is a Buddhist term meaning the world in which unenlightened people live. The character *ro* of *roji* means "dew" (thus the translation Dewy Path for *roji*) but also has broader meanings of being open, exposed, or revealed. Thus *roji* might be said to mean "the place where all is revealed," or, in other words, "the world in which enlightened people live." The White Bull is a term associated with the teaching of One Vehicle, *ichijō* 一乗, which comprises both Hinayana and Mahayana Buddhism. This idea is stressed in the *Lotus Sutra*, *Hoke-kyō*. "White" in the expression "white *roji*" means "pure." Both Yoshino (吉野, written 芳野 in *Kochū Rodan*) and Katsuragi (葛城) are areas of Japan, now within Nara Prefecture, that were famous from ancient times for their beautiful landscapes. English translation based in part on Hirota, *Wind in the Pines*, pp. 240–41. Sen, *Chadō Koten Zenshū*, vol. 4, pp. 414–16.「露地ハ草庵寂寞の境をすへたる名なり、法華譬喩品に長者諸子すでに三界の火宅を出て、露地に居る(座する)と見えたり、又露地の白牛(びゃくご)といふ、白露地ともいへり、世間の塵労垢染を離れ、一心清浄の無一物底を、強く名づけて白露地にいふ、しかれば、本來の心地にして、其心地の外相は、樹石天然の一庭なり、一鳥不啼、雲埋老樹ごときの佳境なり、されば、市中宅辺に自然の地形勝概まれなる故に、木をうる、竹を群し、朝夕の露を愛で、月雪に歩し、深からぬ庭のうちも、おのづから芳野・葛城(かつらぎ)の興をおもひ、むれつゝ來る人をいとひては、花なき林を愛し、心ある友を待ては雪の砌を拂ひなど、其風興におゐてハ述尽しがたし、集雲菴の露地、松下堂の柴門を待合にもちひて、一枚の看板をかけらる、其文如左

一・賓客腰掛に來て、同道人相揃はゞ、板を打うつて案内を報ずべし

一・手水の事、専ら心頭をすゝぐをもつて、此道の肝要とす

一・庵主出請して、客庵に入るべし、庵主、貧にして、茶飯の諸

具不偶、美味も又なし、露地の樹石、天然の趣、其こゝろを得ざる輩ハ、これより速に歸去れ、

一・泄湯松風に及び、鐘聲至らハ、客再び來れ、湯合・火合の差となる事、多罪々々

一・菴内・菴外におゐて、世事の雑話、古來禁之

一・貧主歴然の會、巧言令色入へからず

一・一會始終、二時に過べからず、但し法話・清談に時うつるは制の外なり。」

269. Hirota, *Wind in the Pines*, p. 249. Sen, *Chadō Koten Zenshū*, vol. 10, p. 199.『茶話指月集』「此道を問人あれば、答へていはく、本來禪によるかゆへに、更に示へき道もなし、但わか平生かたり傳ふ古人の茶話を以指月とせハ、をのつから得ることあらんと、かの京極黄門(藤原定家)和歌無師匠只以舊歌爲師。」

270. *Ro* 露 means "to be disclosed" or "to appear," and *ji* 地 means "ground."

271. Translation from Hirota, *Wind in the Pines*, pp. 281–83. Sen, *Chadō Koten Zenshū*, vol. 10, pp. 304–5.『禅茶録』「今の世俗、庭を指て内露地・外露地と稱すれど、義理に於て、甚相違せり、本露地とは、露ハあらはると訓じ、地は心を云り、此自性を露はすの義也、一切の煩惱を離斷して、眞如實相の本性を露す故に、露地といふ、又、白露地と云も同じ、白は清浄なるを云り、此儀を取來て、茶室は本性を露す道場ぞと云意にて、露地とは名づけたるなり、故に露地は、茶室の一名也、又、不毛の赤地の廣莫にして潔浄なるをも、露地と号す、本性に況へたるなり、法華の注に、四衢道中譬四諦觀同會見諦如夫路頭所以名四衢也、若見感雖除思惟仍在則不名露地也、若三界思盡方名露地耳云云、又、道場と云るも、露地と同義也、止観に、道場(皀+刂)清浄境界也、治五佳糖顯實相米云云、如是三界思盡方名露地と出たり、故五佳の煩惱の糖を治め、實相清浄なる本性の米を顯すと云意にて、露地と云ひ、道場と云、異なることなし、又、茶室を別世界など云、是も自心を比したり、語に、世界非世界是を世界と云、應無所佳而生其心なるべし。」

272. *Shokoku Chatei Meiseki Zue* 諸国茶庭名跡図絵.

273. Historical information on Fushin'an comes primarily from Shigemori, *Nihon Teienshi Taikei*, vol. 11, pp. 56–71. Omote Senke 表千家; Fushin'an 不審菴; Zangetsu-tei 残月亭; Tensetsudô 点雪堂.

274. Ura Senke 裏千家; Konnichian 今日庵; Mushikiken 無色軒; Kan'untei 寒雲亭; Yūin 又隠; Rikyūdō 利休堂; Tairyūken 対流軒.

275. Ritsurin Kōen 栗林公園, Kagawa Prefecture, formerly Takamatsu-han; *shinpan* with 120,000 *koku*. Kōrakuen 後

楽園, Okayama Prefecture, formerly Okayama-han; *tozama* with 315,000 *koku*. Koishikawa Kōrakuen 小石川後楽園, Tōkyō Prefecture, formerly Edo, the *kami-yashiki* of the lord of Mito-han; *gosanke* (one of the three families directly related to the Tokugawa) with 350,000 *koku*. Rikugien 六義園, Tōkyō, formerly Edo; the *shimo-yashiki* of Yanagisawa Yoshiyasu, chief advisor (*tairō*) to the *shōgun*. Kenrokuen 兼六園, Kanazawa Prefecture, formerly Kaga-han; *tozama* with 1,025,000 *koku*.

276. See tea records in Nakamura, *Chadō Shūkin*, vol. 5, pp. 275–83.

277 Katsura Rikyū 桂離宮; Gepparō 月波楼; Shōkintei 松琴亭; Onrindō 園林堂.

278. Katsura only became designated as a Detached Palace (Rikyū) in 1886, five years after the property was taken over by the Imperial Household Agency.

279. Shūgakuin Rikyū 修学院離宮; Rinkyūji 林丘寺.

280. Sentō Gosho 仙洞御所; Tōfukumon'in 東福門院; Ōmiya Gosho 大宮御所; Seikatei 醒花亭.

281. Shūsuitei 拾翠亭.

282. Yoshida-ke 吉田家; Hata-ke 秦家; Sugimoto-ke 杉本家; Kojima-ke 小島家.

283. Sankeien 三渓園; Gekkaden 月華殿; Kinmōkutsu 金毛窟; Chōshūkaku 聴秋閣; Shunsōro 春草廬.

284. Tairyūsansō 對龍山荘.

285. Tabuchi-ke 田淵家. Information on the history of the Tabuchi family comes primarily from *Kuni Shitei Meishō: Tabuchishi Teien*.

286. The construction of Shun'insai 春陰斎 was requested by Hisada Sōsan 久田宗参 (1750–1800).

287. Hakusa Sonsō 白沙村荘.

288. Sumiya 炭家; Kawabun 川文; Toriiwarō 鳥岩楼; Tawaraya 俵屋.

289. Ichino, *Chanoyu Koten Sōsho*, vol. 3, p. 177.『数奇道次第』「客人、入さまにたかひにしき仕候て、上座仕人次第ニ入申候、左の手にてくゞりをあけ、敷居に手をつき、まつかどより内のていを見まハし、拠ゆる／＼とはいるへきなり、あとよりはいりし人くゞりをさし、かけかねをかけ申候。」

290. *Chadōgaku Taikei*, vol. 6, p. 371.「昼 堺衆時書院にて振舞給

候て路次口方参候。」

291. Rodrigues, *João Rodrigues's Account of Sixteenth-Century Japan*, p. 156.

292. *Garan*, *samgharama* in Sanskrit, originally referred to a residence for the community of monks and later came to refer to the temple architecture.

293. See note 202.

294. Ichino, *Chanoyu Koten Sōsho*, vol. 3, p. 177.『数奇道次第』「拠先へ入たる人腰かけのまへのふみわけの石に立居方にきを付かんし申候。」

295. Sen, *Chadō Koten Zenshū*, vol. 10, pp. 369–70.『茶湯一會集』「物見の石とて、大ニ平らか成る石あり、爰ニて額・石灯籠・井筒・大木・捨石の類又ハ遠景、何ニても見所あるへし、是をはつすへからす、物を見るときハ、何時も立とゝまりて見るもの也、すへて高聲ニほむるハ悪し、感シたる様よし。」

296. The *machiai-shitsu* is a waiting room within a residence near the *roji*. In some situations, guests are first invited into the *machiai-shitsu* where they change their outerwear and are served a cup of hot water—*hakutō*, *shirayu*, or *sayu*—before going out into the *roji*.

297. The drawing with the *shōgi* appears in "*Chanoyu Hishō*," *Chanoyu Bunkagaku*, March 1999, p. 202.

298. The bark of the Japanese cypress (Chamaecyparis obtusa, *hinoki*) and the Japanese cedar (Cryptomeria japonica, *sugi*) are similar in appearance on the tree but rather different in their method of collection and application. *Hinoki* bark is harvested from living trees that are a hundred years old or more. The first bark is stripped and unused. After that it can be harvested in roughly eight-year cycles, making it very thin and pliant. *Sugi* bark cannot be harvested from live trees and so is collected off felled trees and is correspondingly thicker.

299. For detailed photographs and descriptions of various *chōzubachi*, see Yoshikawa, *Chōzubachi: Teienbi no Zōkei*.

300 Takei and Keane, *Sakuteiki*. pp. 201–3.

301. The parts of the lantern are *hōju* 宝珠, *kasa* 笠, *hibukuro* 火袋, *chūdai* 中台, *sao* 竿, *kiso* 基礎, *kidan* 基壇.

302. Nowadays, copper wire is used under the palm-fiber rope to secure the bamboo.

Tea Text Summaries

The following texts, written between the 13th and 19th centuries, were used in the research for this book. They are all related to tea culture and, usually, have some aspect that is also related to tea gardens. While this list certainly does not represent all texts related to tea gardens written during that period, not to mention those related to tea practice in general, it does include the most important and commonly referred to texts.

The list is in chronological order. Because there were conflicting dates given in various sources for many of the texts, the dates used here are based on those given by Tsutsui Hiroichi in *Chasho no Kenkyū* (pp. 454–517). I have also followed Tsutsui's comments regarding the authenticity of the dates; therefore a date within brackets [ ] means that a date was not specifically given in the original text but was, instead, assigned by Tsutsui and others by assessing the date of death of the purported author and other related information. Dates for records of tea gatherings, *chakaiki* (茶会記), were assigned according to the earliest recorded gathering mentioned within each text. Titles within parentheses ( ) indicate that the text in question had no formal title written on the original manuscript and that the title given here is the one by which the text is most commonly referred to.

Each entry shows the date associated with the text, the romanized name, the name in Japanese, a literal translation of the title in parentheses, alternate names for the text (if any), and the source (or sources) within which the text can be found. The explanations of texts are based on descriptions given in *Kadokawa Chadō Daijiten* as well as other sources.

1211–14, *Kissa Yōjōki* 喫茶養生記 (*The Book of Tea for Health*). Source: Sen, *Chadō Koten Zenshū*, vol. 2.

Written by the Zen priest, Eisai, the text describes the partaking of tea for health but does not refer to the physical setting and, naturally, does not mention a tea garden of any sort.

1350, *Kissa Ōrai* 喫茶往来 (*Correspondence on Drinking Tea*).

Source: Sen, *Chadō Koten Zenshū*, vol. 2.

The authorship is uncertain (and the date could actually be as late as the early 15th century), but the text, which is written in the form of four short exchanged correspondences, describes a type of tea gathering typical of the Kitayama Culture (Kitayama Bunka) of *Shōgun* Ashikaga Yoshimitsu, including the tea arbor and garden of that time.

1435–93, *Inryōken Nichiroku* 蔭涼軒日録 (*The Inryōken Diaries*). Also pronounced *Onryōken Nichiroku*. Source: Takeuchi, Rizō, ed., *Zōho Zoku Shiryō Taisei: Inryōken Nichiroku*.

The official diary of two Buddhist priests who served as advisors to the Ashikaga *shōgun*. Inryōken was the name of the private study of the *shōgun*, which was located in Rokuon'in, a subtemple of the major Zen Buddhist temple Shōkokuji. The diary was kept by Kikei Shinzui 季瓊真蘂 from 1435 to 1466 and by Kisen Shūshō 亀泉集証 from 1484 to 1493, covering the reign of three Ashikaga *shōgun*: Yoshinori (足利義教, 1429–41), Yoshimasa (足利義政, 1449–73), and Yoshihisa (足利義尚, 1473–89). Tea gatherings are not an important feature of *Inryōken Nichiroku* and are only mentioned briefly in passing, but those glimpses give some insight into the physical spaces for tea at this early period.

1448–50, *Shōtetsu Monogatari* 正徹物語 (*Tales by Shōtetsu*). Source: *Nihon Koten Bungaku Taikei*, vol. 65.

A poetic commentary written around 1448–50. The reference at the end to *cha no suki* is one of the first records of the use of the word *suki* in the context of *chanoyu*.

1459–68, *Hekizan Nichiroku* 碧山日録 (*Verdant Mountain Diary*). Source: Takeuchi, Rizō, ed., *Zōho Zoku Shiryō Taisei: Hekizan Nichiroku*.

The diary of Taikyoku (太極, 1421–86?), a Rinzai Zen priest from Tōfukuji temple in Kyōto. The diary covers the years 1459–63 and 1465–68, mentioning various aspects of society and the arts including an early glimpse of an urban arbor.

[1502], (Kokoro no Fumi) 心の文 (Letter from the Heart). Also called Shukō Furuichi Harima Hōshi Ate Isshi 珠光古市播磨法師宛一紙, Kokoro no Shi no Fumi 心の師の文, and Kokoro no Shi no Isshi 心の師の一紙. Source: Sen, Chadō Koten Zenshū, vol. 3. English translation in Hirota, Wind in the Pines, pp. 195–99.

A short letter sent from Murata Shukō to one of his tea disciples, the provincial lord Furuichi Chōnin. The importance of the document lies in Shukō's use in the letter of aesthetic terms such as "chill and withered," hie-kare, and "chill and lean," hie-yase, terms that portend the later use of aesthetic terms like wabi and sabi. Also of importance is Shukō's urging to merge the aesthetics of Chinese (formal) and Japanese (rustic) tastes.

1504–33, Nisuiki 二水記 (The Diary of Two Waters). Source: Dainihon Kokiroku: Nisuiki, vols. 1–4.

The diary of Kyōto aristocrat Washino'o Takayasu (鷲尾隆康, 1484–1533) that covers the years 1504 to 1533. Takayasu comments on various aspects of the arts, including a few remarks about tea—importantly, a mention of Murata Shukō and the use of terms that reflect the development of tea at the time: roji 路次 (entry path/tea garden), sankyo no tei 山居之躰 (appearance of a mountain cottage), and shichūin 市中隠 (Hermitage Within the City).

[1512], Zenpō Zōtan 禅鳳雑談 (Zenpō's Idle Chatter; literally, Zenpō's Miscellaneous Talks). Source: Hayashiya, Nihon Shisō Taikei 23: Kodai Chūsei Geijusturon.

A compilation of various comments made by Konparu Zenpō (金春禅鳳, 1454–1532) to his apprentices over the years 1504–21. Komparu was a nō theater playwright and actor, and his compiler was one of his apprentices, a man named Tōemon 藤右衛門. Zenpō's brief aside about Shukō's taste for a view of the moon half-hidden by clouds is interpreted as an early evocation of the aesthetic taste that will later become known as wabi.

1522–27, Sōchō Nikki 宗長日記 (Sōchō's Diary). Also called Sōchō Shuki 宗長手記. Source: Shimazu, Sōchō Nikki. The text has been translated into English and annotated by H. Mack Horton (Sōchō, The Journal of Sōchō), with additional commentary provided in a companion volume (Horton, Song in an Age of Discord).

Sōchō's visits to the homes of tea masters, especially those of the Lower Capital Coterie, Shimogyō Chanoyu, provide insights into the environment of tea at that time.

[1525], Chōka Chanoyu Monogatari 長歌茶湯物語 (The Chanoyu Epic). Source: Chadō Bunka Kenkyū Dai'isshū.

This long poem about chanoyu is attributed to the dōbōshū Sōami (?–1525) and dated simply by the date of his death. It describes both shoin-style tea as well as sōan-style tea, including a glimpse of a roji, in fact using the word roji 路ち, perhaps for the first time in writing. The mixture of the formal shoin-style tea and the rustic sōan-style tea is indicative of the changes happening within tea culture at the time it was written.

[1533–1650], Matsuya Kaiki 松屋会記 (The Matsuya's Records of Tea Gatherings). Source: Sen, Chadō Koten Zenshū, vol. 9.

The diary of three generations of lacquerware dealers from Nara: Hisamasa (久政, ?–1598), Hisayoshi (久好, ?–1633), and Hisashige (久重, 1566–1652). The three diarists cover over a hundred years of the development of tea, making this text one of the most important, and well-preserved, among the tea records. The small drawings and detailed descriptions of tea utensils, meals served, etc., make it a great resource for students of tea history. However, there are only occasional, short comments on tea gardens and elements within them (water basins and the like), and these occur primarily in the later portion of the text. These comments are important for their historical authenticity, but, as is the nature of records of tea gatherings, chakaiki—which simply record the details of tea gatherings— there is no concise, overall explanation of tea gardens in Matsuya Kaiki.

[1554], Imai Sōkyū Chanoyu Nikki Nukisho 今井宗久茶湯日記抜書 (Extracts of Imai Sōkyū's Tea Diary). Also called Imai Sōkyū Chanoyu Kakinuki 今井宗久茶湯書抜. Source: Sen, Chadō Koten Zenshū, vol. 10 (contains only volume 1 of the two-volume original).

The tea diary of Imai Sōkyū, a wealthy merchant from Sakai with comments on Sōkyū and Furuta Oribe. Volume 1 covers the dates 1554–89 and, although it has numerous comments on tea architecture (irori イロリ hearth, chōzu no ma 手水ノ間 preparation room, etc.), it does not contain any information about exterior spaces.

[1555], (Ikenaga Sōsaku e no Sho) 池永宗作への書 (Tea Writings

of Ikenaga Sōsaku). Also called *Ikenaga Sōsaku Chasho* 池永宗作茶書 and *Jōō Oyobi Ikenaga Sōsaku Chasho* 紹鷗及池永宗作茶書. Source: Sen, ed. *Chadō Koten Zenshū*, vol. 3.

A short record purported to be the teachings of Takeno Jōō as recorded by *Ikenaga Sōsaku*. Of note is a plan-view drawing and description of the entry space to a rustic tea house included within.

1564, *Bunrui Sōjinboku* 分類草人木 (*Classifications of Tea*). Source: Hayashiya et al., *Nihon no Chasho*, vol. 1. Also in Kuwata, *Shinshū Chadō Zenshū*, vol. 8.

A short text that lists aspects of *chanoyu* by classification (*rui* 類), such as Guests 客, Vases 花瓶, and Hearths 風炉・囲炉裏. There is little information on exterior spaces other than a brief mention of the water ladle, *hishaku*, and the entry path, *roji*. Not to be confused with the similarly named text from 1626, *Sōjinboku*.

1572, *Usoshū* 烏鼠集 ("*Crows and Mice*" *Collection*). Also called *Usoshū Yonmakisho* 烏鼠集四巻書. Source: *Chadō Bunka Kenkyū Dai'isshū*.

An early collection of works on *chanoyu* comprising four volumes. The date 1572 appears at the end of the fourth volume, but the entire work was probably finally compiled only during the Keichō period (1596–1615). Many other texts written over the following decades repeat information found in *Usoshū* including *Sukidō Shidai* 数寄道次第 and *Chanoyu Hishō* 茶湯秘抄. The second volume contains many simple drawings of tea rooms, although there is no information regarding exterior spaces. A few occasional comments on the *roji* appear in the text of volume 4 including a comment on the handling of swords upon entry, and the conflicting images of the *roji* as an unplanted, barren space and as a mossy area.

[1586–1613], *Sōtan Nikki* 宗湛日記 (*Sōtan's Diary*). Source: Sen, *Chadō Koten Zenshū*, vol. 6.

The diary of Kamiya Sōtan, a merchant/tea practitioner from Hakata during his visits to the merchant/tea practitioner Tsuda Sōgyū in the capital. It covers the twenty-seven years from 1586 to 1613, important years in the development of *chanoyu* just before and after Rikyū's death. As with other records of tea gatherings, *chakaiki*, Sōtan's focus is on "interior" tea culture such as the hanging scrolls displayed during tea gatherings, which he describes in detail. He does,

however, make numerous, short remarks about the nature of the exterior spaces, including many comments on water basins, occasional aesthetic terms such as *shinzan no tei* 深山ノ躰 ("the appearance of deep mountains"), and descriptions of the tea gardens of Hideyoshi and Rikyū.

1588–1590, *Yamanoue Sōjiki* 山上宗二記 (*Yamanoue Sōji's Records*). Source: Sen, *Chadō Koten Zenshū*, vol. 6. Also in Kuwata, *Yamanoue no Sōjiki no Kenkyū*.

The tea records of tea master Yamanoue Sōji (山上宗二, 1544–590), whose name stems from the Yamanoue district of Sakai where he lived. A primary disciple of Sen Rikyū, Sōji may have served Oda Nobunaga as tea master, and certainly performed that service for Toyotomi Hideyoshi. His ill manners, however, caused him to be exiled from Hideyoshi's service and eventually executed by him. His records of tea, written in the form of six letters during the years 1588–90, focus on descriptions of famous wares, *meibutsu*, and on the tea style of Rikyū. There is a short comment about the colophon written on a portrait of Takeno Jōō by his Zen master. There are some simple plans of tea houses and comments within the text about the nature of the *roji* that, although not prolific, are important due to their historical authenticity, notably, comments about the entry space, *tsubo no uchi*, that was the predecessor of the tea garden.

[1600], *Sōshun'ō Chanoyu Kikigaki* 宗春翁茶湯聞書 (*Sōshun's Notes on Chanoyu*). Source: Kuwata, *Shinshū Chadō Zenshū*, vol. 9.

The tea commentary of Hariya Sōshun (八里谷宗春, or perhaps 針屋宗春). The date of 1600 was written in the colophon but the content points to a somewhat later date. The text has comments on many aspects of tea culture, such as flowers and scrolls and, notably, an entire section regarding the design of the *roji* under the title "Matters Regarding the Design of *Roji*" 露地作様之事. The unclear date of the text notwithstanding, this may be the earliest text that has a section specifically focused on the design of the *roji*.

1602, *Sukidō Shidai* 数寄道次第 (*Circumstances of the Way of Tea*). Source for volume 1: Chizuko Ichino, *Chanoyu Koten Sōsho*, vol. 3, under the title *Sukidō Shidai* 数寄道次第. Source for volume 2: Sōshitsu Sen, ed., *Chadō Koten Zenshū*, vol. 11, under the title *Senrin* 僊林 (see 1612, *Senrin*). Volume 3 does not seem to have been published.

Volume 1 regards Furuta Oribe's *chanoyu*. Some of the terminology particular to Oribe's new *chanoyu* style appear here, such as *kusari no ma*, literally, "connector-room," a room that sat between the formal *shoin* parlor and the rustic *sōan* tea room and reflects the melding of formal and rustic styles that Oribe accomplished as he developed *chanoyu* for the military lords, *daimyō*. The *roji* is not written about at length, but what is of note is the very first entry dealing with the *roji* (in fact the first words of the text are *roji*). This reveals the heightened awareness of the *roji* among tea practitioners at this time. For volume 2, see **1612**, *Senrin*.

1604–12, *Sōhokō Koshoku e Otazunesho* 宗甫公古織へ御尋書 (*Inquiries Made by Sōhokō of Koshoku*). Also called *Keichō Otazunesho* 慶長御尋書. Source: Ichino, *Chanoyu Koten Sōsho*, vol. 2.

Sōhokō refers to Kobori Enshū. *Sōho* is the Buddhist name given to Enshū by his teacher, the Zen priest Haruya Sōen of Daitokuji temple 大徳寺春屋宗園; *kō* is a suffix meaning Lord. *Koshoku* is a contraction of Furuta Oribe's name (*Ko* is the same character as *Furu* and *Shoku* as *Ori*). The alternate name, *Keichō Otazunesho*, refers to the fact that it was written during the Keichō period, 1596–1614. The text records what Enshū asked Oribe directly, or understood through third parties, including numerous glimpses of *daimyō-cha* developing under the influence of Oribe, and Enshū's impression that he himself is the rightful successor of the *daimyō-cha* style of tea. Although there is no section related specifically to the *roji*, there are some occasional comments on elements of the *roji*, such as lanterns, and on the general design of the *roji*, such as the control of external views from the garden.

1612, *Senrin* 僊林 (*The Hermit's Forest*). Source: Sen, *Chadō Koten Zenshū*, vol. 11.

This text comprises volume 2 of *Sukidō Shidai* (see **1602** above). It reflects the changes made as *wabi-cha* (rustic tea) was evolving into *daimyō-cha* (military-lord's tea), especially the relationship between the formal and rustic, using terms such as *gokushin* (extremely formal type), *shin* (formal), and *sō* (informal, rustic). Comments on the *roji* are limited to a few comments taken directly from *Usoshū* (1572).

1612, (*Furuta Oribe Densho*) 古田織部伝書 (*The Records of Furuta Oribe*). Source: Hayashiya, Tatsusaburō et al., *Nihon no Chasho*, vol. 1. Also called *Oribe Hyakkajō Kuritashi-bon* 織部百

ヶ条・栗田氏本 in Ichino, *Chanoyu Koten Sōsho*, vol. 3.

This text is one of the "100-item lists," *Hyakkajō*, of Oribe's teachings. It actually comprises a little over a hundred short, one-line comments on *chanoyu* that are aimed at the novice practitioner. Only a few refer to the *roji*.

[1615], *Ko Oribe Sōdensho* 古織部相伝書 (*Collected Writings of Furuta Oribe*). Source: Sen, *Chadō Koten Zenshū*, vol. 11. Also appears, with slight textual variations, as *Oribe Hyakkajō* 織部百ヶ条 in Ichino, *Chadō Koten Sōsho*, vol. 3 茶道古典叢書3・古田織部茶書2.

As with *Furuta Oribe Densho*, this text also comprises a little over a hundred short, one-line comments on *chanoyu*. None refer to the *roji*. It is important in the context of this book simply because it is believed to have been written by Oribe himself and thus reveals his apparent lack of interest in the *roji*, at least in comparison to other aspects of *chanoyu*.

1620–21, *História da Igreja do Japão* (*The History of the Church in Japan*). Source: Rodrigues, *João Rodrigues's Account of Sixteenth-Century Japan*.

João Rodrigues, a Jesuit missionary from Portugal, lived in Japan from 1577 to 1610. His record, which describes many aspects of Japanese culture, was compiled in Macao in the 1620s but reflects Japanese culture of the late 16th century at the time the practice of *wabi-cha* was being coalesced by Sen Rikyū and others. There are some very detailed descriptions of tea culture, tea architecture, and tea gardens. Because this record was written by a non-Japanese specifically to explain Japanese culture to other non-Japanese it is easily the most thorough and explanatory of the texts from this period.

1626, *Sōjinboku* 草人木 ("Grass, Person, Tree"). Source: Sen, *Chadō Koten Zenshū*, vol. 3.

The odd title *Sōjinboku*—"*Grass, Person, Tree*"—derives from taking the character for tea, *cha* 茶, and breaking it down into its component parts: grass 草 (the top part of the character), person 人 (the middle, roof-like part), and tree 木 (the bottom part). Although the text is long, there is not much associated with the *roji*. The few comments that are made, however, are of interest in that they reflect *chanoyu* at the time the text was written; for instance, it uses terms like outer *roji* 外路地, inner *roji* 内路地, and double *roji* 二重路地. Also found are descriptions of "developed" *chanoyu* customs such as wetting down the garden and seeing a guest off after a tea gathering.

1640, *Chōandōki* 長闇堂記 (*Chōandō's Records*). Source: Sen, *Chadō Koten Zenshū*, vol. 3. Also in Kuwata, Tadachika. *Shinshū Chadō Zenshū*, vol. 9.

The personal records of Chōandō Kubo Toshiyo (長闇堂久保利世, dates unknown). Although the text does not focus on the *roji*, it does discuss a number of people including Furuta Oribe, Yamanoue Sōji (mentioning how he had his ears and nose cut off before being executed), and Hechikan, the stylish fellow with the big red umbrella at the Great Kitano Tea Party.

1641, *Hosokawa Chanoyu no Sho* 細川茶湯之書 (*Tea Records of Hosokawa*). Source: Sen, *Chadō Koten Zenshū*, vol. 11.

There are many texts with similar titles, many of which are primarily or entirely the same in content. They comprise the teachings of military lord Hosokawa Sansai (細川三斎, 1563–1645), as recorded by his student of tea, Ichio Iori (一尾伊織, 1602–89). Many entries relate to the *roji*, and, although most of those entries come in the second and third volume of the three-volume text, the very first items presented in volume 1 (after a short foreword) deal with the *roji*. This shows the importance the *roji* was beginning to hold for tea masters and also reveals that the experience of *chanoyu* was seen as beginning upon entering the *roji*.

[1647], *(Kobori Enshū Kakisute no Fumi)* 小堀遠州書捨文 (*A Simple Note from Kobori Enshū*). Source: Sen, *Chadō Koten Zenshū*, vol. 11. English translation in Hirota, *Wind in the Pines*, p. 289.

A one-page letter written in a poetic manner that touches on the seasons and the need for mixing new and old in tea. Nothing is directly mentioned about the *roji*. What is notable about the letter is that it begins with the words *chanoyu no michi* 茶の湯の道, an expression that will later become shortened to *chadō* or *sadō* 茶道, The Way of Tea, revealing how *chanoyu* was beginning to be perceived as a "Zen-style" art form.

1648–52, *Chadō Shiso Densho* 茶道四祖伝書 (*Writings of the Four Founders of the Way of Tea*). Source: Matsuyama et al., *Chanoyu Koten Sōsho*, vol. 1: *Chadō Shiso Densho*.

A compilation of four tea texts edited by Matsuya

Hisashige (松屋久重, 1566–1652,), the third of the Matsuya tea masters from Nara who kept the tea record *Matsuya Kaiki* (see **1533.** above). Using *Matsuya Kaiki* and other sources, he put together four texts that focus on four masters of *chanoyu*: *Rikyū Koji Densho* 利休居士伝書 (Sen Rikyū), *Koshokukō Densho* 古織公伝書 (Furuta Oribe), *Sansaikō Densho* 三斎公伝書 (Hosokawa Sansai), *Hōkō Densho* 甫公伝書 (Kobori Enshū). The comments on Sansai and Enshū, whose tea gatherings Hisashige attended, are particularly thorough, containing some reasonably detailed plan-view drawings of elements of the *roji*.

[1660], *Koshokuden* 古織伝 (*The Teachings of Furuta Oribe*). Source: Ichino, *Chanoyu Koten Sōsho*, vol. 3.

Koshoku is an appellation for Furuta Oribe. Although the text, other than in the title, does not explicitly say it records his teachings, it is purported to contain teachings of Oribe's style passed on and recorded nearly fifty years after his death. Many short references are made to the *roji* and its use, but the detail and nature of the descriptions reflect the mid-17th century perhaps as much as they do Oribe's own time.

[1661–73], *Chafu* 茶譜 (*Tea Notes*). Source: Original not acquired. Quoted from citations in other sources.

The date on this text is not known with any certainty. It comprises eighteen volumes and, notably for this book, the second volume is entitled *roji* (as is the third volume, although it is about tea vessels and not about the *roji*). The placement of the *roji* at the beginning of the descriptions is indicative of the mentality of tea masters from the mid-17th century onward.

1665, *Sekishū Sanbyakukajō* 石州三百ヶ條 (*Sekishū's 300 Comments*). Source: Sen, *Chadō Koten Zenshū*, vol. 11.

Teachings from the time of Sen Rikyū on down through that of Katagiri Sekishū (1605–73), recorded by an apprentice of Sekishū's. There are some occasional notes regarding the *roji* throughout the text and one extensive, in-depth section focuses exclusively on the *roji*, including some simple drawings of stepping stone patterns and the layout of a water basin. Also, the opening lines of the text are phrased in language taken from Zen Buddhist teachings showing the overt desire on the part of those recording tea practices to link it to Zen Buddhism, something that stems from the mid-17th century.

1666, *Furuta Oribe no Kamidono no Chanoyu no Kikigaki* 古田織部正殿茶湯聞書 (*Lord Furuta Oribe's Tea Notes*). Also called *Koshokukō Kikigaki* 古織公聞書 and *Suki no Sho* 数寄之書. Source: Ichino, *Chanoyu Koten Sōsho*, vol. 2.

Records of Oribe-style *chanoyu* as possibly edited by an apprentice of Kobori Enshū's known as Sakurayama Ichiyū (桜山一有, 1645–1728). There are some occasional notes regarding the *roji* throughout the text and two very extensive, in-depth sections focused exclusively on the *roji*. Like other mid-17th century texts that purport to be records of early-17th-century tea masters, the content is a record of oral tradition and may comprise a mixture of both historically correct teachings and others that developed later and were attributed to those early tea masters.

1688–1704, *Genryū Chawa* 源流茶話 (*Stories on the Origin of Tea*). Source: Sen, *Chadō Koten Zenshū*, vol. 3.

Two volumes, edited by Yabunouchi Chikushin (薮内竹心, 1678–1745), fifth grand master of the Yabunouchi school of tea, this text is a compilation of various teachings on *chanoyu*. Written at a time when tea practice was becoming much more complex, it is an attempt to codify the origins and original practice of tea, at least in terms of how Chikushin perceived that practice. There are some occasional comments on the *roji* and, in the second volume, notes on famous tea masters such as Rikyū, Hideyoshi, Hariya Sōshun, and even some relative unknowns such as Hechikan.

1690, *Sugiki Fusai Densho* 杉木普斎伝書 (*The Writings of Sugiki Fusai*). Source: Sen, *Chadō Koten Zenshū*, vol. 10.

The tea record of tea master Sugiki Fusai (杉木普斎, 1628–1704). It contains many occasional comments on the *roji* as well as a few longer sections commenting on the usual stepping stones, lanterns, water basins, and so on, as well as "developed" details such as the custom of sprinkling water on the *roji* three times. The text is divided into short sections, many of which begin with a comment on the *roji* as it pertains to that section. This positioning reveals the importance the *roji* held at the time of Fusai.

1690, *Nanbōroku* 南方録 (*Records of Nanbō*). Also pronounced *Nanpōroku*. Source: Sen, *Chadō Koten Zenshū*, vol. 4. Partial English translation (Book 1, *Oboegaki*, and part of Book 7, *Metsugo*) can be found in Hirota, *Wind in the Pines*.

Purportedly the tea records of Nanbō Sōkei (南坊宗啓, ?–1624?), a Buddhist priest and supposed apprentice of Sen Rikyū. Nanbō is said to have resided at Nanshūji, a Buddhist temple in Sakai City known for its strong connection with tea masters. However, even though *Nanbōroku* gives the impression that Nanbō was a very close confidant of Rikyū, and although there are some very brief historical records that mention his name at the end of the 16th century, there are no records linking him with Rikyū directly or mentioning him as a tea master. The records of Nanbō were supposedly found and edited by Tachibana Jitsuzan (立花実山, 1655–1708), but recent scholarship proposes that Jitsuzan may well have composed the records himself from oral tradition. Surely the clarity of the language found in the text and the details of *chanoyu* as presented within (including the overt references to Zen practice) are indicative of a late-17th-century voice. *Nanbōroku* is a long text, and, though the *roji* is mentioned a number of times, there is no section devoted entirely to the *roji*. As with other texts of this period, however, the *roji* is often mentioned early on within sections, showing its importance to the author. Also, in this text, both Zen Buddhist and Pure Land Buddhist allegorical imagery is connected directly to the *roji*.

1700, *Kochū Rodan* 壺中炉談 (*Intimate Tea Talk*). Source: Sen, *Chadō Koten Zenshū*, vol. 4. Partial English translation can be found in Hirota, *Wind in the Pines*, pp. 240–41.

Edited by Tachibana Jitsuzan, editor of *Nanbōroku* (see 1690, above), *Kochū Rodan* is considered to be a supplemental text to *Nanbōroku*. One section, "General Points about the *Roji*" (*Roji Daigai* 露地大概), describes the *roji* as a Buddhist "boundary world" as seen in the Lotus Sutra; and another section, "Zen Rules for the Roji and Purity of Tea" (*Roji Seicha Kiyaku* 露地清茶規約) lists seven fundamental points of *chanoyu*. The fact that the list so prominently involves the *roji* shows how it has become an essential part of *chanoyu*.

1701, *Chawa Shigetsu Shū* 茶話指月集 ("Pointing at the Moon" Anthology of Tea Talk). Source: Sen, *Chadō Koten Zenshū*, vol. 10. Also in Hayashiya, et al. *Nihon no Chasho*, vol. 2.

This text is an anthology of the words and deeds of Sen Rikyū as observed by his grandson Sōtan (宗旦, 1578–1658), as told by Sōtan to one of his most important apprentices,

Fujimura Yōken (藤村庸軒, 1613–99), and written down by one of Yōken's apprentices (and son-in-law), Kusumi Soan (久須美疎安, 1636–1728). Many famous anecdotal stories about Rikyū come from this text (such as the one about Hideyoshi and the morning glories in Rikyū's *roji*), and there are also occasional, interesting comments on the *roji*.

1702, *Chanoyu Rokusōshō Denki* 茶之湯六宗匠伝記 (*Records of the Six Masters of Chanoyu*). Source: Original not acquired. Quoted from citations in other sources.

Written by Endō Genkan (遠藤元閑, 18th century?), the text comprises notes on six famous tea masters: Murata Shukō, Torii Insetsu, Takeno Jōō, Sen Rikyū, Furuta Oribe, and Kobori Enshū. Dandelions and doves in Oribe's garden are noted here (as cited in Yabe, *Furuta Oribe*).

1712, *Chadō Kyūbunroku* 茶道旧聞録 (*Old Sayings in the Way of Tea*). Also called *Kyūbunshū* 旧聞集. Source: Original not acquired. Quoted from citations in other sources.

The *chanoyu* of Fujimura Yōken as recorded by his son Seiin (正員, 1650–1733).

1724–1735, *Kaiki* 槐記 (*Pagoda Tree Records*). Source: Sen, *Chadō Koten Zenshū*, vol. 5.

A record of tea gatherings, *chakaiki*, of court noble Konoe Iehiro (近衛家熙, 1667–1736) as written by his physician Yamashina Dōan (山科道安, 1677–1746). Many aspects of *chanoyu* in court society are covered, but the *roji* is given only occasional comments and those only in details rather than comprehensive explanations.

1738, *Chanoyu Hishō* 茶湯秘抄 (*Secret Selections on Chanoyu*). Source: "Chanoyu Hishō," *Chanoyu Bunkagaku* (Kyōto), March 1997: 95–181; March 1998: 137–90; March 1999: 149–218; March 2000: 65–117.

An extensive and detailed text written by Domon Motoaki (土門元亮, dates unknown). Five volumes in all; the fourth volume (found in March 1999) has many comments and sketches (roughly drawn but showing many details) related to the *roji* and tea architecture as well. Although the volume is from 1738, the plans are mostly of tea houses built by early-17th-century tea masters such as Furuta Oribe, Matsuya Hisayoshi, Hosokawa Sansai, and Hosokawa Tadataka (Kyūmu).

1828, *Zencharoku* 禪茶録 (禅茶録) (*Zen Tea Records*). Source: Sen, *Chadō Koten Zenshū*, vol. 10. Also in Kuwata, *Shinshū Chadō Zenshū*, vol. 9.

Purportedly written by Zen priest Jakuan Sōtaku, but this cannot be confirmed. The text, which is not very long and is made up of ten short "chapters" on various subjects, strongly relates *chanoyu* to Zen Buddhism and devotes one chapter entirely to the *roji*, which, in keeping with the whole, describes the *roji* in Buddhist terms. Similar but compressed content is in *Chazen Dōichimi* 茶禅同一味 attributed to Sen Sōtan, but this text does not express the sentiments of Sōtan's era.

[1856], *Chanoyu Ichieshū* 茶湯一会集 (茶湯一會集) ("*Momentary Encounters Within Tea*" Collection). Source: Sen, *Chadō Koten Zenshū*, vol. 10. Partial English translation in Hirota, *Wind in the Pines*, pp. 290–93.

The tea record of Ii Naosuke (伊井直弼, 1815–1860), a *daimyō* at the very end of the Edo period (1600–1868), after which the *daimyō* system was abolished. He records in detail his view on *chanoyu* following the Sekishū style and is particularly philosophical in his interpretation of why *chanoyu* should be practiced. The text is broken into short "chapters" on various subjects, within which are many occasional references to the *roji* as well as one section, entitled "Cleaning and Watering the Roji," that is focused entirely on the elements and use of the *roji*.

Glossary of Tea Garden Terminology

agesu-do 揚簾戸　A lightly built, woven-panel gate that is lifted up to enter.

amigasa-mon 編笠門　A kind of middle gate resembling a traditional rain hat (*amigasa*). See **chūmon**.

an 庵　A rustic structure used as an arbor or hermitage, as in a *sōan*. Also pronounced *iori*.

andon 行燈　A portable wooden lantern, usually set at points along the *roji* to give light.

ara-kabe 荒壁　Rough clay-plaster that acts as the base coat in a wall.

beautiful rusticity　See **kirei-sabi**.

bushi 武士　Men of the military class; *samurai*.

candle-holder stone　See **teshoku-ishi**.

cha 茶　Tea. A beverage made from the broadleaf evergreen plant, Camellia sinensis. Also the cultural practice of drinking tea. It is usually expressed in the honorific, *ocha* 御茶.

chadō 茶道　Way of Tea. See **sadō**.

chaji 茶事　A long tea gathering. Often three to four hours in length, a *chaji* will include a meal, unlike the shorter *chakai*.

chakai 茶会　A short tea gathering.

chakaiki 茶会記　A tea record. These are diary-like texts that record a particular person's tea activities, often the visits they made to other people's tea gatherings.

chaniwa 茶庭　Literally, a tea garden. An understated, path-like garden that acts as an entry way to a tea house. It is also pronounced *chatei*.

cha no suki 茶の数奇　Practitioner of *chanoyu*; literally, "a lover of tea." An early use of the expression *suki* is found in the mid-15th-century text *Shōtetsu Monogatari*. Archaic.

chanoyu 茶の湯　The culture of holding reserved tea gatherings, usually for a small number of guests, at which powdered tea (*matcha*) is served.

chanoyusha 茶湯者　Practitioner of *chanoyu*. See **sukisha**. Archaic.

chatei　Tea garden. See **chaniwa**.

chaya 茶屋　Tea house. The term is used in reference to a place where tea is served casually, perhaps with food or sweets, but not specifically for *chanoyu*. See **chashitsu**.

chayoriai 茶寄り合い　Archaic expression for a tea gathering.

chikushi-gaki 竹枝垣　Fences made of bamboo branches.

chiri-ana 塵穴　Dust pit. Originally used to temporarily deposit small quantities of swept garden debris; in a tea garden, it symbolizes cleanliness and the preparations made by the host for the guest.

chiri-bashi 塵箸　Debris pickers. Resembling oversized chopsticks made of green bamboo, these are placed in the *chiri-ana* along with a small evergreen bough. See **chiri-ana**.

chōzubachi 手水鉢　Water basin. One of the most important elements of the tea garden, the water basin is usually a low-set stone with a basin carved into it at which guests crouch down and take a little water with a ladle to symbolically cleanse their hands and mouth.

chōzu-ishi 手水石　See **chōzubachi**. Archaic.

chōzu-kamae 手水カマエ　See **chōzubachi**. Archaic.

chū-dai 中台　See **ishi-dōrō**.

chūmon 中門　Middle gate. A gate set midway through a tea garden that marks the point of transition from outer to inner garden. Some are light and rustic, such as the *shiori-do*, and some are quite dramatic, like the *naka-gukuri*.

daimyō 大名　Military lord. The hereditary head of a fief or province (*han*). Many *daimyō* became interested in *chanoyu*, including Hosokawa Sansai, Furuta Oribe, and Oda Uraku.

daimyō-cha 大名茶　Military-lord's tea. Developed during the Edo period by Oribe, Enshū, and others, this form of *chanoyu* incorporated more formal aspects.

daisu-cha 台子茶　A formal type of tea service based on the use of a portable "tea shelf" called a *daisu*. Tea as practiced in Song-dynasty Chan (Zen) temples and as imported to Japan in the Kamakura period often made use of the *daisu*.

dōbōshū 同朋衆　Connoisseurs employed at the courts of military lords to advise them on cultural and artistic matters including tea practice.

fumichigae-ishi 踏違石　Waiting stone. A stepping stone set just off a stepping stone path that allows someone to step off the path briefly, or to place on it a hand-held lantern.

fumi-ishi 踏石　Entry stone (literally, stepping stone). A large, flat-topped stone placed just outside the entry to a building, allowing a person to step up into, and down from, the elevated room.

fumisute-ishi 踏捨石　See **fumichigae-ishi**.

fumiwake-ishi 踏分石　Junction stone. A stepping stone, somewhat larger than others, placed at the junction of several paths in the tea garden.

fusuma 襖　Opaque paper door.

gakumi-ishi 額見石　Tablet-viewing stone. A particular stone in a stepping stone path from which the name tablet (*gaku*) that hangs on the tea house gable can be best seen.

gakumi-matsu 額見松　Tablet-viewing pine. A pine tree, the curved trunk of which artfully frames the view of the name tablet (*gaku*) that hangs on the tea house gable.

gaku no matsu 額の松　See **gakumi-matsu.**

garan-seki 伽藍石　Pedestal stones. Large, circular stones—originally used as the pedestals for the large wooden pillars of Buddhist temples—reused as stepping stones in a tea garden.

hanekido 撥木戸　Swinging gate. It is used in a tea garden as a simple, middle gate. Archaic.

hare 晴れ　The official, frontward, sunny, or overt aspects of things. It is the antithesis of *ke*.

hare no cha 晴茶　A modern term used to describe the kind of lavish tea service held in bright open settings that pre-dated the development of rustic tea.

hashigui-gata 橋杭形　A type of water basin made from an old bridge piling (*hashigui*) or made anew to resemble one.

hie 冷え　Chill. One of the aesthetics of linked-verse poetry (*renga*), associated with the development of rustic tea before the advent of the aesthetic *wabi*.

hiroma 広間　A "large" tea room, meaning one over four-and-a-half *tatami* mats in size. kakine

hishaku 柄杓　A bamboo ladle used to scoop water from the water basin in a tea garden.

hiwadabuki-mon 檜皮葺き　A gate with a roof made from finely prepared strips of Japanese cypress (*hinoki*) bark.

hizumi ヒツミ　Distorted. An aesthetic term that describes the strange, warped pottery that appealed to the tea master Furuta Oribe. 歪み Historically written in *kana* only.

hōjō 方丈　Literally, "10 feet square." An appellation for small rustic hermitages as well as for the central hall of Zen Buddhist temples.

ichigo ichie 一期一会　Literally, "one time, one meeting." A communion of people at any particular time that happens only once and never again in the same way.

ichijū-roji 一重露地　One-layer tea garden. A simple garden that, unlike the *nijū roji*, has no middle gate or inner and outer sections.

iemoto-seido 家元制度　Grand master system. This is a hierarchical system of maintaining traditional arts whereby a master passes on both techniques and social credentials to an apprentice, usually his eldest son, who in turn teaches apprentices and passes on the heritage.

ike-komi tōrō 埋込灯籠　A style of stone lantern that has no pedestal stone. The lantern post is buried directly into the ground to control the height.

inkyo 隠居　Recluse. An appellation given to a person who has gone into reclusion that was also used to refer to merchants who had given up the reins of their family business and retired.

iori　See *an*.

ishi-dōrō 石灯籠、石灯篭、石燈篭　Stone lantern. The word refers to any of a number of styles of lanterns made of stone that were originally used as votive lanterns in Buddhist temples and then, with the development of *chanoyu*, were used for their functional and scenic quality in tea gardens. They were typically composed of several separately carved sections including the following (from bottom up): pedestal, *kiso* 基礎; post, *sao* 竿; base stone, *chūdai* 中台; firebox, *hibukuro* 火袋; roof, *kasa* 笠. There are several character combinations used to write *ishi-dōrō*.

kaiseki 懐石　The meal served as part of a tea gathering. Originally extremely simple, such as the meal served to priests in Zen temples, *kaiseki* has come to mean *haute cuisine* in Japan.

kaisho 会所　Literally, "meeting place." The formal reception room or parlor that was used as a setting for tea gatherings in the residences of lords; also the hall that contained such rooms.

kakehi 筧、懸樋　A water pipe, usually made of bamboo (but also wood or stone) that feeds fresh water into a water basin, falling from above and making a burbling sound.

kamado no cha 竈の茶　"Kitchen" tea. These informal gatherings for tea around the cook-stoves (*kamado*) of the kitchen may have set a precedent for the *wabi-cha* tea gatherings.

karaki 唐木　Literally, "Chinese trees." These exotic imported trees used in Japanese gardens included rosewood (*shitan*, 紫檀), ebony (*kokutan*, 黒檀), and kilet (also called Bombay black wood, *tagayasan* 鉄刀木). Also pronounced *tōboku*.

kara-mono 唐物　Literally, "Chinese things." Such luxury items and artwork imported from China to Japan held a place of great importance in the formal *shoin* style tea.

karamono-suki 唐物數奇　A taste for imported Chinese luxury items as well as the style of tea service centered on those items.

kare 枯れ　Withered. One of the aesthetics of linked-verse poetry (*renga*) associated with the development of rustic tea before the advent of the aesthetic *wabi*.

kasa-gata 笠形　A kind of water basin made from the roof (*kasa*) of a stone stupa or a stone lantern.

katana-kake 刀掛　Sword shelf. An open frame, double-layer shelf on which swords are placed before entering a tea room.

katana-kake-ishi 刀掛石　Sword-shelf stone. A flat-topped stone placed just beneath the sword shelf that allows guests to step up and reach the shelf. The stone chosen is often two-tiered and stair-like.

katteguchi 勝手口　Host's entry. The entry from the preparation room (*mizuya*) of a tea house to the tea room itself. It is used by the host and not the guests.

kaya-mon 茅門、萱門　Thatch-roofed gate. It is usually used as a middle gate. The thatching can include *susuki* (Miscanthus sinensis), *chigaya* (Imperata cylindrica var. major), and *yoshi* (Phragmites of various species).

kazari-setchin　See *suna-setchin*.

ke 褻　The private, common, everyday, hidden, or inward aspects of things. Antithesis of *hare*.

kidōrō 木灯籠　Wooden lantern.

kirei-sabi 綺麗さび　Beautiful rusticity. An aesthetic term used to describe the taste of Kobori Enshū.

kirishitan-dōrō キリシタン灯籠　Christian lantern. A stone lantern of the *Oribe-dōrō* style that has carvings symbolic of Christianity on its post or elsewhere.

kiso-gata 基礎形　A type of water basin made from the pedestal of an old stone lantern.

kissa no tei 喫茶の亭　Tea pavilion. A term used in the 14th-century *Kissa Ōrai* for a garden pavilion. Archaic.

kokerabuki-mon 柿葺き　A gate with a roof made from thin shingles of Japanese cypress (*hinoki*) wood.

koma 小間　A "small" tea room, meaning one under four-and-a-half mats in size.

koshikake　See *koshikake machiai*.

koshikake machiai 腰掛待合　Waiting bench. A small roofed bench, usually capable of holding no more than four to five people, placed in the tea garden where guests wait before they are greeted by their host.

kuguri くぐり　Either a crawl-through gate (i.e., *naka-kuguri*) or a crawl-through door into the tea room (*nijiri-guchi*).

kuguri kido くぐり木戸　Crawl-through door into the tea room. An archaic name for the *nijiri-guchi*.

kura 蔵　See *omoteya*.

kuri-ishi 栗石　Gravel. *Kuri* means chestnut, and *kuri-ishi* can refer to small stones ranging from chestnut to fist size. Early-era tea gardens were at times spread with gravel.

kusa no iori 草の庵　See *sōan*.

kusari no ma 鎖の間　A room positioned in between the formal *shoin* and rustic *sōan* tea rooms. The *kusari no ma* symbolizes the bridging of formal and rustic styles that took place during the time of Furuta Oribe.

kyaku-ishi 客石　Guest's stone. A stepping stone on the outer side of the middle gate upon which the guest stands when greeted by the host.

lantern　See *andon*; *ishi-dōrō*; *teshoku*.

machiya 町家　Townhouse. Typically refers to the wooden townhouses that were the residences of urban merchants and artisans containing both residential and store/workshop components.

mae-ishi 前石　Front stone. The large flat-topped stepping stone set in front of the *chōzubachi* on which one stands while using the water.

makkyaku 末客　The guest at a tea gathering who enters last and takes responsibility for finishing things, such as closing and locking the gates of the tea garden. Also called *otsume*.

matcha 抹茶　Powdered tea. New tea leaves are steamed and

carefully ground to produce a fine powder. A small amount is placed in a tea bowl and whisked with a bamboo whisk to make a frothy, somewhat bitter beverage. The culture of powdered-tea service forms the foundation for the culture of *chanoyu*.

merchant   See *shōnin*.

middle gate   See *chūmon*.

mitate 見立て   The technique of reusing old materials in a novel way, such as pieces of old stone lanterns or stupas that are recarved to be used as water basins in the tea garden. These pieces are called *mitate-mono*, literally, "re-seen things."

mitate-mono 見立て物   See *mitate*.

monomi-ishi 物見石   Viewing stone. A stepping stone, usually somewhat larger than others in the path, from which a particular scene can be appreciated, for instance, a tea house plaque or a stone lantern.

mukae-zuke 迎付   The custom of the host of a tea gathering greeting guests in the garden.

mukō-bachi 向鉢   A water basin arrangement (*tsukubai*) with the water basin set at the rear of the arrangement rather than the center (*naka-bachi*).

nagare-tsukubai 流蹲踞   A water basin that is set in the middle of a stream.

naka-bachi 中鉢   A water basin arrangement (*tsukubai*) that has the water basin set in the middle of the arrangement rather than the rear (*mukō-bachi*).

naka-dachi 中立   Midway break. Guests at a long tea gathering take a break midway through and go out into the tea garden to relax.

naka-kuguri 中潜り   A gate placed midway in a tea garden that resembles a section of clay-plaster wall into which a small crawl-through door has been built. Guests approach the door, peek through to see the garden on the other side, and then step up and through the opening.

naka-roji 中露地   Middle tea garden. The middle section of a three-layer tea garden.

nijiri-agari-ishi 躙り上がり石   One of three stones used to step up into a tea house through a crawl-through door: *nori-ishi* (lowest), *ochi-ishi* (middle), *nijiri-agari-ishi* (highest, closest to the entry door).

nijiri-guchi 躙口   Crawl-through door. The guest's entry to a rustic tea house is usually a small door that one must crouch down to enter. This design accentuates the separation between the world inside the tea room and that outside. Some archaic expressions for the same entry include *nijiri-agari* 躙り（にじり）上り, *nijiri-agari-guchi* 躙り（にじり）上り口, *kuguri* くぐり, and *kuguri kido* くぐり木戸.

nijū-roji 二重露地   Two-layer tea garden. A tea garden divided by a middle gate into outer (*soto-roji*) and inner (*uchi-roji*) sections.

niwa 庭   A general term for garden.

niwa-garan 庭伽藍   A large stepping stone made to resemble a pedestal stone (*garan-seki*) on the surface but in fact much thinner and easier to handle than a true pedestal stone.

niwa-mon 庭門   See *roji-mon*.

nobe-dan 延段   A modern term for pathway paving, also known as *tatami-ishi*.

nori-ishi 乗石   Mounting stone. See *nijiri-agari-ishi*.

norikoe-ishi 乗越石   Cross-over stone. A tall stepping stone placed just on the inside of the *naka-kuguri* to step down onto after ducking through the entry door.

ochi-ishi 落石   Falling stone. See *nijiri-agari-ishi*.

omote 表   Front or forward side. Also the formal aspect of something. Tea terms containing *omote* became prevalent during the time of Furuta Oribe as *daimyō-cha* began to develop: e.g., *omote shoin* (formal parlor), *omote no ma* (front room), and *omote-roji* (formal tea garden).

omote tsubo no uchi   See *tsubo no uchi*.

omoteya 表屋   The shop along the street, one of the three structures that make up the typical residence of an urban merchant. The other two are the *omoya*, or residence further back; and the *kura*, or storehouse in the extreme rear of the property. Small gardens based on tea gardens are often built in the open spaces between these.

omoya 母屋   See *omoteya*.

onari 御成   Honorable visit. When an aristocrat or provincial lord paid a visit to someone of lesser or equal standing, it was called an *onari*, and a room designated for the purpose of that visit was called an *onari no ma*.

onari no ma 御成の間   See *onari*.

Oribe-dōrō 織部灯籠   A lantern named after the style of Furuta Oribe. It was distinguished by its cleaner line, lack of ornate carvings, and lack of a pedestal stone, which allowed the post to be buried directly into the ground.

ori-tsukubai 降り蹲踞   A water basin arrangement (*tsukubai*) set in a sunken area and accessed by a few, descending steps. Often covered by a canopy of trees, it offers a cool spot in which to use the water basin.

otsume 御詰 See **makkyaku**.

renga 連歌 Linked-verse poetry. The aesthetics of *renga* poets transferred over to the practice of tea, creating an early precedent for rustic tea (*wabi-cha*). See **hie**; **kare**.

rinkan-chanoyu 淋汗茶湯 The practice of serving tea after bathing.

ro 炉 Brazier. A small fireproof box recessed into the floor where charcoal is burned to heat water for tea.

roji ろぢ, 路地, 路次, 露次, 盧路, 露地 Tea garden. Typically, a small garden that acts as an entry path to a tea house. Developed by tea masters over the course of the 15th and 16th centuries, the form we know today stems from the end of the 16th and early 17th centuries. A *roji* may contain any of the following: entry gates and midway gates to mark passage through the garden; a water basin to cleanse one's hands and mouth; a roofed waiting bench; a stepping stone path; and forest-like evergreen plantings.

roji-guchi 露地口 See **roji-mon**.

roji-mon 露地門 The entry gate to a tea garden. Also called *niwa-mon*, *roji-guchi*, and *soto-mon*.

roji-zōri 露地草履 Tea garden slippers. Made of woven straw (*wara* 藁), rush (*i* 蘭), or bamboo skin (*chikuhi* 竹皮), these soft-soled garden slippers replaced the earlier custom of wearing wooden sandals (*geta*) in the tea garden.

sabi 寂 An aesthetic term that originally meant loneliness but came to mean "rustic yet elegant refinement" in the context of *chanoyu*. It also refers to an elegant patina gained through careful use of an object over time. See **wabi**.

sadō 茶頭 Tea master. A member of the staff of a lord's household whose role it was to prepare tea.

sadō 茶道 Way of Tea. An Edo-period term that refers to the practice of *chanoyu*.

sanjū-roji 三重露地 A three-layered tea garden. This is an uncommon style that has outer, middle, and inner sections.

sankyo no tei 山居之躰 The "appearance of a mountain village." The expression is used to describe rustic arbors such as those used for tea gatherings. Archaic.

sarei 茶礼 Tea rituals. The customs of drinking tea in Song-dynasty Chan temples was transferred to Japanese Zen temples in the Kamakura period (14th century), including formal tea-drinking and tea-offering rituals collectively known as *sarei*. These formed one of the cultural roots of *chanoyu*.

saru-do 猿戸 A simple gate, usually used as a middle gate, similar to a *shiori-do*.

seki-ishi 関石 See **sekimori-ishi**.

sekimori-ishi 関守石 A small rounded stone, tied with a black palm-fiber cord, placed on a stepping stone for use as a marker to block off an unused path in a tea garden.

seki-take 関竹 A length of bamboo laid across two low posts, used as a marker to block off an unused path in a tea garden. See **sekimori-ishi**.

setchin 雪隠 Privy. A rustic yet pristine outhouse built in a tea garden. There are two types: the *suna setchin* (*kazari setchin*), which is only symbolic of the cleanliness and preparation provided by the host, and the *shitabara setchin*, which is a functional privy though rarely put to actual use.

setta 雪駄 Snow sandals. These leather-soled sandals are for walking in snow, and are said to be preferred over wooden clogs because they produce no sound when walking.

shichūin 市中隠 Hermitage in the city. It is an expression used for a place of reclusion within the city itself. It also refers to the person in reclusion, i.e., the hermit in the city.

shichū no sankyo 市中の山居 Mountain cottage in the city. It is an expression used for a place of reclusion within the city itself.

shihōbutsu-gata 四方仏形 A type of water basin made from the pedestal of a stone stupa, four-sided, with simple carvings of Buddhas on all four sides. At times it is pronounced *yohōbutsu* among tea practitioners.

shi'in 市隠 See **shichūin**.

shijin 市塵 The dust of the marketplace. The expression is used to refer to the defilement of human existence.

Shimogyō Chanoyu 下京茶湯 Tea-style of the Lower Capital. It is an appellation for the kind of rustic tea that developed among the merchants in the merchant quarter of the capital (Shimogyō).

shin 真 An expression of formality or control. See **shin-gyō-sō**; **shin no zashiki**.

shin-gyō-sō 真行草 Three linked aesthetic terms describing things that are formal, intermediate, and informal.

shin-kabe 真壁 A method of making clay-plastered walls

in which the post and beam structure is not buried by the plaster but rather is allowed to show.

shin no zashiki 真座敷 A formal sitting room. The expression is used to refer to Murata Shukō's tea room, which had white paper walls and a roof like a Buddhist temple.

shiori-do 枝折戸 A lightly built gate made by weaving a lattice of split bamboo over a frame.

shiro-kabe 白壁 White-plastered walls. *Shikkui* 漆喰 is the name of the white, lime plaster that is applied to the outside of clay walls as a protective and aesthetic finish.

shitabara setchin 下腹雪隠 Functional privy. Also pronounced *kafuku setchin*. See **setchin**.

shitaji mado 下地窓 A lattice window. *Shitaji* refers to the bamboo lath that forms the inner structure of a clay-plaster wall. The *shitaji mado* is supposed to mimic a section of the wall that has not been plastered, revealing the inner lathwork. In fact, the lattice in a *shitaji mado* is a decorative pattern of finer material that is installed for aesthetic purposes.

shōgi 床几 A bench put in a garden as a resting place.

shōgun 将軍 Chief military lord.

shoin 書院 Reading alcove. A shelf in a small alcove set in an outer wall, the *shoin* was a sign of literacy and was included in Zen-temple architecture as well as in the residences of military lords and aristocrats. A room that had a *shoin* in it was also called the *shoin*, and tea performed in those rooms became known as *shoin-cha*.

shoin-cha 書院茶 A formal type of tea service named after the formal parlor (*shoin*) the tea was held in. It is also called *daisu-cha* 台子茶 after the lacquered tea-shelf that was used in the service.

shōji 障子 Translucent paper door.

shōkyaku 正客 The guest at a tea gathering who enters the tea garden first and takes responsibility for initiating things, such as conversation about the tea utensils.

shōkyaku-seki 正客石 A stepping stone in the *koshikake machiai* set in front of the place on the bench where the lead guest (*shōkyaku*) sits; it is placed slightly higher and more forward than the others as a sign of respect.

shōnin 商人 A member of the merchant class.

shujin-seki 主人石 See **teishu-ishi**.

shuro-nawa 棕櫚縄 Black palm-fiber twine made from the bark of the Chinese windmill palm (Trachycarpus fortunei, *shuro* 棕櫚).

sōan 草庵 Thatch-roofed hermitage. A simple, rustic hut—based on the ideals of a hermit's abode—that became the standard architecture for rustic *chanoyu*. Also pronounced *kusa no iori*.

sōan-cha 草庵茶 The style of tea service associated with a *sōan* tea house that applies the aesthetic of rusticity (*wabi*) to all aspects of the tea service: artwork, utensils, architecture, and gardens.

sode-gaki 袖垣 A sleeve fence. It is a short fence, perhaps 1 to 2 meters long at most, the shape of which recalls a draping kimono sleeve.

sode-suri matsu 袖摺松 Sleeve-brushing pine tree. The pine's trunk is so close to a path that one brushes one's kimono sleeve against it when passing.

sode-suri no rui 袖摺類 Any tree, such as the *sode-suri matsu*, whose trunk is very close to a path.

sōsaku-gata 創作形 A type of water basin carved according to a certain design rather than made out of a recycled stone object (*mitate-mono*) or from a natural stone (*shizen seki*).

sotetsu-yama 蘇鉄山 A small hillock planted with cycads (*sotetsu*, Cycas revoluta).

soto koshikake 外腰掛 A waiting bench (*koshikake machiai*) in the outer tea garden (*soto-roji*).

soto-kuguri 外潜 Outer wicket. A crawl-through gate (*kuguri*) in the outer tea garden. Archaic.

soto-mon 外門 Outer gate. See **roji-mon**.

soto-roji 外露地 Outer tea garden. The portion of a two-layered tea garden (*nijū-roji*) entered first on one's way to the inner tea garden (*uchi-roji*) where the tea house is.

stupa A Buddhist tower. Although the word "stupa" can refer to many things, including large architectural towers like those in the Indian subcontinent, here it refers to the smaller carved-stone towers set at Buddhist temples and later used piecemeal in tea gardens. Typically the terms *buttō* 仏塔 or *sekitō* 石塔 are used in Japanese; the word "stupa" can be written *sotoba* 卒塔婆.

sudo no hanekido 簾戸ノ撥木戸 A lightly built swinging gate. Archaic.

sugi 杉 Cedar, Cryptomeria japonica. Used both as plantings in the garden and as an architectural material.

sugikawa-mon 杉皮門 A gate roofed with cedar-bark shingles.

suki 数寄 An aesthetic term meaning taste or style, thus, *karamono-suki* and *wamono-suki*: "a taste for Chinese-style things" and "a taste for Japanese-style things," respectively. The term *suki* was so strongly associated with the practice of *chanoyu* that it came to be a synonym for *chanoyu*. See **sukisha; sukiya.**

sukisha 数寄者　A premodern expression for "tea master." Literally, a "person of tea."

sukiya 数寄屋　A tea house. Initially referring only to those small structures used exclusively for the practice of *chanoyu*, it now more broadly refers to a style of refined residential architecture derived from tea houses.

sukiya tōrimichi すきや通道　A medieval expression for the path to a tea house. Archaic.

suna setchin 砂雪隠　See **setchin.**

sute-ishi 捨て石　A single stepping stone set just to one side of a stepping stone path to add interest and complexity to the design. Literally, "thrown away stone."

sword shelf　See **katana-kake.**

sword-shelf stone　See **katana-kake-ishi.**

tachi-chōzubachi 立手水鉢　An upright water basin, one tall enough to be used while standing. Colloquially, *tachibachi*.

takebuki-mon 竹葺き門　A gate roofed with long pieces of half-split bamboo that overlap each other.

takeho-gaki 竹穂垣　A fence made from bundles of bamboo twigs.

tataki 三和土、叩き土、敲き土　Pounded earth. Entry spaces in rustic buildings were often floored with pounded earth. Properly, *tataki-tsuchi*.

tatami 畳　Rectangular reed mats, approximately 1 x 2 meters (3 by 6 feet) in dimension and 5 cm thick, made from compacted rice straw and covered on the upper surface with a fine mat made of a rush called *igusa*.

tatami-ishi 畳石　An arrangement of flat stones (cut or natural or both) that forms a rectangular section of pavement. Nowadays also called *nobe-dan*.

tea　See **cha.**

tea garden　See **chaniwa; roji.**

teishu 亭主　The host of a tea gathering.

teishu-ishi 亭主石　The stone on the inside of a middle gate (*chūmon*) on which the host stands to initially greet his guests.

teppō-gaki 鉄砲垣　Literally, rifle-fence. A type of fence whose rows of vertical members (usually bamboo) tied to a frame resemble rifles lined up in a row.

teshoku 手燭　Candle holder.

teshoku-ishi 手燭石　Candle-holder stone. A flat-topped stone placed next to the *chōzubachi*, on which a hand-held candle holder (*teshoku*) is placed.

thatch-roofed gate　See **kaya-mon.**

tobi-ishi 飛び石　Stepping stone. Natural stones or pieces of carved granite placed in staggered rows to act as a path.

tōcha 闘茶　Literally, "contest tea." A contest focused on sampling various teas to determine which tea is from which tea-growing region.

toko　See **tokonoma.**

tokobashira 床柱　The main post at the corner of the *tokonoma*.

tokonoma 床の間　Display alcove. This small, understated alcove in a tea room is used to display a seasonal element (a flower) or a thematic piece of artwork (usually a painted scroll or calligraphy).

tōrō　Lantern. See **ishi-dōrō.**

tsubo niwa 坪庭、壺庭、径穴庭　A small courtyard garden, enclosed between sections of a traditional wooden townhouse, usually the shop/residence of an urban merchant or artisan. The typical design contains many elements derived from tea gardens such as water basins and stone lanterns.

tsubo-no-uchi 坪の内　A very small enclosed court or room that acted as a buffer space upon entry to the early medieval tea rooms. At times there were two: one on the "side" (*waki tsubo no uchi* 脇坪の内) that acted as an entry, and one in the "front" (*omote tubo no uchi* 表坪の内) that acted as a tiny viewing garden.

tsuchi-kabe 土壁　A thin wall made of a wood structure, bamboo wattle, and a refined clay-plaster surface.

tsuiji-bei 築地塀　A thick wall made of solid rammed earth.

tsukiyama 築山　An artificial "mountain" or hillock built in a garden.

tsukubai 蹲踞, 蹲い　An arrangement of stones that includes a water basin and is used before a tea gathering to ritually cleanse one's hands and mouth.

uchi koshikake 内腰掛　A waiting bench (*koshikake machiai*) in the inner tea garden (*uchi-roji*).

uchi-mizu 打水　The act of sprinkling water on the garden before, during, or after a tea gathering to evoke a feeling of freshness, as after a light rain.

uchi-roji 内露地　Inner tea garden. The portion of a two-layered tea garden (*nijū-roji*) furthest in from the outer entry—the portion where the tea house is situated.

ukiyo 浮き世   Literally, the "floating world." A figure of speech referring to the impure, mortal world.

umi 海   The central, sunken part of the *tsukubai* arrangement, often covered with gravel, where water can fall and seep into the ground. Also called the *nagashi* (流し).

wabi 侘び   An aesthetic term associated with things that have a subdued patina of age and an inherent naturalness. The rustic form of tea gatherings—which took place in simple tea huts and employed the use of ostensibly non-precious utensils—was called *wabi-cha*.

wabi-cha 侘茶, 侘び茶   See ***wabi***.

wabi-suki 侘び数奇   An older manner of saying *wabi-cha*.

waiting bench   See ***koshikake machiai***.

waki tsubo-no-uchi 脇坪の内   See ***tsubo-no-uchi***.

wamono 和物   Japanese things.

warm-water bucket stone   See ***yuoke-ishi***.

yaku-boku 役木   A plant in a tea garden with a specific function, such as the *gakumi-matsu*.

yaku-ishi 役石   A stone in a tea garden with a specific function, such as the *gakumi-ishi*.

yaku-ju 役樹   An older manner of saying *yaku-boku*.

yamazato 山里   Mountain Village. A term often used in reference to urban tea gardens that evoked the rustic and sentimental quality of lonely mountain villages.

yobanashi 夜咄   A tea gathering given at night.

yohōbutsu-gata   See ***shihōbutsu-gata***.

yojōhan 四畳半   Four and a half mats (approximately 3 m x 3 m). From medieval times, this was the classic size for a tea room and formed a perfect square in plan view. The actual size of most tea rooms, however, is either larger or smaller.

yori-tsuki 寄付   Preparation room. A small structure in the outer tea garden used by entering guests to make preparations for the tea gathering.

yose-dōrō 寄せ灯籠   A stone lantern made from putting together parts taken from other carved stone objects: lanterns, stupas, etc.

yotsugashira 四つ頭   Ceremony of the Four Honored Ones. A ritual held in some Buddhist temples to honor the founders of the temple. A cultural predecessor of *chanoyu*, it includes the ceremonial service of tea.

yotsume-gaki 四つ目垣   A low fence made by tying together stems of bamboo, vertically and horizontally, to form an open, lattice pattern.

yuoke 湯桶   Warm-water bucket. When a tea gathering is held on a cold day, such as in winter, the *yuoke* is placed next to the water basin (*chōzubachi*) to allow guests to warm their hands after using the frigid water.

yuoke-ishi 湯桶石   Warm-water bucket stone. A flat-topped stone placed next to the *chōzubachi*, on which a small wooden bucket of warm water (*yuoke*) is placed.

zashiki 座敷   Sitting parlor. Usually reserved for formal activities, the room is completely covered with *tatami* mats and thus is comfortable for sitting.

zeni-gata 銭形   A water basin shaped like an old coin, *zeni*, namely, one that is perfectly round with a square basin carved in the middle.

zensō 禅僧   A priest of the Zen sect of Buddhism.

Bibliography

BOOKS IN ENGLISH

Berry, Mary Elizabeth. *The Culture of Civil War in Kyōto.* Berkeley: University of California Press, 1994.

———. *Hideyoshi.* Cambridge: Harvard University Press, 1982.

Brower, Robert. *Conversations with Shōtetsu.* Ann Arbor: Center for Japanese Studies, University of Michigan, 1992.

Brown, Kendall. *The Politics of Reclusion: Painting and Power in Momoyama Japan.* Honolulu: University of Hawai'i Press, 1997.

Clunas, Craig. *Fruitful Sites: Garden Culture in Ming Dynasty China.* Durham: Duke University, 1996.

Cooper, Michael. *Rodrigues the Interpreter: An Early Jesuit in Japan and China.* New York: Weatherhill, 1974.

Cox, Rupert. *The Zen Arts.* London: Routledge Curzon, 2003.

Dickins, Victor. *The Hôjôki.* Tōkyō: Sankakusha, 1933.

Elison, George, and Bardwell Smith, eds. *Warlords, Artists, and Commoners: Japan in the Sixteenth Century.* Honolulu: The University Press of Hawai'i, 1981.

Fujikawa, Asako. *Chanoyu and Hideyoshi.* Tōkyō: Hokuseidō Press, 1957.

Hall, John, and Takeshi Toyoda, eds. *Japan in the Muromachi Age.* Berkeley: University of California Press, 1977.

Hirota, Dennis. *Wind in the Pines: Classic Writings of the Way of Tea as a Buddhist Path.* Fremont, CA: Asian Humanities Press, 1995.

Horton, Mack. *Song in an Age of Discord: The Journal of Sōchō and Poetic Life in Late Medieval Japan.* Stanford: Stanford University Press, 2002.

Keene, Donald. *Essays in Idleness: The Tsurezuregusa of Kenkō.* New York: Columbia University Press, 1967.

Kuitert, Wybe. *Themes in the History of Japanese Garden Art.* Honolulu: University of Hawai'i Press, 2002.

Levy, Ian Hideo. *Man'yōshū: A Translation of Japan's Premier Anthology of Classical Poetry, Volume One.* Princeton: Princeton University Press, 1981.

Lu, Yu. *The Classic of Tea.* Translated and introduced by Francis Ross Carpenter. Boston: Little, Brown, 1974.

Moriguchi, Yasuhiko, and David Jenkins, translators. *Hōjōki: Visions of a Torn World.* Berkeley: Stone Bridge Press, 1996.

Moriya, Takeshi. "The Mountain Dwelling Within the City." *Chanoyu Quarterly,* vol. 56, 1988: 7–21.

Nakamura, Toshinori. "Early History of the Teahouse: Part I." *Chanoyu Quarterly,* vol. 69, 1992: 7–32.

———. "Early History of the Teahouse: Part II." *Chanoyu Quarterly,* vol. 70, 1992: 22–40.

———. "Early History of the Teahouse: Part III." *Chanoyu Quarterly,* vol. 71, 1992: 31–44.

———. "Early History of the Teahouse: Part IV." *Chanoyu Quarterly,* vol. 72, 1993: 31–47.

Ōhashi, Haruzō. *The Tea Garden.* Tōkyō: Graphic-sha Publishing, 1989.

Parker, Joseph. *Zen Buddhist Landscape Arts of Early Muromachi Japan (1336–1573).* Albany: State University of New York Press, 1999.

Plutschow, Herbert E. *Historical Chanoyu.* Tokyo: Japan Times, 1986.

Rodrigues, João. *João Rodrigues's Account of Sixteenth-Century Japan.* Edited by Michael Cooper. London: Hakluyt Society, 2001.

Sadler, A. L. *The Ten Square Foot Hut.* Westport, CT: Greenwood Press, 1928.

Sen, Sōshitsu XV. *Japanese Way of Tea: From Its Origins in China to Sen Rikyū*. Translated by V. Dixon Morris. Honolulu: University of Hawai'i Press, 1998.

Sen, Sōshitsu XV, ed. *Chanoyu: The Urasenke Tradition of Tea*. Translated by Alfred Birnbaum. New York: Weatherhill, 1988.

Shōtetsu. *Conversations with Shōtetsu (Shōtetsu Monogatari)*. Translated by Robert H. Brower. Ann Arbor: Center for Japanese Studies, The University of Michigan, 1992.

Sōchō. *The Journal of Sōchō (Sōchō Nikki)*. Translated and annotated by H. Mack Horton. Stanford: Stanford University Press, 2002.

Stanley-Baker, Joan. *The Transmission of Chinese Idealist Painting to Japan*. Ann Arbor: University of Michigan, 1992.

Takei, Jiro, and Marc Peter Keane. *Sakuteiki*. Tokyo: Charles E. Tuttle Company, 2001.

Varley, Paul, and Isao Kumakura, eds. *Tea in Japan: Essays on the History of Chanoyu*. Honolulu: University of Hawai'i Press, 1989.

Watsky, Andrew. "Commerce, Politics, and Tea: The Career of Imai Sōkyū." *Monumenta Nipponica*, Spring 1995: 47–65.

Watson, Burton. *Japanese Literature in Chinese*. Vol. 1, *Prose and Poetry in Chinese by Japanese Writers of the Early Period*. New York: Columbia University Press, 1975.

BOOKS IN JAPANESE

Akatsuki Kanenari. *Saikoku Sanjūsansho Meisho Zue*. Kyōto: Rinsen Shoten, 1991. 暁鐘成『西国三十三所名所図会』京都：臨川書店.

Akisato Ritō. *Miyako Rinsen Meishō Zue (ge)*. Tōkyō: Kōdansha, 2000. 秋里籬島『京林泉名勝図絵（下）』東京：講談社.

Amasaki Hiromasa. *Zusetsu, Chatei no Shikumi: Rekishi to Kōzō no Kiso Chishiki*. Kyōto: Tankōsha, 2002. 尼崎博正『図説・茶庭のしくみ・歴史と構造の基礎知識』京都：淡交社.

Chadō Bunka Kenkyū Dai'isshū. Kyōto: Urasenke Konnichian Bunko, 1974.『茶道文化研究・第一輯』京都：裏千家今日庵文庫.

"Chanoyu Hishō." *Chanoyu Bunkagaku* (Kyōto), March 1999: 149–218. 茶湯秘抄『茶の湯文化学』京都：149–218.

Harada Tomohiko, *Harada Tomohiko Chosakushū Daisan Maki: Chadō Bunkashi*. Kyōto: Shibunkaku Shuppan, 1981. 原田伴彦『原田伴彦著作集・第三巻・茶道文化史』京都：思文閣出版.

Hayashiya Tatsusaburō, ed. *Kadokawa Chadō Daijiten Hon Hen*. Tōkyō: Kadokawa Shoten, 1990. 林屋辰三郎『角川茶道大辞典・本編』東京：角川書店.

———. *Kadokawa Chadō Daijiten Shiryo-Sakuin Hen*. Tōkyō: Kadokawa Shoten, 1990. 林屋辰三郎『角川茶道大辞典・資料索引編』東京：角川書店.

———. *Nihon Shisō Taikei 23: Kodai Chūsei Geijutsuron*. Tōkyō: Iwanami Shoten, 1973. 林屋辰三郎『日本思想大系23・古代中世藝術論』東京：岩波書店.

Hayashiya Tatsusaburō, Yokoi Kiyoshi, and Narabayashi Tadao, eds. *Nihon no Chasho*. Vol. 1. Tōkyō: Heibonsha, 1971. 林家辰三郎・横井清・楢林忠男『日本の茶書・1』東京：平凡社.

———. *Nihon no Chasho*. Vol. 2. Tōkyō: Heibonsha, 1972. 林家辰三郎・横井清・楢林忠男『日本の茶書・2』東京：平凡社.

Hokinoichi Hanawa. *Gunsho Ruijū*, vol. 27. Tōkyō, Zoku Gunsho Ruijū Kanseikai, 1929. 塙保己一『群書類従 第二十七巻』東京，續群書類從完成會.

Horiguchi Sutemi and Inagaki Eizō, eds. *Zusetsu Chadō Taikei*. Vol. 4, *Cha no Kenchiku to Niwa*. Tōkyō: Kadokawa Shoten, 1962. 堀口捨己、稲垣栄三『図説茶道大系・第四巻・茶の建築と庭』東京：角川書店.

Ichino Chizuko. *Furuta Oribe Chasho*, vol. 1 (*Sōhokō Koshoku e Otazunesho, Furuta Oribe Kamidono Kikigaki*). Vol. 2 of *Chanoyu Koten Sōsho*. Kyōto: Shibunkaku, 1976. 市野千鶴子『茶湯古典叢書2・古田織部茶書I』（宗甫公古職へ御尋書、古田織部正殿聞書）京都：思文閣.

———. *Furuta Oribe Chasho*, vol. 2 (*Oribe Hyakkajō, Oribe Chakaki, Sukidō Shidai, Koshoku Chanoyuki, Koshokuden, Chanoyu Rokusōshō Denki*). Vol. 3 of *Chanoyu Koten Sōsho*. Kyōto: Shibunkaku, 1984. 市野千鶴子『茶湯古典叢書3・古田織部茶書2』（織部百ヶ条、織部茶会記、数奇道次第、古織茶湯記、古織伝、茶之湯六宗匠伝記）京都：思文閣.

Itoh Teiji. "Sōanfū Chashitsu no Genryū: Part 1." *Nihon Rekishi*, vol. 101, pp. 21–26. Tōkyō: Nihon Rekishi Gakkai, 1956. 伊藤鄭爾「草庵風茶室の源流・上」『日本歴史』東京：日本歴史学会.

———. "Sōanfū Chashitsu no Genryū: Part 2." *Nihon Rekishi*,

vol. 102, pp. 39–43. Tōkyō: Nihon Rekishi Gakkai, 1956. 伊藤鄭爾「草庵風茶室の源流・下」『日本歴史』東京:日本歴史学会.

Iwasaki Kae, et al. *Shichijūichiban Shokunin Utaawase*. Shin Nihon Koten Bungaku Taikei, vol. 61. Tōkyō: Iwanami Shoten, 1993. 岩崎佳枝他『新日本古典文学大系61・七十一番職人歌合』東京:岩波書店.

Kinsei Fūzoku Zufu. Vol. 3, *Rakuchū Rakugai*, part 1. Tōkyō: Shōgakukan, 1983.『近世風俗図譜・第三巻・洛中洛外(一)』東京:小学館.

Kinsei Fūzoku Zufu. Vol. 4, *Rakuchū Rakugai*, part 2. Tōkyō: Shōgakukan, 1983.『近世風俗図譜・第四巻・洛中洛外(二)』東京:小学館.

Kitao, Harumichi. *Chaniwa*. Kyōto: Mitsumura Suiko Shoin, 1970. 北尾春道『茶庭』京都:光村推古書院.

———. *Kenchiku Shashin Bunko*. Vol. 7, *Chaniwa*. Tōkyō: Shōkokusha, 1954. 北尾春道『建築写真文庫7・茶庭』東京:彰国社.

Kobata Atsushi. *Chūsei Nisshi Tsūkō Bōekishi no Kenkyū*. Tōkyō: Tōkō Shoin, 1969. 小葉田淳『中世日支通交貿易史の研究』東京:刀江書院.

Komatsu Shigemi. *Nihon no Emaki*. Vol. 20, *Ippen Shōnin Eden*. Tōkyō: Chūō Kōron-sha, 1988. 小松成美『日本の絵巻・20巻・一遍上人絵伝』東京:中央公論社.

———. *Nihon no Emaki*. Vol. 19, *Saigyō Monogatari Emaki*. Tōkyō: Chūō Kōron-sha, 1988. 小松成美『日本の絵巻・19巻・西行物語絵巻』東京:中央公論社.

Kumakura Isao. *Chanoyu no Rekishi: Sen Rikyū Made (Asahi Sensho 404)*. Tōkyō: Asahi Shinbunsha, 1990. 熊倉 功夫『茶の湯の歴史・千利休まで(朝日選書404)』東京:朝日新聞社.

———. *Rikyū, Oribe, Enshū: Meihō Nihon no Bijutsu 16*. Tōkyō: Shōgakukan, 1983. 熊倉 功夫『利休・織部・遠州:名宝日本の美術・16』東京:小学館ギャラリー.

Kuni Shitei Meishō: Tabuchishi Teien. Akō City: Akōshi Bunka Shinkō Zaidan, 1995.『国指定名勝・田淵氏庭園』赤穂市:赤穂文化振興財団.

Kusakabe Ryōen. *Hōjōki Shohon no Honbun Kōtei ni Kansuru Kenkyū*. Kyōto: Hatsune Shobō, 1966. 草部了円『方丈記諸本の本文校定に関する研究』京都:初音書房.

Kuwata Tadachika. *Shinshū Chadō Zenshū*. Vol. 8, *Bunken 11-hen jō*. Tōkyō: Shunjūsha, 1956. 桑田忠親『新修茶道全集・巻8・文献篇上』東京:春秋社.

———. *Shinshū Chadō Zenshū*. Vol. 9, *Bunken-hen ge*. Tōkyō: Shunjūsha, 1956. 桑田忠親『新修茶道全集・巻9・文献篇下』東京:春秋社.

———. *Yamanoue Sōjiki no Kenkyū*. Kyōto: Kawahara Shoten, 1977. 桑田忠親『山上宗二記の研究』京都:河原書店.

Matsushita Daizaburō. *Kokubun Taikan*. Vol. 7, *Nikki Sōshibu*. Tōkyō: Itakuraya Shobō, 1903. 松下大三郎『國文大觀・7・日記草子部』東京:板倉屋書房.

Matsuyama Ginshōan, Kumakura Isao, and Tanaka Shūji, eds. *Chanoyu Koten Sōsho*. Vol. 1, *Chadō Shisō Densho*. Kyōto: Shibunkaku, 1974. 松山吟松庵、熊倉功夫、田中周二『茶湯古典叢書1・茶道四祖伝書』京都:思文閣.

Mori Osamu. *Kobori Enshū*. Tōkyō: Yoshikawa Kōbunkan, 1967. 森蘊『小堀遠州』東京:吉川弘文館.

Moriya Takeshi. *Nihon Chūsei e no Shiza: Fūryū, Basara, Kabuki (NHK Books 459)*. Tōkyō: Nihon Hōsō Shuppan Kyokai, 1984. 守屋毅『日本中世への視座:風流・ばさら・かぶき』東京:日本放送協会.

Murai Yasuhiko. *Zusetsu Sen Rikyū: Sono Hito to Geijutsu*. Tōkyō: Kawade Shobō Shinsha, 1989. 村井康彦『図説 千利休・その人と芸術』東京:河出書房新社.

Nakamura Masao. *Nihon no Teien*. Vol. 4, *Cha no Niwa*. Tōkyō: Kōdansha, 1980. 中村昌生『日本の庭園・第四巻・茶の庭』東京:講談社.

Nakamura Masao, et al., eds. *Chadō Shūkin*. Vol. 1, *Cha no Bunka*. Tōkyō: Shōgakukan, 1987. 中村昌生[ほか]編集『茶道聚錦・第一巻・茶の文化』東京:小学館.

———. *Chadō Shūkin*. Vol. 2: *Chanoyu no Seiritsu*. Tōkyō: Shōgakukan, 1984. 中村昌生[ほか]編集『茶道聚錦・第二巻・茶の湯の成立』東京:小学館.

———. *Chadō Shūkin*. Vol. 3, *Sen no Rikyū*. Tōkyō: Shōgakukan, 1983. 中村昌生[ほか]編集『茶道聚錦・第三巻・千利休』東京:小学館.

———. *Chadō Shūkin*. Vol. 4, *Oribe, Enshū, Sōtan*. Tōkyō: Shōgakukan, 1983. 中村昌生[ほか]編集『茶道聚錦・第四巻・織部、遠州、宗旦』東京:小学館.

———. *Chadō Shūkin*. Vol. 5, *Chanoyu no Tenkai*. Tōkyō:

Shōgakukan, 1985. 中村昌生[ほか]編集『茶道聚錦・第五巻・茶の展開』東京：小学館，1985.

———. *Chadō Shūkin*. Vol. 6, *Kindai no Chanoyu*. Tōkyō: Shōgakukan, 1985. 中村昌生[ほか]編集『茶道聚錦・第六巻・近代の茶の湯』東京：小学館.

———. *Chadō Shūkin*. Vol. 7, *Zashiki to Roji: Part 1, Chazashiki no Rekishi*. Tōkyō: Shōgakukan, 1984. 中村昌生[ほか]編集『茶道聚錦・第七巻・座敷と露地(一)・茶座敷の歴史』東京：小学館.

———. *Chadō Shūkin*. Vol. 8, *Zashiki to Roji: Part 2, Kōsei to Ishō*. Tōkyō: Shōgakukan, 1986. 中村昌生[ほか]編集『茶道聚錦・第八巻・座敷と露地(二)・構成と意匠』東京：小学館.

———. *Chadō Shūkin*. Vol. 9, *Sho to Kaiga*. Tōkyō: Shōgakukan, 1984. 中村昌生[ほか]編集『茶道聚錦・第九巻・書と絵画』東京：小学館.

———. *Chadō Shūkin: Index*. Tōkyō: Shōgakukan, 1987. 中村昌生[ほか]編集『茶道聚錦・別巻・索引小事典』東京：小学館.

Nakamura Toshinori. *Seikatsu Bunkashi: Machiya no Chashitsu*. Kyōto: Kyōto Zōkei Geijustu Daigaku Tsūshin Kyōikubu, 2004. 中村利則『生活文化史・町家の茶室』京都：京都造形芸術大学通信教育部.

Nihon Koten Bungaku Taikei. Vol. 29, *Sankashū*. Tōkyō: Iwanami Shoten, 1961.『日本古典文學大系・第二十九巻・山家集』東京：岩波書店.

Nihon Koten Bungaku Taikei. Vol. 30, *Hōjōki*. Tōkyō: Iwanami Shoten, 1957.『日本古典文學大系・第三十巻・方丈記』東京：岩波書店.

Nihon Koten Bungaku Taikei. Vol. 65, *Shotetsu Monogatari*. Tōkyō: Iwanami Shoten, 1961.『日本古典文學大系・第六十五巻・正徹物語』東京：岩波書店.

Noma Kōshin. *Shinshū Kyōto Sōsho*. Vol. 9, *Miyako Rinsen Meishō Zue*. Kyōto: Rinsen Shoten, 1976. 野間光辰『新修京都叢書・第9巻・都林泉名勝図絵』京都：臨川書店.

Ōhashi Haruzō. *Chaniwa*. Tōkyō: Gurafikku-sha, 1989. 大橋治三『茶庭』東京：グラフィック社.

Okuno Takahiro, ed. *Zōtei Oda Nobunaga Monjo no Kenkyū*. Tōkyō: Yoshikawa Kōbunkan, 1988. 奥野高広廣『増訂織田信長文書の研究』東京：吉川弘文館.

Rakuchū Rakugaizu: Miyako no Keishō. Kyōto: Kyōto National Museum, 1997.『洛中洛外図・都の形象』京都：京都国立博物館.

Saitō Tadakazu. *Meien wo Aruku*. Vol. 8, *Chaniwa*. Tōkyō: Mainichi Shinbun, 1990. 斉藤忠一『名園を歩く・第八巻・茶庭』東京：毎日新聞.

Satō Osamu. *Confort Library*. Vol. 7, *Hajimete no Chashitsu: Kyōto, Daitokuji de Kihon wo Manabu*. Tōkyō: Kenchiku Shiryō Kenkyūsha, 2000. 佐藤理『コンフォルトライブラリィ7・初めての茶室：京都大徳寺で基本を学ぶ』東京：建築資料研究社.

Sen Sōshitsu, ed. *Chadō Koten Zenshū*. Vol. 2 (*Kissa Yōjōki, Kissa Ōrai, etc*). Kyōto: Tankōsha, 1956. 千宗室『茶道古典全集・第二巻』(喫茶養生記、喫茶往来、等)京都：淡交社.

———. *Chadō Koten Zenshū*. Vol. 3 (*Jukō Furuichi Harima Hōshi Ate Isshi, Ikenaga Sōsaku e no Sho, Sōjinboku, Genryū Sawa*). Kyōto: Tankōsha, 1956. 千宗室『茶道古典全集・第三巻』(珠光古市播磨法師宛一紙、池永宗作への書、草人木、源流茶話)京都：淡交社.

———. *Chadō Koten Zenshū*. Vol. 4 (*Nanbōroku*). Kyōto: Tankōsha, 1956. 千宗室『茶道古典全集・第四巻』(南方録)京都：淡交社.

———. *Chadō Koten Zenshū*. Vol. 5 (*Kaiki*). Kyōto: Tankōsha, 1956. 千宗室『茶道古典全集・第五巻』(槐記)京都：淡交社.

———. *Chadō Koten Zenshū*. Vol. 6 (*Yamanoue Sōjiki, Sōtan Nikki*). Kyōto: Tankōsha, 1956. 千宗室『茶道古典全集・第六巻』(山上宗二記,宗湛日記)京都：淡交社.

———. *Chadō Koten Zenshū*. Vol. 9 (*Matsuya Kaiki*). Kyōto: Tankōsha, 1956. 千宗室『茶道古典全集・第九巻』(松屋会記)京都：淡交社.

———. *Chadō Koten Zenshū*. Vol. 10 (*Zuiryūsai Nobegami no Sho, Sugiki Fusai Densho, Chawa Shigetsushū, Zencharoku, Chanoyu Ikkaishū, Imai Sōkyū Chanoyu Nikki Nukigaki, others*). Kyōto: Tankōsha, 1956. 千宗室『茶道古典全集・第十巻』(随流斎延紙ノ書、杉木普斎傳書、茶話指月集、禪茶録、茶湯一會集, 今井宗久茶湯日記抜書、等)京都：淡交社.

———. *Chadō Koten Zenshū*. Vol. 11 (*Hosokawa Chanoyu no Sho, Sekishū Sanbyakkajō*). Kyōto: Tankōsha, 1956. 千宗室『茶道古典全集・第十一巻』(細川茶湯之書、石州三百ケ條)京都：淡交社.

Sen Sōshitsu and Nakamura Toshinori, eds. *Chadōgaku Taikei*. Vol. 6: *Chashitsu Roji*. Kyōto: Tankōsha, 2000. 千宗室、中村利則 編『茶道学大系6・茶室露地』京都：淡交社.

Shigemori Kanto. *Nihon Teien no Shuhō*. Vol. 5, *Roji*. Tōkyō:

Mainichi Shinbunsha, 1976. 重森完途『日本庭園の手法・第五巻・露地』東京：毎日新聞社.

Shigemori Mirei. *Chadō Bunko*. Vol. 7, *Chaniwa*. Kyōto: Kawahara Shoten, 1939. 重森三玲『茶道文庫7・茶庭』京都：川原書店.

Shigemori Mirei and Shigemori Kanto. *Nihon Teienshi Taikei*. Vols. 1–35. Tōkyō: Shakai Shisōsha, 1976. 重盛三玲、重盛完途『日本庭園史大系』東京：社会思想社.

Shimazu Tadao, ed. *Sōchō Nikki*. Tōkyō: Iwanami Shoten, 1975. 島津忠夫『宗長日記』東京：岩波書店.

Shin Nihon Koten Bungaku Taikei. Vol. 39 *(Hōjōki)*. Tōkyō : Iwanami Shoten, 1989.『新日本古典文学大系・39（方丈記）』東京：岩波書店.

Shirahata Yōzaburō. *Daimyō Teien*. Tōkyō: Kōdansha, 1997. 白幡洋三郎『大名庭園』東京：講談社.

Shokoku Chatei Meiseki Zue・Chawa Shigetsu Shū. Tōkyō: Kajima Shoten, 1976.『諸国茶庭名跡図絵・茶話指月集』東京：加島書店.

Taigai Kankeishi Sōgō Nenpyō. Tōkyō: Yoshikawa Kōbunkan, 1999.『対外関係史総合年表』東京：吉川弘文館.

Takakusu Junjirō. *Taishō Shinshū Daizōkyō*. Vol. 9. Tōkyō: Taishō Issai-kyō Kankōkai, 1925. 高楠順次郎『大正新修大蔵経・第九巻』東京：大正一切經刊行會.

Takeuchi Rizō, ed. *Zōho Zoku Shiryō Taisei*. Vol. 21, *Inryōken Nichiroku, vol. 1*. Kyōto: Rinsen Shoten, 1953. 竹内理三『増補・續資料大成・蔭涼軒日録・一』京都：臨川書店.

———. *Zōho Zoku Shiryō Taisei*. Vol. 22, *Inryōken Nichiroku, vol. 2*. Kyōto: Rinsen Shoten, 1978. 竹内理三『増補・續資料大成・蔭涼軒日録・二』京都：臨川書店.

———. *Zōho Zoku Shiryō Taisei*. Vol. 25, *Inryōken Nichiroku, vol. 5*. Kyōto: Rinsen Shoten, 1978. 竹内理三『増補・續資料大成・蔭涼軒日録・五』京都：臨川書店.

———. *Zōho Zoku Shiryō Taisei: Hekizan Nichiroku*. Kyōto: Rinsen Shoten, 1982. 竹内理三編『増補・續資料大成・碧山日録』京都：臨川書店.

Tani Akira. *Wakari Yasui Chanoyu no Bunka*. Kyōto: Tankōsha, 2005. 谷晃『わかりやすい茶の湯の文化』京都：淡交社.

Teien Gaku Kōza 2: Chashitsu to Roji. Kyōtō: Kyōto Zōkei Geijutsu Daigaku, 1995.『庭園学講座・茶室と露地』京都：京都造形芸術大学.

Tsutsui Hiroichi. *Chanoyu Kotohajime*. Tōkyō: Kōdansha, 1992. 筒井紘一『茶の湯事始』東京：講談社

———. *Chasho no Kenkyū*. Kyōto: Tankōsha, 2003. 筒井紘一『茶書の研究』京都：淡交社.

———. *Surasura Yomeru Nanpōroku*. Tōkyō: Kōdansha, 2003. 筒井紘一『すらすら読める南方録』東京：講談社.

Tsutsui Hiroichi, ed. *Chanoyu Kaiga Shiryō Shūsei*. Tōkyō: Heibonsha, 1992. 筒井紘一『茶の湯絵画資料集成』東京：平凡社.

Uehara Keiji. *Miyako Rinsen Meishō Zue (shō)*. Tōkyō: Kajima Shoten, 1975. 上原敬二『都林泉名勝図絵（抄）』東京：加島書店.

———. *Zōen Daijiten*. Tōkyō: Kajima Shoten, 1978. 上原敬二『造園大辞典』東京：加島書店.

Washino'o Takayasu. *Dainihon Kokiroku: Nisuiki*. Vols. 1–4. Tōkyō: Iwanami Shoten, 1989–97. 鷲尾隆康『大日本古記録・二水記 1～4』東京：岩波書店.

Yabe Ryōsaku. *Shinshū Chadō Zenshū*. Vol. 7, *Chashitsu Chaniwa Hen*. Tōkyō: Shunjūsha, 1955. 矢部良作『新修茶道全集・巻7・茶室茶庭篇』東京：春秋社.

Yabe Yoshiaki. *Furuta Oribe: Momoyama Bunka o Enshitsu Suru*. Tōkyō: Kadokawa Shoten, 1999. 矢部良明『古田織部・桃山文化を演出する』東京：角川書店.

Yoshikawa Isao. *Chōzubachi: Teien Bi no Zōkei*. Tōkyō: Gurafikku-sha, 1989. 吉川功『手水鉢・庭園美の造形』東京：グラフィック社.

BOOKS IN OTHER LANGUAGES

Empty Vessels, Replenished Minds: The Culture, Practice, and Art of Tea. Taiwan: National Palace Museum, 2001.『也可以清心：茶器、茶事、茶書』中華民國：國立故宮博物院.

Rodrigues, João. *Arte del Cha*. Edited by J. L. Alvarez-Taladriz. Tōkyō: Sophia University, 1954.

Index